REALISM AND ALLEGORY
IN THE
EARLY FICTION OF MAO TUN

STUDIES IN CHINESE LITERATURE AND SOCIETY

Editors
Irving Yucheng Lo
Joseph S. M. Lau
Leo Ou-fan Lee
Eugene Eoyang

REALISM AND ALLEGORY IN THE EARLY FICTION OF MAO TUN

YU-SHIH CHEN

INDIANA UNIVERSITY PRESS • BLOOMINGTON

This book was brought to publication with the assistance of a
grant from the Andrew W. Mellon Foundation.

Manufactured in the United States of America

Library of Congress Cataloging in Publication Data

Chen, Yu-shih.
Realism and allegory in the early fiction of Mao Tun.

(Studies in Chinese literature and society)
Bibliography: p.
Includes index.
1. Mao, Tun, 1896– —Criticism and interpretation.
I. Title. II. Series.
PL2801.N2Z59 1985   895.1'35   84-48486
ISBN 0-253-34950-8
1 2 3 4 5 89 88 87 86

CONTENTS

ACKNOWLEDGMENTS

Two chapters in this book are revised from my previously published articles. A portion of chapter 2 is adapted from "Mao Tun and the Use of Political Allegory in Fiction: A Case Study of His 'Autumn in Kuling'" in Merle Goldman (ed.), *Modern Chinese Literature in the May Fourth Era;* and chapter 6 is a slightly revised version of "Mao Tun and *The Wild Roses:* A Study of the Psychology of Revolutionary Commitment," *The China Quarterly* (June 1979). I wish to thank the publishers for their permissions to use the published materials here.

I am grateful to the Bunting Institute for Independent Studies for Women for a research fellowship in 1977–78. Under the fellowship, I made the trip to China to interview Mao Tun and also completed what are now chapters 6 and 7. I am equally grateful to the National Endowment for the Humanities for a research grant in 1981–82 which enabled me to complete the writing of the chapters on *Eclipse.*

Many scholars and friends have helped in the research and the thinking behind the book. Professor Martin Wilbur read my first draft of the chapter on "Autumn in Kuling" as early as 1973 and offered invaluable criticism on its historical setting. Dr. Marián Gálik, in 1974, gave me the precise date of Mao Tun's departure from Wuhan to Kuling and alerted me to the existence of his several "Letters from Kuling." My special thanks go to Leo Ou-fan Lee, who, over ten years and more, encouraged my continuous research in the early fiction of Mao Tun with his unfailing confidence in its possible merit. His moral support has become the main momentum behind the completion of the book. Iris Pian and James R. Hightower saw me through the first years with their kind concerns, years when I was struggling with my as yet unshaped thoughts and with all the mental agony that went with it. Mary Heathcote applied her enormous patience and editorial experience to the improvement of the style and the organization of the book during the final stage of its writing. I apologize for all the remaining imperfections and flaws that defied the best of her efforts.

The Harvard-Yenching Library permitted me to use its vast collection on modern Chinese literature and history. I want to thank the library staff, especially Mr. George Potter, for making the use of the library and library loans so painless.

REALISM AND ALLEGORY
IN THE
EARLY FICTION OF MAO TUN

INTRODUCTION

Scope of the book

In this book I propose a reinterpretation of Mao Tun's early fictional works—his first novel, the trilogy *Eclipse* (1927–28), the set of five short stories collected in *The Wild Roses* (1928–29), and three historical tales (1930)—a reinterpretation arrived at by taking into consideration their social, political, and biographical contexts. By concentrating on the social context, C. T. Hsia could take these works simply as realistic portraits of the lives of contemporary students, particularly of their amorous and political pursuits, while Ch'ien Hsing-ts'un, a sort of comrade of Mao Tun's, treats the trilogy as practically a disguised political history of the Communist Party during the Great Revolution. My concern is to find a place for both these components, the surface (social) narration and concealed (political) allegory in a framework which includes in addition Mao Tun's own reflections on revolution.

As I see it, the basic conflict in the trilogy is between the beauty of the ideal (the Communist cause) and the ugliness of its failure to attain its goal. How is one to live with failure? One response is the self-delusion of Miss Huan (in *The Wild Roses*). How can one avoid failure, and, in particular, deal with one's enemies (e.g., Pao-su)? It is necessary to deviate from the ideal and use stratagem and deception.

The trilogy was written at a time when Mao Tun was shocked by the sharp contrast between the purity of the ideal of revolution and the unsavory complexity of its attempted execution. He combined a realistic depiction of the effects of the revolution on particular regions and individuals with a layer of allegory presented in terms of the personal relations of the characters that parallel the political struggles within the Chinese Communist Party and its external relations to the Communist International and the Chinese Nationalist Party (KMT). The trilogy summarizes the revolutionary experience from 1926 to the beginning of 1928, and looks for an appropriate response to the discovery that faithful adherence to the revolutionary ideal is an inadequate guide to action.

The negative responses of suicide and self-delusion in *The Wild Roses* can be viewed as an admission of defeat or alternatively as the elimination of weaklings from the revolutionary ranks, leaving it to tougher souls to carry on with the revolution. Love has to be pushed into the background: the ideal must find a way to a more feasible means for attaining the ideal, for the cause can stay alive only if a realistic course can be found. Love gives way to power, for order is brought about only through power. In the historical tales Mao Tun continues the search for a way out by examining the need for deception and submission to leadership. Once these needs were accepted, the right course of revolution was settled for Mao Tun. From then on, the problem was to locate the leaders and to carry out the tasks ordained by the leadership in accordance with Communist premises.

Within this framework the writing of revolutionary literature became a simpler and more manageable endeavor. It was possible to adhere to a form of socialist realism by selecting and portraying actual happenings arranged to support the leaders' interpretation of current events so as to further the current needs of revolution. The famous novel *Midnight* typifies this next stage of Mao Tun's creative work. The earlier fictional works of Mao Tun are a record of his development as a revolutionary writer, dramatizing the choices with which he was faced. As such they constitute a coherent group of his writings, which in turn are an important part of modern Chinese literature from the May Fourth Movement (1919) to the present day.

To produce this group of work Mao Tun had to satisfy several apparently incompatible conditions: (1) He was himself a devoted and active revolutionary; (2) He wanted to reflect in his writing the current history of the revolution; (3) He wanted to go back to fundamentals, and not merely produce examples of what Lu Hsün called (approvingly) "command-obeying literature." At the time Mao Tun was a novice at fiction writing. In resorting to a subtle and complex use of allegory he set himself a formidable task that was carried out only with compromises (such as breaking up one work into three parts) and limited success (as exemplified by the mess toward the end of *Pursuit*). It is not surprising that the many levels of meaning in the resulting works are not easily accessible to the reader. I have tried to make them more accessible by showing the dialectical relation between Mao Tun's texts and multiple contexts, devices and meanings. The difficulties of interpretation are best illustrated by a brief review of my own extended efforts to solve the puzzle.

Puzzles about *Eclipse*

Mao Tun and his fictional works have always held a special fascination for me. The elusive complexity one senses in him and in his works make him particularly challenging. I have never felt that any one of his novels is particularly well-written. Quite the contrary, I have always felt that his novels and stories, especially the early ones, do not hang together well: there are too many desultory episodes in them, too much unexplained violence, and too many eccentric characters encountering mystifying fates. *Pursuit*, the third part of *Eclipse*, is a good case in point. I could not explain the character Shih Hsün, since nothing in the first two parts prepares one for his appearance, nor could I understand the significance of Miss Chang's fantastic therapeutic project. Freud was never an intellectual presence in China: where did Mao Tun get the idea that a release of inhibited sexual energy might restore a person to health?

These and other unresolved puzzles about Mao Tun's early fiction gradually became an obsession. I read his critics and their reviews of his novels, and was puzzled by apparent discrepancies between what Mao Tun said of his own concerns with *Eclipse* and what his critics wrote about it. Where he was concerned with the problems of artistic structure and adequacy of characterization, his critics concerned themselves primarily with the referential world of his text and ideological purity.

Then I discovered from Chang Kuo-t'ao's *Memoirs* that Mao Tun was a member of the Chinese Communist Party, and that he joined the party a month after its founding in Shanghai in July 1921. As I read on in Chang's *Memoirs*, I was struck by certain repeated terms such as *tung-yao* (vacillation) and *tzu-sha* (suicide), which brought to mind similar uses in *Eclipse* and suggested possible connections between Mao Tun's early fictional works and his personal activities as a member of the CCP in the 1920s.

I began to look for evidence that would support such connections, and published the results in an article, "Autumn in Kuling." The evidence there is largely in the form of tropes: emblems, symbols, allegories, which seem to exhibit an internal system and cohere to bring forth a meaningful reading of the text. Further research into the history of the CCP was incorporated in my second article (on *The Wild Roses*) which found correspondences between Mao Tun's own experience and his fictional text.

It was only after these preliminary skirmishes that I finally summoned the courage to tackle directly the formidable and intricate *Eclipse*. Of course I had been thinking about *Eclipse* all along. At one stage I suddenly became aware that my problems in understanding the interrelationship between the parts of that trilogy are exactly those which Mao Tun had been talking about in "From Kuling to Tokyo," where he tells how he went about writing the trilogy. They were problems of artistic structure and of techniques of characterization. Mao Tun said there that he could not quite make an integrated whole of the three stages of the revolution he was portraying in *Eclipse*, and today we see that there is a noticeable hiatus between the first two parts and the third part. The realization that

Mao Tun himself noticed incoherence in *Eclipse* encouraged me to proceed with more confidence.

To lay bare the devices with which Mao Tun constructed his fictional plots from the materials available in the outside world, I am here offering an *explication du texte* of his major novel, *Eclipse*, and the two clusters of short stories. There are a few familiar theoretical concepts which underlie my procedure.

Texts and multiple contexts

The issue of texts in Mao Tun's early fiction cannot be intelligently discussed apart from the question of contexts. Contexts constitute the referential world from which literary texts are structured. In chapter 2 we have a limited problem with the text of the short story "Autumn in Kuling." Whether the middle sections there were actually lost or censored out makes little difference to our reading of the story, given all the clues to the allegory supplied by the author in the story and its postscript. However, the cuts and changes made in the third part, *Pursuit*, constitute obvious contextual interference with the text. In the 1950s, more than twenty years after the publication of the work, Mao Tun was asked to make a "stylistic" editing which affects about one-third of the original work. Large chunks were deleted from chapters 6 and 7; the names of its principal characters were simplified in the interests of "consistency," when inconsistency may have been a deliberate novelistic device. In our reading of *Pursuit* in chapter 5 we shall see that it is not a question of textual variance as such, nor of "stylistic editing" in any common understanding of the term, but a work of free artistic creation brought into conformity with official dogma. *Disillusionment* and *Vacillation* also underwent some "stylistic editing," but not as extensively.

The broadly divergent interpretations of Mao Tun's early fictional works offered by C. T. Hsia and Ch'ien Hsing-ts'un stem from their differing perception of the context (or contexts) of his works.

Until the appearance of Mao Tun's "Memoirs" in the fall of 1979, his membership in the CCP and his activities as a high-level Party propagandist had never been revealed. Yet this information is central to an informed reading of his early fiction. In the absence of such information, critics have little chance to penetrate into the "reality" of the referential world represented in his early fiction.

Hsia's criticism derives from the Western humanistic value system, which claims the right of an individual to pursue freedom, happiness, and self-fulfillment, and he focuses on the development and interaction of the characters in fiction. Here, where men and women share many universals irrespective of race, ideological belief, or religion, he proves himself to be a perceptive and understanding critic. But Hsia does not always distinguish between what is in the literary texts and what is in the referential world; the principle of verisimilitude is literally subsumed.

Ch'ien Hsing-ts'un approached Mao Tun's early fiction from quite another point of view. After a career as a leftist radical, he became a member of the CCP in 1928. He reads Mao Tun's works of the 1920s with an inside knowledge of the latter's early Party membership and revolutionary activities which Hsia could not have. However, this knowledge did not enhance the quality of his criticism. His too is a cultural and historical criticism, in this case one steeped in a Marxist ideology, which regards literature as a vehicle of political indoctrination, and he judges a literary work in terms of its adherence to the current party line.

His ideology has a more restrictive influence on his understanding of literature and on his conception of how an author can design his work. For him what is important is not the meaning but the correctness of a writer's texts, contexts, and devices. Ch'ien distorts the principle of verisimilitude, for he leaves the author no freedom to structure his texts from the materials available in the referential world. Hence, what at first appears to be a difference in the respective ideological positions of the two critics on the issue of a political movement turns out to affect profoundly their implicit assumptions about the role and function of literature in the world in which they reside.

How does one go about determining which information from these multiple contexts (Mao Tun's life, his Party history, his role in that history, his interest in literature, the society of his days) is relevant to his structuring of the texts that concern us? The question of contexts quickly turns into one of artistic design and representation. It is only by examining the fictional works that we can answer the question: If the contexts are multiple, where do the shifts occur?

The artistic design of *Eclipse* and the short stories, as we shall see in chapter 3 and following, is intimately related to how Mao Tun viewed the course of the revolutionary movement which is the subject of his works. Chapter 2 illustrates how Mao Tun first began to structure his literary texts (short poems and a short story) from a welter of contextual materials (literary, historical, and biographical). We also see how the elucidation of such texts has to take into consideration the multiple contexts.

Since some of the contexts are not generally known, I have added a chapter on Mao Tun's life from approximately 1918, the time when he began to be totally politicized, to 1930, when he emerged from a period of despair over the catastrophic defeat of the revolutionary movement at the Canton Commune. In the chapters on *Eclipse, The Wild Roses* and the historical tales, I have provided the more immediate context of Party history, especially the role played by the Comintern.

Outlining the multiple contexts serves to document my allegorical reading of Mao Tun's early fiction, a reading that requires documentary proof. It also supplies the story stuff which Mao Tun transmuted into the plot of *Eclipse*. Events provide only the raw material even for a historian. The context of a literary text is at a further remove from events in their chronological order. It is a distinct sphere of human reality, illuminated by the writer's understanding of the meaning of the events, and organized into an artistic design by means of a set of literary devices so that a new meaning emerges.

The thinning of the text

Devices are an instrument for accommodating a multiplicity of contexts in a single text which may sometimes be distributed, as in the case of Mao Tun's trilogy, into several subtexts. The abundance of contexts increases the "density" of a text. If fewer contexts are present, we get what I would like to call a "thinning of the text" which accompanies a reduction of the contexts and a simplification of the devices. In order to arrive at a fuller understanding of the meaning of a text, it is, however, not sufficient to determine what contexts and devices are present; we have to examine also how the contexts are used in the text and which thematic or character material is the dominant.

Even though (Russian) Formalism is primarily concerned with the study of poetry, I find some of the concepts can also be adapted to look at some principal features of my study in this book.* In terms of devices, the concepts of defamiliarization, temporal rhythm, and parallelism all seem to apply to Mao Tun's artistic designs, particularly in his trilogy. In terms of meaning, the concepts of density, presence, and use as well as the dominant are all quite appropriate. For example, if we look at Mao Tun's creative work from 1927 to 1948, we find that after *Eclipse*, a thinning of the text had set in, largely as a result of his decision to move from a radical (personal and independent) reflection to a "command-obeying literature" stance. Another consequence of this change of purpose (and reduction of contexts) is the shift of attention from the ideals to the feasible measures (largely as determined by the leadership); thematically love gives way to power (which often resorts to deception).

---

*I have borrowed heavily from Victor Erlich's *Russian Formalism* in my attempt to put my interpretation of the early fiction of Mao Tun in a theoretical framework. The terms text, context, device, and meaning are all from Erlich's study of Russian Formalism. I wish to acknowledge full debt to Erlich in the conceptual and critical approach to Mao Tun in this chapter.

Once lies and deception are accepted (as necessary) in the process of revolutionary politics and in its representation in literature, love as a synthetic ordering of human emotions directly in tune with the zestful unmediated pursuit of the ideal is no longer possible. Love by definition is exclusive of lie either as a means or as an end. After *The Wild Roses* Mao Tun never wrote another love story. Throughout the decade of the 1930s, Mao Tun went into an earnest search for an heir to fill the vacancy of love in the emerging mercurial concept of class consciousness. When love resurges in *Putrefaction* (1942), it is represented not as love but as betrayal. Nostalgia, penitence, and atonement do not add up to love as a dominant, for they are deformations of love.

With a predetermined will to survive dominating his vision of the revolution at one end and an equally predetermined conclusion of victorious proletarian class consciousness at the other end, the freedom of formal creation in the text becomes increasingly localized, favoring the representation of the deathbed scene of the oppressing class. This is evident in most of the novels Mao Tun wrote after the three historical tales: *Midnight* (1933), *Polygonal Relations* 1936), and even his rather powerful *Frosty Leaves Red as February Flowers* (1942). What had once been a realm of free formal creation was reduced to a somewhat automatic formula largely based on an externally (by the Party) determined ideology.

Device and meaning

Having identified the contexts of Mao Tun's early fiction, the next step in our critical examination is to try to understand and, if possible, to define the use to which these heterogeneous material and ideas were put in his fictional works. For example, we know that in the early Chinese Communist Movement, there are at least two antithetical views of the goals and process of the revolution, a most obvious illustration being the bifurcated position toward the "United Front" policy with the KMT. Of course, there are also the more striking instances of the Nanch'ang Uprising and the Canton Commune. How are these internal antitheses represented in the literary text? In what images and constructs? How about the relationship of these political positions to the goals of the Chinese Communist revolutionary movement? After all, the avowed goals of "expelling imperialists" and "eradicating traitors" were the same not only for the rival factions of the CCP but also for the KMT. There was, however, a much greater specificity in Mao Tun's own conception of the goals of the revolution. How much of a dominant role for this specificity Mao Tun allows in his representation is an issue that one cannot ignore in a critical examination of the text.

In chapters 3, 4 and 5 I deal in great documentary detail with how Mao

Tun constructed his *Eclipse,* as a novel about the Great Revolution, from the contextual material of his Party history as well as literary sources and literary theories (Chinese and Western), employing a whole array of devices. The devices range from the more familiar ones like puns, symbols, literary allusions, emblems, and allegories to the less familiar ones such as what the Formalist school calls "parallelism" (which Mao Tun used for characterization) and "rhythm" and "density" (which he used in his plot construction). All these devices can be viewed as ways of "defamiliarization" ("creative deformation") which, according to the Formalist theory, functions by using a novel method in representation to make a familiar subject "perceptible" to the readers again.

Defamiliarization

The most noticeable example of Mao Tun's use of this device is his treatment of sex in *Eclipse.* Whether as a device of characterizing the new women types in his fiction or as an allegorical device to represent Party politics, its function of shaking his readers into a new perception certainly is effective. As I see it, what we want to find out, for example in *Disillusionment,* is not so much whether Miss Hui, Miss Sun Wu-yang, and Miss Chang Ch'iu-liu are realistic portrayals of exceptional or even revolutionary women at the time but rather what it is that Mao Tun wanted to render perceptible by throwing their attitude towards sex into bold relief.

Some critics of *Eclipse* who are in the know about the political target to which the device is directed were outraged. Ch'ien Hsing-t'un, for instance, denounced vociferously Mao Tun's use of sex in the characterization of his modern women and the editor of the official edition of *Eclipse* in the early 1950s simply expurgated, ostensibly on puritanical grounds, the more explicit description of it in *Pursuit.*

Throughout Mao Tun's early fiction more local uses of the device of defamiliarization can be found in his seemingly accidental allusions to Western literary sources: Dostoevsky's *Crime and Punishment* and Maeterlinck's "Mona Vanna" in *Disillusionment,* Russian Futurism in the character of Ch'iang Meng in the same novel, and the goddesses of Fate (Greek and Nordic) in *The Wild Roses.* And the creative deformation he exercises over the *Water Margin* sources in the three historical tales further testifies to his innovative ability as an artist in handling the literary material.

Temporal rhythm and plot construction

"Rhythm," the artistic tempo created out of an even flow of chronological time in *Eclipse* and elsewhere, certainly is a central feature of Mao Tun's "plotting device." Critics who insist on an adherence to chronology as a necessary condition of realistic fiction will certainly consider Mao Tun's deviation from the temporal order of events in contemporary history a distortion and a misrepresentation of "facts." Ch'ien Hsing-ts'un again, as the spokesman for those who were in the know about the actual chronology of some of the story stuff used in *Eclipse*, took great pleasure in pointing out such discrepancies as indisputable proof of the novel's weaknesses and flaws. The overnight love affair between Pao-su and Miss Ching in *Disillusionment*, for instance, was criticized by Ch'ien knowingly as happening "too soon." Ch'ien even considered it regrettable that the military action toward the end of the novel did not last long enough. More of it, he said, should be worked into the text. The basis on which Ch'ien offered these "corrections" goes beyond literary criticism and is worth a closer examination, which I shall make in chapter 3.

The relationship between the three parts of *Eclipse* has never attracted much discussion by Mao Tun's critics, in spite of the fact that Mao Tun has made it one of the two foci of his own defense of the work in "From Kuling to Tokyo" (the other being characterization and character types). *Vacillation*, as we shall see in chapter 4, is temporally in parallel to the time period spanned by chapters 7 to 11 of *Disillusionment*. Yet the discrepancies between mass movements as a Party policy and the effects of its implementation was so great that Mao Tun, as a beginning novelist, could not devise a plot structure plastic enough to formally contain within one novel the widely divergent developments of the same theme on two different levels.

To simplify this formidable task, Mao Tun adopted an independent treatment of the actual events of the mass movement in *Vacillation*, which was in large measure dislodged from the context of *Disillusionment*. The appearance of Li Ke and Shih Chun in both books supports my reading that *Disillusionment* deals with the headquarters (allegorically) while *Vacillation* deals with the district level (manifestly). Following this reading, a more significant link is the Futurist Ch'iang Wei-li recovering from a near fatal wound on the battlefield he craved for and loved. I take him as a symbol both for the revolutionary zeal which Mao Tun affirmed and for the casualties suffered on the local level (whether the mass movements depicted in *Vacillation* or the battle in Honan). Mao Tun's affirmation of Ch'iang is revealed by his uncorrupted love affair with Miss Ching, the only admirable love relation in the whole trilogy.

This shift in levels of presentation within *Disillusionment* and between *Disillusionment* and *Vacillation* serves as a magnified illustration of Mao Tun's efforts to control the rhythm and density of his text, thereby making it easier to bring the dominant factors in his representation of the revolution into relief. If *Vacillation* were woven into *Disillusionment*, the mixture would distort the rhythm of the text and displace the dominant in it. The parallel composition in the rhythmic structure of the three parts in *Eclipse* yields a text much richer than critics have so far credited the novel with. A literary text as a system according to the Formalist theory does not mean coexistence of components on the basis of equality. It presupposes the preeminence of one group of elements over the scaling down of others. The notion of the dominant underlies practically all the episodes having to do with villainous characters in *Eclipse.* Their characterization may occupy considerable space in a text such as the character Hu Kuo-kuang in *Vacillation* and Pao-su in the first half of *Disillusionment;* but their importance on the scale of the dominant for a novel on revolution is impressionably foreshortened in Hu's case in his ultimate non-appearance, and in Pao-su in the time allotted to his "overnight seduction plan."

The rhythm in *Pursuit,* that is, its temporal order, is thrown into great confusion because of the violent emotional reaction Mao Tun experienced when he learned about the catastrophic happenings at the December 1927 "Canton Commune" several months after it took place. Chapters 6 and 7 of *Pursuit* are totally out of step, in terms of the temporal order, with the rest of the novel no matter whether we look at them from within the text or outside of it.

The new Miss Wang whom Miss Chang found sick and pregnant in chapter 6 is a phenomenon totally unprepared for. The gory vision of Tung-fang Ming's head bobbing on a ring of blood in the same chapter and the sexual orgy in the following chapter merely serve to shock. Where do they come from? Mao Tun's inability to give a clear account of what is going on in those two chapters and how they fit into the total context of the novel as a whole comes through vividly in his desperate but unsuccessful attempt at getting hold of the time scheme in *Pursuit.*

He tried, I think, to juxtapose the events of chapters 6 and 7 with those in chapters 1 through 5 by evoking the same date, May 3, 1928, to highlight the ironic contrast between the unperturbed pursuits of those allegorical students (in chapters 1 through 5) at the very time when catastrophes are visiting their close classmates (in chapters 6 and 7). Recurrence of the same date here works on the compositional level like alliteration and rhythmical parallelism to convey a note of ironical contrast. The major problem in placing the temporal order is the handling of the Canton Commune which, from what I take to be conclusive evidence, exerted great influence on the construction of *Pursuit,* which was written from April to June of 1928. There was a fairly long interval between the occurrence of the actual episode of the Commune and its being known in Shanghai where totally different types of Party activity were taking place. Mao Tun tried to depict the impact of the Commune in chapters 6 and 7 in a disguised form and shifted the time scale.

What drove Mao Tun to frenzy there was his perceptions of the equally fatal impact on the revolution of the lazy and almost vacuous activities in Shanghai (portrayed in chapters 1 through 5) and the violent but mis-guided sacrifices at the Commune (with its effects portrayed in chapters 6 and 7). Despairing of both kinds of revolutionary effort, he concluded

Pursuit with a despairing final chapter. But before his despair developed into hopelessness in *The Wild Roses*, Mao Tun was still able to discern a difference between the two approaches, which were depicted in *Pursuit* as both mistaken. This distinction may very well be related to the moral distinction he then and later made between those who are damned because they had not loved wisely (Miss Chang and Miss Wang and Ch'iung-hua) and those who were not able to love at all (Miss Chu and Chang Man-ch'ing).

Parallelism and Mao Tun's art of characterization

The effects of Mao Tun's women character types in *Eclipse* are frequently construed by his critics as "daring" and "new," seemingly testifying to his successful delivery of defamiliarization as a device for character portrayal. But whatever this newness means and represents, it is certainly not a uniform object, especially when we consider Mao Tun's statement that his women characters are representative of revolutionary types. Revolution as the dominant central object for fictional representation in *Eclipse* is bifurcated through the device of parallel character types which register multiple reflections and juxtapositions on the level of composition. Synchronic examples are the pairs Hui-Ching and Mrs. Fang-Sun Wu-yang, as well as the quadruplet of Chang Chiu-liu, Wang Shih-tao, Chu Chin-ju, and Mrs. Lu. In addition, there is also the diachronic pair of Chang Ching and Chang Ch'iu-liu. Here again I should like to reiterate that the central critical problem in Mao Tun's fictional characters is not in their presence and their referent in the outside world, but the use to which they are put in the content of the literary text as a distinct sphere of perceived reality.

In the body of this book, I have devoted a great deal of attention to the role of parallelism and the use of the characters in Mao Tun's text. This is another area in which critical discussion has been sparse. Miss Ching, for instance, needs Miss Hui to bring out her relative position in the bifurcated development of love and revolution in time. I have explained in chapter 3 the meaning of parallel love affairs with Pao-su, and in chapter 5 the much denser love affairs of three couples in *Pursuit*. On the whole, women types in Mao Tun's early fiction are, I believe, not just realistic portrayals of *new* women, but generally used to structure the development of the Communist movement on the policy as well as the execution levels. Their adventures with love and sex not only reflect the existing attitudes among young bourgeois intellectuals on the subject, but also denote allegorically Mao Tun's own revolutionary ideals as well as the attitudes of different factions, the successes and the failures in the immediate history of the Chinese Communist Party.

I

FROM SHEN YEN-PING
TO MAO TUN
LITERATURE–POLITICS–LITERATURE

Mao Tun (1896–1981) was one of the most versatile writers and novelists of twentieth-century China. His major novels include the trilogy *Disillusionment, Vacillation,* and *Pursuit,* which was serialized in 1927–28 and published as one novel in 1930 under the collective title *Eclipse; Rainbow* (1929); *Midnight* (1933); *Putrefaction* (1941); and *Frosty Leaves as Red as February Flowers* (1942). In all, Mao Tun published thirteen novels, more than a hundred short stories, a play, two studies of Chinese mythology, two studies of Western mythology, and many articles (more than three hundred) and books on Western literature, thought, and literary theories. He also compiled high-school textbooks of classical Chinese literature and was editor of a number of important literary journals: *Short Story Monthly* in the 1920s, *Literature* in the 1930s, *Literary Front* in the 1940s, *People's Literature* and *World Literature* in the 1950s. In 1949, after the founding of the People's Republic of China, official recognition was awarded to him for the roles he played, first as a pioneer in a new literature that was eminently "modern" and of its time, and later as an untiring literary worker and promoter of cultural exchanges among nations. He became Minister of Culture in 1949 and remained in that office until 1965. He was also Vice-Chairman of the All-China Federation of Writers and Artists, Chairman of the Chinese Writers Union (1949), a member of and later Vice-Chairman of the People's Political Consultative Conference (a non-Party organization devoted to the task of forming a united front of all non-Communist people in China), a member of the Preparatory Committee and then the Executive Board of the Sino-Soviet Friendship Association (and a Vice-Chairman from 1956), and a member of the Board of Directors of the Chinese People's Association for Cultural Relations with Foreign Countries (1954). In 1975 a group of distinguished French writers and scholars nominated Mao Tun for the Nobel Prize for literature.[1]

Mao Tun died on March 27, 1981. In his obituary in the *People's Daily,* the Chinese Communist Party's national newspaper, he was referred to as a "modern Chinese literary giant in the tradition of Lu Hsün." Two weeks later, on April 11, an official memorial meeting in Peking was attended by many living Party leaders such as Hua Kuo-feng, Teng Hsiao-p'ing, Li Hsien-nien, P'eng Chen, Teng Yin-ch'ao (widow of Chou En-lai), Hu Yao-pang, and Chao Tzu-yang and was chaired by Teng Hsiao-p'ing. There a great honor which he had coveted in the last years of his life was conferred on him. Hu Yao-pang, Secretary General of the Chinese Communist Party and the keynote speaker at the memorial meeting, officially restored Mao Tun's party membership, recognizing it retroactively all the way back to 1921, when, as we now know, Mao Tun first joined the CCP.

For the fifty years and more since the publication of *Eclipse* made him a national figure overnight, Mao Tun had not been known as a member of the CCP. He was looked upon in China and abroad as a prominent leftist writer who sympathized with the Chinese Communist movement in China, and who had attained considerable political eminence after the CCP took power in 1949. Because of the very peculiar political situation in China and the even more peculiar Chinese Communist Party politics of the past half-century, nothing was ever openly said about Mao Tun's joining the Party immediately after it was founded in July 1921. His fellow writers and critics, even those who were Party members and sympathizers, were uniformly reticent. Ch'ien Hsing-ts'un, his most perceptive and caustic critic, joined the Party in 1928; Ch'ü Ch'iu-po, a harsh but friendly devil's advocate, was Secretary General of the Party in 1927–28 as well as its leading literary theorist. Nevertheless, their references to the relationships between Mao Tun's literary and his "other" activities were so oblique that the public view of him as a literary man, profoundly sympathetic to the revolutionary cause but never an activist, remained undisturbed. Historians in Japan and Taiwan sometimes include his name on their lists of early Chinese Communist Party members, but his name appears only as a documentary item, unrelated to Party history.

Mao Tun's biographers usually note his various "leftist" activities and record what he did in which year with great accuracy. Klein and Clark's well-researched *Biographic Dictionary of Chinese Communism* (1971),[2] for example, records Mao Tun's working relationship with Mao Tse-tung in Canton in 1925–26 in the Propaganda Department of the Nationalist Party (the Kuomintang or KMT), and notes that in 1957, when Mao Tse-tung was head of state, Mao Tun accompanied his chief to Moscow as an official member of the delegation attending the fortieth anniversary celebration of the Russian Revolution. It also records Mao Tun's working relationship with the Red scholar Tung Pi-wu and Mao Tse-tung's brother Mao Tse-min, when they were editing and managing the CCP-

controlled *Hankow Republic Daily* in 1927, during the Wuhan period of
CCP–KMT collaboration, and with Mao Tse-min in Sinkiang in 1939 for
assignments that were extremely perilous but whose true nature is still a
matter of speculation. His Party membership is not mentioned, however,
nor is the question raised why the Chinese leadership sought out Mao
Tun to work in the volatile area of Sino-Soviet relationships during the
1950s. The *Dictionary* assumes that he was one of the literary luminaries
whose "allegiance" the authorities "were eager to gain."

Thus for over half a century, information about Mao Tun's covert
activities as one of the first CCP members was suppressed. The excitement and struggle surrounding his early career as a young Communist,
his status as a committed revolutionary writer from within the CCP, and
the complex ways he used his life experiences in his work were obscured.
Critics and biographers were interested in Mao Tun primarily as a novelist and essayist on modern Chinese literature, and after 1949, when his
creative writing stopped, they ceased to pay him much attention. Students of Chinese politics, on the other hand, might well have been interested in why he was sought out by the new government for responsibility
in two of its most difficult areas, literature and Sino-Soviet relations. And
his timely replacement as Minister of Culture (by Lu Ting-yi) in January
1965, just before the Cultural Revolution flared up, was surely a further
clue to his closeness to the Party leadership.

In November 1978, without forewarning, Mao Tun published the first
installment of his "Memoirs" in the first issue of a new official journal,
Source Materials on the History of the New Literature, and this timing
looks very much as if the one was designed to introduce the other. The
"Memoirs" do not begin with Mao Tun's family background and ancestry, as is conventional in Chinese autobiographical writing, but with his
first job, as a proofreader and translator in Shanghai; they then dive
speedily into a revelation of Mao Tun's youthful interest in Marxism and
his joining the Communist Party.[3]

The first fifteen installments, published between November 1978 and
May 1982, cover the years 1916 to 1930, a period when the nation, the
society, and Mao Tun's life were all in ferment. It was a document unique
in post-1949 China: no one of Mao Tun's stature had received permission
to lay bare what had been kept under rigorous security for over half a
century.

The true circumstances surrounding the publication of the "Memoirs"
may someday be known, but for the purposes of this book, it is quite
sufficient that we learn from the unchallenged authority of Mao Tun
himself that he became a member of the Chinese Communist Party the
year it was founded and that he worked with its leadership. More
specifically, he worked as a high-level Party propagandist in Shanghai and
then in Canton and Wuhan from 1923 to 1927, and at the same time was

intensely involved with the labor and women's movements and the training of cadres for the mass movements. In Canton in the early months of 1926 he was, with Mao Tse-tung, an eyewitness of Chiang Kai-shek's famous March 20 coup, the Chungshan Gunboat Incident, in which Chiang for the first time asserted military leadership of all the revolutionary forces in China by instigating a Communist naval revolt that he quickly put down.

This and other information about Mao Tun's life between 1921 and 1927, when he adopted this pen name for his first and most important novel, *Eclipse,* provides additional documentary support for the central thesis of this book, formed before the appearance of the "Memoirs," on the primary basis of the novels themselves. The early fiction of Mao Tun consists of allegorical representations of the early Chinese Communist movement in China; it is not merely, as most critics East and West have thought, realistic fiction about young urban intellectuals and their romantic and political adventures.

The "Memoirs" provide an unprecedented amount of information on Mao Tun's early life, his career as a young Communist, his CCP work, and the context of his writings. They also put beyond dispute Mao Tun's political preeminence in Chinese Communist history. Nevertheless, the historical framework that encloses the autobiographical account has some rather serious omissions. The omnipresent role of the Moscow-based Communist International in the early years of the Chinese Communist movement, for example, is almost completely ignored, and we see very little of the personalities and activities of early CCP leaders. Li Li-san, Liu Shao-ch'i, Chang Kuo-t'ao, and Chou En-lai—to name only a few—were all in Shanghai, Canton, and Wuhan in the 1920s. As a high-level Party propaganda and mass movements man, Mao Tun inevitably had constant and close contact with them.

The "Memoirs" are also quite selective about Mao Tun's studies in Western literatures and literary theories. He was careful to document his early interest in Marxism, and quite informative about his studies of Walter Scott and Alexander Dumas (indigenous and Western historical romances and plays are popular in China today and this literary genre seems to have the authorities' approval and encouragement). But Mao Tun's silence about his once fervent interest in Russian literature, especially in the theories of the Futurist school and the poetry of the great Russian Futurist Vladimir Mayakovsky, is noticeable. Similarly, there is little mention of the nineteenth-century German Symbolist playwright Gerhart Hauptmann, on whom Mao Tun wrote a biographical article.[4]

But the area that requires special caution is Mao Tun's discussions of the origins of his own work. In any culture, even one without censorship, writers tend to oversimplify when they try to explain themselves. In his "Memoirs," Mao Tun's selective attention to his own works suggests something more than censorship. He seems to be trying in his later years to revise the essence of his own writing, making it conform to the aesthetics he developed later. His discussion of *Eclipse*, for instance, is so clouded by autobiographical data and superficial equation of Party figures and personal acquaintances with its characters that critics in the future will have a hard time fighting this irresistible autobiographical undertow. And the amount of critical adulation for *Midnight* quoted in "Memoirs XIII," an installment published after his death, is totally uncharacteristic of Mao Tun. The only possible explanation is that the editorial committee for the "Memoirs" wanted badly to stamp *Midnight* as the greatest and most representative, as well as currently the most acclaimed, of his novels.

The venerable Mao Tun painted a partial self-portrait of a young revolutionary and writer in his "Memoirs." The society recreated there is in upheaval, but the old man remembering it is now at peace. With his Party at last in power, he has even become a conformist. Still committed to the Party that he helped to found and that embodied what he held most sacred, he did not want at the end of his life to leave a legacy of dissension. Surely Mao Tun was a patriot of the highest order, persuaded at the age of eighty-two that the most patriotic thing he could do was continue his record of impeccable service by clearing his Party of all possible future charges that it had suppressed the truth about the life and achievements of one of its greatest writers and most devoted members. Nothing in the "Memoirs" was to blemish the Party's image or unsettle the official version of its history.

In Mao Tun's early creative years there had been three levels of censorship: self-censorship, that of the Party, and that of the government in power. Each required him to veil subject matter and content. At the end of his life, with Party and government combined, he still labored under much the same conditions. The "Memoirs" establishes once and for all Mao Tun's importance in the history of Chinese Communism. Nevertheless, in interpreting his early fiction, we will be well advised to examine the new information even more carefully than his earlier autobiographical statements. The creative works themselves, with their imaginative and allegorical subtexts, show us their meaning more clearly than either Mao Tun or his critics can do.

Chinese and Western critics today consider Mao Tun a writer of the realist school and a master of psychological realism. But as he began to write his fiction Mao Tun also used allegory and symbolism to express themes and ideas that he could not express directly.

Allegory and symbolism have a long and honorable tradition in China, and Mao Tun knew the tradition well. He had an extensive background in classical Chinese and had edited, among other classical texts for high-school students, the writings of the philosopher Chuang-tzu and the anthology of ancient poetry *Ch'u-tz'u,* two treasure houses of ancient myth, political allegories, and symbolism. He could write both classical free prose, which is simple and forceful, and parallel prose, which is highly formal and allusive. Hence the allegories and symbols that appear in Mao Tun's fiction can claim their source in traditional Chinese literature, which was as strong an influence as his studies of nineteenth- and twentieth-century European literature or Greek and Nordic mythology.

Mao Tun was a prolific writer, subject to all these influences at one time or another. He also used so many pen names for so many purposes over so many decades—from his first article, "Students and Society," written in classical Chinese and published in *Student Magazine* in December 1917, to his "Memoirs"—that the Japanese scholar Matsui Hiromitsu's noble effort to catalogue his "creative works, critical essays, and prose" has not been completed after more than twenty years.[5] At the beginning of Mao Tun's career many of these pseudonyms were assumed for reasons of practical publishing, to vary the bylines in Commercial Press publications. Very soon they were also used to avoid or postpone government retaliation.

Mao Tun began his literary career when he arrived at the Commercial Press, the largest in Shanghai, in August 1916 to compile anthologies for students and general readers and to translate books and articles written in English, of which he had a working knowledge. His supervisor was an elderly scholar named Sun Yü-hsiu, who had a predilection for writing in the parallel-prose style. Mao Tun was about twenty then, already versed in traditional Chinese literature. When Sun asked him what books he had read in classical Chinese, he was able to answer boastfully,

> What I have come into contact with from my high school days to my Peking University days can be put this way: I read no books that are written after the Ch'in and the Han dynasties [meaning he read only the purest classics]; I consider parallel prose to be the orthodox tradition in writing; I have perused all Thirteen Classics and their commentaries, the works of the pre-Ch'in philosophers, the Four Histories—*Records of the Grand Historian, History of the Former Han Dynasty, History of the Later Han Dynasty,* and *Histories of the Three Kingdoms*—the Collected Works of the one hundred and three writers from Han Dynasty, Wei Dynasty through the Six Dynasties, the [*Prince*] *Chao-ming's Literary Anthology,* the *Comprehensive Mirror for Political Government,* the Nine *T'ung* (encyclopedias of institutions), the *Twenty-four* [*Dynastic*] *Histories* and the poetry and other writings of famous writers.[6]

Allowing for exaggeration, it still represents an impressive classical education, and his knowledge was immediately tapped for his first assignment, to select and edit a collection of Chinese fables and parables.

Mao Tun went on to compile more school and general books, writing introductions in parallel prose. At the same time he was translating such books for popular readership as Edward Carpenter's *Travels in Europe,* which he hoped would relieve Chinese ignorance about how Westerners eat, dress, and live. The following year two things happened that were to exert a decisive influence. One was the transformation of the general-intellectual *Youth Magazine* into the revolutionary *New Youth* under the editorship of Ch'en Tu-hsiu, who later became the founder and first Secretary General of the Chinese Communist Party. The other was the Bolshevik Revolution in Russia. *New Youth,* published in Peking, was faithfully read by Mao Tun and the rest of the young Shanghai intellectuals. When it published Hu Shih's "Draft Proposal of Literary Reform" and Ch'en Tu-hsiu's "Theory of Constructive Literary Revolution," and later Li Ta-chao's two articles on the Bolshevik Revolution and Marxism—"Victory of the People" and "My Understanding of Marxism"—Mao Tun began to develop an active interest in the creation of a new Chinese literature that would be written in the vernacular for the people (as against the earlier tradition of using classical Chinese and writing in conformity with Confucian politics and ethics for an elite class); and in Marxism as a school of thought from the West that advocated social and political changes via revolution. He began to pay special attention to Russian literature and wrote in classical Chinese his first critical essay, "Tolstoi and Russia Today," for the Commercial Press's *Student Magazine* of April 1919.

The May Fourth Movement of 1919, which began as a student demonstration in Peking to protest the government's humiliating concession of Chinese territorial rights to foreign powers at the Paris Peace Conference, soon developed into a nation-wide patriotic "Save-the-Nation" movement. Confucianism was denounced for having been at the very root of all the ills that plagued China in a modern world, and the intellectuals' quest for guidelines in Western literature and politics to cure China's degradation became more urgent. As Mao Tun said,

> That was a period of vigorous intellectual activities. The intelligentsia, influenced by this and that school of Western thought, gobbled down everything that was new coming from the West as if they were famished and dying of thirst. They vied to introduce to China the many "-isms" in Western thoughts and theories. What everybody was thinking was that feudalism in China had to be jettisoned, replacement had to come from the West. Hence "taking over-ism" ['na-lai-chu-i" or appropriating whatever might be useful] was a popular slogan at that time.[7]

In 1920 Mao Tun too was reaching out toward many schools of radical thought in the West. He studied Nietzsche and wrote "The Teachings of Nietzsche," published in *Student Magazine* in January 1920, and he studied anarchism enough to publish "Bakunin and Anarchism" in another Commercial Press magazine that same month. He probed into the social and political institutions of the West and wrote both "The Family in the Future Society" and "The Russian People and Soviet Government" the same year.[8] His interest in "modern," or Westernized, social and political institutions that might be useful for China was soon to be transmuted and given fictional expression. When he was asked to take over the "reform" of the Commercial Press's popular *Short Story Monthly*, which had been dominated by the so-called Mandarin Duck and Butterflies School of fiction (also known as the Saturday School, because *Saturday* magazine was famous for propagating sentimental popular fiction), Mao Tun found a new medium of self-expression.

From 1921, when the first "reformed" issue of *Short Story Monthly* appeared (which for the first time carried a cover illustration—a picture of a newborn baby in its crib), to the second half of 1925, when he "severed his professional tie with literature"[9] to devote himself to the revolution, Mao Tun wrote almost uncountable articles on Western literature. He published essays on realism, naturalism, romanticism, neoromanticism, Symbolism, and Futurism. He read in English translation and introduced to his audience Russian writers (Dostoevsky, Tolstoi, Chekhov, Gorky, Mayakovsky, Kropotkin), French writers (Flaubert, Dumas, Maupassant), and Scandinavian writers. He published literature from Spain, England, America, and "oppressed countries" like Ireland and Poland, as well as Zionist works. To learn, to know, and to assimilate creatively and selectively were the purposes of this enormous literary undertaking, and a more parochial purpose had its place also. He was waging a three-front war with the Saturday School, which resented his attacks on and exposure of their "decadence" and "outdatedness"; with the Creation Society—led by Kuo Mo-jo, Ch'eng Fang-wu and Yü Ta-fu, who had studied in Japan and advocated art for art's sake in creative writing—over questions of aesthetics; and with the *Hsüeh-heng* School in Nanking, which advocated a return to ancient classical literature.[10] As Mao Tun described the excitement from the hindsight of more than sixty years:

> It seems incomprehensible today that one could be so enthusiastic in those days about the literary schools of nineteenth-century Europe. But at the time everybody thought this way: If we are to learn from the West, we have to go to the very root and very beginning of things and cannot stop at having had only a taste. I too, when I was studying Chinese literature earlier, had gone to the very root and very beginning of it. Since I had now shelved all my Chinese books and turned to Europe for borrowings, it was only right that I should begin with Greece and Rome, cutting across the nineteenth century and down to its *fin de siécle* [a favorite phrase of Mao Tun's]. . . . This is the reason I undertook to study Greek and Nordic mythology, Greek and Roman literature, chivalric literature and the litera-

ture of the Renaissance. I was convinced that only in this way could I
select broadly and apply comprehensively, drawing upon the essences of
others to transform them into flesh and blood of my own. And only in this
way would I be able to create epoch-making new literature.[11]

When Mao Tun set out to realize this lofty ambition, he did indeed
draw upon the "essences" of both Chinese and Western literature. And he
used them to their fullest in his earlier novels and short stories. Critics in
the West as well as in China have always considered *Midnight* to be (1933)
Mao Tun's most important novel. His reputation as a creative writer rests
primarily on this, his only translated novel[12] and on several short stories
of that period which have also been translated and which deal with the
same theme: the imminent fall of the traditional Chinese social order.[13]

Less well-known but even more significant in political as well as literary terms is a group of significantly different novels and short stories
written between 1927 and 1933. These works, on which the present study
will focus, include his first and most controversial trilogy, *Eclipse;* five
short stories collected in *The Wild Roses* (1929), which was politely ignored at the time and barely acknowledged in the "Memoirs"; a set of
three historical tales (1930), "Lin Ch'ung the Leopard Head," "Great
Marsh District," and "Stone Tablet"; and "Autumn in Kuling," an enigmatic story published in 1933 but arguably written much earlier. When
Eclipse appeared it received enormous attention, including extensive and
prolonged attacks from critics on the radical left. The three novels were
denounced as weak in plot and characterization, lacking authenticity in
their depiction of the revolutionary spirit. The standard critical line of
later years is that *Midnight* represents the peak of Mao Tun's artistic
achievement, whereas the earlier works are qualitatively inferior and artistically unsatisfactory. Such criticism obscures the true nature of these
novels and stories and distorts the perspective from which Mao Tun
meant them to be read. The themes and characters in these novels, in fact,
recur often in Mao Tun's later works, which indicates that they represent
something profound and lasting in Mao Tun's creative consciousness. The
question, of course, can always be asked whether the more popular and
better received works of a writer are necessarily intellectually and thematically the more important and interesting. In Mao Tun's case, the
answer is no.

One can readily discern two dominant themes in all his thirteen novels:
socialist revolution in China and the economic disintegration of the old
order. Of the two themes, the former is much closer to Mao Tun's heart;
it appears in *Eclipse* and the other earlier works. Later, he returned to the
theme of revolution for better understanding and further clarification. In
Rainbow (1929), Mao Tun looked further back into the past, into the
experience of pre-May Fourth youth, in search of an answer to the ques-

tion why and in what sense the May Fourth Movement and the Great Revolution of 1925–27 were necessary and inevitable. Thirteen years later, in *Frosty Leaves as Red as February Flowers* (1942), by portraying a stifling family life early in the century Mao Tun demonstrated why, long before the May Fourth Movement and the Great Revolution, young people had already found it impossible to continue living with the old system. In *The Wild Roses,* as well as two less successful short novels, *The Road* (1930) and *In Company of Three* (1931), Mao Tun's own inability to accept the catastrophic failure of his party in the 1925–27 revolution was vividly expressed in the failure of his fictional characters to achieve full self-realization. *Frosty Leaves,* along with *Putrefaction* (1941), a novel about the insidiousness of the KMT secret police system, becomes part of another trio when we add *Tempering* (1948), Mao Tun's last novel. Like *Midnight, Tempering* is set in Shanghai. The structural thinking that underlies these three novels parallels that of the trio published in the late 1920s and early 1930s, *Eclipse, Rainbow,* and *Midnight.* The 1940s trio represents Mao Tun's last effort as a creative writer to try to understand, represent, and come to terms with the most momentous phenomenon in modern Chinese history: the tragic necessity of the Communist revolution. It was necessary because of the stagnant social condition within *(Rainbow, Frosty Leaves)* and capitalistic and imperialistic exploitation from without *(Midnight, Tempering).* It was tragic because of the human faith, love, and ideals woven into the revolutionary movement *(Eclipse, The Wild Roses)* that made it perennially vulnerable to intrigue, tyranny, and betrayal by comrades and enemies alike (the three historical tales, *The Road, In Company of Three, Putrefaction*).

Mao Tun made only one known attempt at large-scale representation of the post-1949 socialist reconstruction effort in literary form. It was a movie script about the national campaigns against corruption and bureaucracy, written in the 1950s in Shanghai, before the campaign to suppress intellectual freedom and criticism of government and Party leadership began in 1957. The script never saw publication nor was the movie produced; Mao Tun is said to have used the sheets of his manuscript as lining for his spittoon, till every bit of it was used up.[14]

To understand Mao Tun and to appreciate his contribution to modern Chinese literature, we need to reassess his most misunderstood works, the novels and short stories published between 1927 and 1930. It will also be useful to examine the historical framework in which they are set and rediscover some of the issues that provoked such stormy criticism in the late 1920s from Ch'ien Hsing-ts'un and Ch'ü ch'iu-po and from the less understanding but more vociferous Fu K'e-hsing.

The first area to explore is the life of the man himself, from the time he joined the Chinese Communist Party to the time he settled on the significant pen name Mao Tun—Contradiction—for his creative writings.

His activities and experiences as a dedicated Communist worker in these early years are intimately related to his early fictional works, all of which deal with the Communist movement. Many of what his contemporary critics regarded as flaws in these novels are best regarded as something more than artistic failings. They are reflections of Mao Tun's mixed feelings about the uncertain future of his Party and about the morality of certain revolutionary tactics (such as agitation, violence, and deception) adopted by its leaders. Almost alone among the Communist writers of the May Fourth era, Mao Tun tried to articulate his profound personal skepticism about his Party's governance by international Communist authority and the correctness of its national leadership, which was torn by incessant infighting and fitful changes of line.

In his fiction of 1927–30, such flaws as "inconsistent" characters (Wang Shih-t'ao), undependable authorial variations in involvement with them—from passionate closeness to a cold "overdistancing" which is most noticeable in his characterization in *Pursuit* and *Vacillation* respectively—uneven emphasis on plot development (between the first half and the second half of *Disillusionment* for example), the problem of the Jamesian unreliable narrator in "Suicide," the discrepancy in scale of representation and scale of value in *Vacillation,* and the allegorical meaning of his women characters, which could not but escape the attention of any reader who did not know of the historical facts involved, stem from a young writer's struggle to shape his material to his creative will. Other flaws may be regarded in the 1980s as genuine artistic failures: the obscuring effect of his "profile" technique rather than full exploration in the characterization of Li K'e, Shih Chün, and Fang Lo-lan; the sudden and anachronistic shift from the real time of Chang Man-ch'ing and Wang Chung-chao in *Pursuit* to the remembered, psychological time of Wang Shih-t'ao and Chang Ch'iu-liu without adequate preparation, and the failure to give even a minimal representation of Lung Fei who has been instrumental in the death of Wang Shih-tao's lover, Tung-fang Ming. In these works Mao Tun is grappling with the overwhelming task of trying to create a form, for his reader and probably for himself, that gives some order, purpose, and meaning to the anarchical bloodshed spreading around him. The resulting perception, especially in *Eclipse,* comes painfully close to Yeats's terrible vision in his poem on the Irish Easter Rising, "The Second Coming": "The best lack all conviction, while the worst / Are full of passionate intensity." Mao Tun's fictional men and women, such committed revolutionaries as Tung-fang Ming, Shih Hsün, and Wang Shih-t'ao, die, commit suicide, or sell their bodies to survive, and miscreants like Hu Kuo-kuang *(Vacillation)* and Dean Thorn *(The Road)* often carry the day. Mao Tun's comrades and comradely critics would have preferred it otherwise. They wanted unblemished, ever victorious protagonists who whatever the strictures of censorship could symbolize an unblemished revolution. Mao Tun's own life, especially his years in the Party, tells us much about why the young writer could not oblige.

Mao Tun was born in Chekiang Province, Central China, in 1896. His name was Shen Te-hung and his courtesy name Yen-ping.[15] His father died when he was ten, and in 1914, at the age of eighteen, he left his large gentry family in Wu Village, Tung County, to enroll in the first year of preparatory study at Peking University.[16] After two years at the university, financial hardship at home forced him to leave. In 1916 he went to Shanghai, the cultural capital of China and its most westernized city, and through family connections got his first job with the huge Commercial Press. His career, like that of many men of letters at that time, began almost at once to be divided between literature and politics.[17]

Between 1918 and 1920, when Shen was writing for the Commercial Press's trade periodicals—*Student Magazine, The Ladies Journal,* the *Intellectual, Tung-fang tsa-chih (East Magazine),* and "Lantern of Learning," the literary supplement of the Shanghai newspaper *Shih-shih hsin-pao,* he developed a burning interest in socialist thought in general and Communist literature in particular. He joined a Marxist study group in 1920, when such groups were being formed in Shanghai as preliminaries to formal Communist Party organization.[18] Such groups were of course illegal under the Peking government of Tuan Ch'i-jui, but the foreign concessions of Shanghai offered more political freedom.

Mao Tun's household then consisted of his mother, his wife, K'ung Te-chih, and himself. In the spring of 1918, in compliance with his mother's wishes, he had married a girl from Wu Village. She was illiterate at the time, recognizing only the character "K'ung," her maiden name, and the numbers one to ten.[19] After the marriage, Te-chih went to live with her mother-in-law in the village and began to learn to read and write classical Chinese under her tutelage. Mao Tun went back to Shanghai alone after the marriage; he had only a month's paid leave and barely enough income to support himself. As he became increasingly busy with his new literary activities and political involvements, and still so short of money—or time—and even with his salary raises that he did not go home for New Year's at the end of 1920, his mother began to worry about his life among the sophisticated women of Shanghai. She wrote him a stern letter telling him to find an apartment as soon as possible so that she and his wife could come and live with him in Shanghai. Mao Tun, who had just agreed to reorganize the *Short Story Monthly* for the Commercial Press, was busier than ever, but he could not argue with his mother. Wife and mother arrived in Shanghai later that winter and his mother immediately took charge of managing the household, leaving Te-chih time to continue her studies.[20]

The arrival of his womenfolk apparently did not change the direction of Shen Te-hung's Shanghai life. "Before I was twenty-five, I led a peaceful and stable life under the supervision of my mother. In the ten years since, my friends have exerted a great influence."[21] Shen Yen-ping was twenty-five in 1920. His friends then included many literary figures who were to become famous writers of the May Fourth generation. There was Chou Cho-ren, a polished essayist and a younger brother of Lu Hsün; Cheng Cheng-tuo, editor of *Shih-shih hsin-pao's* literary supplement and later of *Short Story Monthly*, who was also a respected scholar and historian of Chinese vernacular literature; Hsü Ti-shan, a poet, philosopher, essayist, and short-story writer who showed a strong intellectual preference for Buddhist philosophy; and Yeh Sheng-t'ao, an editor, writer, and teacher of Chinese literature and creative writing. Yeh wrote one of the first novels of the May Fourth era, *Ni Huan-chih*, which Shen read and reviewed at length in his "On Reading *Ni Huan-chih*." In 1921 these young litterateurs founded the Literary Association, which was based on their common belief that literature is part of life and for the people.

At the same time he became part of this circle, Shen also became close to such political activists in Shanghai as Ch'en Tu-hsiu, editor of *New Youth* and a founder of the Chinese Communist Party; Li Ta, editor of *Communist Party Monthly* (a short-lived journal of only five issues) and another founding member of the Party, as well as principal of the first Chinese Communist school, the Common People's Girls School, when it was set up in Shanghai toward the end of 1921 as a training center for the women's movement; Shih Ts'ung-tung, a Marxist theorist; and Yü Hsiu-sung, leader of the Communist Youth Corps.[22]

Under pressure from the warlord government in Peking, many of the May Fourth leaders left the capital for Shanghai in 1920. Ch'en Tu-hsiu, one of the first to arrive, reopened his magazine *New Youth* there and openly promoted basic knowledge about Marxism and Soviet Russia.[23] In the succeeding months he talked with a number of young intellectuals, and in July he predicted to a friend that if the Shanghai Communist Party nucleus were formed immediately, Yü Hsiu-sung, Shen Yen-ping, and seven others would undoubtedly join. The Shanghai Communist Party nucleus was formed in August 1920 and Shen Yen-ping joined the following year, after the Party was formally organized at the First National Congress[24] in Shanghai in July 1921.

Shen's younger brother, Shen Tse-min, who had been studying hydraulic engineering in Nanking, also arrived in Shanghai in May 1921. Much against the wishes of his mother and brother, Shen Tse-min had abandoned engineering for literature and politics. In July he went to Japan to study, and when he returned to Shanghai the following year, his brother sponsored him for membership in the CCP. From then on, the two brothers worked together in the revolutionary movement as well as in propagating modern Chinese literature. Shen Tse-min did many translations from Russian literature which were published in *Short Story*

Monthly and *Tung-fang tsa-chih*. One of his most impressive articles was "Characteristics of the Russian Citizen as Seen from the Russian Literature," which was published in *Tung-fang tsa-chih* in 1921. In 1926, Shen Tse-min went to Moscow to study at Sun Yat-sen University, which was then headed by Pavel Mif. Later he became an important Party propagandist during the Mif and Wang Ming era in the early 1930s.[25]

Shen Yen-ping was a patriot who believed in saving the nation through political change. Marxism offered an intellectual solution and the success of the Bolshevik Revolution offered proof of the feasibility of Marxism for China. At first he tried to understand, through Russian and German literature, the distant causes and forces in history that generated revolution and war and, above all, the psychology and the philosophy that made World War I and the Bolshevik Revolution historical facts. Before he actually engaged in any concrete organization work, he had read Bakunin, Kropotkin, Nietzsche for intellectual ideas, and Hauptmann, Maeterlinck, and the nineteenth-century Russian masters for prerevolutionary psychology and conditions of life.

Still in intellectual ferment as a Party member Shen Yen-ping gave the impression of being a prudent man.[26] He began Party organizational and propaganda work in 1921 and became involved with the Shanghai labor movement in 1922. That same year,[27] he began teaching English at the newly founded Common People's Girls School. His six women students included the beginning writers Ting Ling and Wang Chien-hung, as well as his own wife, Te-chih. In late 1922 Shanghai University was opened as a cadre training center under the politically safe presidency of Yü Yu-jen, a pro-left KMT member. The following year Shen began teaching Marxism and fiction there. Ch'ü Ch'iu-po, who had just returned from a journalistic assignment in the USSR, was also teaching at the university, and Shen Yen-ping met him for the first time.

In September 1922, a party underground weekly, *Vanguard*, was founded, with Ts'ai Ho-shen, an active CCP propagandist, as its editor. Demanding freedom of speech, assembly, press, and religion, *Vanguard* was the first CCP-sponsored publication that bluntly proposed revolution as the means to overthrow the Peking government. The Party had already moved well beyond study groups. *Vanguard*'s four slogans were unification of China, peace, freedom, and independence. From then on the CCP had two forums for its programs—*New Youth* for theoretical guidance and *Vanguard* to point the way to practical action.[28]

Shen Yen-ping's position in the CCP became increasingly important after the Party's Third National Congress, in January 1923. That congress was the first to endorse—at the insistence of the Communist International and over vehement protest—a policy of collaboration with the KMT. Also at the insistence of the Comintern, it ordered all CCP members to join the KMT as individuals. After a special branch meeting in

Shanghai on July 8, at which these policies were again heatedly discussed, Shen was elected a member of the Executive Committee for the Greater Shanghai Region. He was charged with the unsavory mission of persuading his fellow CCP members to join the KMT and also with overseeing the well-being and success of the collaboration, the "united front policy" through which KMT and CCP together were to carry out a revolution against the warlords and strive for national unity under one democratic government. The Executive Committee was reorganized in September and the National Movement (the United Front KMT-CCP) of which Shen was now Committee Chairman, expanded its activities to include organizing the workers, peasants, students, women, and even businessmen.[29]

In early 1924, the Shanghai Executive Department of the reorganized and expanded KMT was formed, and Mao Tse-tung, another CCP founder, became secretary of its Organization Department. At about the same time, the Executive Committee for the Greater Shanghai Region underwent another reorganization: Shen Yen-ping and his brother were both on the five-member Committee, and Shen Yen-ping was accountant and secretary. In addition to his committee and united-front work, Shen Yen-ping in March of 1924 took on the editorship of a supplement in the KMT newspaper in Shanghai, the *Republic Daily*. He also wrote on the average one article a day for the supplement, under the heading "Candid Sketches of the Society." Not surprisingly, his contributions to *Short Story Monthly* diminished.[30]

Shen did not slacken his pace in his work for the labor movement, however. The Secretariat of the Chinese Labor Unions, established in 1921 with headquarters in Shanghai, was for many years one of the most active CCP organizations. Shen participated in the workers' education program and helped organize strikes, which were often led by Liu Shao-ch'i, the famous organizer who was later to become head of state in the Communist government before he was toppled as a "capitalist roader" in the 1960s. Liu was also a faculty colleague of Shen's at the Common People's Girls School.

In 1925, violence in Shanghai provided the impetus for what became the national May Thirtieth Movement. This movement is always noted in Chinese Communist history as the beginning of the era of mass awakening and the end of Franco-American style bourgeois-democratic revolution. In mid-May a young Chinese worker named Ku Chen-kung was killed by Japanese guards and security people at a Japanese-owned cotton mill. Denial of demands for punishment of his killers and compensation for those killed and wounded in the subsequent protest caused a furor among students, workers, and merchants. On May 30, great crowds of students from Shanghai University and other schools, laborers, women workers, and ordinary citizens marched down Nanking Road, the center of the business section, and there were mass killings and arrests by soldiers and police. The people were furious and the call went out for "Three Strikes": students to strike the schools, workers to strike the factories, and merchants to strike the city's businesses.

Shen Yen-ping participated in the Nanking Road demonstration and the May Thirtieth Movement that grew out of it. His familiarity with workers' lives and his firsthand knowledge of events associated with the movement are vividly expressed in the factory scenes in *Midnight* and in the last chapter of *Rainbow*. This familiarity also caused him in his article, "On Reading *Ni Huan-chin*," to voice acute disappointment that the novel's protagonist, Ni Huan-chih, failed to respond positively to the anti-imperialist tide of the May Thirtieth Movement. The disappointment, we now see, was deeper than that of a disinterested literary critic.[31] The same article contains one of his angriest outbursts against the Creation Society, which asserted that literature, like a beautiful poisonous plant, is for beauty only and not for any utilitarian purpose. Shen remarked that its members, notably Ch'eng Fang-wu and Kuo Mo-jo, would be infinitely better off if they had stepped out of their "snail shells" into the streets with the May Thirtieth Movement.[32] Again the intensity of feeling is stronger than a doctrinal feud with antagonists of the Literary Association would evoke.

Because of his labor organizing and other radical activities, Shen Yen-ping became an embarrassment to the *Short Story Monthly* and was removed from the masthead in 1923.[33] From 1923 to 1925, although he was still officially in charge of the magazine's "Literary News from Overseas" section, his literary work was noticeably reduced. It ceased almost completely in the second half of 1925, and in December, when the Nationalist Party set up a Shanghai Municipal Headquarters, Shen Yen-ping became chief of its Propaganda Department. Toward the end of that month, five members of the headquarters staff were elected delegates to the KMT Second National Congress at Canton, the seat of Chiang Kai-shek's Nationalist Government. Shen Yen-ping was one of the five. Thus it was late 1925 when he "severed" his tie with literature and devoted himself wholly to the revolution. One of the last pieces he finished before going to Canton was entitled "On Proletarian Literature."[34]

During the turbulent years 1926–27 Shen Yen-ping the revolutionary was transformed into Mao Tun the revolutionary novelist. The next time we meet him in a literary context is with the appearance of *Disillusionment*, which was serialized in the September and October 1927 issues of the *Short Story Monthly*. Under his striking new pen name the author of *Disillusionment* wrote with an immediacy and exaltation that took the literary world by storm. *Vacillation* (January–March 1928) and *Pursuit* (June–September 1928) followed. Feverish, despondent, and neurotic, the as yet unidentified author of these works did not recall the thoughtful, prudent Shen Yen-ping of earlier days. The world reflected in these three novels was immensely different from the world that had inspired the reasoned arguments of such essays as "Naturalism and Modern Chinese Fiction," and "The Duties and Efforts of Students of the New Literature." Only the most advanced and boldest of the younger Chinese writers had anything like his confessional intensity. Mao Tun's life in the mid-1920s yields a better understanding of that transformation than any inferences from the literary theories he adhered to at one time or another. The process of transformation was recorded by Mao Tun himself in "Remarks on the Past,"[35] an autobiographical essay that is much more intimate than the later, official "Memoirs."

This 2500-word article, published in 1933, reveals a dimension of Mao Tun's life up to 1928 with all the emotional coloring that is now expunged from the "Memoirs." It also offers clues to the complex style that he devised for his early fiction to elude the censors by developing a narrative flow that on the surface betrays nothing that might provoke censorship. This narrative style uses facts as well as metaphors and symbols, and it advances action simultaneously with political allegory. In "Remarks on the Past," we see that the setting is also both factual and allegorical. Kiukiang, for example, is factual, and so is Kuling, but the "hospital" and the "Supervisory Department" are as allegorical as the guests who stay there:

> The year 1926 is a year I probably will never forget. After New Year's Day of that year, my life lost its tranquillity. I was one of the passengers on board the ship *Awakened Lion*.[36] There were five of us traveling together.
>
> Since I left school, I had worked as an editor in a book publishing company. This was how I became involved with literature. But from the time I stepped onto the *Awakened Lion* on New Year's Day in 1926, my professional tie with literature was severed.
>
> Canton in those days was a huge furnace, an enormous whirlpool—a colossal *contradiction*.[37]
>
> In March, this furnace, this whirlpool, violently exploded.
>
> In the middle of April, I returned to Shanghai. I had no job then, but was very busy. My health was much better in those days. Frequently I ran around for a whole day and did not even feel tired; I even felt like doing something more afterward. So I began my research in Chinese mythology, a world apart from my daytime occupation, which I found helpful for balancing physical activities. Meanwhile, I thought of using what spare time I had left to try my hand at writing a novel. This was because the mentality and outlook of several women at that time attracted my attention. It was on the eve of the Great Revolution. Students with a bourgeois background and women intellectuals felt rather strongly that if they did not join the revolutionary party, they would be wasting their learning. Furthermore, they entertained strong illusions about revolution. They walked into revolution on the strength of those illusions. Actually all they

did was to stand on the periphery of revolution and look in. There were also women who sought revolution because they had been frustrated somehow and were indignant as a result—they added a dash of skepticism to their illusions. Standing shoulder to shoulder with them were still other, totally different types. Together, they presented very strong contrasts. And my urge to write a novel grew stronger by the day . . .

I remember one evening in August. I had just come out of a meeting and was on my way home. It was raining hard. There were no pedestrians and no automobiles; raindrops fell pitter-pat on my umbrella. The person walking next to me was one of the women who had formerly attracted my attention. During the meeting, she had talked excessively. Her face was still flushed with excitement. As we walked, I suddenly felt inspiration surging inside me. Had it been possible, I think I would have grabbed a pen right then and there and begun to write in the rain. That night, after I got home, I was able for the first time to formulate an outline of the novel I had wanted to write.

This is how, once again, I resumed my traffic with literature on a "non-professional basis" after I had broken my "professional" tie with it.

The outline I made at that time later became the first half of *Disillusionment*. A whole year went by from the time the outline was formed until I actually began writing. During that year, I was caught up in the torrents of the revolution. I never had the time to revise my outline. In January 1927 I arrived in Wuhan. I forgot all about the outline. I also forgot all about the fact that I even had the urge to do creative writing. At that time, Wuhan, too, was an enormous whirlpool, a colossal contradiction. And the women I had encountered in Shanghai also turned up in Wuhan. In this time of whirling crisis, their natures were exposed even more clearly. . . . Finally that colossal contradiction again exploded. I watched many people showing their true faces, and I watched many "modern women" lose control of themselves, become depressed, and go under. I left Wuhan and went to Kuling to recuperate. In the third-class cabin on board the ship *Hsiang-yang-wan*, there was a berth with two light blue skirts for curtains. They were meant to obstruct people's views but they had the contrary effect of arousing attention. In that crowded third-class cabin, I ran into two women whom I had met before in Shanghai and then in Wuhan. They were going to Kiukiang [in Kiangsi Province, where the fighting between the CCP and the KMT generals for control of the area was very fierce in summer and fall of 1927]. They told me that there were quite a few acquaintances of mine aboard the same ship. The outline I had written and left in my apartment in Shanghai suddenly surged up in my consciousness. Since I had nothing to do, I let it occupy my mind again.

I stayed in Kiukiang for half a day and then went on up to Kuling. The first thing I did after settling in a hotel room was to pick up the old tune again. The result was the "newsletters from Kuling." . . . Less than four days after we arrived in the mountains, the two friends who came with me from Hankow left. . . .

When we first arrived, a lot of old acquaintances were still there. The Grand Hotel of Lushan was filled with people who had fled Wuhan. At the end of July, they left in separate groups. Then three others came, stayed only one day, and went off to some cave in the deep white clouds to seek refuge from the din. The once bustling Lushan grew quiet. Two friends stayed on—both women. One was in the hospital and I visited her. But we had exchanged no more than a few words when she lowered her voice and said, "This is not the place to talk." The other stayed at the Supervisory Department *(Kuan-li-chü)* as a temporary guest of Mrs. Lin. It was she who told me what had been going on in the Lushan. When the autumn winds blew, I returned to Shanghai. I dug out the year-old outline from a pile of paper and read it over and decided that it had to be revised and cut.

I sat down and began to write; what came of it were *Disillusionment* and *Vacillation*. . . .

Thus it is not by coincidence that I made three women the protagonists of *Disillusionment*. Those who do not know me will probably try to guess who these three women are. They may even want to compile a "key." However, those who know me and my friends, men and women, will probably understand that these three women are not three individuals but many individuals—they are three types. Miss Ching is the type that receives most of my attention. The other two are just for support or contrast. I admit that I have not portrayed any truly revolutionary women. For this I deserve to be criticized.

"Remarks on the Past" is itself a mixture of fact, metaphor, and political allegory; it is not merely personal reminiscence or straightforward auto-biographical account. Mao Tun had let his organizational tie with the CCP lapse in late 1927, but in "Remarks" he was still writing about the CCP and therefore had to use indirect methods of expression to protect himself and his friends. On the whole, he used the actual time and geographical location for the historical events presented: from January to April 1926 in Canton; April to December in Shanghai; January to July 1927 in Wuhan; end of July to mid-August in Kiukiang and Kuling. But what actually happened during this time and in these places is presented indirectly, not on a single level or in uniform terms. The cataclysmic events that swept both Canton and Wuhan are presented in strikingly similar metaphors as "a huge furnace" and "an enormous whirlpool, a colossal contradiction" that "exploded." The policy-making that went on first in Shanghai and then in Wuhan and Kuling, from which such events evolved and on which subsequent actions revolved, is presented in a much more complex narrative structure. Within this narrative structure, there is a realistic "cover" of research in Chinese mythology and a retreat to Kuling. There is also an allegorical underpinning in the allusions to "meetings" and "women."

To trace the extremely complex historical events that underlie this deliberately vague narrative is a first step in understanding the similar narrative method in the short story "Autumn in Kuling," which will be analyzed in the next chapter as an illustration of the method of interpretation used throughout this book. "Remarks" develops around the voyage from Wuhan to Kuikiang that Mao Tun actually took. Such a conspicuous clue strongly suggests looking more deeply into his activities in Canton and into the historical events of 1926–27.

Mao Tun reached Canton in January 1926. From January to April he was Secretary in the Propaganda Department in the Central Executive Committee of the KMT, first under its nominal chairman Wang Ching-wei and then, after February 1926, under Mao Tse-tung, who succeeded Wang as Acting Chairman.[38]

When Mao Tun arrived in Canton, the CCP had already gained a foothold in high-level KMT governmental organizations. The Propaganda Department in which he served was, predictably, under CCP control.

Under Mao Tse-tung, Mao Tun edited *Political Weekly,* a KMT newspaper founded in 1925. He wrote several articles for it on the theory of the sovereignty of the state, and he lectured on revolutionary literature in the political training class organized by the Central Propaganda Department. He followed the expansion of Party activities from cell work to training school programs.[39] Under the cover of his job as secretary, he conducted training and educational programs for Party cadres as well as "ground-level" organizing among the masses. Party work during these revolutionary years was frequently conducted within the schools, and schools provide the setting and protagonists for much of Mao Tun's early fiction, in which meetings among students—both in *Eclipse* and elsewhere—parallel Party meetings where policies and objectives are discussed and actions planned.

This parallel between fact and fiction helps explain why meetings and personal relationships among students in Mao Tun's novels and stories received so much attention from Communist critics such as Ch'ien Hsing-ts'un, Ch'ü Ch'iu-po, and Fu K'e-hsing. When Ch'ien, for instance, criticized Mao Tun for obscuring the "main subject" in chapter 5 of *Disillusionment* with his "method of indirect presentation"—meaning that he had presented only a partial view of characters and events—the reference is to exactly one such "meeting" in one such "school," when in the disguise of student debate, important resolutions about the CCP-KMT collaboration and KMT membership for all CCP members were voted on.[40] And when Ch'ien attacks Mao Tun's portrayals of the women characters in *Pursuit,* it is obvious that the criticism does not really relate to literary issues but to a historical frame of reference from which these characters derive their symbolic meaning as representative of Party policies and their political future.[41]

More than once in later years, Mao Tun himself mentioned that during these revolutionary times he had been in close contact with all levels of the Party.

> Between 1925 and 1927, I had considerable contact with the nucleus lead-
> ership center in the revolutionary movement. My post enabled me to have
> frequent dealings with ground-level organizations and the masses. Hence
> in every sense I should have been able to have an overall understanding [of
> the revolutionary movement].[42]

The "leadership center" is the CCP Central Committee, and the
"ground-level organizations" are local party cells. The perspective in Mao
Tun's early fiction is not one of a keen, disinterested observer, as previously assumed by his readers and most critics, but that of a committed
Party member, who, having participated in Party policy-making, was in a
privileged position to present to the world "an overall understanding"
and a penetrating analysis of the revolutionary movement.

Hence the revolution that Mao Tun "observed and analyzed" in the
three parts of *Eclipse* corresponds not so much with the overall National
Revolution of 1926–28, led by the KMT in alliance with the CCP, as with
the Chinese Communist movement in that early stage. Only in this light
are we able to explain Mao Tun's deep emotional involvement with the
dilemmas and tragic fate of his fictional characters: in reality they are his
comrades. And only this approach to the subject matter of his fiction also
explains why such prominent CCP leaders and leftist critics as Ch'ü
Ch'iu-po and Ch'ien Hsing-ts'un took so much interest in even the most
minute details in his early novels and short stories.[43] Mao Tun's contemporary defense ironically anticipates the critical uproar over *Pursuit* at a
time when misfortune and defeat had overtaken many of his old friends:

> One who will not be bent by external forces may lose his mind with
> disappointment at the perverse behavior of those he loves. One day such
> matters may become known. This is what gives my writings a deeply
> pessimistic hue, and colors them with a basic tone of lugubriousness and
> agitation.[44]

The metaphors of the twice-exploded contradiction Mao Tun referred
to in "Remarks on the Past" are obviously related to the developments in
the Chinese Communist movement. Two dates stand out in relation to
the "contradictions": March 20, 1926, and July 1927. Are these chosen by
chance? On March 20, 1926 and July 15, 1927, the KMT and the CCP
confronted each other in two crucial tests of power. The first confrontation, Chiang Kai-shek's Chungshan Gunboat Incident was a setback for
the Chinese Communist expansion within the KMT; the July 15 "Wuhan
debacle" marked the permanent split of the CCP from the KMT left, and
it was followed by large-scale persecution and massacre of Communist
members and followers. Mao Tun viewed these two defeats—the two
explosions mentioned in "Remarks"—as inevitable consequences of the
tension and conflict that arose out of the "colossal contradiction." In

their respective suggestions of burning violence and inexorable self-encircling action, they lead to an inevitable end.

In the series of negotiations that followed the Chungshan Gunboat Incident, Chiang Kai-shek demanded that important CCP members be removed from responsible KMT posts and stipulated rigid restrictions on CCP participation in the KMT government.[45] CCP control over the KMT Propaganda Department was dissolved in early April, and shortly afterward Mao Tun returned to Shanghai.

From mid-April to the end of 1926, Mao Tun continued his work in the CCP Propaganda Bureau in Shanghai. The "August meeting" in "Remarks" is both a profile of the Second Enlarged Plenum in Shanghai (July 1926) and a composite of the many meetings held earlier on the central controversy that preoccupied all ranking CCP members: the policy of collaboration between the KMT and the CCP. In Mao Tun's foreshortened representation, the reasserted "contradiction"—the collaboration policy—stretched out painfully and inevitably toward a second "explosion," which occurred in Wuhan on July 15, 1927, when the Nationalist Government at Wuhan officially announced its expulsion of the CCP.

It is obvious from the early history of the Chinese Communist movement that the Comintern had a direct hand in formulating and directing CCP policy toward the KMT and many other party matters, such as the organization of mass movements and the interpretation of revolutionary trends.[46] In retrospect, we can say with considerable certainty that the Comintern's interpretation of the situation in China from 1922 to 1928, and its resulting strategy of collaboration with the KMT, led to the disasters that befell the CCP in March 1926 and July 1927. This factor was more important in the Party's setback than Chiang Kai-shek's personal ambitions or his turn from Soviet aid to a campaign for peace with the Japanese. Mao Tun was certainly aware of every Comintern intrusion into CCP policy decisions. It is inconceivable that he should write about these years without giving the Comintern a prominent role. The natural questions to ask, then, are: In what image is the Comintern role cast? And who are the most prominent figures in the climactic scenes in Shanghai "on the eve of revolution" and in Wuhan in July 1927? The answer is "the women."

It was the modern, emancipated women of Shanghai, with their radical ideological outlook, who attracted Mao Tun's attention. It is a woman who, walking home with Mao Tun after the meeting in August 1926, reveals to us through her flushed face and excited talk the important issues that must have been raised and discussed in the meeting. The modern women acquaintances Mao Tun knew from Shanghai and Wuhan days were on board ship when he retreated from Wuhan to Kiukiang. Two other women acquaintances were there when Mao Tun went to Kuling to recuperate—one in the hospital, the other a guest at a shadowy

"Supervisory Department." To deserve such intense concern, who are these women? They must represent something persistent and essential in Mao Tun's revolutionary experience. "Remarks" tells us that these women have to do with the revolution of 1926–28, with ideology, and with types; they are composites of women Mao Tun knew during the years he served as party propagandist and organizer of mass movements.

The women in "Remarks" are symbolic participants in the actual revolutionary history of the 1920s. They represent images of the dominant CCP leadership groups, including the group following Comintern policy, committed to conflicting political positions. Some opposed, some compromised with, and some exploited the collaboration policy; some supported and some advised toning down the radical peasant movements in Hunan and Hupeh provinces in the first half of 1927.

The main women characters are much better realized in Mao Tun's fiction than in such autobiographical essays as "Remarks." But in his fiction he so often shifts from a close-up of the individual to the movement of a group, and on to an analytical survey of revolutionary history, that to follow his trail, these works must be read on many levels at once. The real women of "Remarks on the Past" correspond to the two women characters Old Ming encounters in "Autumn in Kuling."[47] They serve as the bridge between Mao Tun's two worlds, of reality and fiction. They are also an indispensable key to an enlightened reading of the themes and of the meaning of both the characters and the character relationships in them, and the next chapter is devoted to a study of that story.

II

"AUTUMN IN KULING"
FROM LIFE TO FICTION

"Autumn in Kuling," an undated short story, was first published in installments in the journal *Literature* in 1933.[1] In a footnote Mao Tun revealed that the story originally had nine sections, but sections five to eight, "for reasons unknown, disappeared the night after it was written." He added, "I would have found them if I had wanted to look for them, but I did not feel like looking, nor was I up to rewriting the missing parts."[2] What he did instead was make the original section nine the new concluding section five.

As a work of imaginative fiction, "Autumn in Kuling" is not entirely successful, but there are several reasons why it is a useful microcosm of the young Mao Tun's developing fictional method.

First, it is short—some 20,000 to 25,000 words in its published version. The four middle sections almost certainly disappeared because the work was a thinly veiled report on current history.[3] The story's brevity becomes an advantage when connections between history and Mao Tun's fiction are sought; there is less concealment to uncover, and fewer links to reconstruct. It offers a rare opportunity to observe closely how Mao Tun used fiction to satisfy his irrespressible urge to write about contemporary history, despite all the practical difficulties of dealing with such sensitive matters under the various levels of censorship.

Second, the story is illuminated by its autobiographical companion, "Remarks on the Past," also published in 1933.[4] The parallels between the two provide enough clues to establish the historical subtext in the fictional work as the cluster of events surrounding the retreat of the Chinese Communists from Wuhan in the second half of July 1927 and the famous Nanch'ang Uprising of August 1, which has since been declared the official memorial day to mark the founding of the Chinese Red Army. Certainty about the subject matter of the story greatly facilitates our study of Mao Tun's fictional technique of using political allegory and symbolism.

Third, it offers a way to begin discussing what Mao Tun himself said in

"My Understanding" about the importance of characters in fiction and of the relationships between characters.

Fourth, "Autumn in Kuling" is a prime example of Mao Tun's way of dealing with women in literature. Unoppressed women were a rare phenomenon in modern Chinese writing of the 1920s, even for the most revolutionary and the most sympathetic of writers. The women in Lu Hsün's stories are almost without exception victims of institutionalized oppression. And Ting Ling's Miss Sophia (1928),[5] a bold image of and a confessional outcry for freedom from traditional bonds—sexual as well as educational—is a feverish, tubercular heroine who exemplifies not so much freedom as the frustrated urge for freedom. Mao Tun's women characters, by comparison, are by far the most emancipated, free, and healthy; they are the only women in major Chinese fiction of the period who actually move outside family settings and still remain realistically convincing as characters. Their behavior is unfettered by traditional notions of chastity and docile womanly virtues, and they are accountable only to their inner sense of responsibility. Certainly they are frequently excitable creatures, and we also get clues to this in Mao Tun's non-fiction—such as the scene in the autobiographical "Remarks on the Past" in which a woman, flushed of face, is walking in the rain beside Mao Tun and talking in great excitement about a political meeting. But she, like her fictional counterparts, is never patronized, and Mao Tun is clearly aware of what revolutionary struggle for emancipation of the oppressed meant for women. Traditional Chinese literature is not used to educated women with a degree of freedom; even Mao Tun's contemporaries did not know quite what to do with them. Mao Tun was to go on in his novels to make his women much more real than in either "Remarks on the Past" or "Autumn in Kuling." And we shall see in his women characters a degree of concern for their total emancipation that not many activists in those days paid much attention to.

"Autumn in Kuling" also seems from internal evidence to be Mao Tun's first attempt at totally imaginative fiction. It marks the end of his first politically active period, and it may sensibly be read as his first attempt to recreate imaginatively the four years of revolutionary development that he had experienced. For the first time, too, Kuling, a summer resort town up in the mountains, the beautiful Lushan range in Kiangsi Province, begins to take on the aura of a private symbol for Mao Tun. He used it often in the early part of his career as a writer; it was a touchstone that evoked the Chinese Communist movement during the years of the Great Revolution.

The publication date of the story gives no clue to when it was written. Many of Mao Tun's stories are dated in footnotes or datelines, but this one is not. Evidence that it was written some time before publication is abundant, however. First, there is the first-person "I" passage in the footnote about the sections that disappeared, which calls attention not only to censorship but also to the timing of publication. Then there is the name of a character in the story, Master Cloud (Yün shao-yeh), which links him quite unambiguously to many other occurrences of the name Cloud—rich in symbolism in Chinese literature—in Mao Tun's other writings during his three-week stay at Kuling or about events that took place then.

According to his first and highly emotional defense of *Eclipse*, "From Kuling to Tokyo," and also to his autobiographical "Remarks on the Past," and his "Memoirs IX," Mao Tun went from Wuhan to Kiukiang on July 23, 1927, immediately after the CCP-KMT split, on orders from the Party. He was on a secret assignment to deliver a draft for two thousand dollars to a contact in Kiukiang and possibly also to attend one of the Party's planning conferences, for which the Lushan area was a favored setting. The next day he made the short journey up to the mountain resort town of Kuling with a few friends. They were told that there was another route down the far side of the mountain that could take them to Nanch'ang. He suddenly fell ill with a severe case of dysentery. His wife, who was pregnant, had already gone back to Shanghai, a safer place than Wuhan at the moment, and his friends now departed also. Mao Tun stayed behind in Kuling till mid-August, recuperating. During that time he heard about the Nanch'ang Uprising and about meetings between generals and politicians of the KMT Left Wing from a woman coworker named Fan Chih-ch'ao, who was also in Kuling after the Wuhan retreat. An active man, Mao Tun was suddenly reduced to inactivity by illness and by the need to conceal his presence in Kuling. He had time on his hands.

Illness is a time when people think a great deal; it is a time to confront death and to think over the past and the future, perhaps feverishly. In his forced state of physical inactivity, Mao Tun was certainly not intellectually idle. Things were happening just over the mountain. The revolution was at a turning point. Many of his comrades were braving death at Nanch'ang; some were trying to carry a share of the action underground via a secret journey back to Shanghai. All were in acute danger. While his body was immobilized, his head was filled with excitement—the known and unknown movements of his friends and comrades; the future of the Party and the revolution; the bad news portended by the meetings there and then in Kuling between such KMT Left Wing leaders as Wang Ching-wei, Yü Yu-jen, and the no longer supportive army generals Chang Fa-k'uei and Huang Ch'i-hsiang (which he learned about from his colleague Fan Chih-ch'ao).[6] Mao Tun could not but be obsessed by the possible outcome of all this.

In "From Kuling to Tokyo," as well as "Remarks on the Past" and "Memoirs," we are told that while he was in bed he was reading a collection of essays by Maurice Maeterlinck, *The Buried Temple,* and translating a short novel, *Their Sons,* by the Spanish novelist Eduardo Zamacois.[7] "From Kuling to Tokyo" offers the clearest account:

> In the summer of 1927, I stayed in Kuling to recuperate from an illness; five or six of us had gone there together originally, but later on they left the mountain, one after the other, some going further back into the mountains to visit scenic sites, leaving behind my sick self to be attacked by insomnia every night. Listening in the quietness to the rattling of the windows in the mountain wind, my head aching, I read M. Maeterlinck's collection of essays, *The Buried Temple,* and spent the short summer nights thus without ever shutting my eyes.

We also learn that other thoughts about the immediate affairs around him demanded even more of his attention. His reaction to them was first expressed in several nonfiction "newsletters" he dispatched to the *Hankow Republic Daily* and later treated allegorically in "From Kuling to Tokyo" in his account of an encounter with a certain Miss Cloud:

> But I often looked up several acquaintances who had remained at Kuling or had just come to have a chat. Among them was a Miss Cloud, who was in "the second phase of pulmonary consumption." For this Miss Cloud, "the second phase of pulmonary consumption" was very important, not because the "disease" had actually damaged her health, but rather because the dark shadow of the "disease" had created in Miss Cloud a wavering state of mind which alternated between pessimism and excitement. She also spoke of her own life experience, which to my ear sounded like a medieval romance—not that it was not ideal but rather too ideal. It produced in me an interest to study this "melancholy and bedridden Miss Cloud," as people called her. She said that her life could be written into a novel. That was unquestionably true. . . .

This Miss Cloud is certainly not any real person whom Mao Tun actually met in Kuling. If Fan Chih-ch'ao provides a partial model for her, then it is highly conceivable that the account of the Nanch'ang Uprising that Fan gave Mao Tun provides a partial model for Miss Cloud's experience which struck him as a medieval romance. Mao Tun could not fail to recognize the romantic aspects of the gallant, doomed rebellion. Miss Cloud is of special interest here, however, for the clue to an approximate dating of "Autumn in Kuling" provided by her name. For "Cloud— "Yün"—as a character appears continually in Mao Tun's writing of the period and does not reappear after this cluster of works which revolve around his thoughts and experiences of the Kuling period.

There are at least five other pieces written by Mao Tun between July 24, 1927, and November 1931 in which the name Cloud appears as a person. The texts of four are available but the content of the other two, which are oddly unavailable, can be inferred from the titles. The two unavailable pieces are both "Newsletters from Kuling," which, according to "Remarks on the Past," were the first things Mao Tun wrote "after settling in a hotel there." One, he says, is about a story he heard from a certain Miss Cloud on the subject of "catching fleas,"[8] a most incongruous subject under the circumstance. But if Mao Tun was inspired to write about it at that juncture, we may infer that this tiny blood-sucking insect carries some allusion to current events about which he felt scornful enough to joke in a mock-heroic mood. The other newsletter, "Master Cloud and the Straw Hat," was published in the *Hankow Republic Daily*'s "Literary Supplement" of July 29, 1927.[9] Of course, it would be possible to do elaborate speculative exercises on the allegorical meaning of "Cloud" and "Straw Hat," drawing upon other work by Mao Tun for support. But for the present I will only note that the light, mocking tone suggested by the title is quite consistent with the light, mocking tone we can infer from the flea-catching story of the same period.

The third piece in which Cloud appears as a person is a poem, "Goodbye to Younger Sister Yün," dated August 12 and published August 19, 1927:

> Sister Cloud, my half-pound of black tea is already finished,
> My five hundred cigarettes are finished,
> I have finished translating a novel of forty-thousand words . . .
> The summer season is nearly finished,
> All the tourists have spent their zeal,
> And all the roads have been traveled on.
> Everything that can be said has been said.
> Money is finished.
> All is finished, finished.
> I can now leave.
> I have reaped nothing from this trip,
> Except that I have drunk half a glass of "nectar [of the gods],"
> I have watched several cascading waterfalls,
> I have roamed over many wooded hills,
> I have also experienced profoundly the grief of disillusionment!
> When shall we meet again?
> How do I dare speculate? . . .[10]

So the mocking tone continues. The poet is grievously disillusioned but nonetheless remains hopeful that he and Sister Cloud will meet again.

Shortly after dispatching the poem, Mao Tun left Kuling to return to Shanghai. It was at this time that he became separated from the Party organization and was no longer on the front line.[11] Once in Shanghai, he went into hiding with his mother and wife on the third floor of a small house in Ching-yün Lane—where Lu Hsün was soon to become his neighbor. During the subsequent months—from the end of August 1927 to June 1928—he was active on a different front, writing the trilogy *Eclipse*. In June 1928, ostensibly for reasons of personal safety, he left for Japan. But no sooner had he arrived in Japan than attacks on *Eclipse* began. He quickly responded with "From Kuling to Tokyo," and we can see from the content of the piece that Mao Tun was still deeply concerned with those who had remained on the front line (or had died there). He could not stop reliving those years when he too was at the heart of the Party organization. This continuous inner involvement with events after the events themselves are past accounts for much of the creative energy Mao Tun displayed in his Japan years (1928–1930). Miss Cloud appears again in "From Kuling to Tokyo," but the allegory has lost its light-hearted tone: the benign mocking that informed the Kuling "newsletter" and the goodbye poem a year before is no longer there. The Miss Cloud of July 1928 is critically ill and her mind is no longer playfully dabbling with catching fleas but alternates "between pessimism and excitement." And this state of alternating pessimism and excitement continues when Cloud next appears as a young man from a land-owning peasant family in the short novel *In Company of Three*.

The mysteries surrounding Mao Tun's Cloud character are far from the only mysteries in his early writings. For example, the publication date of the minor novel *In Company of Three*, whether by coincidence or not, is similarly "clouded." The official version in "Memoirs XII" is that the novel was written in the second half of 1931. This is consistent with Ch'ü Ch'iu-po's remarks in an early review that the latter part of the novel was written in the fall of 1931 because in it Mao Tun referred to the Japanese invasion of Manchuria in September 1931.[12] The time Ch'ü Ch'iu-po and Mao Tun gave for the writing of the book would put the publication date no earlier than December 1931. However, two Shanghai editions of *In Company of Three*—each called "first edition"—give the publication dates as, respectively, March of the 18th year of the Republic, which is March 1929, and October of the 20th year of the Republic, which is October 1930.[13] Such confusion about the dating of *In Company of Three* certainly allows us to reconsider the dating of "Autumn in Kuling."

Internal evidence—the story itself—is as important as all these elusive Clouds.

The development of tone and style in the works in which Cloud appears as a character—from the light-hearted mocking tone of the "flea" newsletter, "Master Cloud and the Straw Hat," and "Goodbye to Younger Sister Cloud" to the pessimistic and excited tone of "From Kuling to Tokyo" and *In Company of Three*—places "Autumn in Kuling," with its light-hearted, carefree, tourist-minded Master Cloud, in the July–August group. Its spirit is in tune with the first three, and there is a clear division between the feverish gaiety of these four works and the driven quality of the other two. The young man Cloud in *In Company of*

Three, especially, belongs to an altogether different political era, when it is important to assert peasant background and peasant class-consciousness.

Theme and tone argue that "Autumn in Kuling" was written not long after "Master Cloud and the Straw Hat," probably in the first week of August 1927, after the Nanch'ang Uprising had been put down and the Southern March of retreat had begun. We may safely assume that the story was withheld from publication at the time because of multilevel censorship of the parts, now missing, that logically would have dealt with the uprising. Mao Tun would have acceded to the deletion not only out of Party loyalty but partly because as a beginner at fiction he was not entirely confident of his own skill at portraying such a momentous event. Possibly, too, since he was planning a novel about the Great Revolution, he hoped to incorporate the material in it. Then *Eclipse* took shape and the story did not fit in after all. But when Mao Tun returned from Japan the political scene had changed, and when he became editor of *Literature* in 1933, he had a place to publish his work somewhat more freely. No doubt he also felt much more confident of its reception—even though it was based on events six years earlier—now that he had earned a reputation with the trilogy. Whether out of nostalgia or lingering defiance or both,[14] he quickly serialized the safer parts of "Autumn in Kuling" in the September, November, and December issues of his magazine.

The "Cloud" allegory is worth looking into a little further because it is so intimately woven into this unique period in Mao Tun's life, when he was being transformed from a revolutionary into a creative writer. It crystallizes in one image the widely divergent sources of inspiration—literary, biographical, geographical, political, and ideological—which Mao Tun was to draw on continuously for allegories and symbols in his early fiction.

The making of the Cloud allegory begins with Kuling, a real place high enough in the mountains for real clouds to be very close. The time was July–August 1927, a turning point in the history of the Chinese Communist revolution. Mao Tun, too, was on the verge of a critical change. Out of action for the first time in years, his mind preternaturally alert despite his debilitated body, he listened to all sorts of plans about what was to be done in the aftermath of the disaster at Wuhan. Friends came and then disappeared into the clouds on the mountain above the town. Men and women were all busy talking about goals and action. Physically inactive himself, Mao Tun had just the right perspective for contemplating his friends' plans. The old ideological framework, the old Party line that had informed everybody's actions with a sense of reality, had just fallen apart. New slogans for a new line were yet to be formed. The Nanch'ang Uprising, for example, was being planned and was surely to take place soon. But would it really usher in the new, third phase of the Chinese

revolution, the "soviet phase," with identifiable geographical areas transformed into soviets and governed on Communist principles? Or was it
merely to be words all over again?

As the clouds floated among the mountain ranges, and people floated
busily in and out of them, and words floated around seeking incarnation
into concrete history, a literary idea also began to float in Mao Tun's
mind, agitating and pushing to take shape. From his vast knowledge of
literature, Mao Tun was trying hard to summon a literary motif, a tradi-
tion-rich image, to give fitting expression to this enormous contradiction
he saw all around him: the concreteness of people's actions and the unreality of their goals. This agitated search finally settled on the encom-
passing figure "cloud."

There is at least one well-known use of "cloud" in Chinese literature
relevant to the case in point. The Chinese use is embedded in the Taoist
tradition of "taking off to the clouds" ("yün-yu)," in which a Taoist
disciple would from time to time take leave of mundane concerns and, for
the benefit of his spirit or his health, journey to some distant place, a high
mountain where clouds gather. This Chinese use aptly captures one aspect of Mao Tun's ironic view of the ever self-rejuvenating revolutionary
slogans and activities that indeed took leave of reality when called on to
do so for the sake of spiritual—read ideological—truth. However, this
use alone is a bit too pretty to carry the full weight of Mao Tun's condemnation of such behavior. From his studies of English, Mao Tun no doubt
understood the dual meaning of the common phrase "head in the clouds,"
which implies pure and lofty thoughts along with the inability to see
one's immediate circumstances. In addition, Mao Tun knew at least two
specific Western uses of "cloud" that address his concerns very well.

Vladimir Mayakovsky, the Futurist poet laureate of the October Revolution, whom Mao Tun had studied and written about, in 1915 wrote a
long poem, "The Cloud in Trousers," in which he glorified the coming
revolution and the victory of the proletariat. The poem begins:

> Your thought,
> musing on a sodden brain
> like a bloated lackey on a greasy couch,
> I'll taunt with a bloody morsel of heart;
> and satiate my insolent, caustic contempt . . .
> Come and be lessoned—
> prim officiates of the angelic league,
> lisping in drawing-room cambric . . .
> If you wish,
> I shall rage on raw meat;
> or, as the sky changes its hue,
> if you wish,
> I shall grow irreproachably tender:

> not a man, but a cloud in trousers!
> I deny the existence of blossoming Nice!
> Again in song I glorify
> men as crumpled as hospital beds,
> and women as battered as proverbs.[15]

There were several Chinese translations of this poem, and Mao Tun certainly knew it for he mentioned it in the section on Mayakovsky and Futurism in his *Outline of Western Literature*,[16] and later on borrowed from it the metaphor for revolution of a crown of roses and thorns to use in his *Wild Roses* stories. Mayakovsky's "Cloud" had a specific meaning as a metaphor for "proletarian revolution" and its nebulous ideology. When we juxtapose Mayakovsky's "Cloud" with the contemporary meaning of "straw hat" in Shanghai journalism, a picture emerges that helps to explain the allegory for both "Master Cloud and the Straw Hat" and "Autumn in Kuling."

Shanghai, where Western journalism arrived early, had both Western-style newspapers and illustrated journals. The *Tien-shih-chai Illustrated News* was a famous publication by the Commercial Press that used drawings to comment on the social and antisocial activities of Westerners and the Western military. There were scenes from the 1884–85 Sino-French war over Annam, for instance, and at the other extreme, a long-gowned foreign woman playing the piano in a Western-style drawing room with a poodle jumping by her side. When Mao Tun became editor of the *Short Story Monthly*, one of his innovations was to include several pages of illustrations accompanying its world news section. He was thus familiar with the cartoons and drawings of Shanghai young men wearing a still Western-style straw hat that advertised their Western pretensions. Mao Tun took over the hat as a symbol of empty pretensions to Western learning in a number of his early works. In *Pursuit*, for example, he scornfully refers to a Party man's lofty speeches about education as "big-hat" talk—a lot of empty air under the hat that is too big for the head. This usage provides a clue to the allegory in the title "Master Cloud and the Straw Hat." A young revolutionary named Cloud (a possible surname in Chinese) decked out in this cheap imitation of fashionable foreign attire, the symbol of an imported ideology. It could well be Mao Tun's commentary on the Comintern influence incongruously superimposed on the Chinese revolutionary movement.

The second Western use of "Cloud" comes from Aristophanes' satirical play about Socrates, *The Clouds*, which Mao Tun summarized in his *Outline of Western Literature*, giving it his own emphasis. His synopsis shows that: A bankrupt old man goes to seek instruction from Socrates on how to hoodwink his creditors. As they are talking, in comes a women's chorus, the "Clouds." The old man takes them to be gods, but

Socrates says, "They are clouds in the sky but lazy people still look upon them as goddesses. To us philosophers and theoreticians, we extract from the clouds ideas, language, and philosophy." Unable to understand Socrates' philosophical talk, the old man fetches his son to take his place. The son soon becomes an accomplished sophist and confuses all the creditors with his nonsense. He does many outrageous things and finally beats up his father, defending the logic of his actions every step of the way. The old man is so incensed by the consequences of Socrates' teaching that he burns Socrates' Academy and his home to the ground. It is easy to see in Socrates' teaching an analogy to the effect of Soviet Russia's doctinaire ideology on China, resulting in outrageous behavior for the learner.

The "Cloud" is a complex symbol combining several important elements of Mao Tun's revolutionary experiences in the years immediately preceding his Kuling stay, where he began his career as a creative writer. Gradually and one by one, aspects of this welter of experience begin to assume human forms and appear as characters, several of them bearing this densely allegorical name Cloud. As the pattern develops, women Clouds generally represent abstract ideals and goals and men Clouds represent implementation of such ideals and goals on the level of action. "Autumn in Kuling," with one such Cloud among its characters, belongs to this period of Mao Tun's writing. Cloud does not appear again as a character after *In Company of Three.* In our analysis of "Autumn in Kuling," we shall see that Mao Tun's major themes are already present in it, themes that will be developed and presented more successfully, in greater depth and fuller realization, in the rest of his early fiction.

The story opens with a scene at Pier Six on the Hankow waterfront. The date is July 23, 1927. Three men are seen boarding the Japanese ship Hsiang-yang-wan to go to Kiukiang.[18] In the third-class cabin the three are cursorily introduced to the reader: Old Ming, a journalist, Old Sung, an exiled KMT member from Chekiang who recently came from Shanghai, and Master Cloud, apparently a young tourist but a friend of Ming and Sung. The three meet a number of acquaintances and exchange ambiguous remarks on the current political situation and military developments. A light blue skirt strung up in the third-class cabin as a makeshift screen calls their attention to the presence of two women acquaintances, Miss Wang and Miss T'ao. They too are going to Kiukiang, to take the train from there to Nanch'ang.

In Kiukiang, the three men spend two very confusing and frustrating days. First they have trouble finding the people they had arranged to meet. Then their plans change repeatedly in less than half a day. Miss Wang and Miss T'ao appear, somewhat unexpectedly, in the same hotel. The train to Nanch'ang has been delayed because of the need to transport soldiers.

In the last section, the former section nine, the scene abruptly shifts to

Kuling. A week or so has elapsed. Two of the three men, Ming and Master Cloud, are still on the scene, playing chess in a hotel. "Where do you think Old Sung and the rest of them are now?"[19] asks Ming. "Don't they say that once beyond Fuchow, it is all wild mountains? We are in the mountains too, but theirs over there must be more interesting." Cloud has no answer, and the two men muse silently about their friends and about their own situation for a while. Finally, they decide to go back to Shanghai in two or three days.

The plot of "Autumn in Kuling" thus summarized tells very little about the events presented, much less the significance of the characters. There is much bustle in the story, but none of it has any clear direction. We are not told anyone's background or what kind of work any of them is doing now. The reason for the trip to Kiukiang is not known, and the encounters with the women seem to be casual and without significance. The final episode in Kuling, instead of answering these questions as endings normally do, introduces yet other mysteries, the business of Old Ming and Master Cloud in Kuling, and of "Old Sung and the rest" in the mountain areas near Fuchow.

"Autumn in Kuling" has never attracted much critical attention; probably because of its apparent pointlessness, any clue to an intelligent reading was lost when the middle sections vanished so mysteriously. But the similar trip described in the nonfiction "Remarks on the Past," published in the same year, throws considerable light on the story. Mao Tun himself had traveled from Wuhan to Kiukiang on the ship *Hsiang-yang-wan*, and from "Master Cloud and the Straw Hat" we know that he left Wuhan on July 23, 1927, the same day the *Hsiang-yang-wan* departed from Hankow in the opening scene of "Autumn in Kuling."

Such striking coincidence inevitably suggests a connection between the actual and the fictional trips. Other details, down to the color of the woman's skirt strung up in the cabin, indicate that the two trips are one and the same. (There are two light blue skirts in "Remarks" and only one in "Autumn in Kuling.") In both cases the skirt belongs to one of the two men that Mao Tun, as well as characters in the story, had known from his Shanghai days. Later in "Remarks," Mao Tun says he went from Kiukiang to Kuling; two of the three male characters also go from Kiukiang to Kuling. From Kuling, Mao Tun left in less than two weeks' time to go back to Shanghai; the two men also decide to do this at the end of "Autumn in Kuling."

Such coincidences cannot be accidental. The author evidently links "Autumn in Kuling" to his autobiographical "Remarks" and relies on these links of detail to reveal the larger common historical context that was his main concern and real subject. Reliance on external information to reveal the deeper subject matter, and use of selected details to pinpoint the larger historical framework, occur repeatedly in Mao Tun's early fiction, especially in the *Wild Roses* stories and their prefaces. It is also true of the trilogy *Eclipse* and Mao Tun's two articles in defence of it, "From Kuling to Tokyo" and "On Reading *Ni Huan-chih*."

"Autumn in Kuling" in fact deals with a small, clearly identifiable cluster of historical events: the retreat of the Chinese Communists from Wuhan in the second half of July 1927 and the famous Nanch'ang Uprising of August 1. A comparison of these events with the time, place, and sequence of events in "Autumn in Kuling" shows that the story is indisputably a fictional representation of current history, and that the literary technique, far from being purely realistic, is broadly allegorical.

"Autumn in Kuling" begins on July 23, 1927, when the retreat was already under way and the plan for the Nanch'ang Uprising had been made final. It ends in Kuling around August 8,[20] when the uprising had been defeated and the remnants of the Red Army had reached Fuchow, its final stop on its retreat, the Southern March to Kuangtung.

Hankow, Kiukiang, and Kuling are the settings of the fictional events in the order they occur. Nanch'ang and Shanghai are mentioned as the two separate destinations of the retreating personnel from Wuhan after they gathered in Kiukiang. Mao Tun uses specific place names (Chengchou in section 2, Mahweiling in section 4, and Fuchow in section 5) to anchor the political perspective of the story. These place names identify important military events in the history of the Chinese Communist movement at that juncture. They are emblems of the historical events associated with them. Mahweiling, a strategic military area near Nanch'ang, signifies Chinese Communist troop movements during the Nanch'ang Uprising; it was controlled by Chinese Communist forces under command of Nieh Jung-chih.[21] Fuchow, in the eastern part of Kiangsi Province, was the first stop of the surviving forces moving south around August 5;[22] Chengchou evokes painful memories of T'ang Sheng-chih, the powerful Hunan military governor who from the CCP point of view betrayed the revolutionary cause on May 29, and the Chengchou Conference of June 10–12, when Feng Yü-hsiang, the "Christian General" who controlled the Northwest Army, met with the leaders of the Wuhan government to discuss their common interest against the CCP, a meeting which foreshadowed the expulsion of the CCP from the Wuhan government in July.[23]

In "On Reading *Ni Huan-chih*," Mao Tun complained that Yeh Shao-chün, the author of the novel, failed to make clear which political party the title character belonged to: "Ni Huan-chih at that time probably had already joined a certain political party. But from chapter 22 on, the activities of Ni Huan-chih do not clearly reflect his group background; as a result, they become the insignificant action of one individual. This greatly affects the basic orientation of the novel."[24] "Autumn in Kuling" presents a concrete example of how Mao Tun suggested the group—or political party—background of *his* fictional characters by placing their activities in historical times and places and a well-defined political community.

In 1934, in an essay on the writing of fiction, "My Understanding [of Fiction Writing]," Mao Tun discussed the significance of character and human relationships in fiction:

> The prime goal in fiction writing is people. One has to have people before one can have a starting point. . . . One cannot single out one character from the others and study him separate and apart. . . . It is not sufficient to just have people; there have to be relationships among people. It is these relationships among people that constitute the theme in a work of fiction.[25]

"Autumn in Kuling" highlights both the characters and the relationships among them. As Mao Tun intended, the story's theme emerges not so much in any one individual's character and action as in relationships, and once these relationships are shown, the characters' "group background" and the nature of their activities become clearer.

There are three main characters in "Autumn in Kuling": Old Ming, Old Sung, and Master Cloud. One can infer from the Chinese custom of addressing someone as "Old" ("Lao") to show respect that Ming and Sung are older than Master Cloud. They are probably in their late thirties or early forties, whereas "Master" Cloud would be in his early twenties.

Old Ming had worked in a newspaper office in Wuhan (like Mao Tun himself) before he left for Kiukiang. He is said to have inside knowledge of why everybody is going to Kiukiang.

Old Sung recently arrived in Wuhan from Shanghai. He is specifically introduced in the first section as an "exiled KMT member from Chekiang Province, and not an X-tang [CCP member]."[26] Old Sung "does not clearly understand" what he was sent to Kiukiang to do. But once there, he is the one most busily engaged in all sorts of ambiguous business. Toward the end of section 4, he is ordered to attend a "meeting" in Nanchang, and in the concluding section he is said to be in the "mountain area near Fuchow."

Master Cloud is an even more elusive character.[27] The symbolism of the name Cloud more or less links the central action (the missing part) to some high revolutionary goal. But as we have him now, aside from his ringing laughter, his sportive air, and his persistent presence throughout the story, nothing very definite can be said about his business or his status. The only clue to what he represents in "Autumn in Kuling" is his preoccupation with Lushan—the meeting place of all kinds of political groups in the last days of July 1927.[28]

Individually, none of these three characters seems particularly significant. But in examining their activities in the perspective of their "group background" and their relationships with other characters, a different picture emerges.

The reason for their departure from Wuhan is presented in the opening scene at the Hankow waterfront and later in a morose statement made by Old Sung. The juxtaposition of a Japanese gunboat in the river with the *Hsiang-yang-wan* at Pier Six speaks silently of the tense political situation in Wuhan during the last hours of the CCP presence there. The departing *Hsiang-yang-wan* signifies the retreat of the Communists, and the presence of the Japanese gunboats is meant to show that the KMT government at Wuhan has already compromised with foreign powers and abandoned the cause of the National Revolution. Sung's sullen complaint that he should not have come all the way to Wuhan from Shanghai to face this "rotten mess of a situation" represents the prevalent feeling among CCP members and their fellow travelers at that point.

In section 2, there is a clear portrait of the political party to which the acquaintances of the *Hsiang-yang-wan* passengers belonged. Ostensibly it deals with a number of trifling incidents on the night of July 23 in the third-class cabin. The two casual encounters between Old Ming and his acquaintances and the incidental glimpses of other passengers are Mao Tun's way of delineating their "group background." In the first encounter between Old Ming and a leftist youth named Hsü, Hsü's conversation reveals the most recent political development that led up the Wuhan retreat. His excited, disjointed conversation also reveals something about the business that awaits the *Hsiang-yang-wan* passengers in Kiukiang. "I sent you a telegram from Chengchou," he tells Ming,

> It was sent to the newspaper office. Did you get it? Damn it! That Honan Province was certainly a godforsaken place. The Red Spear Society! The Blue Spear Society! And whatnot, you name it! The local bullies and evil gentry certainly had their way there. But Old Ming, are you going to Kiukiang too? Damn it, we'll give them hell when we get to Kiukiang.[29]

Hsü is not merely a sketch of an overenthusiastic leftist youth, undoubtedly a common type in the revolutionary ranks at that time. Nor was he created to enliven the realistic cabin scene on board the *Hsiang-yang-wan,* although he fulfills that function equally well. Over and above such realistic assignments, Hsü also presents the political past and future of the *Hsiang-yang-wan* voyage. His remarks about the unenlightened people in Honan, the resistance of the local secret societies to Communist propaganda against the landowners and local powers—the "bullies and evil gentry"—and the compromise his "Director Teng" is eventually compelled to make, succinctly summarize the political developments that caused the passengers to board the *Hsiang-yang-wan* for Kiukiang. Giving them hell in Kiukiang refers to the prospective Nanch'ang Uprising, and for Hsü to mention it off-handedly in public suggests that the other passengers not only know about the plan but are also participants. The offstage "Director Teng" is Teng Yen-ta, a real person who was head of the Political Department of the Fourth Army, which fought most valiantly in the Northern Expedition, and which was infiltrated by the CCP.[30]

The encounter between Old Ming and his two women acquaintances serves a similar purpose of underlining their common political background. Miss Wang is someone Old Ming knew in his schooldays in Shanghai. Miss T'ao is a member of the Committee for the Women's Movement in Hupeh. "School" and "Committee for the Women's Movement" imply CCP organization and policies. Miss Wang and Miss T'ao are going to Kiukiang only to get a train for Nanch'ang: obviously they are intimately involved either in plans for the Nanch'ang Uprising or in plans for the secret retreat back to Shanghai.

Thus section 2 presents an overview of the people who constitute the political community. There were KMT leftists like Hsü and women CCP activists like Miss Wang and Miss T'ao. The other passengers include Old Li and his group, as well as a young man who speaks with a heavy Cantonese accent. The name Old Li strongly suggests Li Li-san, who first conceived the idea of the Nanch'ang Uprising and was on its Front Committee, and the young man with a Cantonese accent easily leads one to think of the Communist troops from the Fourth Army, the main force in the planned uprising gathering near Nanch'ang, which included many Cantonese. The ship's passengers are bound together in a common destiny by their common past (Shanghai and Wuhan) and they are heading toward a common future (Kiukiang).

Sections 3 and 4 deal primarily with the situation at Kiukiang. Section 3 is set in the early morning of July 24, just after the ship arrives, and section 4 that evening. War clouds, which have long hovered on the horizon, are now descending over the city of Kiukiang. Soldiers are everywhere. They crowd the train station, pack the outgoing trains, march in the streets and shout slogans like "long live X X X [Wang Ching-wei]," "Down with X X X [Chiang Kai-shek]."[31] These scenes reproduce most realistically the commotion in Kiukiang in the days immediately before the Nanchang Uprising.[32] The Front Committee, with Chou En-lai as its chairman, which was to direct the field action of the uprising, had been formed. Its general headquarters was in Nanchang, and military operations had already begun. But the Party leadership in Wuhan had not yet decided whether the uprising was advisable. The Central Committee in Shanghai was also undecided. It was still meeting secretly with Soviet advisers and Comintern representatives, and as late as July 26 the committee sent an envoy (Chang Kuo-t'ao) to halt the military action. This lack of synchronization between political and military arms is portrayed in the confusion and frustration of Old Sung and his two women coworkers in Kiukiang.

In sections 3 and 4, all the important characters have congregated in a hotel in Kiukiang. By bringing them together in one hotel, Mao Tun seems to be modeling the Hua-yang Hotel in the story on the real Grand Kiangsi Hotel in Nanch'ang, which was the headquarters of the Front Committee, and thereby making it the center of the collective activities of his fictional characters.

In the concluding section, what must have been the climax of the story—the Nanchang Uprising—is over. Anything Mao Tun saw in Lushan or learned from his woman acquaintance at the Supervisory Department (in "Remarks on the Past") has been deleted from the story. There was probably no conceivable way Mao Tun could have treated the uprising and the Southern March honestly and to the satisfaction of either the Party or the KMT. The other details used in the story were mostly forgotten by the time it was published, but even in 1933, the Party, still under Comintern control, could not conceivably have sanctioned an act of such magnitude as the Nanchang Uprising, which flew straight in the face of Comintern authority; and the KMT, whether in 1927 or 1933, was not likely to tolerate the publication of a story about so treasonable an act.

The plan of retreat can, however, be reconstructed from the itineraries of the three main characters in the published story. Old Sung's itinerary from Shanghai to Wuhan to Kiukiang, Nanchang, and Fuchow traces the assemblage of forces for the Nanch'ang Uprising and the escape route of the Southern March. Old Ming's and Master Cloud's itinerary from Wuhan to Kiukiang and then Lushan-Kuling to Shanghai follows the retreat route of the Wuhan Office of the CCP Central Committee from Wuhan to Shanghai.

As a work of literature, "Autumn in Kuling" satisfies in many ways Mao Tun's own prescription for modern Chinese fiction. Its subject matter is thoughtfully chosen: for a CCP member of the 1930s, what could be more important than the CCP's unprecedented attempt to break free of Comintern interference, abandon the "suicidal" policy of collaboration with the KMT, and establish its own Red Army? Its theme reflects Mao Tun's conception of the spirit of a revolutionary epoch and is concerned with the life and destiny of far more than the few individuals portrayed. "Autumn in Kuling," mutilated though it is, gives convincing early evidence of Mao Tun's sensitive experimentation with political allegory couched in realistic terms.

III

DISILLUSIONMENT

Disillusionment, the first part of the trilogy *Eclipse*, was written in late August and September 1927, after Mao Tun came back to Shanghai from his involuntary stay in Kuling. It was serialized in the September and October issues of the *Short Story Monthly* that year, to much acclaim and considerable criticism. Ch'ien Hsing-ts'un, especially, felt it portrayed vacillation rather than disillusionment. In mid-1928, from his party self-imposed exile in Tokyo, Mao Tun wrote his first statement about this volume:

> I was only writing about the general disillusionment people felt at the time when summer was passing into autumn in 1927. Before that time, most people entertained some illusions about revolution, but at that juncture they experienced disillusionment! And what excitement there had been when it was about to arrive, as if the Golden Age would be here on the morrow. But the morrow had come and gone, and the day after the morrow was gone too. All hope for the success of one's ideals was gone and new sufferings increased inexorably. And everybody sighed in his heart, "Oh! Is this what it's all about?"
>
> Thus came disillusionment.
>
> This was a universal situation. At that time those who had been sincerely and earnestly looking forward to the revolution all suffered this kind of disillusionment. This was true not only of the petty-bourgeois class, but also of the impoverished peasants and workers. This is disillusionment and not vacillation. After disillusionment, one may become more negative or more positive. But there is no vacillation.[1]

For the author, then, the novel is about disillusionment, not about the vacillation that, he believes, comes only after disillusionment—and that will be the title of the second novel in the trilogy. Furthermore, the focus here is on the disillusionment he witnessed and undoubtedly felt in the summer and fall of 1927. We may note also that these events are not recollected in tranquility but recreated immediately after they occurred, while the author was in hiding, unable to leave his house, as a direct result of these events. Thus the first thing to look for is the specific illusions about the revolution that are to be dispelled in the course of the story, and their embodiment in individual characters.

Disillusionment has fourteen chapters. The first eight are set in Shanghai and tell the story of a group of students in "S University." The central relationships are those between two women students in their early twenties, Chang Ching and Chou Ting-hui, and each of their relationships with a young man named Pao-su. The last six chapters, set in the tri-cities of Wuhan—Wuch'ang, Hankow, and Hanyang—follow the same group of students as they become participants in the mass movements of workers and peasants after the National Revolutionary Army took over Wuhan in October 1926 on its Northern Expedition. The Northern Expedition was led by the joint forces of the KMT and the CCP with the aim of overthrowing the warlords in the Yangtze River area and farther north, thus uniting China. In Chinese Communist history, it is frequently called the Great Revolution. The expedition, under Chiang Kaishek's command, started from Canton in July 1926. Its initial successes were gratifying to all participants, but the continuing power struggle between the KMT and the CCP quickly undermined their "united front." This struggle was to culminate in the Shanghai Massacre of April 12, 1927, and the expulsion of the CCP from the KMT government at Wuhan on July 15, 1927. Large-scale purges followed, and the split between the two parties of the national revolutionary force became irrevocable.

In the first eight chapters of the novel, the "illusion" of unity is expressed in the love relationships of the characters; in the last six, social movements and political work in the National Government in Wuhan are the subjects of illusions. As the omniscient author—the usual mode in both classical and modern Chinese fiction—Mao Tun is free to move from one character's perception to that of another in the same scene.

The First Half: Disillusionment in Shanghai

The novel begins in Chang Ching's room off campus with a dialogue between the two former high-school classmates, Miss Hui and Miss Ching. Miss Hui has studied abroad; she is just back from two years in France, much disillusioned by her experience with men both at home and abroad. Chou Ting-hui has acquired a cynical attitude toward people and her environment. She does not like Shanghai: In addition to foreigners, most of the objects of her contempt are working and propertyless people. She has a philosophy about men:

> "Mankind is selfish, intent on cheating and making use of others. Ching, let me tell you, men are all scoundrels. They have nothing decent in their

minds when they approach us. You'll be throwing a shining pearl in the latrine if you ever show a man your true feelings."[2]

Hui believes men have to be dealt with on their own terms and made use of for one's own purposes.

Hui is in a sense a creature of circumstance. In the first chapter we not only hear her philosophy, we also learn that she is not really master of her own life. Ching knows from a letter Hui wrote her earlier, on May 21, that she is out of work and has been turned down by all prospective employers. Her older brother has no respect for her because she studied abroad but got no academic degree. Her mother wants her to come home and marry. Hui, however, wants to room with Ching while she continues to look for a job.

Miss Ching's has been a different family environment; so far she has lived an unsullied life. She is the one who still indulges in "illusions," although disillusionment with her year's work in a provincial student movement is what impelled her come to Shanghai. She now has the illusion that studying will somehow provide a way, but she has no clear idea about the purpose of her study, whether it is for the advancement of scholarship or a means of making a living. It seems mostly to be an escape from her general disenchantment with "movements," and from her former classmates, many of whom have abandoned their original goals in the student movement and are now beginning to make useful social contacts and have love affairs. Ching's mother, unlike Hui's, has never tried to arrange a compulsory marriage for her. For Ching, man-woman relationships "had always been hiding behind a silk screen of dignity, holiness, and gentleness. She had never lifted a corner of the screen to find out what it is. She neither desired nor dared to lift the screen."[3] But Hui forces her to take a look, and she is amazed to find that underneath "such a lovable face as Hui's, there lurks such abhorrent ugliness."

Chapter 2 introduces two male classmates of Ching, Pao-su and Li K'e. It begins with Ching noticing a faded red blouse on the porch and becoming curious about its owner, her landlady, who was married a year ago. Ching wonders about the married life of that young woman:

> Once the virginal dream is over, the inevitable commonplace begins to descend on you from above, crushing you, forcing you to abandon all ideals, cease all illusions, yield to it until your very existence is denied. Helplessly exposed to the instinctive drive of the male, you have to annul the dignity, holiness, and ideals of a virgin. Your virginal idealism is an eternal contradiction of the everyday reality of a young married woman.[4]

The thought reminds Ching of Hui and her former fondness for her. Ching knows now that she is the more fortunate of the two, having neither the pressure to earn a livelihood nor the nagging criticism of her family. She decides to take Hui in.

In the afternoon, Pao-su makes an unexpected visit. He brings Ching the news that the university is to devote all of the next week to publicity work for the Anniversary of the Abolition of the Unequal Treaties. He also informs her that there are rumors that she is in love and that he is her lover. Pao-su mildly deprecates the rumors, saying that he is not even part of her group. Ching reminds him that he has always been against "free love" (meaning courtship without parental authorization and supervision), for all that he admires Kropotkin. She does not declare herself on the subject, but we shall see that she is capable of "free" behavior and does not worry about her "reputation." On his way home, Pao-su meets Li K'e, who notices that Pao-su has just come from Ching's room and appears to be pleased with himself.

Chapter 3 is set a week or so later, on the first anniversary of the May Thirtieth Movement. Most of the students go to the memorial rally, but Pao-su, Ching, and Hui have gone to a movie theater where Dostoevsky's *Crime and Punishment* is showing. Pao-su is wearing a Western suit and a flashy necktie. "He was fond of wearing red ties. It was said that there was a reason behind his fondness for red ties."[5] His dress and his student pallor impress Hui favorably, and they get on like old friends.

In the theater, Pao-su finds Ching less attractive than formerly. Next to Hui she appears plain, even haggard. During an intermission they discuss the nature of crime and the meaning of punishment. Hui says that people are forced into crime by their environment; there was nothing wrong with Raskolnikov's killing the two women, since it was to relieve the pressure of poverty on himself and his mother and sister. What she cannot understand is why, having killed her, he did not take more of the money for his trouble. Pao-su agrees with Hui and expresses sympathy for criminals; they are pitiable, not detestable people. Ching is of a different opinion. She concedes that Raskolnikov's act of murder was motivated and not a wanton act, that he had reasoned and found it justifiable to kill for the sake of saving more people. Her question is why he suffered pangs of conscience after the murder. These speculations are interrupted as the movie starts up again, and the author comments, "Movies are like human history. It too leaves you with only a very brief interval when you can discuss and deliberate, but before you reach any conclusions, the show goes on. Hence you never get a satisfactory answer."[6]

In the next chapter Pao-su takes Hui to dinner in the French Park in Shanghai's French Concession. Later, out in the park, Pao-su declares his love for Hui, and they kiss. For such students this is a daring love scene. It is late when Hui gets back to Ching's room, but she cannot sleep, and memories of her past crowd her mind.[7] Soon Hui sinks into a dream. She is in the French Park again, and Pao-su is lying with his head in her lap.

Not far away, by a tree, is a boy of about three—their child. As she raises her hand to pat the boy's head, a man suddenly appears behind the child, shouting at her, "I'll kill you, you shameless creature. Did I ever mistreat you when you were away from your country? And you run away from me without my knowledge! Who is this bastard? Take this, and this!" He is hitting her with his walking stick. She feels as if her skull has broken under the blows. Furious, she picks up a huge rock at her feet. Then she wakes with a start.

Lying awake and thinking about her dream, Hui asks herself whether Pao-su is worth her giving herself completely to him. Her answer is no; he is just like the men she has met before. Ever since a man named Lü abandoned her—whether in France or earlier is not clear—she has been committed to the idea of retaliation. She will flirt with men, but there will be no love. About having been wronged she feels only anger at not taking enough revenge, never grief or remorse.

Having come to the conclusion that "there is nothing wrong with her past strategy," Hui gets up the next morning and tells Ching about her dinner with Pao-su, omitting the intimate details. When Pao-su comes again, she treats him as though nothing had happened. Pao-su is bewildered; "he had planned his next step already."

Several days pass. Then, in chapter 5, there are two episodes on the S University campus. Pao-su, still puzzled beyond endurance at Hui's rejection, runs into Li K'e and suddenly remembers that Hui and Li come from the same town. He knows nothing about Hui except that she was a student in Paris for two years and is a former classmate of Ching. To find out more about her he asks Li K'e about his home town.

> "Don't you come from Yü-huan? How long have you been away?"
> . . .
> "Yes, my home is at Huang-po in the prefecture Yü-huan. I was home only three months ago."
> . . .
> "Oh. Then you probably know Miss Chou Ting-hui, who also comes from your town" . . .
> Li K'e smiled. Pao-su shivered, not able to tell whether the smile was friendly or not.
> "Do you know her?" Li K'e, the "rational man" returns the question.[8]

As Pao-su briefly ponders what Li K'e said and did not say, he hears the sound of bells summoning students to a special meeting.

The meeting is in classroom 3: "Everybody knows that whenever the bell rings and no class hour is scheduled, it means that everyone is supposed to come to this classroom." The occasion for this special meeting is a discussion of Miss Wang Shih-t'ao's triangular love affair. The chairman is asking for a vote on prohibiting Mr. Lung Fei from courting Miss

Wang, who is in love with Mr. Tung-fang Ming. The students' opinions are divided. The majority is for an order to desist. But Mr. Shih Chün, a big gun on campus, says that Miss Wang's idea of finding another girl friend for Lung is no help, and he proposes that she be punished for getting into such a situation. Finally, the proposal to prohibit Lung's courtship is unanimously passed with a show of hands, but the vote on Shih Chün's motion is postponed.

Chapter 6 sees one resolution of the triangle between Pao-su, Ching, and Hui.

Hui suddenly leaves to go home. Ching thinks that Hui's suddenly going home must have something to do with Pao-su, but there is no way for an outsider to know exactly what is involved. She is restless and irascible. Everything gets on her nerves. The landlady is scolding a child. A couple is quarreling. "A fly is dashing itself against the glass pane on the window on the west side of the room. Seeking the light, the fly keeps trying to force itself through the blocked exit, emitting a spasmodic frantic humming."[9] Ching feels weighed down by all the ugly things that have been happening around her. They "gathered themselves into a huge black column and whirled in front of her eyes. She would like the earth to be destroyed. She would like to commit suicide. She could not endure a minute longer this endless ugliness and darkness." She covers her face with her hands, muttering the word "destruction" over and over. Tears drop from between her fingers.

Her thoughts turn to Hui. Probably Hui's mother is finding her a fiancé again. Then she thinks of her own mother. Is any other mother as loving as hers? "It is motherly love that brings warmth and comfort to society and light to life." Ching suddenly regrets her own aloofness toward the outside world and remembers a piece of presumably kind advice from Pao-su, that she is too much by herself.

Sunlight comes in through the western window. The fly has stopped buzzing. A light knock at the door, and there is Pao-su. "The first thing that struck Ching's eyes was that bright-red tie. . . . Whether it was a reflection from the red tie or for other reasons, Ching all of a sudden flushed red."[10]

They talk about Hui, and Pao-su tells Ching that he had a heart-to-heart talk with Hui that sent her home. He found out from a classmate, he says, that Hui has been married several times and had had many affairs. Her behavior in the French Park caused him a great deal of suffering later, when she told him she was only flirting and was not serious about him.

Ching, believing Pao-su, does not know what to think of Hui, whether to pity or condemn her. Knowing that Hui has been hurt once, Ching decides that Hui is now taking her revenge on all who came later. Ching pities Pao-su but feels that Hui is probably even more pitiable, being the victim of fate.[11] When Pao-su laments that he should not have hurt Hui so by getting angry with her, Ching suddenly warms toward him. She responds to his lovemaking at once, and Pao-su stays the night.

After Pao-su leaves the next morning, Ching begins to analyze what took place. She is sure that her part in it was not a passive one. Then she thinks about her home town and her mother. The fields, the rice-sprout songs, the water buffalo and their boy riders all come to her mind in their pastoral tranquillity. A dream scene unfolds. She is in her home town just as she was seven or eight years ago, reading a newly founded youth magazine.[12] Mother is coming out of the door, followed by Pao-su and a puppy. Mother has her usual kindly smile on her lips. In that illusory state, Ching finds herself also smiling sweetly. But "reality" pushes the silk curtain of "illusions" aside, and Ching walks over to her desk to write down her thoughts. As she rummages through the pile of notebooks and books on the desk she comes upon a small leather notebook she has never seen before. On the cover is a strip of paper with the following line from Kropotkin: "In any age, between the reformists and the revolutionaries there can always be found anarchists *(Modern Science and Anarchism)*."[13]

As she turns the pages in the notebook, a photograph of a woman falls out. Written across it are the words "To dear Pao-su, June 9, 1926, Chin-ling." She also finds a love letter from the same woman, and she reads it. She remembers that June 9 was the day on which Pao-su demanded an answer from Hui. She begins to pity the girl in the picture and feel relieved for Hui. Then she comes across another letter folded into the notebook:

> Your letter has been received. I am remitting another hundred dollars to you. His Excellency the General considered your report by and large empty of content. From now on, you are expected to observe more closely and you must find out the organization's headquarters and the names of the leaders. Otherwise I will be unable to help you further and you will have problems with your subsidy. Do your best.
>
> (Signed) Kuo-liang, June 2.[14]

Ching feels utterly betrayed. Her lover of the night before is a spy for a warlord general. She has lost her virginity to a shameless impostor. She cannot stand it any more; she feels terrible physically and emotionally. She knows she must run away. As a modern educated woman, she will go to a hospital.

In the next chapter we find Ching in the hospital, ill with scarlet fever. She has been there ten days and has passed the critical stage. During her recuperation in the month following, Ching thinks a great deal about fate.[15] Her self-confidence recovers somewhat as she listens every day to the news of the Northern Expedition's movements which a doctor reads to her. Wu P'ei-fu, the warlord who controls Central China, is losing ground and the Nationalist Army has taken over Hankow. The doctor does not seem to understand the good news in the paper's statement that the "people" helped in the victories of the Nationalist Army, especially "the people" in Hupeh and Hunan provinces of Central China.[16] A letter from Ching's mother dated September 10 brings different news. She is leaving Changsha, the capital of Hunan, to go to her sister's home, and she advises Ching to stay in the hospital instead of coming home. A few days later, Ching learns that Li K'e and other classmates are all in the hospital: Chao Ch'ih-chu, the loud student Shih Chün's girl friend is there; so is Wang Shih-t'ao, who had her troubles with the two suitors. They tell Ching that Shih Chün's proposal to punish Wang at the classroom 3 meeting was defeated.

When the news comes that the Nationalist Army, still fighting its way north, has captured Kiukiang, near Nanch'ang, Li K'e and others think everybody should go to Wuhan, now the center of the Nationalist Government, to work in the mass movements there. This gives Ching a new problem to agonize over. Should she join the new revolutionary movement in Wuhan? Can she allow herself to hope again and perhaps be defeated again?

Ching decides to try for a new life in Wuhan. "Enthusiasm, light, and a dynamic new life were opening their arms to her, waiting. After her disappointment in love, she now turned her eyes to 'social services,' anticipating consolation" and "a degree of happiness in living."[17]

What the Students Are Really Studying

These eight chapters have components that call for explanation in the light of Mao Tun's own experience and also of the CCP's development since its founding in 1921.[18] For example, Mao Tun himself returned from Canton to Shanghai after March 20, 1926, and left for Wuhan around January 1, 1927. Hence the period covered in the eight chapters coincides roughly with his own stay in Shanghai before he went to work in the new government in Wuhan.

In "From Kuling to Tokyo," Mao Tun clearly stated what the novel is *not* about. First, it is not about the "conflict between love and revolution." Second, it is not about "the vacillation toward revolution of the petty bourgeois." Mao Tun did not "wish to ridicule the petty bourgeoisie, nor to use Miss Ching as a representative of the petty bourgeoisie." Several years later, in "Remarks on the Past" he added that the content of the first part of *Disillusionment* bore closely upon his personal experience with the Great Revolution in the year 1926. Since Mao Tun was then a CCP activist, the historical frame of reference for the first half of *Disillusionment* is the major policies that concerned the Party leadership in 1926.

The central issue for the early Chinese Communist movement was the collaboration between the CCP and the KMT. This collaboration did not originate with the CCP but was decided upon by the Comintern, and almost all ranking members of the CCP strongly objected to the policy throughout its course, from 1923 to 1927.[19]

A "democratic united front" was first proposed at the First Congress of the Toilers of the Far East, held in Moscow and Petrograd in January 1922, and was relayed to a plenum of the Shanghai branch of the CCP by Chang Kuo-t'ao upon his return from the congress. Many members strongly opposed the plan as unfeasible in practice and detrimental to the integrity of the Party. At the same session, the leadership, reacting to the uproar, demanded stronger Party discipline and ideological training to insure conformity to the Party line. Shen Yen-ping was among those who protested against such Party dogmatism.[20]

At a special plenum of the CCP's Central Committee at West Lake, Hangchow, in February 1922, the policy of CCP-KMT collaboration was again discussed. All five members of the Central Committee were present and spoke against it. Maring, the Comintern representative, overrode their objections by invoking international discipline, and the Central Committee acceded under pressure.

The Chinese Communist Party officially adopted the policy of entering the KMT at the Third Party Congress in the summer of 1923.[21] Party members began to join the KMT on an individual basis without giving up their CCP membership. Their double status soon became a source of serious conflict.

After the Third Party Congress, the position of leading CCP members remained polarized on the issues of collaboration and Party discipline. One group still demanded immediate withdrawal from the KMT. The orthodox Party line as dictated by the Comintern, however, remained the same: to maintain organizational relationship with the KMT for the long-term goal of the Chinese National Revolution. CCP members were told to gradually take control of the KMT governmental organs and military forces and to strengthen their influence among the masses. When Voitsinskii came to China in late 1923, to replace Maring as Comintern delegate, he brought a different emphasis to the collaboration policy, encouraging independent development of the CCP as well as development within the structure of the KMT.[22]

As top-level leadership was shifting its strategy, tactics were also being formulated on the operational level to strengthen the Communists' position in the KMT. These included alliance with the Left Wing of the KMT and organization of Communist Party factions in the KMT. Programs for further organization of mass movements among workers, peasants, and women were also developed.

The KMT, as could be expected, was increasingly alarmed by these tactics. From the time Sun Yat-sen first agreed, in 1923, to admit individual Communists into his party, the KMT had taken measures to guard itself against excessive Communist infiltration and expansion. In November and December of 1925, some months after Sun Yat-sen's death, a group of Right Wing KMT leaders, known as the Western Hills Group, made a serious attempt to expel CCP members and reduce Soviet influence in the KMT; their effort was soon defeated by the Left Wing of the KMT. On March 20, 1926, however, the Left-Wing KMT military leader Chiang Kai-shek, who then had the full support of the Moscow government and its representative Borodin, carried out his March 20 *coup d'état* and succeeded in curbing the expansion of the CCP while establishing his own claim to leadership of the KMT forces.

CCP and Comintern reactions to the March 20 coup differed radically. Soviet Russia was conciliatory toward Chiang, who had not entirely disowned his own Soviet connections, whereas the CCP leaders took the setback hard. They began to view collaboration as not only contradictory but ominously "suicidal."[23] Much of the CCP leadership was again clamoring for immediate withdrawal from the KMT, but they failed to prevail against the Comintern line. There were heated arguments and flushed, angry faces at the Second Enlarged Plenum in Shanghai in July 1926, the meeting that for Mao Tun was the genesis of *Eclipse*. But in spite of all, a resolution in favor of continued CCP-KMT collaboration was passed. Measures aimed at placating the KMT were also rammed through, including downplaying radical organization of peasants and workers and a specific prohibition against the peasant movement's taking land by force.

Disillusionment depicts the process by which the Chinese Communists' first illusions about the Nationalist Revolution were dispelled. In the world of the novel, CCP activities are given the fictional form of student activities at a university that is probably modeled on the CCP's real Shanghai University. Two kinds of student activities stand out in the first part of the novel: the triangular love affair of Miss Ching, Miss Hui, and Pao-su (chs. 1–4 and 6–7); and the student meeting in which issues of general concern are discussed and voted upon (chs. 5 and 8). In Chinese society, then as now, it is hardly conceivable that students would make a public issue of their fellows' love affairs, and the very implausibility of the scene invites an allegorical interpretation.[24] But the parallels with the reality of the political world, combined with the course of the central characters' love affairs in the rest of the novel, show that this elaborately developed episode is intended to apply to rivalry on another level.

Ching in *Disillusionment* is a sort of mirror image of Hui. The two women followed the same course until their high-school days ended. Many of Ching's activities in *Disillusionment* get their meaning from the constant contrast with Hui. Viewed apart from Hui, Ching fits C. T. Hsia's description of her comfortably—she stands for

> the discrepancy between individual effort, which avails little, and the general prevalence of anarchy [in the Great Revolution years 1925–27]. In Mao Tun's scheme, the young participants in the Northern Expedition are fired by the dual ideal of personal emancipation and patriotic service. Ching's failure to realize either is partly a matter of sensibility, but more important, it is also the inescapable reaction to a state of affairs that are a caricature of purposeful action.[25]

Taking *Disillusionment* as a novel about the experience of individuals in the revolution during 1925–27, Ching is everything that Hsia has said. But if Ching, as Mao Tun himself specified, is not merely an individual but a type, and if *Disillusionment* is not merely a novel based on the experience of individuals in the revolutionary movement but instead expresses a collective experience of the revolution as a whole, then we have to assess Ching's role in relation to that of Hui as well as in relation to the roles of the other characters. We need also to take Mao Tun's own experience into consideration and interpret the plot and characterization in *Disillusionment* on the two levels he intended: the realistic level of individual experience, which is what the novel is ostensibly about, and the allegorical level, dealing with the collective experience of the Chinese Communist movement, which is the deep subject.

The comments of Ch'ien Hsing-ts'un, himself an insider, offer some assistance:

> In part 1, chapter 5 depends too much on the method of profile painting, leading one to regard the chapter as irrelevant and [overlook] the very special purpose of the writer in writing it. In chapter 7, the discovery [of the notebook] comes too soon, [and] the method is not satisfactory. The letter should not have been found in a book that Pao-su carried with him all the time; it should have been in his clothing or some other place. The place of discovery ideally speaking should have been somewhere else also [meaning other than Ching's room].[26]

Chapter 5, in which the student assembly discusses Miss Wang Shih-t'ao's triangular love affair is an apparent digression from the main plot, but Ch'ien's statement that Mao Tun had a "very special purpose" here suggests that there is a key to the puzzle. What is it there in chapter 5 that made Ch'ien so concerned that the reader not miss it? Again, chapter 7 brings the main story of the relationships of Pao-su and Ching and Hui to a plausible resolution, but Ch'ien Hsing-ts'un criticizes the event that provides the denouement.

If we follow Ch'ien's lead, we notice interesting correspondences between the times and places suggested by chapters 5 and 7, and key events in the development of the policy of collaboration with the KMT from the May 30th anniversary in chapter 1 to just before the Nationalist Government moves from Canton to Wuhan in chapter 8.

The collaboration policy was first decided upon by the *Third* International and, after heated debate, was adopted officially by the CCP at the *Third* Party Congress in the summer of 1923. These three "three's" lend significance to the otherwise pointless detail of classroom 3, the setting of the student assembly. The students' public debate about how Wang Shih-t'ao is to treat her two suitors (whether she should accept the one as a suitor when she is already in love with the other) becomes integral to the novel when it is viewed as representation of the question raised at the Third Congress, whether a CCP member should at the same time take KMT membership. The two-suitor policy is voted down at the student assembly, and there is even a proposal to punish Miss Wang. The debate and the vote accurately represent the feeling of the majority of the CCP members at the Third Party Congress, and it can even be said that Mao Tun is not merely indulging in wishful thinking but carefully setting the historical record straight.[27]

The role of Pao-su on the allegorical level is easy to recognize.[28] His red necktie and the photograph and letter he carries in his pocket notebook unmistakably identify him as a representative of the faction of the KMT Left that was under Chiang Kai-shek's control in Canton. Chiang's faction in 1927 not only commanded the military forces represented by the Whampoa Academy but had also moved to occupy Nanking by June 2, the date of the "Kuo-liang" letter.

In the first half of *Disillusionment*, Mao Tun is representing the opposition of the CCP leadership to the policy of collaboration with the KMT. The argument against collaboration, presented allegorically in the student debate, was that the CCP was already committed to the cause of socialist revolution in China (just as Wang Shih-t'ao had already fallen in love with Tung-fang Ming); expedience was no excuse for parleying with the KMT (Wang Shih-t'ao, in the opinion of the student majority, should not have flirted with Lung Fei simply because she was too weak-willed to resist the opportunity). History, of course, turned in quite a different direction. To see how Mao Tun represents this development, we must turn to the other triangular love relationship in the novel, the one involving Ching, Hui, and Pao-su on the surface level.

This relationship is the product of circumstances. Hui's philosophy of love, like her approach to all human relations, is based on expediency. Her flirtation with Pao-su, which develops in a simulated foreign setting, the French Park, is colored by distrust and motivated by retaliation; it cannot and does not lead to fulfillment. Hui's foreign connections are not adventitious. Combined with other details—her birthplace, her age, the color of her clothing (purple, which is an excessive red), and her philosophy of love—they make a significant allegorical pattern.

Hui, we remember, is a native of Huang-po. In the history of the Chinese Communist movement, Huang-po is a meaningful place name; it was where the CCP-organized peasant movement was strongest in 1926. The radical land reform carried out at Comintern instigation in Huang-po and Huang Kang in Hupeh Province in the spring and early summer of 1927 was the direct cause of the catastrophic rupture of the CCP-KMT alliance in July. Less publicized in later years than Changsha in Hunan Province (Ching's birthplace, which is near Hsiang-t'an, Mao Tse-tung's birthplace), where the peasant movement was led by indigenous CCP people and organized by Mao Tse-tung on his own initiative, Huang-po carries an unfortunate association with arbitrary orders from abroad. Thus her geographical origin also identifies Hui with a foreign source that dictates policy.[29]

As to Hui's age, she is twenty-four at the beginning of the novel, and the year 1924 saw some vital political developments in the early Chinese Communist movement. That was when the reorganized KMT officially accepted the CCP in the Nationalist Government at Canton and also when members of the CCP were officially ordered to join the KMT. The double-membership issue was not merely a matter of policy but of practical experience, and it underlies the Ching Hui Pao-su triangle.

The CCP leadership objected to the policy on grounds of principle as well as practicality, which made it all the more distasteful to the Party members charged with implementing it. This foreign imposition of an impossible, unethical political partnership is translated into Hui's nightmare after her evening with Pao-su. Hui's dream tells us that her disastrous love affair left her with a child of three—the years 1924–27—and there is also a threatening personage from her past who makes it impossible for her to have a genuine relationship with any other man.

To find symbolism in Hui's age is not as far-fetched as it may appear. Not only is it a time-hallowed custom in Chinese literature to use numbers as symbols, but there is a corollary in Ching's age, which is twenty-one, the year the CCP was founded. Ching represents a different conception of the CCP in the political alliance with the KMT—she is not trying to exploit Pao-su but truly taking joint responsibility for what becomes an illusory love affair. Accordingly this affair follows a different course, and Ching suffers more severely through Pao-su than Hui has done. She loses not just one round in political parleying but almost her ideal in love.

There are no illusions about possible fulfillment in Hui's philosophy of love. It is at best a pose for pleasure and self-gratification and at worst an expedient. Its goal is always the maximum gain for the self. Her flirtation with Pao-su is in essence no more and no less than a match between two masters schooled in the art of political expediency; neither side intends sharing or giving. In Pao-su's account, the skirmish comes to a speedy end when Pao-su suspects that Hui has had numerous affairs with other men and confronts her with his suspicions. We have no way of knowing whether fear of discovery of his own secret by a woman he now sees as worldly-wise is in Pao-su's mind when he, as he reports, confronts Hui with her undeclared past. Mao Tun never explores Pao-su's inner feelings. What we do know is that Hui promptly leaves Shanghai after the confrontation, and Pao-su, feigning innocence, continues his quest with a new target: Ching.

It is a curious fact that in the 1928 polemics between Mao Tun and his critics on the extreme left (with Ch'ien Hsing-ts'un as the most vocal representative) neither side took the trouble to argue over the ideological correctness of Hui. Her political role in *Disillusionment* was seemingly agreed upon. Mao Tun made only one noteworthy statement about Hui and her type in the trilogy in his first defense of the trilogy, when he wrote that her type did not represent "superficial women."[30]

Both Ching and Hui represent the CCP. The CCP during the Great Revolution years was by no means an undivided whole. Inner-party politics and factional struggles were constant. In 1926, the critical issue was the CCP-KMT alliance, and there the Party had always been split. The group that Hui represents saw it simply as an inevitable evil that could be rationalized as Raskolnikov rationalized his killing of the two old women in *Crime and Punishment*: it was the act of a superman done with the amoral conviction that the merit of the goal takes precedence over all conventional considerations of right and wrong. Ching represents the position which could not bear to see the Party's will subjected to force of circumstance: the CCP should not be a tool in a conspiracy of foreign design. How to present these conflicting views in fictional form was only part of Mao Tun's problem, for the Party's will to self-determination was not borne out by its actions. What was Mao Tun to do?

In 1922, when he was studying the plays of the Belgian playwright Maurice Maeterlinck, Mao Tun had been particularly intrigued by one of his plays, *Mona Vanna*, which poses two questions: Can a woman remain spiritually chaste when her body is sullied? Should a woman sacrifice her body as bravely as she would her life, to save others and her country? Maeterlinck's answers to both were in the affirmative. Soon in a transposed context of political reality, Mao Tun as a Party propagandist had to deal with analogous political problems: Could the spirit of the CCP remain pure if its principles were compromised? Should the CCP sacrifice purity to serve a larger goal?[31] And these problems, encapsulating the revolutionary consciousness throughout the period 1925–27, were reviewed in the fictional context of *Disillusionment* on more than one level.

Mao Tun first presents these questions on a moral plane, when his characters offer their opinions about Raskolnikov's moral responsibility (chapter 3). Pao-su's argument shifts responsibility from Raskolnikov himself to the invincible power of external circumstances. Hui then raises the claim that a moral goal justifies immoral means. But Ching, by considering Raskolnikov's guilt, brings moral responsibility back to the human self. Thus three answers are suggested to the question of how to reconcile the humanity of a goal with an inhumane action, but no definitive answer is given.

Then the questions are presented on the political plane, when the student assembly debate stands for a debate on Party principle (chapter 5). Here the contention centers on the question of the acceptability, in principle, of one person having two loyalties at the same time. The discussion and vote shows a majority rejection of the idea of two loyalties. Purity of principle is asserted for the individuals and, by analogy, for the Party.[32] One can well imagine how such an idealistic defense of Party principle, regardless of later compromises, appealed to CCP members. Even Ch'ien Hsing-ts'un a few years later accorded that chapter his rare approval: "Its method of representation is vivid and fascinating."

The third plane is the historical and realistic one: How were the questions resolved in action? Here we have to look at another set of triangular love in the novel. Ching and Hui, regardless of their different attitudes toward love, both have a relationship with Pao-su, just as the CCP, in spite of intra-Party policy disputes, made an alliance with the KMT. Whatever their reservations about such a policy, members of the CCP did join the KMT in 1924; and in spite of Chiang Kai-shek's Canton coup in 1926 and his Shanghai Massacre in April 1927, they continued to serve in the Nationalist Government in Wuhan. But Chiang's faction was dissociated with the continued collaboration. To justify the March 20 coup, Chiang claimed to have discovered a conspiracy by the CCP (as Pao-su claimed to have found out about Hui's hidden past): limitations were imposed upon CCP activities within the KMT government, and the Soviet advisers were expelled from Canton (paralleling Hui's departure from Shanghai). Then the Shanghai Massacre occurred. This convinced even the Soviet advisers and Comintern representatives that Chiang was not a dependable partner in the collaboration. Thus after his overnight affair with Ching Pao-su disappears from the scene, and the redness of his tie contaminates Ching and becomes the redness of her scarlet fever.

The affair with Pao-su takes a physical toll on Ching's health. She is hospitalized and is weighed down by a crushing sense of fate. But she accepts her share of responsibility in the affair. It does not matter, after the fact, whether it was out of innocence or ignorance or illusion that Ching went to bed with Pao-su. The important thing is that she had not been passive. She was temporarily immobilized by her physical and mental weakness. But she quickly recommitted herself to the revolutionary life at the exhortation of her old company of classmates. Accepting her role in the social movements, she once again reached out for fulfillment of her original ideal.

The political parallel to Ching's recommitment occurred soon after Chiang Kai-shek's massacre in Shanghai. Calling Chiang a traitor and expelling him from the KMT, as was done on April 17 in a communiqué signed by both Wang Ching-wei, soon to be the leader of the Wuhan government, and Ch'en Tu-hsiu, secretary general of the CCP, did not solve the problem. The question remained whether continued collaboration with the KMT Left now in power in Wuhan was still feasible.

As far as is known, the CCP leadership was just as averse to an alliance with the new leader of the Left KMT as they had been to the alliance with Chiang.[33] The politicians and generals of the Wuhan regime seemed to them no more trustworthy than those of the right-wing KMT. At a Politburo meeting held in Hankow before the Fifth Party Congress of April 27, 1927, Ch'en Tu-hsiu announced that cooperation with the KMT was becoming more precarious every day. On the surface, conflict with the KMT seemed to be over such problems as the peasant and land-distribution movement, but the true contest was for hegemony. To the CCP leadership, the choice was clear: the party must now either abandon the fight for hegemony or break with the KMT Left at Wuhan since the attempt to undermine the KMT from within had been disastrous. Unfortunately, the decision was not theirs to make.

The Fifth Party Congress convened in the wake of the April 12 massacre and Chiang's subsequent large-scale purges in Shanghai, Canton, and Peking.[34] There were heated arguments between Borodin, the Soviet government's adviser to the KMT, and Lois, now the Comintern representative to the CCP, about the direction the Chinese revolution should take and what was to be done about the peasant movement. Borodin still urged collaboration with the KMT and moderation in the mass movements, while Lois demanded increasingly radical, indeed violent, takeovers. The CCP casualties among both cadres and the rank and file had been staggering. Most of the members present at the Fifth Party Congress saw no way out for the CCP in either Borodin's or Lois's position.[35] As they were still vacillating between continued collaboration and a decisive break with the KMT, advance or retreat in the peasant movement, the warlord forces struck again.[36]

On May 21, General Hsü K'e-hsiang, long incensed with the CCP peasant movement, carried out a military coup against the CCP and the Peasant Association in Changsha. Immediately the angry calls for withdrawal from the KMT were renewed. But on June 1 a letter from Stalin himself arrived in Hankow. There was to be no withdrawal. The CCP was instructed to step up its operations: the part of the peasant movement it controlled was to start confiscating land and its military cadres were to take control of the KMT armed forces.[37] The Stalin letter immediately became known to Wang Ching-wei, thanks to Lois, and his Wuhan government quickly decided on its course of action. The expulsion of the CCP from the Wuhan government was announced on July 15; purges and massacres followed.

In the brief month and a half before the expulsion, the predominant mood in both the CCP leadership and its local provincial offices was a mixture of confusion, vacillation, and disillusionment, a mood vividly portrayed in the second part of *Disillusionment.*

The Second Half: Students in the Field

In the second half of *Disillusionment,* Ching, in the company of Hui and many of her university classmates, becomes active in the revolutionary center at Wuhan. The year is 1927.

Critics have noted that the second part of the novel is not as well constructed as the first. It may be that Mao Tun decided it would be too tedious to fashion yet another love triangle so like the previous ones. In reality, little that happened at Wuhan in the spring and early summer of 1927 differed from what had already happened in Canton and Shanghai. The CCP-KMT alliance continued, with Wang Ching-wei as the partner instead of Chiang Kai-shek. The covert struggle between the KMT and the CCP for control of the military, the labor unions, and the peasant associations went on as before. The Comintern and the Kremlin still issued directives that were remote from Chinese reality and that pushed the CCP ever closer to the breaking point with the Wuhan government.

In the novel, the disastrous outcome had already been presented once, when the March 20 coup and the April 12 massacre (and possibly the July 15 debacle too) were telescoped in Ching's allegorical scarlet fever after her lovemaking with Pao-su. (Hence Ch'ien Hsing-ts'un's comment that Pao-su's betrayal is found out too soon). The surface action, the endless bustle in Wuhan over mass movement activities depicted in chapters 9–11, was no longer the central drama of the Great Revolution. The real center in the spring and summer of 1927 had shifted to the countryside and the escalating peasant movement—the story that will be told separately in *Vacillation.* But in the second half of *Disillusionment* there is still one episode pertaining to the Wuhan period that Mao Tun could not leave unrepresented, and that was the Nanch'ang Uprising of August 1, 1927. The Nanch'ang Uprising and the Southern March, in which the remnants of the first Red Army escaped after the uprising was crushed, form the basis for three of the six chapters in the second half of *Disillusionment*, providing a climactic ending to the increasingly disoriented narrative in the last six chapters of the novel.

To all ranking members of the CCP, whatever their attitude toward the role of the Comintern, the Nanch'ang Uprising was a glorious historic event. "Autumn in Kuling" was a clear though somewhat elliptical and offstage fictional representation of the uprising. The representation in the last three chapters of *Disillusionment* is still allegorical, but closer to the passion and will that inspired the revolutionary action. These scenes, portrayed before the apocalyptic Canton Commune was known to Mao Tun, bubble with an energy that the short story lacks, an energy exuberantly concentrated in the name symbol of Ching's work partner, the battalion leader Ch'iang Meng, whose style Wei-li means Power by Force Only.

The Wuhan phase of *Disillusionment* begins with a surprise reunion between Ching and Hui on April 20, 1927, the day the Wuhan government launches its Second Northern Expedition from the military academy in Nanhu, a section of Wuch'ang. It ends when Ch'iang Wei-li leaves Wuhan to join the Southern March to Swatow and Canton, and Ching, accompanied not by Hui but by her university classmate Wang Shih-t'ao, starts back to Shanghai. There is a strong contrast between chapters 9–11 and chapters 12–14, between ineffectual revolutionary activity (Hsia's "caricature of purposeful action") and the purposeful romantic episode that concludes the book.

Chapter 9 is devoted to the ceremonial launching of the Second Northern Expedition and to the appearance of Hui, which signifies the continuing hand of the Comintern and Borodin in CCP politics at Wuhan. In chapter 10, a large assemblage representing the whole political spectrum of CCP leadership is complete on the Wuhan stage. One by one Ching meets her former classmates: Tung-fang Ming and Lung Fei, still rivals for Wang Shih-t'ao's attention, are now political workers; Wang Shih-t'ao is now a representative of the women's movement; Li K'e, Shih Ch'ün, and Chao Ch'ih-chu are affiliated with the labor organizations; and Hui is a salon hostess among the foreigners in Wuhan. Contradictions mark everything people are doing in Wuhan; the pursuit of pleasure seems to be the common denominator in this wartime setting. Ching gets sick again in the ambience of self-indulgence among revolutionaries.

> As she lay idle in her sickness, thoughts rushed through her mind. It seemed as though everything she had experienced in the past half-year spoke of contradiction in life. On the one side there was tension in the air, and revolution; on the other this general weariness and depression. All activities were mechanical, making one wonder if they were no more than

empty gestures. Yet exhaustion was everywhere visible. Was this not
weariness? Lovemaking became an epidemic. People madly sought
gratification of their desires, novel sexual stimuli. . . . Nevertheless, these
were symptoms of weariness. In a subdued atmosphere, the images of
weariness take the form of despondency and negativism; in a tense atmosphere, they become sexual pursuit. The so-called love-affair, as a result,
became a sacrosanct excuse.
    Contradiction! Everywhere contradictions![38]

In the midst of such contradictions does the revolution really march
on? Ching had her moments of doubt, but she still had her illusions also.[39]
    In chapter 11, Ching is confronted with a dilemma. Tired of life in
Wuhan but dependent on the company of her two "sisters," Hui and
Wang Shih-t'ao, she does not feel like going home to Changsha, where, as
her mother now writes to suggest, she could do the same type of work.
She has become close to Wang Shih-t'ao, but Wang is soon to join her
lover Tung-fang Ming in Kiukiang, near Nanch'ang. Ching cannot go to
Kiukiang because Hui objects, but she has no intention of moving in with
Hui and becoming her roommate again. After prolonged discussion, all
three women agree that it would be best for Ching to become a nurse at
the military hospital in Wuhan.
    In the historical context, at the time Ching is ruminating over her
sickness and doubts, her unwillingness to room with Hui and her inability to follow Wang to Kiukiang (a veritable state of vacillation), the
Chinese Communist movement is suffering serious losses in Hupeh and
Hunan provinces and the uneasy two-party collaboration in the Wuhan
government is becoming increasingly precarious. Vacillation is the keynote on the scene. And the effects were most immediate and concrete in
the area of military movements. A showdown in terms of brute force was
imminent and the stage was set for Ching, in the fictional context, to
unite herself with the allegorical "Power by Force Only."
    In history, military attacks by anti-Communist warlords increased in
number and strength in the spring and summer of 1927. Hsia Tou-yen, a
lower-ranking military commander, led an attack on May 17 on Wuhan
which nearly unseated the Wuhan government. Hsü K'e-hsiang's May 21
Mutiny at Changsha followed,[40] and his rebellion had broad repercus-
sions among other generals who, like him, owned land in the countryside. The Wuhan government refused to take action against the Hsü
mutiny because of its displeasure with the labor and peasant movements
radicalized by CCP agitation (see *Vacillation*). Instead, it began suppression by disbanding the peasant associations in Huang-kang and Huang-
p'o, the two largest in Hupeh province.
    In the novel, the news that western Hupeh province is under siege (ch.
12) and the message from Changsha that CCP reinforcement is needed
there (in the form of the letter from Ching's mother) register only periph-

erally on Ching's sensibility, which is weakened by illness. But these reports reflect the result of military action against the peasant movements in Hunan and Hupeh provinces and the confusion and ineffectualness of the CCP leadership in Wuhan. The break between the CCP and the KMT Left is in the offing. However, this will not occur before Ching and Ch'iang Wei-li become united in a genuine romance of spontaneous love and free will.

Ch'iang Wei-li, when he first appears on the scene in chapter 12, is a wounded soldier back from the North China front. From his account of the battle of Lin-ying in Honan Province, we learn that he has been with the Second Northern Expedition force fighting Chang Tso-ling in Honan at the same time Hsia Tou-yen was besieging Wuch'ang. Mao Tun has dexterously brought the two battlefronts of the CCP together in chapter 12; news of the losing battle from the reports Ching reads to Ch'iang Wei-li, and the victory that Ch'iang reports to Ching. The latter is used to convey the fact of the CCP's active participation in the Second Northern Expedition, although the numerical strength of these forces did not make them important to the general public.[41] However, historical record notwithstanding, Mao Tun was most conscientious to preserve in Ch'iang's characterization the discrepancy between the physical condition of the CCP military and the poetry of its aspiration. Ch'iang Wei-li is not portrayed as physically robust and his devastated body testifies to the untold story behind his narrated victory.

Three armed forces came together in the Second Northern Expedition in 1927—Chiang's force from Nanking; the Sixth Army of T'ang Sheng-chih and the Fourth Army of Chang Fa-k'uei from Wuhan; and Feng Yü-hsiang's army from Shensi. There was a concentration of CCP cadres in Chang's Fourth Army. The CCP contingent suffered heavy casualties in the battles against Chang Tso-ling in Honan during the second half of May, but victory brought the Party no material gain. So in *Disillusionment*, we see

> Ch'iang Wei-li returned from the battlefield wounded: Shrapnel fragments had cut off his left nipple, and left three or four deep cuts in the lower part of his left breast. The army doctor said that this battalion leader of ours would have become a dead war hero if the cuts had gone a fraction of an inch deeper.[42]

Ch'ien Hsing-ts'un, a die-hard extreme leftist, applauded what had been done in this chapter; he only wished the author had done the same in the next, working more "military action into it."[43] Ch'ien's wish is understandable. The CCP forces that led the Nanch'ang Uprising two months later included those that had participated in the Second Northern Expedition. The suppression of the peasant movement in Hunan and Hupeh by the warlord generals and the lack of KMT acknowledgment of CCP participation in the Second Northern Expedition had convinced many of the ranking CCP members in summer 1927 that the only way that the CCP could ever come to its own was to have an army, a banner, and a slogan of its own. And time was running out. On May 29, a few days before the Second Northern Expedition scored a conclusive victory against the northern warlords, powerful elements in the combined armies openly turned against the CCP. First Tang Sheng-chih, commander of the Sixth Army and the most powerful of the "progressive" warlords, announced his anti-CCP stand. Shortly afterward, at the Cheng-chou Conference on June 10, 1927, his position was supported by another hitherto "progressive" warlord, Feng Yü-hsiang, and by the KMT representatives from Wuhan. The stage was set for a thorough purge of the CCP, the only question was when.

But Mao Tun refused to let these circumstances entirely explain the dynamics of CCP policies and actions. The founding of a Red Army came about as the crystallization of a whole complex of factors. Some were external—the new pressures from the KMT and the warlords—but there were also critical internal factors, and these inform the last part of *Disillusionment.*

The union of Ching and Ch'iang Wei-li in the last chapter is literally a union between a sick body and a sick political consciousness. But on a different level, it is also a tender romance consummated in a fulfilling love relationship. Ching is passionately in love with Ch'iang Wei-li, a fanatical Futurist as well as a warrior. Their union,

> on the part of Miss Ching, was a white-hot love, arising out of a mingled compassion and respect; it was voluntary and self-conscious, not emotional or impulsive. One might say of the Futurist that he was attracted and moved, but it might be said that their love was only another phase of his Futuristic activities; heaven only knows what was actually going on. But in that first week the two hearts were joined, it was undeniably a spontaneous love, a love of Naturalism, not a Futuristic one.[44]

Ch'iang Wei-li and Ching spend a week in Kuling, a week of "total forgetfulness, devoted to a whole-hearted pursuit of carnal pleasure."[45] This was precisely the time when the CCP forces were gathering in Kiuchiang and Nanch'ang to form the Red Army and initiate its first independent action, the Nanch'ang Uprising. No wonder Ch'ien Hsing-ts'un would have preferred another description of military action.

Mao Tun, however, did not adopt a realist's approach and end *Disillusionment* with a climactic battlefield scene. Had he done that the result might not have been complimentary in realistic terms either, because the Nanch'ang Uprising was a military failure, and the subsequent Southern March was *de facto* a military retreat. At the time, the real significance of the Nanch'ang Uprising to the CCP had little to do with the surface military action, and everything to do with the fact that it was a spontaneous act of total free will of the Party, conceived without interference from the Comintern and carried out, Futurist style, voluntarily by such dedicated leaders as Li Li-san, Chou En-lai, Yeh T'ing, and Ho Lung. These men first organized the Front Committee for the uprising, then led the rank and file of the Fourth Army, and ultimately founded the Red Army. No matter how the military action itself turned out, the two important things were this will to freedom and the determination to use speed, brute force, and destruction as the means of action.

Mao Tun ingeniously found a means to represent these two facets of the Futuristic poetry of those days in the white-hot "voluntary and self-conscious" love of Ching for Ch'iang Wei-li and in Wei-li's craving for battlefield destruction and his ultimate march back to duty. Writing in August and September of 1927, back in Shanghai and disillusioned with the fiasco of his party's coalition with the KMT but nonetheless yet unburdened with the agony and despair to come out of the gory Canton Commune, Mao Tun was still hopeful that his comrades' Southern March would build a base for future action. Hence Ching's romance with Ch'iang Wei-li has a level of light-heartedness that marks only the writings of Mao Tun of the pre-Canton Commune days.

Mao Tun's interest in Futurism, like his many other interests in Western literature and literary theories, was more than a scholarly one. It was a part of his life-long struggle to bring about revolutionary change in China and his literary comrades' apparent inability to assimilate either Soviet Futuristic literature or the Soviet model of proletarian literature for China's use concerned him for many years.[46] In the early 1920s Futurism bespoke for Mao Tun the poetry and romance of the Bolshevik Revolution. He had great admiration for the power of Futurism, as represented especially by Mayakovsky, although he recognized that, as Wang Ch'iung-ch'üan, a friend and literary collaborator, wrote in *Short Story Monthly*,[47] "Futurist poetry gathers its material from the clamor of an industrial work site, the roar of racing cars; and all noise of hubbub and commotion. Its goal is to smash the stagnant, passive, and unhealthy spirit; in effect its only poetic reality is the Dionysian state of unbridled life force."[48] And Mao Tun knew anything unbridled can promise perils as well.

There are a number of parallels between Ch'iang Wei-li's characterization and his creator's early study of Mayakovsky. For examples, Mao Tun believed Mayakovsky's claim that he enlisted in the army during World War I and that he enlisted not for patriotic motives but to give full vent to his passion for bloody destruction. This of course could well have been part of a pose that Mayakovsky was fond of assuming in his pre-October-Revolution writings, but Ch'iang Wei-li claims the same when talking to

Ching. His battlefield speech impresses us in almost the same manner as Mao Tun's praise for Mayakovsky's "150,000,000." "This is a great and powerful poem," he wrote in "The Current State of Futurist Literature" in 1922.

> It seems to represent the fearless, destructive spirit of the Bolshevik Party. After you have read the poem [or, heard Ch'iang's speech], you may hate it, you may like it, but you will not be able to remain indifferent to it, devoid of reaction. It pierces your heart, demanding that you pay attention to it and take a position.[49]

In destruction there is a possibility for rejuvenation. Bolshevism could be the "spiritual dynamics" which the Futurist poetry celebrates, a kind of dynamism that brings "a blood transfusion for those paralyzed by the old Russian nihilism."[50] But when transplanted, what it can be for China, even as Futurist poetry, is by no means certain.

> Steam, light, electricity, the speed and power they represent, have already become part and parcel of the consciousness and subconscious of modern man. Since art is the essence flowing out of man's consciousness, only accidentally arrested in this or that form, it is obvious that speed and energy cannot be kept out of the artistic domain. Futurists say that the sound of a motor car is more pleasing to the ear than music written by classical composers.[51] Maybe it is to their ears. In that case, one has nothing to say to that. . . . [But] the rapid disappearance of the Futurist School has come about because man's worship and awe of machine power are already passé. . . . Because it praised machine civilization, it took it upon itself to destroy everything else with all its might. The Russian Futurist School now puts destruction of the old at the center of its program; it has already ceased its earlier praise of machine civilization.[52]

Futurism, when serving as a guiding principle for action, or, worse, for revolutionary action, is a frightening philosophy, with its blind hacking away at all obstructions lying in the way to the future. In 1925 in his article "On Proletarian Literature," Mao Tun was already calling attention to the distinction between revolutionary literature, which aims to destroy, and true proletarian literature, which portrays the people's quest for freedom. More specifically there, he warned against any "ism" in literature that turns away from present-day reality and entrusts its goal to an unknown future. This warning was repeated in another article in the same year, "The New Missions of Writers." He warned writers not to abandon real life to describe the future ideal world.

> We cannot put aside wants and needs . . . and if we are unable to grasp what the needs and wants of the present generation are, then we cannot

trace the right road of the future, and then the ideal of the future society we carry within our heart is but a medicine that does not heal the disease.[53]

In the characterization of Ch'iang Wei-li as an allegorical representation of the goals of the Nanch'ang Uprising, we see the tension between two unresolved forces: one striving for a better life in a better future, and the other pulling it blindly, almost against its will, into the abyss of destruction in the warring present. Ch'iang's excited speech about the battlefield—a faithful reproduction of Russian Futurist poetry—does not portend well for his promised reunion with Ching.

> I still want to go to battle. To me the battlefield is a stronger temptation than any other temptation. It concentrates a man's experience in life. Hope, encouragement, fury, destruction, sacrifice—all these experiences which would otherwise require half a lifetime to savor, I can get on the battlefield within a few short hours. Life on the battlefield is life at its liveliest and most changing. It is also the most artistic: the thrilling whistle of the flying bullets from a carbine; the ghost-like qock, qock, qock of the machine gun—even the bravest cannot help but wince at the sound of a machine gun; it sounds really ugly. The roar of a cannon is like the bass drum in an orchestra, keeping the beat. Ah, the breath of death [in battle] is more intoxicating than the breath of the sweetest wine.[54]

And when asked what sends him to the battlefield, Ch'iang says:

> I adore Futurism in art. I go after strong stimulants. I sing hymns to bombs, cannons, revolutions—all that expresses violent destructive force. I became a revolutionary because I was tired of the everyday round and that is also why I enlisted in the army. The battlefield is the best setting for Futurism: strong stimulants, destruction, change, inane killing, worship of brute strength, everything you can think of is there. . . . To tell you the truth, I like to fight, not for any reason, but because I thirst after strong stimulants; I don't care whether I win or not.

The last scene in *Disillusionment* sees Ch'iang Wei-li marching off to southern China with his leader Tung-fang Ming to an uncertain future, while Ching and Wang Shih-t'ao return to Shanghai together to await reunion with their lovers. But these reunions never materialize; destruction strikes instead. A few months later, the opening scene of *Pursuit*, back in Shanghai, does feature a Miss Wang and a Miss Chang, but Tung-fang Ming and Ch'iang Wei-li are absent. The failed promise of reunion tells us that Ch'iang Wei-li will never come back. The perversion of means has finally affected the nature of its goals. Between Canton and Shanghai, Ch'iang Wei-li's Futurism has changed as much as European Futurism changed on its way from Italy to Russia to China. Celebration of force for the purpose of creation of a new future has been perverted to blind destruction.

Disillusionment was completed just three months before the prophecy of blind destruction was fulfilled in the Canton Commune, a blind uprising of workers ordered by the Comintern to supply proof for its prediction of a "rising tide" of revolution in the new-China-to-be. The romance of Chang Ching, reviewed in the context of the Canton Commune, becomes the grotesque and gory revitalizing project of Chang Ch'iu-liu in *Pursuit.* And in *Pursuit,* Tung-fang Ming returns only in a nightmarish vision and only with a blood ring around his neck.

IV

VACILLATION

Vacillation, part 2 of the trilogy *Eclipse,* is, according to Mao Tun, "a story set in a town in Hupei along the Upper Yangtze River Valley" in January–May of 1927.[1] Its theme is the vacillation experienced by participants in the revolutionary activities when the revolutionary struggle was fierce."[2] In his 1928 defense of the trilogy, Mao Tun went on to say that there was no protagonist in the novel: Characters in it are "representatives" of phenomena that were prevalent at that time. And it was a very disturbing time, since "the period covered by *Vacillation* represents the most momentous stage in the history of the [Great] Revolution in China, the vacillation of revolutionary ideas and revolutionary policies from the leftist tendency to the emergence of infantile leftism, from coping with infantile leftism to the ascendancy of rightist thoughts, and finally the great reaction."[3]

This volume too was written while the author was in hiding in Shanghai and was published almost immediately—January–March—in *Short Story Monthly.* Mao Tun, ever the intellectual activist, was well aware of Lenin's castigation of infantile leftism as a fatal inability among the more extreme Communist party members to understand that diverse tactics were required to accomplish the historical mission of different phases of the Communist revolution, tactics that are not always explicable in straightforward ideological terms.[4]

To present the phenomenon of vacillation and the ensuing "infantile leftism" Mao Tun intended to use an objective, noninterpretive descriptive method to point up the most typical elements of the revolutionary situation described in the novel. The invisible framework enveloping the story is drawn tightly: neither the policy-making process in the central Party organization in Wuhan—which was not only the seat of the united-front government but the capital of Hupei Province—nor the final eruption of mass violence in the little country town moves above a reporting of the fictional bare facts. The former is embodied in the arrival of orders from Wuhan carried by two special commissars, Shih Chün (chapter 6) and Li K'e (chapter 11); the climactic eruption is a local riot (chapter 11).

The internal entanglements of the central Party apparatus that were at work behind the objectives of the "cause" are beyond the story's scope; what is brought to life are characters and situations that do not carry their own rationale beyond the façade of conflicting personal interests. Yet the drama of the revolution, which the characters in *Vacillation* neither understand nor are able to direct, unfolds around the interplay of their interests and around their interpretations and attempted manipulations of the vacillating "revolutionary ideas and revolutionary policies" of town and central CCP organizations. The authority carried first by Shih Chün and then by Li K'e is cloaked in dispassionate objectivity; there is no overt comment on their correctness or usefulness. The local scenes of the Businessmen's Union and the peasants' and women's movements are described in more detail, but again with no overt judgments of right or wrong.

The questions that arise from the drama—How are these events (and similar events elsewhere) affecting the CCP and the Great Revolution? How have they shaped the later course of the revolution?—are not answered in the story. In this sense, it provides only a case study of how vacillation in the ideas and policies coming out of Wuhan affected the daily lives of local people in a small town and the surrounding countryside—people the CCP through the "Great Revolution" intended to emancipate and lead.[5]

The twelve chapters in *Vacillation* are organized around two central episodes: a strike of store workers that leads to Shin Chün's investigation with its prescribed-in-advance "Solution" (chapter 6); and, later, the riot that Li K'e's arrival precipitates (chapter 11). The alliances of local interest groups in the two incidents, though sometimes overlapping, are different. The first set of issues concerns disputes between labor and petty bourgeoisie businessmen whose base is primarily in town; the second set, which concerns the women's and peasants' movements, involves people all the way out into the countryside.

In the labor-proprietor disputes of the first six chapters, the local interest groups are represented by Hu Kuo-kuang, a well-connected political opportunist and *arriviste* to the gentry, and Lu Mu-yu, the black-sheep son of a bold scholar-gentry family. In theory, Hu and Lu should have been prime targets of the revolution: both are veritable *lieh-shen* (evil gentry). But in fact their social and economic standing gives them the advantage in the revolutionary power game.

In the last half of the novel the interest groups are much more complex. Once land and women are brought into the picture, all the imbalance and inequity of this microcosmic Chinese "feudal" society become visible. Concubines, nuns, land ownership, husbands' rights—all these are aspects of the intractable concept of property ownership that the revolution was coming to demolish. It was truly terrifying, as Mao Tun said in "On Reading *Ni Huan-chih*," to see what cruelty the people in even that small a town were capable of once their ownership rights were threatened.

The drama (the impact of the revolution on the daily life of one small town) and the theme (the vacillating revolutionary ideas and policies that shaped the impact) are elaborately interwoven.

The Town (Chapters 1–6)

Hu Kuo-kuang's devious climb to power occupies center stage in the beginning chapters of the novel. In chapters 1 and 2 we learn that Hu has one wife, one concubine, one delinquent son, and one bondsmaid—a typical "feudal" family awaiting emancipation. He frequents the Clear Wind Pavilion teahouse, where the dregs of the old world's politics congregate, and he courts the friendship of Lu Mu-yu, who often visits local brothels. Normally one would not think of Hu Kuo-kuang's way of life and daily activities as anything that could be called criminal. But January– May of 1927 is not a normal time; revolution has come to the county and its norms and values are undergoing violent changes. What was once the source of privilege and power to the upper class—for example, land and other forms of property—is now evidence of counterrevolutionary crimes members of that class have to answer for. Workers, peasants, and women, the community members who have never enjoyed equitable rights, are to benefit from the revolution and receive their overdue share of privileges.

Hu Kuo-kuang is expectedly threatened by the loss of his possessions—his concubine as well as his money. He quickly takes stock of his time-tested survival techniques and devises a way to weather this new wave of revolutionary upsurges, as he had done once before, when the Manchu Dynasty fell:

> Two months ago, he was still blabbing in the Clear Wind Pavilion about General Wu [P'ei-su, one of the warlords], notwithstanding that the country office had already hoisted the flag of the Nationalist Government. He was a time-tested old fox. In the year *hsin-hai* [1911], when the New Army mutinied in the provincial capital and occupied the armory at Ch'u-*wang't'ai*, scaring [the Manchu governor] Jui-chen away, he was among the first in the county to cut off his queue.[6] At that time he was only thirty-four years old. His father, a member of the board of trustees for the county orphanage, was still alive. He had not yet bought this concubine Golden Phoenix; and his son was barely three years old. With a silver-plated lapel pin of some political party or other, he began to pass himself off as a member of the gentry class in the county. Since then, personnel turnover in the provincial government had been once every two years on the average,

and in the county government once every year and a half. But his position as a member of the gentry has never come under threat. He saw with absolute surety that as long as there is need for county chiefs, there would be need for gentry folk like himself. Without the gentry, there could be no government bureaucrats. His "iron rice bowl" [guaranteed usefulness as part of the gentry] would never crack. Hence when the county office changed its flag to that of the Nationalist Government, and quite a few posters appeared on the walls at the Temple of the Local God advocating "Down with the Local Ruffians and Evil Gentry," he remained unperturbed and continued to air his views about General Wu and General Liu Yü in the special section of the Clear Wind Pavilion.[7]

To Hu Ku-kuang now the game is basically the same. Only the names have changed. Whereas formerly you hankered after the honorific address *ta-ren-lao-yeh* (Your Excellency My Lord) now you run for *wei-yüan* (committee member). Thus when Hu's cousin Wang Jung-ch'ang, a local storekeeper, comes to see him about the new regulations, Hu quickly sees in Wang's problem the exact opportunity he needs to get into the new game.

Wang Jung-ch'ang is a timid, law-abiding small businessman. Recently the county Party organization notified him that all businessmen must join the Businessman's Union and make public the names of the store owners and managers, the year the store started to do business, and the amount of its capital. The last item is particularly frightening; Wang Jung-ch'ang sees in it nothing less than the beginning of *"kung-ch'an,"* communizing private property. Hence his pathetic plea to Hu Kuo-kuang:

> Some say that it won't come to communizing private property; that all they want is to have us join the Businessmen's Union, to vote. By the end of this month there is going to be an election for Businessmen's Union representatives. Cousin Chen-ch'ing, you know me, I understand only business, I'm no good at all at committees and elections. I'm deathly afraid of walking into meetings and associating with government officials.[8]

Hu Kuo-kuang quickly volunteers his services, telling his cousin that he will be glad to stand in for him as the owner of the store, join the union, and deal with those committees and elections on Wang's behalf. Wang could not be more grateful. Thus begins Hu's career as a revolutionary.

Hu joins the store owners' union, and at once tries to get himself elected to its standing committee. To that end he forms an alliance with his drinking buddy Lu Mu-yu. The trade-off is that if Lu helps Hu get elected, Hu will help Lu in his amorous pursuit of the widowed store owner Ch'ien Su-chen. Lu Mu-yu's father was a respected scholar in the community, many of whose former students now hold key positions in the county government and Party organization. Through the Lu family's connections, therefore, Hu Ku-kuang becomes acquainted first with

Chou Shih-ta, one of father Lu's students and a member of the county Party's standing committee, and then with Fang Lo-lan, head of the County Bureau of Commerce and the Party member in charge of labor affairs. The "Party" ostensibly refers to the KMT, because it was the only legal party at the time *Vacillation* was published and therefore the only party Mao Tun could openly mention. But he need not be talking about the KMT only. The allegory could very well cover his CCP comrades who at the time of the story were still working under cover in the KMT government and its party organization.

The Party man Fang Lo-lan, head of the Commerce Bureau and responsible for maintaining labor-business stability, has a very important role in the central drama of *Vacillation*. Like Hu Kuo-kuang, he will have a decisive impact on the two key public events. However, while Hu Kuo-kuang concentrates in himself all the murky local forces that will try to make the revolutionary movement a fiasco, Fang Lo-lan embodies the preposterous vacillating and conflicting policies and ideas that beset the movement internally.

Aside from members of the Lu family, who serve as the bridge between their two separate worlds, Hu and Fang share no other apparent common ties or acquaintances. They are brought together through conflicts in their respective positions concerning the mass movements. Fang first meets Hu during one of these moments of conflict, as Mao Tun begins in chapter 3 to introduce Fang Lo-lan and his world.

Fang Lo-lan, an intellectual turned revolutionary, is thirty-two years old. He has been happily married for four or five years, ever since he graduated from the university. Now he has a son of four or five, and a wife whom he still loves dearly though she has fallen somewhat behind the times. On the day Hu first comes to his house, to ask for his backing in the election, Fang Lo-lan happens to be upset by the alluring image of another woman, a certain Sun Wu-yang. This is the first time such a thing has happened since he married. Sun's image is competing for his attention with Hu, who, loudly protesting his innocence, wants his name cleared of recent accusations of being "evil gentry," which are about to cost him his otherwise assured position on the standing committee of the Business Men's Union. Fang, knowing Hu's background, has no patience with his plea of innocence, and refuses to help. After Hu leaves, Fang is still haunted by his breathtaking encounter with Sun Wu-yang. As he sits in his living room,

> A vision, taking form in front of his glazed eyes, finally assumed concrete form: prominently facing him now was no longer the holly bush but a woman's long dark-green coat, dotted all over with small red stars the size of red holly seeds. Suddenly they acquired life. The red stars set in dark green all began to explode; they raced and they hopped. Like sparks

bursting out of fireworks, they vied to shoot upward, gathering in the end
into a somewhat larger dot of crimson red at the collar of the woman's
dark-green coat. This crimson-red dot, too, presently broke open, revealing two rows of lovely pearls. Ah! This is a smile, the alluring smile of a
woman. Above that smile, under crescent eyebrows, was a pair of dark,
lash-sheltered eyes from which radiated a green-yellow light. . . .

"Wu-yang, you are my light of hope. I cannot help going with you."

From that day on, Fang Lo-lan's life becomes irrevocably entangled with
that of the repulsive, opportunistic Hu Kuo-kuang, whose ambition to
become a power in the revolutionary camp keeps him close to Fang, and
with his Party coworker, the seductive, free-loving Sun Wu-yang.

Trouble with the store workers soon flares up. Encouraged by the
organization of a Workers' Union, a workers' patrol, and other Party-
sponsored movements favoring the work force, the employees make
three unprecedented demands on their bourgeois employers: (1) a pay
raise of 20 to 50 percent; (2) no layoffs; (3) no lockouts for any reason.[9]
Lu Mu-yu, newly elected to the Businessmen's Union Standing Committee, is preparing a speech, hoping to get in first on the pro-labor side
before the Party takes a public position. Of course, Lu recruits Hu Kuo-
kuang to draft the speech. The time is close to the end of the last month
on the lunar calendar (still used in such agricultural communities). This
means it is about the beginning of February 1927 on the solar calendar.
The labor movement is gaining momentum; the atmosphere in the town
is tense. The workers' patrol is regularly seen in the streets and with them
are teams of boys carrying clubs and wearing strips of red cloth around
their necks.[10] One day, when the Workers Union is holding a parade, a
group of thugs suddenly dash out of the Clear Wind Pavilion to break it
up; street fights ensue. The next day the union patrol begins to carry
guns, and three hundred reinforcements are sent in by the neighboring
peasant associations to help out. A showdown between the workers and
the proprietors is imminent.

At that very moment Fang Lo-lan is caught in a two-front crisis. Ch'en
Chung, a high-school classmate who is now a member of the Party's
standing committee, comes to his house with Chou Shih-ta to discuss the
labor problem; and Fang's wife, Lu Mei-li, has just quarreled with him
over a handkerchief given to him by Sun Wu-yang, and is in tears. With
the assistance of Ch'en Chung and Chou Shih-ta on the labor problem,
and of two other family friends, Miss Liu and Miss Chang—one a former
schoolmate of Mrs. Fang and the other a member of the county Women's
Association—with Mrs. Fang, both crises are temporarily resolved. On
the political front, it is decided that tomorrow there will be a joint meeting of the various people's organizations. Representatives from the Businessmen's Union, the Workers' Union and the Women's Association will

discuss and resolve the labor question. Mrs. Fang is somewhat pacified by Miss Chang and Miss Liu, who persuade her that Sun Wu-yang is a notorious flirt and that the handkerchief carries no more meaning than a passing whim. Fang Lo-lan, swearing innocence, presents Mrs. Fang with the very handkerchief that caused the domestic storm, and wins a reluctant smile from her.

The next chapter describes the joint meeting where alignments among people from both the Party and the local groups became well-defined as three proposals are put on the table. The scene is very factual, with the "lines" set out clearly and no attempt to show the emotions of any of the participants. The style is that of "minutes of the meeting." Lu Mu-yu of the Businessmen's Union, joined by the chairman of the Workers' Union, Lin Pu-p'ing, proposes that all three of the Workers' demands be approved and a special committee be set up to see that they are carried out. The proposal is seconded by another representative of the Businessmen's Union. Lin Tzu-ch'ung of the Party organization then proposes that consideration of the three specific demands be suspended until the special commissar from the provincial capital, who is expected any day, arrives to resolve the whole matter. But in the meantime there should be an active purge of the "local ruffians and evil gentry" and "suppression" of conspiratorial, reactionary store owners. This proposal is seconded by Sun Wu-yang of the Women's Association. Fang Lo-lan then makes a third proposal: (a) gradual, not precipitous pay raise; (b) layoffs to be permitted with the consent of the Workers' Union; (c) requests to close a store to be considered by the county Party organization after investigation by a special committee of representatives from the people's organizations; (d) street patrols by workers and youth to be called off to forestall general panic; and (e) no unauthorized arrests of store owners. The proposal is seconded by Ch'en Chung and Chou Shih-ta.

As the proposals are being argued, a report of street rioting is brought in. Wang Jung-ch'ang has been caught smuggling merchandise out of his store, and his cousin, Hu Kuo-kuang, has denounced him in an open speech in front of the store. He has suddenly become an exemplary "revolutionary" store owner. The incident not only sways the meeting to support Lin Tzu-ch'ung's proposal for immediate purges and for leaving the workers' demands to the Wuhan envoy, but, even more important for subsequent events, it also cements the "revolutionary" comradeship between Lin Tzu-ch'ung and Hu Kuo-kuang. Hu's revolutionary zest seems to have found in Lin Tzu-ch'ung a backer on the level of Party policy; and Party policy as voiced by Lin seems in turn to have found in Hu Kuo-kuang a man of action on the grass-roots level.

Subsequently a telegram from the capital arrives. Forbidding rash action, it goes directly against the grain of the motion just passed, furthers the confusion, and puts Fang Lo-lan on the spot. Unable to act on these orders because the local conflicts are already in motion, he has no answers to the businessmen for whom he is responsible when they ask: After the wire arrives, why weren't the patrol team and the youth groups ordered off the streets? Why weren't the reinforcements from the peasants' associations sent back? Is the Workers' Union truly under the command of the Party? What attitude does Fang's Bureau of Commerce take toward the current action against the business sector? The credibility of the Party in general and Fang's own authority in particular are assaulted from both sides. Fang is totally frustrated, and his colleagues Ch'en Chung, Chou Shih-ta, and P'eng Kang share his frustration. They began to feel somewhat the way Mrs. Fang feels, behind the times and hopelessly lost in a rapidly changing world.

Then Shih Chün arrives, the special commissar from Wuhan. Shih Chün, we remember, was Chao Ch'ih-chu-s boyfriend in *Disillusionment,* the student who voiced loud objections to the triangular love affair between Wang Shih-t'ao, Tung-fang Ming, and Lung Fei. Now he appears in the troubled county as a special representative, authorized to handle the local labor dispute. Outspoken and forthright as before, he offers his characteristic direct solution with a resounding crack of the whip:

> "What the people in the Provincial Capital have in mind for the store workers' problems are (1) a pay raise; (2) no layoffs; (3) prohibit any disruption of business by storeowners' lockouts. This is how it's done in Hankow, and this is how it's done in the outlying counties. The only difference is in the details, such as how much of a pay raise is a real pay raise."[11]

Of course, the solution Shih Chün has brought corresponds straight down the line with the first proposal, made by Lu Mu-yu and Lin Pu-p'ing. Party authority as represented by Shih Chün has inadvertently played into the hands of people like Lu Mu-yu and Hu Kuo-kuang. Fang Lo-lan, Chou Shih-ta, and Ch'en Chung try to reason with Shih Chün, arguing for some degree of moderation in the treatment of the owners, but Shih Chün only becomes more determined. The peasants' army isn't needed in the labor struggle, he says flatly.

> Tomorrow we'll call a meeting to announce the policies of the Provincial Party organization and settle all measures of implementation on the spot. That should take care of it. If there are store owners who want to object, or local ruffians and evil gentry who want to make trouble, we will have them arrested and taken care of right away.[12]

Once the labor policy is spelled out and the method of execution is decided upon, all that is left for Shih Chün to do is to meet with representatives of the various factions in the peoples' organizations. It is thought-provoking that the two he especially wants to talk with are the new revolutionary zealot Hu Kuo-kuang and the flirtatious Sun Wu-yang. Hu's visible devotion to the revolution impresses Shih Chün tremendously, and right after their meeting he decides to recommend Hu for membership in the standing committee of the county Party organization. His talks with Sun Wu-yang are longer, and they are as much concerned with Sun Wu-yang herself as about the kind of revolutionary policies Shih has brought with him.

Shih Chün sees Sun Wu-yang three times after the settlement of the labor policy, and each time she is with a different man. The first encounter is at Shih Chün's guest house, and Sun is with the Party leader Lin Tzu-ch'ung. In this scene, Lin and Sun flirt with each other as Sun sings the "Internationale" over and over. Neither Lin nor Sun seems to have much respect for another person who is present, a man by the name of Chu Min-sheng, although Sun seems to be on rather intimate terms with him. The meeting is cut short because all must attend a tea reception for Shih Chün at the Women's Association, and there Sun is alone with Fang Lo-lan for a few minutes. During those brief moments Sun suddenly becomes a different person, all understanding and sympathy for the family trouble Fang has had because of her handkerchief. When Fang leaves, he is totally intrigued by this complex and multifaceted woman.

Shih Chün is supposed to meet Sun for a third time just before he leaves town, but he cannot find her. Looking around for her, he thinks he may have seen her in a yard with a flowerbed, just turning the corner of the house with some other person. But the train is leaving and he had no time to continue the search. Just as his train is pulling out of the station, Sun Wu-yang comes running up, followed by the mysterious Chu Min-sheng. Her dress is rumpled, she is flushed and panting, and there are petals of crushed chrysanthemum in her hair.

The people on the platform to see Shih Chün off are talking about a new topic. The local labor problem seems settled for the moment; the pressing question now is the peasant movement and the rumor about "communization of wives and concubines." What is the Party's policy on the movement?

The County (Chapters 7–12)

The second half of *Vacillation* begins, like the first half, with a prelude of private dealings between Lu Mu-yu and Hu Kuo-kuang: This time it is Lu Mu-yu's turn to expect Hu Kuo-kuang's assistance in his affair with the widow Ch'ien Su-chen. Lu and Ch'ien have become lovers and Ch'ien needs the help of people on revolutionary committees to safeguard her business and her property from the greedy hands of her relatives. Hu Kuo-kuang, thanks to the patronage of Shih Chün, is now an elected member of the Executive Committee of the county Party organization. Both Lu and Hu are in place to capitalize on the next wave of revolutionary development in the county.

Spring is in the air and the peasant movement in the countryside is steadily on the rise.

> Since the end of the last lunar year, Peasant Associations had been formed in the nearby countryside, Nan-hsiang. Peasants actually became organized and rumors accordingly followed. The first rumors were about the "communization" of property because at that time the peasant associations were investigating the distribution of land ownership among the peasants. But the rumors quickly turned into "men for draft and women for sharing." Hence peasants at Nan-hsiang had been in a state of fright as they spent their pathetic lunar New Year Days. There were incidents of assaults on the peasant associations, which caused the county association to dispatch a special commissioner by the name of Wang Cho-fan to Nan-hsiang for an investigation.
>
> What had happened was not difficult to bring to light. The ones who had been spreading the rumors were the local ruffians and evil gentry; and the ones misled were the peasants. However, if you tried to argue that there had been no "sharing" of wives, the peasants were not going to believe you. It was clear as daylight to all that there was a Communist Party. Thus it went without saying that all property was to be shared, and that since wives are a form of property, it would make absolutely no sense to the peasants to say that wives were to be exempt from sharing. That would be downright double-dealing.
>
> Special Commissioner Wang was an able man. Therefore, within a week of his arrival at Nan-hsiang, peasants there had added another slogan, "Those with extra wives are to share their wives," to the one they already knew by heart, "Land to the tillers."[13] In China there are always extra women and unattached women. For one man to have two wives makes one wife "extra," of course, and widows not remarried and nuns without husbands are of course "unattached." Now the peasants of Nan-hsiang were going to compensate for these deficiencies by sharing the extras and making full use of the unattached.

As it happened, on the same spring day that Lu Mu-yu consummates his love affair with the widow Ch'ien, a mass meeting of peasants raises the demand to "share" the concubines and bondsmaids in the households of "local ruffians," and to "share" the nuns too. A group calling themselves the Association of Husbands Rights is outraged and armed with hoes, clubs, and spades, tries to break up the session. Violence ensues.

When reports of the incident come to the county Party organization, reaction is again threefold. The Lu Mu-yu and Hu Kuo-kuang alliance, fearing personal loss and lusting after personal gain, proposes an all-out

women-sharing program in the name of unrelenting revolutionary struggle. According to them, "Why should there be a revolution if revolutionary policies are always meted out in half measures?" Miss Chang and
Sun Wu-yang, representatives of the Women's Association, see the institutions of concubinage, nunnery, and slave-bondsmaids as in principle
inhumane and believe "emancipation" is in order. However, they want a
simultaneous skills-training program so that, once freed, the women will
be able to make a living instead of falling back into a second slavery. Fang
Lo-lan and Ch'en Chung are opposed to the Hu-Lu proposal of abrupt
all-out women's "emancipation," but they have no counterproposals.

But as the meeting goes on, the discussion shifts from whether there
should be such an all-out movement to how it can best be carried out.
Long, exhausting argument results in two resolutions. The first is that
"all bondsmaids are to be emancipated without exception; concubines
over forty are allowed to remain in their former masters' homes; nuns are
to be emancipated without exception but old nuns may choose to remain
nuns; widows under thirty who have no children will be emancipated
without exception, whereas the others may continue their widowhood."
The second resolution is that "the problem involving women-sharing at
Nan-hsiang will be assigned to the Women's Department of the county
government and the Women's Association of the Party organization for
joint investigation; the investigation is to be completed within a week. A
Women's Care Center is to be established to take care of the women after
they are emancipated." Once the resolutions are passed, Hu and Lu
immediately put their heads together and decide to get Widow Ch'ien on
the staff of the Women's Care Center, through Chu Min-sheng and Sun
Wu-yang. The Women's Care Center is soon set up, and, indeed, Ch'ien
Su-chen serves under Miss Liu of the Women's Association as the center's
general manager which greatly enhances her social and political status,
thus putting a crimp in her relatives' scheme to grab her property.

As dozens of nuns, widows, and bondsmaids begin to arrive at the
Center, Fang Lo-lan is caught in another quarrel with his wife, this time a
much more serious one. Recently Mrs. Fang seems to have been behaving
strangely, and Fang feels that communication between them has somehow
ground to a halt. For a short period after the handkerchief misunder-
standing, their relationship as husband and wife swung back to normal,
but as soon as the Women's Care Center was established, it went sour
again. Not only is Sun Wu-yang again implicated in their domestic
trouble, but rumors are also circulating that Sun Wu-yang had a notorious and insatiable appetite for men, any man. However, as far as Fang
Lo-lan is concerned:

> It was true that he adored Sun Wu-yang more and more every day. He
> categorically refuted all talk and observations about her that came from a

negative standpoint. He discovered a growing number of good qualities in her: her vivaciousness and innocence of guile was attractive, but what was even more winning were those taciturn moments in which she was unspeakably melancholy. Whenever he chatted with Sun Wu-yang, he felt his heart pounding. However, he could still keep himself under control because he was exceedingly conscious of his responsibility as a husband and would not allow himself to take another step closer to Sun Wu-yang. Hence he firmly believed that his wife's remoteness had nothing to do with Sun Wu-yang. Nevertheless, he had become more and more inclined in recent times, unconsciously so too, to go to Sun Wu-yang for healing when he was vexed by the rebuffs of his wife. One might say that Sun Wu-yang had *de facto* become Fang Lo-lan's solace, except that Fang was not conscious of that himself and was seeking it over and over again unknowingly.

May 1, Labor Day, is approaching, and Fang Lo-lan's frequent visits to Sun's room, which have drawn many well-intentioned warnings from Miss Chang, finally provoke Mrs. Fang to an explosive confrontation. Mrs. Fang wants Sun Wu-yang out of Fang Lo-lan's life, or else she herself will leave. Further defense of Sun Wu-yang's character only intensifies her anger and jealousy. The situation in the Fang household has reached an impasse. "There is no need to mention the past any more," says Mrs. Fang, and

"there is no need to say who is right and who is wrong. You are the only one who knows whether you love Sun Wu-yang or not; I am not going to care any more. The relationship between you and me can no longer continue. Of course I am an old-fashioned person, having no belief in 'isms'. The education I received was of course not modern, but it does teach me one thing: I do not wish to be fooled by others nor am I willing to be hoodwinked by others. It teaches me another thing also: Do not stand in other people's way. In other words, 'Do not harm others while reaping no benefit yourself.' I see it even more clearly now, I have been in the position of harming others while reaping no benefit myself. Why should I bother? I might as well give everybody a simple, quick solution."[14]

Mrs. Fang's simple solution is obviously a demand for a divorce. Fang Lo-lan is flabbergasted. Never for a moment, not even with all his dissatisfaction, had the idea of replacing Mrs. Fang with Sun Wu-yang ever crossed his mind.

"Mei-li, we have been husband and wife many years now. Middled-aged and with a child of four, that the word 'divorce' should have been spoken and heard truly cuts me to the quick. Mei-li, if you still recall the happy days we used to have together, or even the happy days we had not so long ago, how can you bear to say that you want to divorce me?"[15]

But Mrs. Fang will not be dissuaded. She does not rely on her emotions and she did not come to the idea of divorce on impulse; hence the argument of past love cannot change her mind about something she has decided upon after long, serious thought.

Mrs. Fang, however, after repeated pleading by Fang Lo-lan, finally consents to remain in the same house with him, though in separate rooms and only on a tentative basis. Fang thereupon is able to turn his attention again to official duties, and that forces him not only into the company of Hu Kuo-kuang, now the acclaimed veteran revolutionary in the county, but, what is worse, also that of Sun Wu-yang, now the confirmed source of his domestic troubles.

The month of May in China is replete with memorial days: May 1, May 4, May 7, and May 9.[16] On each of these memorial days there is a mass rally; and during each of these Hu Kuo-kuang gets up on the platform and flaunts his revolutionary zest with fiery speeches. On one such occasion Fang Lo-lan and Sun Wu-yang manage to escape from the rally and speech to the nearby *Chang-kung-ssu,* to cool off in seclusion from the noonday sun. Their conversation quickly turns to the subject of Sun Wu-yang's many men. Wu-yang is quite frank about herself. She denies having been in love with Chu Min-sheng; what happened, according to her, was that she had been seen with him a lot and people simply began to talk. As to Fang Lo-lan, her feeling is significantly different. She has heard about his argument with his wife and wants Fang Lo-lan to try for a reconciliation.

"Listen to me, you have to find a way to make her happy. Even for my sake, you have to find a way to make her happy. You two cannot divorce, I do not approve of your divorcing. You have the most respect for me and maybe you understand me the best. Of course I am grateful for that but I cannot love you. No, don't feel bad. Listen to me. It is not that I love someone else. There are quite a few sticking to me, playing around. I am not afraid of playing around with them in return; I am made of flesh and blood, I have my instinctive drive. At times I cannot help myself. . . . But my sexual drive cannot bind me to anything. Therefore there has not been a single person for whom I have felt love; there were only those with whom I have had passing affairs. Lo-lan, do you think I am terrible? I am wicked? Maybe I am, maybe I am not. I don't care either way. I am just having my fun. But I will not let others suffer for it, or hate me for it. I especially do not want to see another woman suffering on my account. I know the suffering of a woman who is deprived of love. Maybe there have been some men who suffered on my account. But I have no pity on those who had no respect for me and suffered on my account anyway. This is my philosophy of life, my philosophy of how to cope in this world.

"Lo-lan, I trust you a lot. To tell you the truth, I am used to my freedom, I cannot be anybody's wife any more. Therefore, even if you love me passionately, I cannot return your love. You are too good. I do not want you to suffer because of your love for me, and on top of it, to have your wife suffer too. Now cancel your idea of divorce quickly. Come with Mei-li to see me, affectionately, the two of you. Or else I will not talk to you any more from now on. Lo-lan, I can tell that you have a fancy for my body. I am happy to offer you a few minutes of satisfaction."

She embraced Fang Lo-lan, whose forehead was covered with cold sweat. With only a thin layer of silk covering them, her soft breasts pressed against Fang Lo-lan's heart, which was throbbing violently. Her burning lips closed on the numb mouth of Fang Lo-lan. And then she let go and walked away with a light step. Fang Lo-lan stood there totally befuddled.

The next day Fang Lo-lan goes to see Sun Wu-yang again, ready to sacrifice everything for her. But Sun Wu-yang will not hear of it; she tells him to forget about sacrifices and go quickly to his business of making up with his wife. When Fang Lo-lan gets home, he finds a note from Ch'en Chung about the Peasant Association's demands for waiving taxes and levies as a part of the reform movement. The county Party organization has called a meeting to discuss the matter. Fang, just rejected by Sun Wu-yang and now pressed by urgent calls of duty, cries out in agony and desperation to his wife, "Mei-li, Mei-li, please forgive me. Please let me have some peace of mind to serve the revolution."[17] Mrs. Fang's resistance melts; harmony, for the time being, is restored to the Fang household.

The next day, Fang Lo-lan also learns from Ch'en Chung that new troubles have arisen from the worker-store-owner confrontation and from the Women's Care Center. The store owners have been secretly withdrawing their investments and making off with the money. The Women's Care Center, with Ch'ien Su-chen in the lead, is turning into a semiofficial brothel, with practically every woman in it taking on two or three lovers. Worse, Hu Kuo-kuang, the newly elected revolutionary committee member, is behind everything. In addition, rumors are spreading that the provincial government, incensed by what it has learned, has ordered the county Party organization, the Workers' Union, and the Peasants' Association disbanded, and is sending police to arrest the Executive Committee of the Peasants' Association. Apparently the Party is disavowing all the radical reforms so recently introduced.

However, at the scheduled Party organization meeting, the demand for waiving taxes and levies on the peasants is passed as if nothing were happening outside. At the same time, the rumors of arrests have come true: the county police have come and arrested three members of the Executive Committee. Threats of force are made on both sides, and a major showdown between the Peasants' Association and the county mayor is imminent. Hu Kuo-kuang, perceiving an opportunity to displace the mayor and seize the job for himself, comes out strongly on the side of the

Peasants' Association. He also sees that inciting a riot to protest the
Party's failure to obtain release of the prisoners will give him the leverage
he needs to unseat Fang Lo-lan. Hu becomes even more active and vocal.
At a mass demonstration threats of violence develop into real violence.
Fights break out between the police force from the county government
and the Peasants' Association army. Tension escalates and fear descends
on the inhabitants. While the Peasants' Association army is surrounding
the police-guarded county office building and petitioning for the release
of their imprisoned members, Hu Kuo-kuang is making a heroic speech
to Fang Lo-lan at a Party meeting, demanding the prisoners' release and
the mayor's resignation. There is a deadlock. Just at this juncture, a
special commissar from the provincial capital appears among the petitioning Peasants' Association members. It is Li K'e whom we met as the
"rational man" in *Disillusionment*, the native of Miss Hui's home town.
He has come to take command of the crisis.

Li K'e moves quickly and efficiently. He obtains the prisoners' release
and the mayor remains in office. Li K'e has with him an order to arrest
Hu Kuo-kuang as a revolutionary impostor and *bona fide* "evil gentry."
Ch'en Chung advises caution: such drastic action as arresting Hu might
not yield the desired result. But Li K'e is contemptuous of caution. He
insists that it is absolutely essential to know when force is necessary in a
revolutionary situation. "The greatest mistake here in the past," Li K'e
tells Fang Lo-lan and Ch'en Chung,

> "comes from a lack of clear understanding. When something happens, one
> hesitates and stands indecisive, not knowing whether to use force or to be
> lax. Sometimes one acts as if one were lax; in fact, it is simply a cover for
> not having understood things clearly and hence lacking the audacity to
> take action, because when one is lax, one is still acting. On the other hand,
> one sometimes acts as if one were strong; in fact, that is also a cover for not
> having understood things clearly, and hence one acts unthinkingly. The
> upshot is that one always ends up acting provisionally, with neither
> foresight nor advance planning. From now on, we all have to have a clear
> understanding of things. When we need to act, if the time is not ripe, it will
> do no harm to proceed as if we were slack, but we will be acting
> nonetheless, not forgetting to take action."[18]

Hu Kuo-kuang, however, does not wait for Li K'e to work out his
theories of clear understanding and acting with strength or with slack-
ness. He sets the Businessmen's Union up to challenge Li's denunciation
of him and has the provincial representative beaten up at a union meeting.
The Peasants' Association, too, is ready for action, and government
troops are moving down the Yangtze River Valley in anticipation of a riot.
Li K'e, Fang Lo-lan, and Ch'en Chung have another consultation at a
Party meeting in the besieged county building.

Fang and Ch'en are gravely worried that the Party organization will not be able to handle the military showdown because it has no control over the government armies. But Li K'e, totally unperturbed, continues to issue his instructions from "above":

> The most crucial thing is that the Party has to be resolute. It has to take the initiative, putting down the reactionaries by force of the patrol groups and the peasant armies. Tomorrow at the meeting, the following things will have to be done: (1) immediately put under arrest the local bullies and evil gentry hidden in the town and all suspects; (2) get rid of all local vagabonds and hoodlums; (3) request the mayor to hand over his police guards to the Party organization—it is absolutely not right to have the police guards serve as the personal guards of the mayor himself.[19]

Fang and Ch'en are completely taken aback. Li K'e must be delirious. The proposals may be theoretically sensible, but how are they to be carried out?

Before the Party has time to finish its discussion of Li's proposals, the riots break out, led by "local vagabonds and hoodlums." The Women's Association is the first to be attacked; almost all the emancipated women in the area are killed or brutalized. Then the mob turns to the Party organization building in the county town. As the workers' patrol team and the county police come to dispel the mob, Fang Lo-lan suddenly has an epiphany:

> The account since the first lunar month this year will have to be squared sooner or later. You have deprived people of their means of existence, stirred up hatred among men; now it is time for you to eat the bitter fruit. You forced people into a dead end with nowhere to turn, so they turned on you. Have you forgotten the old saying that cornered animals will not stop fighting? You have turned too many people into your enemy with your too simple words: "local bully, evil gentry." You have chased away old-style local bullies and replaced them with new-style revolutionary flag-waving hoodlums. You ask for freedom and get despotism. You may call it rigorous suppression, but even when it works, it is nothing more than another form of despotism which you will not be able to control. Hear this! Be magnanimous, be moderate. Only with magnanimity and moderation will you be able to do away with vendettas. Now your guns have shot five or six persons. What purpose does that serve? It will serve only as a bridge to more terrible vendettas.[20]

The epiphany comes too late. By now the town and much of the country are aflame. The violence and the approach of the "enemy army" force members of the Party organization to flee their homes.

Mrs. Fang and her husband escape to a deserted convent, where Sun also finds her way. The novel ends with a hallucinatory vision that Mrs.

Fang has. She first sees a spider hanging on a thread in the air whose body soon turns into a suffering human face, which in turn, explodes into innumerable similarly suffering faces of those killed in the riots. The hall of worship in the nunnery itself is suddenly transformed into a tall, ancient building, cracking and falling and finally crashing into a ruined pile of fragmented tiles and broken beams. From the pile a streak of blue smoke begins to ascend to the sky. A band of little creatures emerge in the smoke and gradually their faces grow to look like those of Fang Lo-lan, Ch'en Chung, Miss Chang, and many other people Mrs. Fang has known. Then the pile suddenly rises from the ground and reassembles itself into one mass in the air. The mass pounces on those little creatures and send them running, escaping in all directions. Then a black heart appears in the midst of all, throbbing, expanding, eventually swallowing everything and destroying everything. Moaning, Mrs. Fang falls to the ground.

Realism as Allegory

Vacillation is more direct than *Disillusionment*. It shows the "vacillation or revolutionary ideas and revolutionary policies" within the revolutionary camp—the CCP—through concrete experiences in specific revolutionary activities. Several of the important episodes in the story, Mao Tun said, are based on news dispatches from the countryside that he could not publish in the Party press at that time.[21] This realism should make interpretation of the novel rather straightforward. But nevertheless interpretations both of its theme and of its subject matter vary widely.

C. T. Hsia, whose insight into the psychology of characters in modern Chinese fiction is generally admirable, writes of Fang Lo-lan:

> The local Kuomintang representative . . . A man of tortured conscience . . . further paralyzed by his wife's silent reproach of and increasing alienation from him under the suspicion that he has formed a liaison with his coworker Sun Wu-yang. Obsessed with his marital crisis, Fang Lo-lan is utterly powerless to prevent the demagogues both within and outside the Kuomintang from turning the proposed reforms topsy-turvy.

And he sees Hu Kuo-kuang as "not merely a demagogue and voluptuary; he is the powerdriven man bent on self-aggrandizement. . . ."[22]

Ch'ien Hsing-ts'un criticized it for presenting a "wrong" picture of the political reality of the day. His reading of the same male characters yields a different picture. Ch'ien says of Fang Lo-lan:

> In terms of characterization, the author failed. In places he uses the "profile" technique, thus making criticism impossible. Such a representa-

tional method frequently obstructs one's perception of the merit of a character. In short, Fang's actions and ideas show the ills and ineffectualness and the compromises [people make] with situations . . . there are too many like him—a follower of the so-called Golden Mean.

And about Hu Kuo-kuang:

> An opportunist like Hu Kuo-kuang is puny and peripheral in the course of revolution. Mao Tun had seen opportunists tens or hundreds of times worse than Hu Kuo-kuang in the Hunan-Hupeh region. It is a pity he did not depict those. . . . the reality of those opportunists lies in their secret conspiring with the warlords and bureaucrats, buying off the fallen masses, using feudalistic ploys to expand their own power, agitating and controlling and laying snares for their rivals, buying influence at the top level, and going so far as to secretly hit it off with the imperialists. We get no inkling of all these prevalent phenomena in *Vacillation.* . . . There are no woman revolutionaries. Sun is decorative, romantic, new-woman type, an ornament for the revolution.[23]

After Hsia's and Ch'ien's comments, the author's own statements about the characters in *Vacillation* come as rather a surprise. For one thing, he defends his "profile" technique (meaning not presenting a full view and in depth), saying it was the only way he could depict the situation. And about the characters, after saying that there is no protagonist in the novel, he writes:

> There are many opportunists like Hu Kuo-kuang; they are more leftist than anybody. Many of the highly unpopular cases of infantile leftism were actually their work. I portrayed a Hu Kuo-kuang because this was also a phenomenon in vacillation. . . .
>
> Fang Lo-lan is not a protagonist either. My original intention was to make him a representative figure in *Vacillation.* He differs from his wife. Mrs. Fang does not know how to deal with the disturbances in the current situation. . . . She cannot be said to be either vacillating or not.
>
> Fang Lo-lan is the opposite. Although he and his wife are alike in not seeing clearly the nature of the era, he has assumed the role of an important figure in the Party organization; he has no choice but to spend his time confronting problems, so that his thoughts and actions are seen to vacillate a great deal. He not only vacillates in Party affairs and mass movements, he also vacillates in love . . . the love episode between him and Sun Wu-yang is probably not something adventitious.
>
> Moreover, if one remembers that *Vacillation* is about "vacillation," and Fang Lo-lan is its representative and Hu Kuo-kuang has no more significance than playing a supporting role in the phenomenon of vacillation, then it is probably not a technical flaw that Hu Kuo-kuang does not appear again at the end of this piece. . . .[24]

Ch'ien Hsing-ts'un and Mao Tun are seeing different novels. Ch'ien's central complaint about Mao Tun's incomplete presentation of the political reality of 1927 is that Mao Tun did not include in his depiction of the phenomenon of vacillation a full-scale presentation of its role in the overall picture of the revolution. Ch'ien would have liked to see in *Vacillation* what Mao Tun had deliberately excluded; the genesis of the Party's internal entanglements which were at work behind the events of the story. Fang Lo-lan and Hu Kuo-kuang, instead of merely representing aspects of vacillation, should have been directly related to the original cause and hence held accountable for the success or failure of ideas and policies. In the novel the cause was entirely veiled in the objective authority of Li K'e and Shih Chün and unexamined in the fictional reality.

If we do not demand along with Ch'ien that *Vacillation* offer up the full-scale political reality of the revolution in 1927, but approach the novel as portraying "part of an organic structure," as Mao Tun himself suggested, we see that the entire drama falls into the time period of the second half of *Disillusionment*, and that its vacillations reached their highest pitch exactly at the juncture when, in *Disillusionment* Ching decides to go to Wuhan to work for the revolution.[25] The ascendency of Hu Kuo-kuang's career and the sundry vacillations of Fang Lo-lan correspond in time to Ching's increasing discouragement with the contradictions she sees in the revolutionary organizations and the insufferable "love frenzy" her coworkers are indulging in. Hui and her love philosophy also reappear at this juncture. Therefore, whether in the novelistic context of the trilogy or in the life context of the revolution, *Vacillation* is an illustration of how in reality rather than theory, the vacillating revolutionary ideas and policies coming out of Wuhan as a result of intra-and inter-Party struggles could push the revolution along a course of destruction.

Critics who want to read *Vacillation* realistically, as a slice or cross-section of the Great Revolution, are likely to arrive at a pessimistic conclusion about the future of the revolution. C. T. Hsia, who does read it this way, says

> Mao Tun ably mirrors [Fang Lo-lan's] futility in his marital crisis: Mei-li, bitterly unhappy in her inability to adjust to the present and step boldly into the unknown future, stands for tradition, while, like Hui, Sun Wu-yang is the modern nihilist who, having shed traditional manners and pieties, is merely carried into the vortex of the Revolution. In this symbolic scheme, the decrepit convent in which Fang Lo-lan and the two women finally seek refuge stands for an old and decayed China. At the very end of the novel Mei-li has a nightmarish vision of the fall of this structure, whose crash stamps out any sign of resurgent life underneath.[26]

But to the "Futurist" critics, if they exist, death and destruction of the past is but a resounding trumpet call for a bright and even better future.

Mao Tun the "contradictionist" understood that also, as he showed us in the last two chapters of *Disillusionment* in his portrayal of the tender romance of Ch'iang Wei-li and Miss Ching. By setting the development of *Vacillation* in the context of as well as parallel to the second half of *Disillusionment* in time and its ending immediately before the romance of Wei-li and Ching, Mao Tun the novelist-artist has skillfully brought together in his plot design two different levels of fictional representation of the Great Revolution: the level of realistic depiction of the disheartening revolutionary present in the summer of 1927 and the level of poetry, Futurist style, of possible fulfillment in the revolutionary future ensuing. As to the question whether the Futuristic ending of *Disillusionment* is a more probable portrayal of what awaits the Communist revolution next, or is the symbolic prostration of Mei-li a more authentic projection, we will not have the answer till the appearance of *Pursuit*, the third and last part of his trilogy.

Meantime, in relating the subject matter and characterization of *Vacillation* to the national political drama of the time, the issues that concern us most in our understanding of this fictional representation are still those emphasized by Mao Tun himself. What does he mean when he says that *Vacillation* is about "vacillation," that there is no protagonist in *Vacillation* and that he could depict the situation only by resorting to "profile" sketching?

First of all, "*Vacillation* is about vacillation" seems to mean that it would be wrong to equate the phenomenon of vacillation with the entire course of the revolution, as Ch'ien Hsing-ts'un and C. T. Hsia both do, and thus to try to see its representatives as symbols of revolution and revolutionary ideals for the whole of China. Unlike *Disillusionment*, in which revolution is a quest for ideals, *Vacillation* is intended mainly to dramatize the practical consequences of vacillation in one concrete and specific historical context. The portrait thus resulting is, as he says, only a profile, only one aspect of the revolution and its significance cannot be fully grasped except in the total structure of the trilogy. Therefore, when we move from the subject of revolution (allegorized in *Disillusionment*) to the subject of vacillation (dramatized in *Vacillation*), we cannot overlook the thematic and technical differences in the two works: an allegorical cross-section view of the whole is not the same thing as a profile view of the whole.

Here Mao Tun presents a small Hupeh county as if it were a self-sufficient and closed world. His characters included not only representatives of the vacillating revolutionary policies (such as Fang Lo-lan and Lin Tzu-ch'ung) but also representatives of the opportunities vacillation affords for the seizure of power (by the likes of Lu Mu-yu and Hu Kuo-kuang). Without Fang Lo-lan and Lin Tzu-ch'ung and the conflict in their positions, Hu Kuo-kuang and Lu Mu-yu could not have taken advantage of the momentum created by the mass movements. This makes the significance of a character like Hu Kuo-kuang, though not the character itself, contingent on the vacillation between Fang and Lin. It should therefore come as no surprise that Mao Tun denied Hu Kuo-kuang the status of a protagonist in *Vacillation.* Moreover, since the characters themselves are also profiles—not even Fang is drawn full face, though he does have two aspects—the author saw no need to bring Hu or Lu back on the scene after they had done their work of inciting reaction.

Vacillation in the CCP policies on mass movements was not limited to the theoretical contentions portrayed, for example, in the triangles in *Dissillusionment.* In the first half of 1927, the vacillations of the leadership were felt all the way down the organizational line to the very ground level of isolated rural counties. This is what created the split between the Fang Lo-lan faction, which includes Ch'en Chung and Chou Shih-ta, and the Lin Tzu-ch'ung faction, supported by Sun Wu-yang; and it dramatically affected the form and direction of all three mass movements portrayed in *Vacillation:* first the labor movement (chapters 1–6), then the peasants' and women's movement (chapters 7–11). Mao Tun carefully built his characters and their influence circles in the chapters leading up to the confrontations, beginning with Lu Mu-yu and Hu Kuo-kuang (chapters 1–5) who will benefit from the vacillation of the Fang and Lin groups on the first labor issue. But in chapters 7–10 Mao Tun concentrates more on portraying the conflict between Sun Wu-yang and Fang Lo-lan, which builds up to an explosion not only in Fang's household and within the Party organization at the county office building, but also outside, between the revolutionary peasant army and the women's organization on the one hand, and the government army and the Husbands' Rights Association on the other.

While conflicting policies on the mass movements—whether to further radicalize or curtail them—are being argued around the conference table, they are being reinterpreted in action by the actual masses themselves, among whom opportunists and dregs of the old county community predominate. With vacillation as the collective protagonist of the novel, and with its theoretical and practical levels organically integrated, there can be no individual protagonists. The love affair between Fang Lo-lan and Sun Wu-yang not only represents one facet of vacillation in the revolutionary policies each of the two expresses, but also intimates the inextricably interwoven relationship between the two opposing policies within the same revolutionary camp.

Sun Wu-yang, like Hui in *Disillusionment,* embraces a philosophy of revolution that is thoroughly political and strongly controlled and directed by the Comintern. The least subtle of many hints comes when she keeps singing the "Internationale" over and over when flirting with Lin. Sun's position, articulated through Lin in the county Party organization, is what offers Hu Kuo-kuang the golden opportunity to make his way into the local power circle; hence twice in the novel Sun appears in Hu's eye as "a pile of eye-dazzling silver."[27] On the other hand, to Fang, she is the "other woman," not quite part of his domestic household and not quite at the center of the Party—she has to speak through Lin Tzu-ch'ung or through Miss Chang and Miss Liu of the Women's Organization. But she is the source of his trouble both within his family and in his public domain of responsibility. Sun appears to Fang first as specks of red stars against a background of green (symbolic of the Party's presence), then as a pair of glittering green-yellow eyes (green-yellow identifies the eyes of a foreign species) as he looks up from the stars to a point at the top of the vision.

In chapter 6, when Shih Chün arrives to take charge of the flaring labor dispute, Sun is shown as flirting with three men at once: she plays with Lin Tzu-ch'ung whose position on mass movements reflects her own; she infiltrates the consciousness of Fang Lo-lan, whose position on mass movements contradicts her own; and she rolls in the grass, so to speak, with Chu Min-shen, whose name suggests the "Min-sheng-chu-i" in the Three People's Principles of Sun Yat-sen of the KMI (Sun being the first to conceptualize the land and peasant problems and incorporate them in his political theory and platform for action). Sun Wu-yang's meddling with all factions in the government and in Party affairs, being part of and yet not really responsible for what takes place in the novel, admirably captures Mao Tun's vexation with the ubiquitous presence of the Comintern in the internal affairs of the CCP.

Sun Wu-yang is also used to show the relationship between the rioting masses and the revolution as a whole. Whether the obtrusion of Sun Wu-yang into the domestic life of Fang Lo-lan is eventually going to prod Mrs. Fang to catch up with the times or not, we never know. What we do know is that Mrs. Fang will not be able to remain in her old serenity and refinement any more. Her home has been destroyed in the riot and the convent where she and her husband take refuge also collapses in her vision of the destiny of her old world. If she does not catch up with the times, her husband will probably disappear also, if not with the symbolic collapse of the old order, then with the irresponsible, alluring, and enigmatic Sun Wu-yang. What road will Fang Mei-li choose? The novel ends on this note of uncertainty and challenge.

Vacillation itself, like Mrs. Fang, stands at a crossroads in the revolution. A year after it was published, Mao Tun wrote in explanation or justification, "Mrs. Fang does not know how to deal with the disturbances in the current situation,

> she is confused and lost, and she perceives that the turbulent new situation
> is pregnant with contradictions, so that she feels somewhat disillusioned

and depressed. She has completely failed to enter into the new situation and the new era; she cannot be said to be either vacillating or not.

The old order with all its beauty and tranquility (Mrs. Fang) can be no more; its decadent life style (Lu Mu-yu) is gone too. But is Sun Wu-yang an acceptable replacement for Mrs. Fang in the future world of Fang Lo-lan? Mao Tun did not make this clear. But the two mounds of eyes in Fang Lo-lan's hallucination after the riot (chapter 11) offer a powerful image of the disaster brought upon the entire Party by the green-yellow eyes of Sun Wu-yang. They are the eyes of those who died in the riots.

Wu-yang is not a name symbol suggestive of dependable partnership. There is a man by the name of Ch'in Wu-yang in the famous story of Ching K'o from *Records of the Grand Historian.*[28] Ching K'o was waiting for a friend, who would assist him in assassinating the king of the State of Ch'in. When the friend did not arrive in time, he left with Ch'in Wu-yang as a substitute. Ch'in's nerve failed at the crucial point and the attempt failed; both he and Ching K'o died in vain. The name Wu-yang suggests a parallel between that ill-fated partnership and the equally unproductive association between the CCP and the Comintern. Both involve the fate of a nation: the State of Yen in one case, and an independent socialist China in the other.

Ch'ien Hsing-ts'un, who was dissatisfied with almost everything Mao Tun did with his characters in *Vacillation,* also disliked Sun Wu-yang:

> Sun Wu-yang has no philosophy of revolution. There are few women who work for revolution who know what revolution is all about. Sun Wu-yang has only a love philosophy. Her philosophy is one of retaliation against philanderers. Is she a revolutionary? We doubt it. We have no need of her kind of women Party members who indulge in lovemaking and are oblivious to revolution. . . . But this is again a prevalent phenomenon today: there is an abundance of women revolutionaries who specialize in love, but a paucity of women revolutionaries who devote themselves exclusively to revolution. Sun Wu-yang's philosophy of life is one that builds itself on sex and love, there is no career in it.

On the novel as a whole, Ch'ien pronounced a more general judgment:

> It has no healthy revolutionaries. The message of the book is unclear. If we compare the work with the happenings in 1927, we cannot arrive at a conclusion as to who is right and who is wrong. It has not paid sufficient attention to political reality. For example, the ones who were brutalized were not the opportunists or the reformists but the revolutionaries. The book presents just the opposite.[29]

Ch'ien Hsing-ts'un, a new arrival in the radical camp after the Wuhan retreat, would have liked to see some heroic portraiture of the Great

Revolution. He had not had Mao Tun's working experience with the revolution from its inception, and, without that, he naturally resorted to exhortation when the political reality of earlier days did not live up to revolutionary intention. But when Mao Tun went on in his next novel to paint what Ch'ien had demanded of *Vacillation*—a picture of the damaged and brutalized revolutionaries—Ch'ien's shrill call rang out again. There are no "healthy revolutionaries" in *Pursuit* either. Mao Tun's portrayal of the final phase of the Great Revolution is desperate—bereft of illusions and no longer even vacillating. But in *Vacillation* and in the interweaving structural relationship between *Vacillation* and chapters 9–11 of *Disillusionment*, Mao Tun managed to transmit a double-edged message about the sinister and destructive political reality of the revolutionary present for the CCP at Wuhan, and a tender, loving, spontaneous, and passionately committed revolutionary future for the forces leading out of the Nanch'ang Uprising southward.

V

PURSUIT

The third novel in the *Eclipse* trilogy was written in April–June 1928. The period it encompasses, August 1927 to June 1928, saw a series of unremitting catastrophes for the Chinese Communist movement. The retreat to Swatow of the Southern March forces in October 1927 was followed in December by the bloody three-day Canton Commune. The Autumn Harvest Uprisings led by Mao Tse-tung in eastern Hunan in the fall of that year were succeeded by the defeat of the Hai-lu-feng Soviet in rural Kwangtung and the assassination of P'eng Pai, its brilliant young leader.[1] In the cities, the KMT White Terror that followed the Wuhan split has taken the lives of many Communist leaders: Li Ta-chao was arrested and executed in Peking in October 1927; Chang T'ai-lei died in action during the Canton Uprising; the two sons of Ch'en Tu-hsiu were martyred in Shanghai; and Hsü Pai-hao was also sacrificed there, in one of the blindly ordered city strikes of the last months of 1927.[2]

By the time *Pursuit* was completed, all Mao Tun's hope for a strong Red Army and a "soviet" base in the South was extinguished. The future of the Chinese Communist revolution hung precariously, like "a spider on a thread," as Mao Tun had prophetically portrayed it in the last scene of *Vacillation*.

Inside the CCP there was constant reassessment and change of policy in response to the terror. At the August 7, 1927, Emergency Conference of the CCP in Wuhan, at the Enlarged Session of its Central Committee on November 9 in Shanghai, as well as at the Ninth Plenum of the Executive Committee of the Comintern in February 1928 in Moscow,[3] the defeats had been evaluated in terms of the theory of "rising and falling waves."[4] There were, it was held, rising and falling waves in the revolutionary situation in China, marking the beginning and ending of different phases of the Chinese Communist revolution. On these grounds the "subjective" failures of the CCP leaders were identified and castigated. Ch'en Tu-hsiu was severely criticized at the August 7 Emergency Conference. His "rightist opportunism" was said to have aborted the CCP-led mass movements, and he had failed to take proper advantage of the "rising waves" in the Chinese revolutionary situation. Thus he had not completed the historic mission of the "second, bourgeois-democratic phase" of the revolution, seizing power from within the KMT armies and government. Ch'ü Ch'iu-po replaced Ch'en as Secretary General and the Comintern delegate Besso Lominadze was made co-leader.

The Comintern now predicted an imminent surge of rising waves, and Ch'ü, urged on by Lominadze, soon issued bold calls for "armed uprisings on every hand."[5] Thus the Chinese Communist revolution began its tottering journey from the "bourgeois-democratic revolution phase," under the rubric of the united front, to a "proletarian revolution phase," whose new historic mission was to establish soviets under the slogan of proletarian hegemony.[6] In December, with the CCP-organized and worker-led uprising in the city of Canton, which was intended to mark the beginning of the third, or soviet phase in the Chinese Communist revolution, that journey came to an abrupt end. Though the Red Army and the Canton citizenry fought heroically, the uprising was speedily and ruthlessly suppressed by the counterrevolutionary forces led by the Kwangtung warlords. The Party base in South China was nearly destroyed, and the staggering casualties dealt a nearly fatal blow to the young Red Army, Party morale was very low, and the Comintern in Moscow was forced to reexamine its China policy.[7]

At the time of the August Emergency Conference, Mao Tun was still in Kuling, recuperating and awaiting secret passage back to Shanghai. By the time the Autumn Harvest Uprisings and city strikes began under the new Ch'ü-Lominadze leadership, he was in hiding in Shanghai, in low spirits but not despairing, being "still in the grip of the stubborn will to live."[8] News of the Southern March and the uprisings trickled in, probably through old friends at Shanghai newspapers and publishing house and certainly through comrades at the underground Party headquarters in Shanghai.[9] The news was not good, but the momentous tragedy of the Canton Commune was still in the future. Mao Tun began writing *Disillusionment* in August; at the same time he "roughed out" the outline of *Vacillation* and *Pursuit*. In the projected outline, as Mao Tun put it in "From Kuling to Tokyo," *Pursuit* was to depict the unwillingness of modern youth "to withstand loneliness and their attempt to make yet a final effort at pursuing their original goal."

This early outline, briefly described but never used, cherishes a picture that is considerably more optimistic than the novel itself became. In September the outlook for the Southern March was still promising; it had just scored a resounding victory in Kianssi under the able command of the future general Liu Po Ching. Ho Lung, too, whose bandit origin and operating style had made both marching cadres and the rank and file uneasy, had acquitted himself exceedingly well in battle and was formally recruited as a Party member. The march was pushing forward to Ch'ang-ting in Fukien, on its way to meet P'eng Pai at Hai-lu-feng in Kwangtung

to form the first Chinese soviet. Mao Tse-tung, too, with whom Mao Tun
had worked in Shanghai and Canton, had escaped capture after the Autumn Harvest Uprisings, and was hiding in the Chingkang mountains on
the Hunan-Kiangsi border, rebuilding his forces. These exploits were
indeed the stuff of "medieval romances."[10]

But between October 1927 and April 1928, news about the Southern
March and the ill-planned uprisings became everywhere steadily worse.
By the time Mao Tun actually began writing *Pursuit*, the Canton Commune had been destroyed and the Ch'ü-Lominadze leadership had been
dismissed at the Ninth Plenum of the Comintern Executive Committee in
Moscow. The revolution had deteriorated so much that an honest novel
could no longer present the period as a "final effort at pursuing their
original goal." Mao Tun, fully aware of his change of tone, wrote in
"From Kuling to Tokyo":

> I myself love this piece very much, not because it is well-written, but
> because it expresses a period of depression in my life. . . . *Pursuit* is not any
> longer than *Vacillation*, but it took twice as much time to write, two solid
> months not counting the days spent on interruptions. I could not proceed
> very quickly, because I was undergoing a period of spiritual depression at
> that time; in an instant my mind would dash back and forth between
> conflicting ideas, my emotions would suddenly ascend to an incandescent
> pitch, and just as suddenly drop to icy coldness. This was because at that
> time I met several old friends and learned about a number of heart-rending
> events from them; those who can stand unyielding in the face of strong
> forces can still be made to despair and go mad over the perverse acts of
> those dear to them. These events may come to light in the future. This
> imbued my work with a pessimistic color and brought about the inter-
> weaving of both sorrowful and rousing strains in it. *Pursuit* is just such a
> wild and disorderly mixture. My moods, which went up and down like
> waves, are revealed between the lines, from the first page to the last page.[11]

In a deep personal sense, *Pursuit* is Mao Tun's elegy to his dead comrades, who laid down their lives at the bidding of a blind and callous
leadership. As he began writing, his last rays of hope for the future of the
"Great Revolution" had been extinguished. His condemnation of events,
his rage, and the weight of his grief brought up a voice of despair that was
without hope for grace or for redemption:

> The basic tone of *Pursuit* is extremely pessimistic; the large and small goals
> pursued by the characters in the book are, without exception, thwarted. I
> even went so far as to describe the failure of a skeptic's attempted suicide—
> the most minimal kind of pursuit. I admit that this basic tone of extreme
> pessimism is my own, although the dissatisfaction with the existing situa-
> tion, the frustration and the searching for a way out on the part of the
> young people is an objective reality. If one says that this shows how my

thoughts are behind the times, then I do not understand why blindly crashing like flies against the window pane should not also be considered behind the times. Likewise, I will admit to the charge that I am only negative and do not give my characters a way out; but I myself cannot believe that making oneself into a phonograph shouting "This is the way out, come this way" has any value or can leave one with an easy conscience. It is precisely because I do not wish to stifle my conscience and say things I do not believe—and I am not a great genius who can discover a trustworthy way and point it out to everybody—that I cannot make the characters in my novel find a way out. . . . From the beginning I have never approved of what many people for the past year or so have confidently called "the way out." Hasn't it now already been proved clearly that this "way out" has become almost a dead end?[12]

The fact that Mao Tun could no longer follow his original plan for *Pursuit* is the reason why the novel departs from the straightforward plot line of *Disillusionment* and *Vacillation*. The intention of using and developing the student-Party worker cast from *Disillusionment* is radically distorted. Characters disappear—Miss Ching, Wang Shih-t'ao's lover Tung-fang Ming, the Futurist Ch'iang Wei-li, the students-turned commissars Shih Chün and Li K'e. Yet two of these major characters are symbolically present, with altered names that signify the terrible alterations in their lives. Miss Chang Ch'iu-liu of *Pursuit*, though no longer the Miss Chang Ching of *Disillusionment,* is still connected by the surname; the suicidal Mr. Shih Hsün of *Pursuit* cannot be the noisy, positive Shih Chün of *Disillusionment* and *Vacillation* but again the surname has been kept.

The changing fortunes of the Party are also reflected at other levels. Money, or the lack of it, assumes a new dominance as a symbol of the desperate need for material resources. Love and love affairs have become overwhelmingly destructive. Chang Ch'iu-liu perverts love with her sexual adventure; the "ugly-voiced" Chu Chin-ju destroys love with her lies; and love is over for the beautiful Lu Chün-ch'ing when her face is disfigured by an accident.

Some of the characters from the two earlier novels meet an unhappy fate: Wang Shih-t'ao, her lover killed, has to resort to prostitution for a living. Ch'ao Ch'ih-chu, too, adopts that profession to keep herself and her lover alive on the subsistence level. New characters appear without explanation, representing the now fragmented revolution, and the people of the novel are no longer bound together by a concerted goal. A deep chasm has developed, separating the world of Chang Man-ch'ing, for instance, from that of Miss Chang Ch'iu-liu and her old "west-side" student group. All these dramatic, indeed drastic, changes in plot and character are made silently, with only the most oblique references in the novel. Mao Tun never explained these amazing changes anywhere, although he made an equally oblique comment about them in his defense of the trilogy:

> [The characters] were all unwilling to spend their days unthinkingly and without purpose; they all wanted to pursue something but in the end they all failed; even Shih Hsün's goal of committing suicide failed. I feel very apologetic about having written such a depressing novel. What I had to say went from bad to worse. But please forgive me, I really could not exorcise all this away. I could only let it be written down as it is, a sort of memorial.[13]

So Mao Tun was still continuing to depict the Great Revolution and its aftermath, seeking to make do with the good intentions of his characters for what was lacking in their actions. Not surprisingly, he provides more speeches, private thoughts, and dream visions in *Pursuit* than in either *Disillusionment* or *Vacillation;* emphasizing this subjective factor in his characterization. Finally, though, events subvert all intentions, and reality destroys the original purposes of all the characters' pursuits.

Tsui-ch'iu (Pursuit), which means literally questing after,[14] contains eight chapters. It is considerably longer than *Disillusionment* and somewhat longer than *Vacillation.* Chapters 1 and 2 introduce two young men, Chang Man-ch'ing and Wang Chung-chao, and their outlook on the present and future of the revolution. From chapter 3 on, the futility of their goals is gradually exposed. Chang Man-ch'ing has chosen the education of modern youth as his new career, aiming to point a "way out" for the coming generation through the teaching of world history. Wang Chung-chao wants to enlighten the public; he has ideas about how to reorganize the "social reporting"—news of local events and sketches of urban life—of a local newspaper, so that its content will authentically register the "pulse of the cities" and serve as an index of the health of the nation. Moreover, both of them have found an ideal woman to whom to entrust their love: Chang Man-ch'ing has met a faculty colleague, Chu Chin-ju, and Wang Chung-chao has a girlfriend, Lu Chün-ch'ing, from a genteel family in Chia-hsing (the Shanghai suburb where the the CCP was actually founded).

But as the novel goes on, the goals of the two men become "illusory bubbles," and their loves too eventually yield only shock, disappointment, and bitterness. Chang's courtship of his "ideal woman," Chu Chin-ju (literally meaning "bearing a resemblance to Red"), and their subsequent married life is one of the most grotesque and degrading of all the love stories in the trilogy. By comparison, the affair between Pao-su and Ching is a romance. Even the free-love attitude of Miss Hui and Sun Wu-yang, and the unabashed sexual encounter that Shih Hsün and Chang Ch'iu-liu will have later in *Pursuit,* are more sympathetic, for here at least the characters are honest with themselves.

Chapter	Characters		Events	
I	Chang Man-ch'ing Wang Chung-chao	Chang Ch'iu-liu and the "West-side" group: Wang Shih-t'ao, Ts'ao Chih-fang, and Lung Fei. Shih Hsü	Ch'ang Man-ch'ing tells Wang of his new pursuit in education.	The west-side group plans an association. Shih Hsün appears, a changed man. The group goes to see the movie *Souls of Late Party Members*.
2	Wang Chung-chao		Wang Chung-chao's pursuits: journalistic reform and the courtship of Miss Lu Chün-ch'ing	
3	Wang Chung-chao Chang Man-ch'ing	Shih Hsün Chang Ch'iu-liu	Wang goes to Chiu-hsing to visit Miss Lu. Chang shows minimum concern over Shih's suicide attempt, and becomes fully aware that the love between him and Miss Chang is already a thing of the past.	Shih Hsün attempts suicide. Chang Ch'iu-liu visits Shih in the hospital and takes care of his bills.
4	Wang Chung-chao (Tsi-nan Incident of May 30, 1928)	Chang Ch'iu-liu and the west-side group	Wang notices the resemblance between Miss Lu and Miss Chang; his reform plan for his section of social news is frustrated. He receives an invitation from Ts'ao to a meeting and an invitation from Man-ch'ing to a debate.	The west-side group is in trouble; the Association is disbanded; members complain that Ts'ao is too domineering. Lung Fei tries to make love to Miss Chang and is rebuffed.

Chapter	Characters	Events
5	Chang Man-ch'ing Chu Chin-ju Wang Chung-chao	Man-ch'ing introduces Miss Chu to Wang and Wang notices the resemblance between Misses Chu, Lu, and Chang. The debate as the setting to the love scene between Man-ch'ing and Miss Chu	Miss Chang expresses her reservations about Miss Chu.
6	Wang Shih-t'ao, Chang Ch'iu-liu, Tung-fang Ming (dead), Ts'ao Chih-fang; Chao Chih-chu		Miss Wang, broke and pregnant, tells Miss Chang about Tung-fang Ming's death. Chao Ch'ih-chu has taken to prostitution. Ts'ao Chih-fang agitates in the street about the Tsinan Incident; Miss Chang rebuffs his love-making and also turns down his invitation to banditry.
7	Wang Chung-chao		Chang Ch'iu-liu Wang Chung-chao receives a letter from Miss Lu; her father has agreed to their getting engaged in a week.	Tragedies befall members of the west-side group: Chang Ch'iu-liu has a hallucinatory vision of Tung-fang Ming's death,

Chapter	Characters	Events	
	Chang Chi'iu-liu	Wang receives a wedding invitation from Man-ch'ing; he and Miss Chu are getting married in three days.	and Wang Shih-t'ao takes up prostitution as a means of living.
		Wang is invited by Miss Chang to a picnic to meet a new friend on the same day as Man-ch'ing's wedding.	Shih Hsün dies as a consequence of Miss Chang's revitalization project. He is to be the "new friend."
8	Chang Man-ch'ing	Man-ch'ing's wedding takes place on time, in the same afternoon of the day when Shih Hsün dies.	Chang Ch'iu-liu has contracted syphilis from Shih Hsün but remains rebellious.
	Wang Ch'ung-chao	Man-ch'ing's ideal woman turns out to be a vulgar, materialistic person; his ideal of educational pursuit also turns out to be a fiasco.	
	Chu Chin-ju		
	(Lu Chün-ch'ing)	Wang Chung-chao's ideal love is punctured by a telegram informing him that Miss Lu has met with an accident.	

Parallel to the degradation of Chang's and Wang's goals is another set of pursuits chosen by a group of people who are veterans of the Wuhan days of the Great Revolution. These include Wang Shih-t'ao's attempt to continue her past love affair with Tung-fang Ming into the future by nourishing the baby inside her, and Chang Ch'iu-liu's pursuit of revitalization for a demoralized comrade. Shih Hsün no longer has a pursuit of his own, but Ts'ao Chih-fang, Chang Ch'iu-liu, and Wang Shih-t'ao do.

Given such a decentralized and multilinear surface plot, it seems helpful to first have a diagram of the fragmentized story of *Pursuit* and then follow the individual pursuits of the main characters in the summary and discussion proper, cutting across chapter lines and forsaking the preceding format of chapter-by-chapter synopsis. Simultaneity in the novel is employed to underscore intertwining events, suggesting cause and effect. For examples, in chapter 3, Wang Chung-chao's going to Chia-hsing is linked to Shih Hsün's suicide attempt by simultaneity in time, and Shih's suicide in turn intertwines with his recollection of a certain Miss Chou and France, thus relating Shih and *Pursuit* obliquely to Chou Ting-hui and *Disillusionment*. In chapter 7, the three invitations Wang receives on the same day are similarly intertwined by their simultaneity (and thereby suggesting causal relationships) with the deaths of Tung-Fang Ming and Shih Hsün and Wang Shih-t'ao's choice of prostitution.

There is no central point of view in *Pursuit* except that of the omniscient author. Or in Mao Tun's terms, there are no "positive characters." Those who at first seem positive are disqualified as the discrepancy grows between their words and deeds. First, however, all the characters in *Pursuit* are introduced in chapter 1 in a group scene that sets the stage for them.

Reunion in Shanghai (Chapter 1)

As the story opens, we find Chang Man-ch'ing talking to his former classmate Wang Chung-chao in a scene reminiscent of Miss Ching's conversation with Miss Hui in the opening chapter of *Disillusionment*. The subject is still "What am I to do?" but the time has changed from pre-Wuhan to post-Wuhan days, and the setting from S University to the parlor of an alumni club for its former students. Chang Man-ch'ing, who has just come back to Shanghai—presumably from southern China—is telling Wang about his year of revolutionary work:

> "Chung-chao, you used to say when I was at the university that I pursued my vision without sparing any effort. Yes, each of us has a vision we strive for. However, when your goal turns into an illusory bubble, would you rather endure the pain of disillusionment and go ahead and puncture the

bubbles, or would you rather deceive yourself and go on dreaming sweet dreams? For me, I would rather accept the sadness of disillusionment. Therefore, although I hate what happened last year, yet at the same time I am still thankful for the year's mixed tears and laughter, songs and sobs. My pessimism—yes, I confess I am a bit pessimistic—does not stem from my vanished vision; rather it is for the insight I gained into the "sickness of the time!"

Chang Man-ch'ing goes on to tell Wang what he means by the phrase:

"Chung-chao, do you know what is meant by the 'sickness of the time' today? It is exactly the *fin de siècle* ennui that we used to speak of. Of course it is a Chinese style *fin de siècle* ennui. Last year I went to so many places . . . and I saw this sickness everywhere; as someone once said, wandering youths all feel ennui. But our ennui consists mainly of the sadness of disillusionment, the anxiety to do good and the impulses and urges toward decadence. Their ennui is different. Their ennui is that they do not know what will happen from one day to the next, and hence become as restless as if they were sitting on a blanket of needles. Not a single one of them dares to say how long his life is going to last; everybody is concerned only with the here and now. When interests converge, they unite; when interests conflict, they part, quite irrationally, without aim, and without principle: but their words sound just as beautiful to the ear.

"Chung-chao, tell me if you think there is anything one can do about all this? I do not even dare to believe in a purpose for this race of ours; for even if a purpose exists, as claimed by a lot of overoptimistic and over-idealistic people today, it exists only as a form of self-rationalization, or self-deception. Even if it were not self-deception, I still do not dare believe it can be translated into reality."[15]

While Chang Man-ch'ing is revealing himself to the patiently listening Wang Chung-chao, there is a commotion at the west end of the room. With much excitement and group spirit, several young people are discussing what to do next. Their Canton and Hunan accents signify that they are survivors of the Southern March, the Autumn Harvest Uprisings, and the Canton Commune.[16] A proposal to organize themselves into an "association" has been made, overriding Ts'ao Chih-fang's boisterous suggestion that all of them should go to the mountains and become bandits. Miss Chang Ch'iu-liu disagrees vehemently with Ts'ao. Agitated but undaunted, not at all resigned to disillusionment but with little confidence in banditry, she proclaims:

"We as a group are all fond of action and detest inaction. But in this time of great change, we are placed in the position of doing nothing. It's not that we can't find work to do: if we have no shame, we can get along fine. We've thought about the idea of shutting ourselves in and studying; but we are not superhuman. We have burning emotions; when all around us is enveloped in fire and blood and when demons and goblins are on the loose, we cannot quiet our hearts and attend to our studies. Everywhere and all the time we hear about deeds of heroism carried out. Our hot blood boils every minute, every second, but there is nothing for us to do. We are not qualified to be great lords and masters; we do not know how to be bandits and robbers. In this time of great change, we are the equivalent of zero. We are almost unable to believe that we are still alive. We sit idle from morning to night, brooding, brooding. We while away half our day at this alumni club, and while away our evenings at a dance hall. When we are driven beyond tolerance by our frustration, we laugh and shout at the top of our voice. With tears in our eyes, we abandon ourselves to romances. But who is to say that we choose willingly to squander our lives this way? We still want to march forward. This is the background to our plan for the organization of an association."[17]

When Miss Chang finishes her speech, members of the group excitedly propose ideas for the draft charter of the prospective association. Participants in the discussion including Miss Wang Shih-t'ao, whom we have met in *Disillusionment;* Lung Fei, the less important part of Miss Wang's triangular trouble, and Hsü Tze-ts'ai, also from *Disillusionment;* and the new figure, Ts'ao Chih-fang, who was two classes junior to Chang Man-ch'ing in school and who has just proposed that they all become bandits as a "way out." Their contradictory proposals include (1) a magazine to comment on "current affairs;" (2) members' engagement in "social movements;" (3) a new sort of "united front" with other political groups; and (4) prohibition of triangular love relationships.[18]

Their idea of an association, however, stirs no sympathetic response in Chang Man-ch'ing, veteran of a year's work in the "social movements." He has seen enough of associations already, he explains, and no association of this kind has ever worked. Sooner or later and without exception, all such organizations either become the tool of some ambitious politician or come to a quick end. He feels condescending toward this lost, hotheaded group.

Chang Man-ch'ing thinks that he himself, by contrast, has something constructive mapped out, nothing like the group work the association plans, and nothing like the dangerous lawlessness of Ts'ao Chih-fang's banditry. His goal is "education," the instruction and guidance of the younger generation through classroom study. It is a noble calling, he believes, for it is in the youth—youth in high schools or, even better, youth in elementary schools—that hope for the future of China lies.[19]

Thus step by step Chang Man-ch'ing is distancing himself from the "west-side circle" of his youth and installing himself safely in a position of authority on a separate plane. It is from that elevation that he sees the surviving enthusiasts from the bygone Wuhan days as a "decadent, self-destructive, and self-abandoned lot."

At this point a former classmate of his, Shih Hsün (whose name literally means History in Cycles), comes in unexpectedly and cynically punctures Chang's thoughts:

> And their course reads: when seventeen and eighteen, rebuild society; when twenty-seven and twenty-eight, try to get along with society; when thirty-seven and thirty-eight, tread on the heels of society; and when forty-seven and forty-eight, drag society backward from behind.[20]

Chang Man-ch'ing is shocked at the changed thinking as well as the changed appearance of his former classmate. The zealot Shih Hsün has become a near-skeleton, a hopeless man. The other young people are overjoyed to see Shih Hsün; they gather around him, embracing the newcomer and fondly pulling him this way and that. But Man-ch'ing quickly regains his composure and begins to look upon the convivial group as "fear-inspired" children huddling together for mutual consolation.

Toward the end of the first chapter, the group, boisterously pushing and shoving, crowds out the door to go again to their favorite movie, Souls of Late Party Members.[21] Chang, staying behind with Wang Chung-chao and Shih Hsün, continues to ruminate upon the difference between himself and the group, and how far, for example, he has gone beyond people like Miss Chang. Only a year ago he and Miss Chang could easily have fallen in love with each other. He can still remember how, the evening before he left for "the affairs of state," he and Miss Chang kissed in the moonlight tenderly and passionately.[22] But now, he muses,

> Even if Miss Chang is still the same Miss Chang, even if her pretty smile appears a second time, still radiant with deep affection, I, Man-ch'ing, am no longer the same Man-ch'ing. How capricious life is![23]

Chang Man-ch'ing has shed his old infatuations with politics and political women. He has resolved to devote himself to something that progresses slowly, something that does not yield quick results, and has also resolved that his ideal mate will not be one of those "loud, self-styled martyr types," but someone "gentle, quiet, not prone to empty talk and not ashamed of humble endeavors."[24]

Chang Man-ch'ing's Pursuit (Chapters 1, 5, 8)

Once the new directions of his work and personal life are outlined, we find Chang Man-ch'ing keeping only a minimal contact with his former classmates. For example, in chapter 3, after Shih Hsün's first suicide attempt, he agrees to pay part of the hospital bill but shows none of Chang Ch'iu-liu's deep concern for his old friend. And his brief meeting with Ch'iu-liu does nothing to bring back his romantic feelings of the year before.

In chapter 5, Chang's two pursuits converge in apparent success—portrayed so grotesquely, however, that one senses the author's deep irony.

Chang Man-ch'ing arranges a debate for his history class. The topic, chosen by his faculty colleague Miss Chu Chin-ju, carries a patently "international" tone: "Where will World War II break out." A certain Dr. Gold *(Chin)* is invited to be the debate referee. Dr. Gold is a social scientist who, as Miss Chang presently remarks sarcastically, specializes in "painting a gold-colored idealism over what are in reality commonplace facts."[25] The debate, which the author sets up perfunctorily and in fact never actually portrays, is obviously not the main subject of the chapter. The central attraction is Chang Man-ch'ing's courtship of Miss Chu Chin-ju.

Chu Chin-ju is first introduced through the impressions of Chang's friend Wang Chung-chao the journalist, then through the sensibility of his former girl friend, the self-invited and hostile Miss Chang, and finally through Chang Man-ch'ing himself, in the form of his martyr-like acceptance of Miss Chu as his ideal woman.[26]

The scene is a reception room where the guests assemble before the debate. Wang Chung-chao, at first sight of Miss Chu, is caught by surprise at the close physical resemblance between her and his own girl friend. However, on closer acquaintance subtle differences began to show themselves. The greatest observable difference between the two is in the texture of their voices. Chung-chao

> could not understand why there was such a dissonance between the voice of Miss Chu and her appearance. The tone of her voice, flat and broad to begin with, was further coarsened by a grinding hoarseness, evoking a most unpleasant lead-heavy and gagged feeling even when it attempted a gentle whisper.[27]

Miss Chang who invites herself to the debate does not linger over looks or voice. She sees a deep and deplorable duplicity in Miss Chu. There is nothing, absolutely nothing, that remotely resembles the new "ideal woman" Chang Man-ch'ing recently described to her. "In this slender and externally attractive figure, there is only shallowness, meanness, vileness, and small-mindedness."[28] Feeling sorry for Man-ch'ing, Miss Chang decides to warn him about her presentiment.[29]

But Chang Man-ch'ing has no choice even at this early stage of his love. He sees how angry Miss Chu is at Miss Chang's presence and friendship with him, how her "gray complexion" turns to a "sinister glow of seething anger" when Miss Chang acts the mischievous tease with him.[30] And when he tries to explain his relationship with Miss Chang, her voice, originally coarse, becomes unbearably harsh, "a gritty grinding that makes his hair stand on end."[31] The reasons which they finally give each other to finalize their pledge are grotesquely devoid of passion and ideal.

> "I cannot but love you," Miss Chu said in a low voice, glancing sideways at Man-ch'ing as if she had been wronged. Two circles of pink began to show at her temples. She turned halfway toward him, holding out her hands as if waiting for Man-ch'ing to embrace her.
>
> "Out of ethical considerations, I, too, cannot but love you," Man-ch'ing said with determination. Suddenly what Miss Chang had just said to him flashed across his mind, knocking out of him the courage to embrace Miss Chu. He merely picked up her hand and kissed it once. The sound of a bell came from afar, reminding them that the debate was starting and that Man-ch'ing was expected there as the chairman.
>
> Picking up Miss Chu's hand and kissing it once again, Man-ch'ing walked out of the room, his arm locked in hers. But when they came to the short hallway, Miss Chu quietly freed herself and let Man-ch'ing go a few steps ahead of her; thus they entered the auditorium one after the other.[32]

The seduction of Miss Ching by Pao-su and her courtship by Ch'iang Wei-li, the remembered honeymoon of Fang Lo-lan and his wife, and the orgiastic sexual encounter of Chang Ch'iu-liu and Shih Hsün which will occur later all help us to evaluate the meaning of love in the trilogy. If these other pursuits of love are to be ruled failures or excesses, then how are we to describe the outcome of Man-ch'ing's courtship of Miss Chu, which will result in a miserable marriage for him? In the final chapter of the novel, we will find the couple finally married. After the wedding, Miss Chu turns out to be even less the "gentle, quiet" type. Man-ch'ing finds her to be greedy and banal and interested only in worldly gain.

> Man-ch'ing felt that the shadow of his ideal woman was fading farther away from Miss Chu by the day. But Miss Chu had already become his "sacred partner for life." Social conventions as well as moral teachings prohibited him from thinking any irregular thoughts. He had no choice but to bear this heavy load and keep going. Meantime, self-consolation, that miraculous cureall, began to stir in his heart. He hoped he would never find out any more of Miss Chu's defects; that was all he could ask for.[33]

His courageous statement in the opening chapter that he "would prefer to stand the pain of disillusionment and go ahead to puncture the bubble . . . rather than deceive" himself has by the end of the novel become a statement of unrelieved irony. In the final chapter we learn also that his career has been subverted by the school authorities: educating the minds of the young has become a process of brutalizing their minds by an unswerving indoctrination that stifles all intellectual curiosity. The only excuse Man-Ch'ing can find is probably in the statement that, near the end of the novel, he wishes he could make to Wang Chung-chao, "Chung-chao, you may not be the exception either."

Sadly enough, the pursuit of Wang Chung-chao has not been exempt from failures.

Wang Chung-chao's Pursuit (Chapters 2, 3, 4, 8)

Wang Chung-chao is a journalist, an editor at a Shanghai newspaper.[34] Not coincidentally, one of Mao Tun's duties as a Party newspaper editor during the Wuhan period was exactly what Wang Chung-chao in *Pursuit* is hoping to do: to select and organize incoming news in such a way that its publication would create the impression that the revolutionary "tides" are pushing forward succesfully toward a historical destiny. In the years of the Great Revolution and afterwards, newspapers and other forms of mass communication—wall posters, for example, in *Vacillation*, and soapbox speeches by characters like Ts'ao Chih-fang in *Pursuit*—were all politicized. As in *Disillusionment*, schools and student meetings are Mao Tun's fictional representation of Party leadership meetings where top-level decisions were made and transmitted to the cadres. In turn, the mass media in *Pursuit* function as his fictional representation of the Party communication system that disseminated the decisions and instructions to the public, often in altered form. When we compare the careers of Wang Chung-chao and Chang Man-ch'ing with Mao Tun's work in the Great Revolution years, we see a connection emerging from their otherwise totally unrelated undertakings: Wang Chung-chao is Chang Man-ch'ing's propaganda agent in the Party structure.

For his classroom history lessons Chang Man-ch'ing needs raw data from Wang Chung-chao's news items to substantiate his theses. The conversation between Wang Chung-chao and Chang Man-ch'ing in the opening chapter, about the vacuousness that underlies almost every exalted pursuit, contrasts sharply with the casual joke made by the "west-side" people, who six chapters later, pleased that the slogan of "the united front" has lost its "old popularity," propose banditry as a way of life (and material for history). Banditry usually means taking to the mountains, like the heroes of the traditional novel *Water Margin*, who operated out of reach of official authority for group self-preservation. Mao Tun's contemporary reference here is no doubt to the peasant movement, as exemplified in the Autumn Harvest Uprisings, which have a similar goal of self-preservation and the same romantic, heroic idealism of the old banditry. By the same token, a conversation between Wang and Chang in chapter 5 about the vacuousness of teaching material for contemporary history also acquires a new significance.

According to Chang, all information about contemporary life that comes from newspapers has either been heavily edited or is told from a subjective viewpoint, and therefore has little connection with day-to-day historical reality of the time.[35] This is more than a disillusioned statement made by a pedantic theoretician of "modern history" to a detached, and similarly disillusioned, but nonetheless still committed and over-cautious professional journalist. Chang's opinion bears directly on our understanding of the internal working of the revolutionary leadership at the top and the revolutionary strategies of propaganda and organization during the Wuhan and post-Wuhan period. Mao Tun's portrayal of the interrelationship in the career quests of Chang and Wang, and of the self-deception and empty slogan mongering involved in both, unmistakably reflects the author's view that false information and inflated propaganda not only destroys the cadres' confidence in the Party's integrity and affect the morale of the rank and file, but also reduce the revolutionary movement to an empty facade.

Wang Chung-chao therefore plays a strategically, if not dramatically, important role (just the reverse of Hu Kuo-kuang in *Vacillation*). As a fictional character he is rather pale. His defeat and disillusionment have none of the drama and the glamor of Chang Man-ch'ing's or Chang Ch'iu-liu's, and his quest is as fatally flawed as that of any other character in the novel. Unassuming and unimposing, Wang has received little attention from critics, but we cannot overlook the fact that he is the one character in *Pursuit* who keeps his presence of mind and his analytical and critical ability from beginning to end.

Wang Chung-chao is also the one character who at all times is consciously aware of the nature, limitations, and inherent perils of the quests of those around him. Artistically he supplies one of Mao Tun's vantage point in the conceptual scheme of *Pursuit*. From this vantage point the disorganized world acquires a perspective and the other character types derive their relative positions. As he begins to realize the failure of his own pursuit, he is also the reader's vantage point, from which we may assess the lack of significance of the surrounding characters' pursuits.

Wang Chung-chao is an observer rather than an actor. From his first appearance, he lacks the charismatic air that characterizes most of the other characters. He listens to the self-satisfied sophistry of Chang Man-ch'ing with critical detachment and to the agonized outcries of Chang Ch'iu-liu and her group with sympathetic understanding. Wang is not carried away by rhetoric, and in response to Ts'ao Chih-fang's sarcasm about his modest proposal of journalistic reform, he merely says,

Why should we bring in such large problems as saving the country? Man-ch'ing, you are probably right in pointing out that public opinion today has very little dignity and freedom left to it. Yet insofar as a personal profession and making a living is concerned, the world of journalism still has its lure. Here, of course, I am speaking only of a person's limited choice of a profession, nothing so ponderous as the large question of saving the nation. Recently I've gotten so sick of those big-hat names. The bigger the hat, the more empty the head. To me the most substantial thing one can do today is to save oneself: to save oneself from frustration and aimless wandering, and to save oneself from futile endeavors and rashness. To be a healthy person one should at least be equipped with superior common sense, a cool head, a sharp eye for details, and a forbearing spirit.[36] The reason why I prefer journalism is exactly because the life of a journalist can turn me into such a person.[37]

How much self-irony is woven into this portrait of Wang Chung-chao we do not know. What we do know is that Mao Tun, at the time of writing *Pursuit*, undoubtedly shared Wang Chung-chao's abhorrence for those who specialize in big-hat names and content-empty slogans and who thereby contributed decisively to the Wuhan and Canton disasters.

Chapter 2 is almost exclusively devoted to a depiction of Wang Chung-chao's working environment[38] and his pursuit of love and career. Wang is courting a beautiful girl whom he met at a party at her school. Her name is Lu Chün-ch'ing and she comes from Chia-hsing where her authoritar-ian old father still lives. Wang Chung-chao understands that if he is to court Miss Lu, he must first make something of his career, so that her old father will view him favorably. Wang's pursuit of journalistic reform becomes interwoven with his pursuit of the beautiful Miss Lu.

Wang Chung-chao, in charge of the page-four "social news" section of his paper, plans to reorganize methods of news-gathering and train a new staff. He wants investigative reporters who will go out into society to collect news, then analyze it, and present an overall picture that captures the "pulse of urban life." He tells his boss, the editor-in-chief:

> The essential materials for the page four . . . are (1) disorders in society—kidnaping, robbery, rape, strikes, divorce, and so on. (2) social entertain-ments—movies, plays, dance halls, and the like. These two contrasting areas reflect the bewilderment and frenzy of modern life, provide us with the pulse of urban life, and allow us to make our diagnosis of the state of health of our society.
>
> But the data we have in front of us today did not come from our own special search. They were passively supplied to us, not actively gathered on our own initiative. Therefore I find them only a mass of contemptible garbage. There is not much news value in them, and even less social significance. Of course, one can hardly blame everything on the data. Most of our field reporters are not equipped with much knowledge of the

social science [Marxism]. Moreover, they are not perceptive; they cannot see behind an event to find the issue at the core. If we want to make this garbage pile shine, we can no longer rely upon the old reporters we have; we have to have trained reporters out in the field. . . .[39]

The editor-in-chief, however, wants none of the troubles that he knows would come with such new, responsible reporting. Neither the authorities nor the rich and powerful, he says, want any news about strikes or sex or violence that would stir up unrest in their areas of control. Wang Chung-chao, of course, is distressed to see that the real readership his superior has in mind for their newspaper is not the general public but rather the staff of other newspapers in the city. The purpose of their work is not to communicate with society at a basic level but to outdo the next paper in retailing insipid prepackaged items.[40]

After the meeting, Wang Chung-chao goes back to his desk and falls into one of those reveries during which Mao Tun allows us into the inner truth of a character's personality:

> Chung-chao sank into deep thought with his head in his hands. But he could not think clearly, blood kept humming in his ear, creating all sorts of sound waves. Among them there was the sound of the marrow-chilling sarcasm of Shih Hsün, the pent-up, impatient outcries of Ts'ao Chih-fang's group, and the weary groans of Chang Man-ch'ing. All these sounds raced violently around inside his skull, each trying to take full control of him, ravenous and greedy. It seemed that there was a phonograph disc spinning at top speed right under the middle of his skull,[41] making a grinding, gritty sound that combined all the different sounds in question. Yes, there was such a thing spinning there, spinning, and spinning faster, till all phrases and words blurred into one single deadening noise. He felt a dizzying headache.

Suddenly all noises die down, leaving only the cold voice of Shih Hsün ringing out:

> "Life is a tragedy; all ideals are empty; hopes are phony; and what lies ahead of you is only darkness, darkness. Your groping is futile. Will you still not admit to the frailty of mankind? Will you still not admit your own frailty? Before disappointment overtakes you, you act as if you were someone brave. But look what's happening to you now. You used to take such pride in being practical, not pursuing extravagant hopes. But now, isn't your practicality pretty hollow? Even your most limited hope cannot escape the fate of being turned into a dream." Chung-chao lifted his head, puckered his lips, and blew through them. At the same time he shook his body as if he wanted to shake away that skeptical, pessimistic shadow [of Shih Hsün] and he admonished himself thus: "In our lives, there were originally threads of light and threads of darkness. The path of man's life was originally overlaid with thorns. But those who succeeded know how

to use the light of hope to illuminate their journey and how to use the flame of patience to burn away those thorns." As if to rebuke the Shih Hsün of his imagination, he thought to himself, "The world has never seen a man who is born brave; all brave people develop through discipline. The setbacks one suffers in the present are to be welcomed. Life that is too easy is mediocre. Whatever can be gotten easily cannot be valuable. If we have to take our journey step by step anyway, why not take just half a step to begin with? To take half a step, after all, is better than taking no step at all." He again consoled himself. "Everything has happened as you expected. Why get so nervous? Isn't it true that you are already able to coolly confront all the turns of events in the world and not get pessimistic? Then why can't you be patient with this little obstruction?"[42]

Wang cheers up after this long period of introspection and begins to see that the prospect for his dual pursuit is not entirely hopeless. Even without the editor-in-chief's explicit support and even without the help of additional trained staff, he can still write his own articles, his "impressions" of urban realities.

In the fortnight following, he writes and publishes a series of eight "impressions" of dance halls and other scenes. His editor-in-chief then calls him in for further instructions. This time Wang is politely but firmly told that he has to stop these "impressions" of his, to cut out all such troublesome reporting and print in its place boilerplate, preprinted advertisements, for imported goods and the like.[43]

Dejected at this further curb, Wang gives in without much struggle: he has already written enough innovative "impressions" to win Miss Lu's father's favorable opinion, and he and Miss Lu will soon be formally engaged. He will not lose much by giving up that type of reporting, and besides, he has not found in the dance halls the kind of information he was looking for. He had expected to find:

> the tears hidden behind loud laughter, the frustration behind decadence, the defiance that seeks to sample the meaning of existence in sensual stimuli, the cries of despair that pierce through the grey veneer of life. He had looked upon the meteoric rise of the dance halls in Shanghai as the equivalent of the *Sturm und Drang* Expressionism of post-World War I Berlin and expected to find in it a natural explosion of the disillusioned and vacillating human heart in gloomy and callous surroundings. . . .
>
> Instead, Wang had found vile sexual license, ugly trading of gold for sensual gratification. These of course were not the data he had wanted for his feature "impressions." He had met only one person who could conceivably symbolize for him the target of his quest—Chang Ch'iu-liu. But to write her up in his "impressions" and make her the personification of all he wanted to bring out simply seemed inappropriate.[44]

Finally, Wang Chung-chao decides to forget about his plan to reform journalism which appears increasingly dishonest to him. From then on, one phase of his pursuit is quietly abandoned as he dangles between an inability to go forward and an unwillingness to resign his job. For the rest of the novel Wang Chung-chao becomes only the objective observer, quietly noting the disasters that overtake the lives and crush the ideals of his friends and former classmates.

Shih Hsün's first attempted suicide, for example, falls on the same day Wang Chung-chao goes to Chia-hsing to visit his ideal love (chapter 3); and Wang's return from Chia-hsing coincides with three events inside and outside of the revolutionary camp: the internal quarrel and disbandment of the "west-side" group as reported to him by Chang Ch'iu-liu, Chang Man-ch'ing's invitation to the debate in his "school" on where the next war will start, and the Tsinan Incident of May 3, 1928, in which Japanese soldiers murdered Chinese civilians in Shangtung Province. The interrelationship of the first two is underscored by the simultaneity in time, and their respective responses to the third reflects the divided stand of the Party on a national issue.

Further disasters occur all at once as Mao Tun telescopes the last two chapters of the novel to rush everyone to his or her fate. Wang attends the Cannon Bay picnic party of Chang Ch'iu-liu and Shih Hsün (chapter 7), and the wedding of Chang Man-ch'ing and Chu Chin-ju (chapter 8), on the same day.[45] On that day also, Shih Hsün finally succeeds in killing himself and Chang Man-ch'ing discovers that his bride is a travesty of his ideals. As the pursuits of all those around him culminate in tragedy or disappointment, Wang receives news of the reward of his own pursuit of love: his Miss Lu's beautiful face has been disfigured in an accident and she is in critical condition.

All these dire events involving the young people and their pursuits have their counterparts in CCP history. The ones that are of particular relevance to our discussion of Wang's pursuit here are of course the events tied by simultaneity of time in the fictional context to his visit of Miss Lu in Chia-hsing and to Miss Lu's accident and disfigurement.

The name of Wang's fiancée Lu Chün-ch'ing immediately reminds us of the Lu family in *Vacillation* and the mass movements in the countryside. And the name Shih Hsün effectively brings back the image of Shih Chün, also in *Vacillation*, who misdirects the mass movements. The simultaneous appearances of Shih Hsün and Miss Lu in chapter 3 allegorically registers the continuous presence within the CCP of mass movements on both the slogan and the action levels. But in *Pursuit* they are no longer centrally staged. The value of their actions is drastically undercut by the ineffectualness of their means: Wang's pursuit of Miss Lu depends on a series of very subjective "impressions" of urban life, and Shih Hsün's suicide uses an obsolete token of love linked up with the fading memory of a woman reminiscent of Miss Chou Ting-hui of *Disillusionment*.

In this way Mao Tun recast in *Pursuit* in May–June of 1928 CCP's continuing attempt at mass uprisings in the wake of the various suicidal attempts since May and June of 1927, making a montage of its past heroism and present unreality. In the changed context of 1928, the once vivacious hero of the Wuhan period has become a mere shadow of his former self. But even at that the developing events do not allow the shadow to live long. A new love affair was brewing, at the headquarters, between the new CCP leadership and the new Comintern representative. A new slogan of the "soviet phase" was being concocted.

As we know, Moscow's order in the fall and winter of 1927 for the CCP to begin acting on the new slogan (viz., the "soviet phase") meant literally the death in action of many valiant and dedicated CCP cadres from the Pre-Wuhan days. So Shih Hsün, who narrowly survives his own suicidal attempt in chapter 3, has to die a blood-spitting violent death in the midst of a revitalization project, on precisely the same day when the Party ideologue Chang Man-ch'ing weds his international history in-structor colleague in the "School." In other words, what calamity that has not been accomplished for the Party by the mass movements depicted in *Vacillation* (recast as Shih Hsün's suicide alongside with Wang Chung-chao's pursuit of Miss Lu in chapter 3) is finally accomplished by the mass uprisings at the Canton Commune ordered by the Comintern (the orgy at Cannon Bay taking place simultaneously with a wedding involv-ing the gritty-voiced Miss Chu in chapter 7).

Mao Tun was despondent at the historical happenings. But before he let the final catastrophe in the novel sweep away all known romances and pursuits of his characters, he stopped the clock of time, took a pause, and made an undeletable record for history of the terrible passion and beauty that had gone into the making of this momentous tragedy of the Canton Commune. His fictional representation of the degrading and wrong-headed pursuits of Wang Shih-t'ao (chapter 6) and Chang Ch'iu-liu (chapter 7) which we will examine next reiterates a same conviction, as he has earlier voiced through Miss Ching in her overnight affair with Pao-su, of the historical responsibility involved in the implementation of a revo-lutionary tactic: that Miss Wang and Miss Chang are responsible for their action, they are not passive prey of their circumstances, they have ac-tively participated in the making of history, be its outcome disorder or fulfillment.

Wang Shih-t'ao's Pursuit (Chapter 6)

Chapters 6 and 7, devoted to the pursuits of the two main women characters, Wang Shih-t'ao and Chang Ch'iu-iliu, are the two most heav-ily censored chapters in the current official edition of *Eclipse*. In chapter 6, Wang Shih-t'ao's half-hearted flirtation with Lung Fei is deleted as is the section on her hard choice of a future life of prostitution.[46] In chapter 7, Chang Ch'iu-liu's vision of Tung-fang Ming's martyrdom has been drastically pruned, as has the lengthy description of her love-making with Shih Hsün, the disbandment of the "west-side" group association, and the attempted suicide of Shih Hsün. All these come together to provide the context to Wang's change and her lover's death.

The first persons who appear in chapter 6 are Chang Ch'iu-liu and Ts'ao Chih-fang. Miss Chang, having just listened to Man-ch'ing's debate, is on her way to visit Wang Shih-t'ao. She has heard that Wang has been ill for two weeks and has no money. On the way she is attracted by a commotion. She saw Ts'ao Chih-fang standing on a platform in the street exhorting a gathering crowd about the recent Tsinan Incident (neither Chang Man-ch'ing nor Wang Chung-chao who are so keen about educating the young and reporting news to the public show comparable concern for the incident). Ch'iu-liu exchanges a few words with Ts'ao and both resume their separate but related missions.

When Miss Chang arrives, the Wang Shih-t'ao who meets her eyes has aged considerably and her silvery laughter has grown leaden. Wang tells Miss Chang that her lover Tung-fang Ming is dead and she is carrying his child. She also confides to Miss Chang that before Tung-fang Ming left, he had told her that he had chosen to go to the countryside a second time because her flirtation with another man had freed him from the last worry he had, which till then had always been his worry for her. Once freed, he was ready to die.

Wang says that after she learned of Tung-fang Ming's death, she contemplated death herself, but finally rejected the idea, being convinced that their children will take over their torch.[48]

Ch'iu-liu asks no questions about the lost lover but concentrates on the future. What will Shih-t'ao do now that she is alone and without resources?

> Miss Wang lowered her head and did not answer. When it came to the question of the future, she was not really all that confident. She was already less confident about how she was going to solve the problem of her livelihood in the present. Had there not been this pregnancy, she might still be able to manage for herself. But it was obvious that this unborn baby was going to drag her down in the days to come. For example, she could accept the love of anybody who happened along and rely on his financial support. This, of course, could be easily accomplished. But this was the same as being "married off to someone," just as her parents had once wanted to marry her off.[49] At that time, because of her determination to be independent and free, to pursue her own goals, she had rebelled against her parents and left her family to keep from being thus married off. Now, was she to turn around of her own accord and be married in the name of the very same sacred ideals she then entertained? This time it would be a

marriage by her own will, but was that going to be any better than being married in accordance with someone else's wish? The man who would be able to provide for her financially would by definition not be one of her poor friends. There would necessarily be conflicts in the way they thought and her way of thinking would necessarily be scorned. . . . Once again she thought of abortion. That would enable her to roam the world freely and to carry on her struggle. . . .[50]

On the surface, Wang seems to be pondering over the choices available to her for sustenance. But what Wang is really deciding here at the level of political allegory, is whether she should defect—exchange her revolutionary ideal for material support as some of her comrades had done by choosing outside support in exchange for the impoverished independence of the Party—or leave the Party to form another political alliance. The choice she finally decides upon is neither marriage nor abortion but prostitution—a way of purchasing her long-term freedom and independence with a short-term selling of her body. She tells Ch'iu-liu that she has heard that her former classmate Chao Ch'ih-chu, the girl friend of Shih Chün, has been doing that for some time. Chang Ch'iu-liu is appalled by such a choice, but Wang Shih-t'ao has already made up her mind. With the life and future of her child inside her and with Chao Ch'ih-chu's example supporting her choice, she will not be alone in making this temporarily degrading concession for survival. She defends herself accordingly to Chang Ch'iu-liu.

> Chao Ch'ih-chu and her lover are literally penniless. Neither of them has been able to find a job. Since they are not allowed to work for revolution anymore, they have lost their means of livelihood. Ch'ih-chu hit upon this very natural recourse. Is it not true that the ultimate means of making a living for a woman is to sell her sex? She said that she would under no circumstances compromise her ideas and beliefs, but in order to maintain this independence of her ideas and beliefs, and to conserve their physical selves for the sake of resuming their struggle someday in the future, prostituting her body once or twice in the present is a totally immaterial consideration.[51]

Chang Ch'iu-liu is at once moved and persuaded by the moral strength of her friend's conviction. She thinks,

> Why should [Chao Ch'ih-chu] feel pain? She has the backing of a public cause and she has the self-confidence of her firm moral beliefs. She definitely will not feel the pain. Only those who loiter and vacillate, leading a life of contradiction and remorse, will feel the pain.[52]

We have mentioned previously that in his 1921 article on Maurice Maeterlinck, Mao Tun had raised the questions of the value of women's chastity and the value of sacrificing chastity for a greater cause.[53] Now, in his fictional exploration of Miss Wang's choice, the questions resurge. And Miss Wang's answer is just as positive. Once again the issue of woman's virtue is enlisted here allegorically to support a political decision in a revolutionary situation.

In depicting Wang's choice of a way of life, Mao Tun's emotions, over and above his political conviction, were deeply involved. The question of sacrificing for a larger cause in the summer of 1928 is not as hypothetical as is the case with his 1921 literary study of "Mona Vanna." What agony it must have been to him to entrust to words the covert reality behind Wang Shih-t'ao's situation—that the glorious goal of universal emancipation of the oppressed was now forced to the level of bare survival, and that its future was as precarious as the life of an unborn baby in a prostituting mother.

But not even Wang Shih-t'ao's predicament is the complete equivalent of how deeply into the mire of desperation the revolution had sunk by the summer of 1928. Immediately following Wang's story we come to the even more heart-rending love adventure of Chang Ch'iu-liu and Shih Hsün, the accompanying violence and passion of which almost made Mao Tun lose control of *Pursuit* in his fictional representation of the wrong-headed courage, devotion, and bravado of his dearest comrades.

Chang Ch'iu-liu's Pursuit (Chapters 6, 7, 8)

Chang Ch'iu-liu is a very different "type" from the other characters in *Pursuit*. She is the Futuristic present, harking back to the passionate romantic union between the warrior Ch'iang Wei-li and the trusting Miss Ching of *Disillusionment*. She is dynamic, enigmatic, and reckless, at once passionate and compassionate. Defending her against Ch'ien Hsing-ts'un's charge of unrevolutionary behavior and licentiousness, Mao Tun wrote that if women like Chang Ch'iu-liu are "not revolutionary women, neither are they merely superficial and licentious women."[54]

The first thing we note about Chang Ch'iu-liu is that she is the only character in the novel who shows deep concern for others. She is the author's means of deepening all the characters by infusing their intellectualized pursuits with her own emotional intensity. Ch'iu-liu is the one who visits Shih Hsün at the hospital and arranges for her schoolmates to pay his hospital bills. It is to her that Shih Hsün confides that he has tried to kill himself because his vitality has been drained by an attack of appendicitis. Again, when Wang Shih-t'ao is making her sad decision to become a prostitute, it is Ch'iu-liu who visits her to offer comradeship and support.

From the novelistic viewpoint, Chang Ch'iu-liu provides a second perspective, after Wang Chung-chao, for a reading of the fictional events. She affirms emotional truths that, for technical and historical reasons, are not available to the male characters in the novel. Her disenchantment with Chang Man-ch'ing, for example, runs even deeper than Chang's disenchantment with her. She does not merely complacently dismiss Chang's new pursuits, she refutes them. She feels that Chang's "big-hatted" theory of education has no contact with reality and is as hollow as the base of Wang Chung-chao's news data. She has no respect whatever for Man-ch'ing's "ideal woman." Persistently, relentlessly she exposes the ugliness of Miss Chu's voice and the total absence of genuine love between Man-ch'ing and Chu Chin-ju. Miss Chang's condemnation of Miss Chu is as eloquent as it is absolute, and her charges find staunch support in the more objective observations of Wang Chung-chao.

Miss Chang's evaluation of the different pursuits of the others persuades us with its simplicity and intuitive perception. We are led to see the serious self-deception in Chang Man-ch'ing's courtship and the equal if not greater destructiveness in his education theory, as compared to the limited, personal damage of Shih Hsün's self-destruction—and even the Futuristic affirmation of her own revolutionary project to rescue Shih Hsün through sexuality.

In addition to her accurate perceptions of others, Miss Chang's unconditional compassion for Wang Shih-t'ao and Tung-fang Ming, and her totally unselfish scheme of remaking Shih Hsün, finally entitle her to her creator's defense that she is not a superficial or simplistically "romantic" woman. In Mao Tun's fictional representation, her affair with Shih Hsün is imbued with a tender lyricism that expresses not conventional eroticism but an infinite comradely love, a sense of the irretrievable loss that characterizes the foolhardy martyrdom of a committed revolutionary.

In chapter 6, after Chang Ch'iu-liu leaves Wang Shih-t'ao, Ts'ao Chih-fang bursts into her room to demand that she prove herself by running off with him to a life of "banditry." Miss Chang, though caught nearly naked, refuses both his advances and his partnership offer but afterward feels uneasy. Self-doubt makes her ask herself whether it was cowardice that caused her hesitation:

> She had never been a cowardly or base woman. She was a person of complete self-control and self-confidence. But what happened a moment ago seemed to prove that she was just a tiresome word-mongering person. She had suddenly fallen into the pitfall of cowardice and could not extricate herself. This brought on a sorrow that was embarrassing, unjust, and more than she could bear. It was only an impulse of curiosity that made her behave as she did. In the past few days, she had been completely under the dictates of that impulse and has been deeply enthralled by it. She wanted to bring a miracle to pass, namely, to remake the skeptic, Shih Hsün. Three or four days ago, when she first started on this project, there were quite a number of difficulties. The thoroughly disillusioned Shih Hsün did not

lend himself easily to a revivification effort, but this had just made Miss Chang more determined . . .[55]

In the next chapter, we find a complete picture of the inner and external life of Chang Ch-iu-liu.

At the beginning of chapter 7, Wang Chung-chao has received a letter from Miss Lu saying that her father has finally agreed to their union. Wang then has a premonition that something will prevent this marriage—which is symbolized by a dream that the warmhearted Chang Ch'iu-liu has forged the letter,[56] but then the disturbing resemblance between Miss Chu and Miss Lu flashes across Wang's mind.[57] He suddenly remembers that Chang Man-ch'ing too is getting married and that the wedding is only two days away. Wang is pleased that, compared to Chang Man-ch'ing, he is definitely getting the more ideal woman. There is no question that Miss Lu is prettier and has a sweeter voice and a better personality. With his own wedding in mind, he goes to visit Miss Chang Ch'iu-liu, and for the first time becomes conscious that Ch'iu-liu also has a dreamlike resemblance to his fiancée. In this section we have a hint of the two kinds of resemblance of the women types in *Pursuit:* that between Miss Chang and Miss Lu (their similar revolutionary ideals) and the superficial resemblance between Miss Lu and Miss Chu (which connects the inherent hollowness of their lover's pursuits).

When Wang Chung-chao arrives at Miss Chang's he is greeted with no comparable good news. The first thing he learns is that Wang Shih-t'ao has in fact confirmed her decision to make a living by prostitution. Miss Chang has seen it. But Wang Chung-chao, though a professional journalist specializing in just such events, seems to be not at all interested in such real-life news. Miss Chang then says,

"Since it doesn't affect you, you'd better not ask any questions. What has happened to Wang Shih-t'ao may make people indignant and sorry for her. But I myself feel choked. A better way of putting it would be that I feel suffocated, suffocated with that infernal suffocation one feels when one smells the stench of a rotting corpse."[58]

Then she drops the subject and goes on to Miss Chu:

"Chung-chao, have you ever heard Man-ch'ing talk about his 'ideal woman'? . . . It's an open question whether Man-ch'ing's ideal is right for him or not, but whatever his ideal is, this Miss Chu certainly comes nowhere near it. I have spoken my mind to Man-ch'ing but he never pays any attention to me. He has finally taken this impostor Miss Chu to be his real ideal. Chung-chao, do you know, Man-ch'ing is an overcautious person. He must have given a lot of thought to this matter of Miss Chu. Yet he still cannot escape being deceived by her imposture. This is how fate plays with human beings."[59]

When Miss Chang mischievously suggests that his Miss Lu might also turn out to be as much a disappointment as Chang Man-ch'ing's "ideal woman," Chung-chao quickly denies the possibility:

> "When a person hoists the standard of his ideal in the air and pursues it, he may get something that looks like his target but actually is not. This is because his eyes are already dazzled by his own ideal and he can never see reality with a cool mind. I do not set up any standard to begin with. I am not one of those ambitious people who think they are living in the best and most beautiful of ideal worlds. I am not that kind of dreamer. I pursue only what my reason tells me is beautiful and good. I first look with my cool, observant eyes to locate beauty, and then I apply my entire self to the quest. Therefore, in my case there may be failures but not disappointment. But now I am completely triumphant."[60]

Chang Ch'iu-liu is skeptical but she is not going to argue. She extracts Wang's promise to come to a picnic two days later and meet a "new friend" of hers. They do not mention that Chang Man-ch'ing's wedding day is also two days later, but the coincidence is certainly designed.[61]

After Wang leaves, Miss Chang sits on her window sill and, thinking of her friend Shih-t'ao, has a waking dream of Tung-fang Ming's death,

> A piece of floating cloud moved aside, and the golden sunlight poured on Miss Chang. Her flimsy dressing gown was transparent and the slight undulation of her breasts could be vaguely seen. Terrible mental pictures once again enveloped her. Night before last, she had seen a man and a woman walking by with their arms around each other's waists. That woman had looked very much like Wang Shih-t'ao. . . . The next day she purposely went to see Miss Wang about it, mentioning what she had seen the night before. Miss Wang confessed. . . .
>
> Miss Chang let out a breath uneasily. She opened her eyes wide and firmly focused on the sun that just showed its face from behind floating clouds. As if this radiant star in the sky were her enemy, even though it donned such an aggressive mien she was unwilling to flinch or show any timidity, and she stared directly into it. But in a few seconds she began to feel dizzy. She could not help closing her eyes.
>
> A number of airy red circles emerged at the edge of her field of vision. Following them was the sorrowful stricken face of Wang Shih-t'ao, squarely on top of each of the red circles. Then, the scene changed again. Flickering, flickering, miraculously magnifying, it congealed into a horrifying face. Ah! It was the horrifying face of Tung-fang Ming, his teeth clenched tight. The red circle, supporting Tung-fang Ming's head, looked exactly like a bloody line encircling his neck. Miss Chang opened her eyes in fright. . . .
>
> . . . The blood-dripping red circles continued to dangle in front of her eyes. She began to feel goose pimples on her smooth skin. . . .
>
> "That's strange. I have never let anything haunt me like this." She questioned herself coolly. "Is this a revelation of my latent timidity? But

this is totally without rhyme or reason. Of course, the profound sorrow of Wang Shih-t'ao's situation is also an unforgettable fact. Did this tragic fact stir up such compassion that it brought on this abnormal reaction? Is it because of that burning compassion that I cannot chase away the image of the blood-dripping red circles, that I become so frightened and lapse into timidity? It never occurred to me before that indignation and fright are two sides of the same thing. Is it because when I think about Wang Shih-t'ao I become indignant, and when I am indignant I become frightened?"[62]

The vision of Tung-fang Ming leads Miss Chang to the thought of Chao Ch'ih-chu, who preceded Shih-t'ao into prostitution. Thinking of both women, Ch'iu-liu decides that to sacrifice the present for the un-known future, as they have done for somewhat different reasons, is a passive morality not congenial to her taste. She herself will have nothing to do with a passive morality. To her

> the first rule of morality was to respect yourself. This she called "initia-tive." It had been her standing opinion that to toy with men bespoke the amorality of women, but to be toyed with by men, even for a defined goal, was not worthy of her consideration, let alone acceptance for the sake of an indefinite and unknowable future.[63]

Upon that thought Miss Chang gets up and goes out to look for Shih Hsün.

Shih Hsün, though still far from well, is ready to join in her plan of revitalizing him. The two decide to go at once to a hotel on Cannon Bay on Shanghai's Wu-sung Harbor. They will have two days before the picnic to which Miss Chang has invited her group and Wang Chung-chao. Provided with ample money and wine, they take the train to the ominously named center of Shanghai's seashore defenses.

> When they arrived at Cannon Bay, Shih Hsün had sobered up completely. He still did not say much. They sat by the riverbank for a long time, watching the foreign gunboats and merchant ships entering and leaving the harbor busily. It was night. The silvery beams of the half-moon bathed the bay. They sat on the hotel porch. The Wu-sung-Shanghai train roared by. The long, sad whistles of the steamboats came from the river. The army sentinels on the nearby boulevards shouted a question every now and then. Aside from these noises, everything else was quiet, in deep slumber. The two of them exchanged only a few insignificant remarks, nothing like a lively conversation. A silent tension spread between them. Their hearts were dwelling on the thing that was about to take place. They had expected it to take place for a long time. But its final arrival threw them, as instru-ments, into a palpitating anxiety. . . .[64]

Shih Hsün and Miss Chang retreat to their room and the daring, vio-lent, unrestrained lovemaking begins, with "the voluptuous and healthy body of Miss Chang" contrasting sharply with "the skeleton-like emaciated Shih Hsün." The aphrodisiac wine supplies the passion that Shih Hsün could not otherwise summon. On the second night,

> Under the cover of wine, they forgot the past, and no longer worried about the future. Their hearts and their souls were wholly immersed in the unrestrained pleasure of the flesh of a brief fleeting instant. . . . The moonlight was even better than last night, but they did not go to the porch; They just shut themselves in their room and drank. Nothing untoward occurred, except that Shih Hsün was even more excited. [Outside] this night too passed quietly, lightfootedly, while the lovers were under the violent stimulus of wine and in the eddies of passion. As they had the night before, they lost consciousness in extreme exhaustion.
> Not long afterward sunlight came to the earth again. It pierced through the window screen, peeping onto these two intoxicated beings and invoking blessings on them. . . . The life in retreat of the past three or four months, together with all the vital energy accumulated during that period, had been poured out in the two or three hours of last night, beyond all precedent.[65]

When morning comes they are hurried back into reality. The picnic is held on schedule and everybody from chapter 1 except Chang Man-ch'ing and Wang Shih-t'ao is there to celebrate the birth of a new Shih Hsün. As merriment is in full swing, Shih Hsün suddenly falls to the ground. Blood gushes from his mouth; he is taken to the hospital and in a few hours dies just as Chang Man-ch'ing's travesty of a wedding is taking place.

A few days later Chang Ch'iu-liu tells Wang Chung-chao that she has contracted syphilis from Shih Hsün, and just as Wang Chung-chao is comparing his own good luck with Miss Chang's misfortune, a telegram arrives informing him that Miss Lu has been critically injured and disfigured.

As the novel ends, the goals and the pursuits of all the major characters have turned to dust. The dreams were delusions, and the survivors are aware that they were. Wang Shih-t'ao's baby may have a slim chance for life; Miss Lu may survive the accident; and Chang Ch'iu-liu may be cured—but these rays of hope are dim indeed in the dark present.

The Real and the Symbolic

Pursuit is clearly not a natural development from *Disillusionment* and *Vacillation*. Some events in this novel do not show the characteristics of a rational world; their meaning is repressed in the realistic setting of the novel and they acquire lucidity only when we follow the inner thoughts of the characters into the underlying psychological world where a different order of time exists and a different interpretation of events is possible. While references to current historical events seem to be anchoring the surface action in the historical present, they in fact are more truly read as indices to decisive turns of events in the recent past, events that elucidate the present.

The Tsinan Incident of May 3, 1928, for example, is one of such realistic points of reference. It appears twice in the novel: once in chapter 4 when Wang Chung-chao is shuttling between Shanghai and Chia-hsing, and once in chapter 6, when Ts'ao Chih-fang is giving his soapbox speech. Superficially it provides a setting in time for the events in *Pursuit*, pointing to the development of the Great Revolution up to May 1928. This time reference serves a practical purpose when it comes to the identification of the Party theoretician behind Chang Man-ch'ing: we will find Ch'ü Ch'iu-po and not Ch'en Tu-hsiu or Li Li-san.[66] But thematically, it is also used by Mao Tun as a novelistic device to imprint another chapter of Party history during the Great Revolution years that is not likely to appear in the official version. Its twice occurrence actively registers for Mao Tun how by May 1928 the CCP leadership (represented by Chang Man-ch'ing) and its Propaganda Department (Wang Chung-chao) had done an aboutface and turned away from crying national issues in their dogged and empty pursuits of newly concocted slogans from Moscow (debate in Chang's school and instruction for Wang to advertise imported goods), and how only a small group of old-time revolutionaries (the "west-side" group) still persists in their old tactic of mass agitation and in their effort at seeking national emancipation.

Ts'ao Chih-fang's soapbox speech scene, otherwise a dangling digression from the plot line of *Pursuit*, becomes thus centrally related to the overall theme and structure of the trilogy. The Great Revolution, after all, is not merely an account of the intricate Party politics at the headquarters. The Tsinan Incident and Ts'ao Chih-fang's street scene, therefore, by breaking away from the domination of Party politics as represented by the pursuits of Chang and Wang in chapters 1 to 5, manage to take the story line of *Pursuit* back to the concrete and join it to where *Disillusionment* ends—Tung-fang Ming marching off to the south.

Mao Tun apparently had great difficulties, in chapters 6 and 7, in handling the story of Tung-fang Ming and what his death signifies to the future of the revolution and to the surviving coworkers. Time and reality in these two chapters become more and more confused as Mao Tun tries to step back from the present (i.e., May 1928), retracing from the news of Tung-fang Ming's death to the monumental tragedy of the Canton Commune behind it, and then to the selfless devotion and comradely love that finally transform that apparent act of blind heroism to a drama of passion and of love. The narrative rewinds in chapters 6 and 7, and scenes are exposed in their reversed order.

The news of Tung-fang Ming's death comes from Wang Shih-t'ao, but the circumstances surrounding it becomes known only later in Chang Ch'iu-liu's hallucinatory vision. We know he died in action in the Canton Commune because he appears in Chang's vision with a bloody ring around his neck. The red ring came from the strips of red cloth which the insurgent Chinese Communists tied around their necks for identification during the uprising in Canton—an ironic contrast to the blood-red tie Pao-su wears in *Disillusionment* and a reminder of the red neckerchiefs the youth groups wore in *Vacillation*. But when suppression started, the red ring left by sweaty neckerchiefs unmistakably identified the cadres as well as the rank and file to the counterrevolutionary forces. Leaders and followers alike were rounded up by the thousands and executed in the streets.

What is of interest to us today, beyond uncovering the historical events behind Tung-fang Ming's death, is, of course, how Mao Tun, as an active coworker at the time, reacted to this bloody event and to its impact on the Great Revolution. We do not normally find out from revolutionary slogans or Party propaganda what the Party leadership really felt about a political blunder of this order. Mao Tun, fifty years later, eschewed the whole issue in his "Memoirs." But in *Pursuit*, his method of "profile painting" and his use of political allegory and private symbolism offer some sharp side views.

In Chang Man-ch'ing's renunciation of his past relationship with Miss Chang and in his subsequent pursuit of Miss Chu, we have a political allegory, portrayed by Mao Tun with notable abhorrence, of the CCP unfeelingly closing its chapter on the second phase (the democratic-bourgeois revolution) and entering into the third "soviet phase." And in Wang Chung-chao's busy reorganization of his news section to phase out the "united front" slogan in order to promote another revolutionary tide, we have another allegory of the Party's propaganda organ being forced into synchronizing its action with the new Party line.

But what about the second phase just closed and the comrades sacrificed for its closing? Are they to be so easily deleted from the memory of history just because another "big-hatted" slogan has been advanced to take their place? In 1928 Mao Tun could not bear to see it so. Chapters 6 and 7 are his testimony. The mixture of lyricism and abandonment in his depiction of Chang Ch'iu-liu and Shih Hsün's love affair leaves an indelible record of genuine human passion. The Cannon Bay episode, an interlude out of the temporal order of the events surrounding it, reveals Mao Tun's inconsolable grief at the martyrdom of his beloved comrades. Through its irrevocable sense of loss, Mao Tun salutes the "Souls of Late Party Members" who sacrificed themselves unflinchingly in the mad December days in Canton. Their noble but misguided attempt to revitalize the Party is mirrored in Ch'iu-liu's doomed plan to revitalize Shih Hsün.

As he wrote later, "Those who can stand unyielding in the face of strong forces can still be made to despair and go mad over the perverse acts of those dear to them." These dead comrades were more real to Mao Tun in the fictional present of May 1928 than what was going on around him in actual life. The silvery moonshine that bathes the couple the night before they plunge into their wild pursuit, and the golden sunlight that blesses their deathlike slumbering bodies on the morning of the picnic day intertwined to form Mao Tun's personal wreath of thorns and roses on the unmarked graves of his martyred coworkers. But for the lovers as for the insurgents, the noonday reality has quickly overtaken the poetry of passion.

The sexual encounter of Chang Ch'iu-liu and Shih Hsün strongly reminds us of the week of similarly abandoned lovemaking of the Futurist Ch'iang Wei-li and Miss Ching in Kuling at the end of *Disillusionment,* and Mao Tun used a similar vocabulary to describe their intense pursuits of the pleasures of the flesh. In both cases, they are allegorical representations of the two self-willed albeit reckless military adventures by the CCP in the second half of 1927: the Nanch'ang Uprising and the Canton Commune. Yet the consequences of the two pairs of selfless and hence self-asserting lovers are drastically different. The "future" toward which Ch'iang Wei-li and Tung-fang Ming marched off together has become utter devastation in the Cannon Bay episode: the cyclical history of blind uprisings that Shih Hsün represents has finally consumed itself in action; the revolutionary vision of an emancipated political Party and military force, in the second instance, loses its ability to reproduce itself, as Chang Ch'iu-liu believes she has,[67] and the seed of a future life for the revolution is imprisoned in the prostituted present of Wang Shih-t'ao.

It is not a bright picture, but Mao Tun had to make it: "I feel very apologetic about having written such a depressing novel. What I had to say went from bad to worse. But please forgive me, I really could not exonerate all this away. I could only let it be written down as it is, a sort of memorial." The question of crime and punishment in *Disillusionment,* whether a human being can be absolved of crime committed for a public "superhuman" cause, is given one answer in the symbolism of the reverent movie title of "Souls of Late Party Members." But still, if one can be morally absolved of his crime by his own selfless sacrifice, how about the effect of the crime on others? To Mao Tun, the ultimate intentions of the comrades who led the Canton Commune were beyond question, but his reading of the goals of the Great Revolution did not permit him to forgive deplorable tactics. For in adopting a tactic one is, knowingly or not, committing one's self to a particular view of history. And if one's view is partial, or if what one counted on betrays one, one is still responsible for the outcome. And it is this drama of historical responsibility that Mao Tun is laying bare for us in his portrayal of the pursuits of Chang Ch'iu-liu and Wang Shih-t'ao. Although the emotional crisis at the time disabled Mao Tun from exploring further into the drama, he has by no means given it up. In *The Wild Roses* stories which will be discussed in the next chapter, we shall see that most of the personal drama of love and love politics there are his studies in fictional form of the ways he and other members like him have found of living with that responsibility, or of avoiding it.

Chapter 6 and 7, therefore, reenact, in their break from the story line of chapters 1 to 5, Mao Tun's refusal to reconcile the death of his comrades with the lie of a new revolutionary era beginning. The narrative there is violently thrown back to the past, retracing through the memory and nightmarish vision of Miss Wang and Miss Chang to the point when the explosive and self-destructive plunge of Chang Ch'iu-liu and Shih Hsün takes place. In this way, Mao Tun manages to join, somewhat belatedly as the news of the Canton Commune has come to him so belatedly, one course of development of the Great Revolution back to when *Disillusionment* ends, a course for which he would never have forgiven himself had he let it be distorted into a dress rehearsal for the fiasco of a third revolutionary phase.

Allegory and Symbolism

Allegory and symbolism, as we know, work on many levels throughout *Eclipse*. In *Pursuit* their interaction is especially subtle and intricate. On the verbal level, they include the witty labeling of "big-hat" and "phonograph disk," equally self-defeating slogans of two of the revolutionary camps—the theorists and the disoriented activists. Political allegory infuses the dramas of the characters and their pursuits: Chang Man-ch'ing the Party ideologue; Wang Chung-chao the reformist Party propagandist; and Wang Shih-t'ao the devastated hope for the future of the revolution.

The novel is replete with such political meaning. There is the allegorical representation of the bloody three-day Canton Commune in the orgy at Cannon Bay, and the rift over the united-front policy in the *internal disease* of appendicitis that brought Shih Hsün to physical exhaustion and abortive suicide.

Name symbolism is plentiful in *Pursuit*. The family name Shih (History) is shared by two characters in the trilogy: Shih Chün (History Handsome), a symbolic presence of mass movement leadership within the CCP in *Disillusionment* and *Vacillation*, and the transformed suicidal history Shih Hsün (History in Vicious Circles). Such name symbolism also extends to suggest Mao Tun's conception of the total structure of the trilogy: how the events in the three novels related to one another in history and in ideals, and how the events in *Pursuit* in particular relate to the history and ideals portrayed in *Disillusionment* and *Vacillation*. The two most important name symbols in this connection are Tung-fang Ming and Chang Ch'iu-liu, each of which signifies a broad network of interrelations and transmogrifications.

The name Tung-fang Ming (East is Bright, meaning dawn and symbolizing hope for a new future) alludes to the title of a play *Vor Sonnenaufgang* (originally entitled *Der Saemann*—the *Seed Sower*), by the German playwright Gerhart Hauptmann (1862–1946), which was translated in Chinese as *Tung-fang wei-ming* (East is Not Yet Bright).[68] Tung-fang Ming, who made the Southern March after the Nanch'ang Uprising in *Disillusionment,* is the allegorical seed-sower for the Communist-led revolution, sowing the seed of a politically independent future with his military action. In *Pursuit,* the sower is destroyed. The responsibility for his death, strangely enough, is directly attributed to his lover Wang Shih-t'ao. The name Wang Shih-t'ao also carries symbolism of a sort, alluding via the two characters in the first name *"shih"* (poetry) and *"t'ao"* (T'ao Ch'ien, a poet and a self-supporting farmer-intellectual who lived at a time of great political unrest, 365–427) to the mass movements in the countryside. Wang was to await for Tung-fang Ming's return in Shanghai. But in late 1927 and early 1928 there is no reunion between the military and the masses. Because of Shih-t'ao's weakness for Lung Fei (whose name symbolism I have not been able to read), Tung-fang Ming again went away to the countryside and Shih-t'ao was reduced to nourish his "seed" with the most degrading of means.

Tung-fang Ming, the Seed Sower, has meantime died a phoenix death. His Party role is resurrected in *Pursuit* in the person of the "big-hat" theorist Chang Man-ch'ing. That Chang Man-ch'ing is a successor, though an impostoring one, of Tung-fang Ming can be seen in a play on their names. Man-ch'ing was the courtesy name of Tung-fang Shuo, a jester and attendant to the Han Emperor Wu-ti. This pun, joining the two characters via the name of Tung-fang [Ming] and [Chang] Man-ch'ing, joins as well the empty shell of a once genuine hope to the pretentious claim of a new Party line. It is quite in tune with Mao Tun's view of what has been transacted at the time.

Chang Ch'iu-liu's resurrection from the ashes of Chang Ching of *Disillusionment* is analogous to the transformation of Tung-fang Ming into Chang Man-ch'ing. "Ch'iu-liu" means "autumn willow." It carries an allusion to a pair of poems in the eighth century between two lovers separated in war. In the poem "Chang-t'ai Liu" ("The Willow of Chang-t'ai"), the T'ang poet Han Yi (*circa* 755) addresses his love thus:

> Willow of Chang-t'ai, Willow of Chang-t'ai
> Are you as green as you used to be?

> Your long branches may be dangling still
> Picked no doubt by another's hand.

And the lady responds with her poem:

> The willow (liu) branch has kept its fragrance.
> Too bad it is only used to say goodbye.
> A leaf falls in the wind, autumn (ch'iu) is here.
> Even if you came now, it would not be worth your picking.[69]

To those who are familiar with the story behind the poems, the allegory is transparent. The autumn willow (Ch'iu-liu) stands symbolically for the lady's image of herself after she was kidnapped by a barbarian general. And the contemporary parallel lies obviously in the constant interference of the Comintern in the internal affairs of the CCP, which, in a sense, contaminated the purity of the Party like the barbarian general sullying the purity of Lady Liu with his attention and favor forced on her. In the fictional context of the trilogy, the foreign interference is the principal factor that underlies the allegorical transformation of Chang Ching, the revolutionary ideal of 1927, to Chang Ch'iu-liu, the revolutionary ideal of 1928. Perhaps Chang Ching did not reappear in Shanghai, as the reader was promised at the End of *Disillusionment*, because the change between her course of action after August 1927 and her course after December 1927 was so great that the disparity could not be contained within the same character. Mao Tun tried to keep Wang Shih-t'ao the same person and the result is artistically unsatisfactory.

One last point in Mao Tun's characterization of political women in the novel that is worth our attention is his revised understanding of the relationship between the Comintern and the CCP, a revision poignantly represented in his characterization of Chang Ch'iu-liu. In "From Kuling to Tokyo," he refers to Miss Chang as belonging to the same type as Hui and Sun Wu-yang. But if we look more closely, we will see that Chang Ch'iu-liu differs from the other two in a very important way. First of all, she is not promiscuous. She turns her back on Chang Man-ch'ing and rejects the advances of Ts'ao Chih-fang. Love for her is no longer represented as a matter of expediency. Ch'iu-liu directs her love to a definite goal—to revitalize Shih Hsün. Secondly, she is genuinely concerned for Wang Shih-t'ao's and Shih Hsün's well-being, and her concern is qualitatively different from Sun Wu-yang's flirtatious good will toward Fang Lo-lan or from Hui's philosophy of love. Something has been cleansed from the character of Hui and Sun Wu-yang to make the characterization of Chang Ch'iu-liu different—and when we look closer, we find that it is the foreign element that has gone out of her physical and psychological make-up. Chang Ch'iu-liu has no "foreign" connection (like Lady Liu in the poem being finally delivered from the barbarian's custody and reunited with her poet-lover.) That part of her psyche has been recast into a separate character, Miss Chu Chin-ju, a type we have never met before in the other two novels.

The appearance of Miss Chu in *Pursuit* marks a decisive turning point in Mao Tun's political consciousness. He begins to appreciate the difference between international communism as a tool for power politics for a foreign country and as a genuine revolutionary goal for China. Later on, when Mao Tun emerges from exile to reopen the question of the "seed" of the revolutionary future for China in his fiction, he will not forget his determination to cast out the image of the "foreign" Comintern from the characterization of his revolutionary heroes and heroines.[70]

VI

THE WILD ROSES
THE PSYCHOLOGY OF
REVOLUTIONARY COMMITMENT

Soon after completing *Eclipse* in the spring of 1928, Mao Tun went to Japan, where he stayed until April 1930. Shanghai was still not safe for him, and he was so mentally and physically exhausted that perhaps, as in his summer stay in Kuling, he needed to be off the front lines, literary as well as political. He was one of many Chinese dissidents and revolutionaries who have sought refuge in Japan, of whom K'ang Yu-wei, Liang Ch'i-ch'ao, and Sun Yat-sen are the most recent and the best known. Japan was particularly inviting in 1928, because China and Japan had mutually waived passport requirements for their citizens and it was possible to make the trip without alerting the authorities.

Mao Tun's friend, the scholar and former Party member Ch'en Wang-tao, helped arrange a third-class passage for Mao on a Japanese ship and provided him with a "moderate sum" of Japanese money. When he sailed in early July, he left his wife, mother, and two children in the Chin-yün Lane house in the care of his loyal friend Yeh Sheng-t'ao.[1]

The ship docked in Kobe and Mao Tun took the train from there to Tokyo. He was met by Ch'en's girl friend, Wu Shu-wu, who took him to a medium-priced hotel in Tokyo. He had no sooner settled in than he was visited by the Japanese secret police. When Ch'en Ch'i-hsiu, former chief editor of the KMT's *Central Daily* in Wuhan, came to visit his fellow émigré, Mao Tun asked why the Japanese secret police should honor him with their attention. Ch'en laughed and said,

"Aren't you famous? You were in Canton during the Chungshan Gunboat Incident and you were in Wuhan last year. That made you conspicuous. Naturally the Japanese intelligence watches you. They must have your photograph on file. Probably they spotted you when you arrived in Kobe. But you don't have to worry. If you come to Japan only for political refuge and don't engage in other activities, they will be considerate."[2]

136

During the five months that Mao Tun lived in Tokyo, Ch'en Chi-hsiu visited him frequently, and since Ch'en was still in touch with Chinese politics, he kept Mao Tun informed in the development of the KMT and the CCP. A cousin, Ch'en Yü-ch'ing, who had been in Tokyo since 1925, also visited every once in a while. But Mao Tun was essentially incommunicado, and he missed his family and close friends in Shanghai. In addition, he had to support both himself and his family. So he wrote, for practical as well as for personal reasons. In the twenty-one months he was in Japan, he completed and sent back to Shanghai for publication seven books on Chinese and Western mythology and literature. He also wrote and published one novel, *Rainbow,* seven short stories, a dozen or so essays, two articles defending *Eclipse,* one long article on Gorki (for the first issue of the magazine *Middle School Students*), and several other, shorter pieces.[3]

In December 1928, partly to economize, he moved to Kyoto, where another friend, Yang Ching-hsien, helped him find inexpensive lodging. Yang Ching-hsien and his wife returned to China in July 1929. Eight months later, Mao Tun too started homeward.

Mao Tun's Japan period was not outwardly eventful. He was physically even farther away from the center of action than he had been during the fruitful three weeks at Kuling. But the series of catastrophes that had befallen his party in 1927–28 continued to torment him.[4] Having seen from afar the victorious sweep of the Chinese Communist revolution in our time, it is hard for contemporary Western readers to recapture the tragedies of that revolution during the 1920s. Battles were lost, political rivalries undermined the health and vitality of Party leadership, comrades were killed: the cause often seemed hopeless. Mao Tun's mood when he arrived in Kobe was such that even the whistle of a bean-curd peddler could evoke painful memories of the recent past: "The whistle sound, the trembling sound so much like the trembling battle bugle sound on a reduced scale, reminds me of the past in a different world, a past that hangs on like mist and cloud." But the exile could not allow himself to fall into self-pity, he quickly added, "No, not really. What is past leaves only a faint, faint scar; everything else has been wiped out by the solemnity of the present and the glow of the future."[5]

Although Mao Tun had let his formal ties with the Party lapse, its politics followed him to Japan, and attacks in Shanghai on his trilogy provoked him to write "From Kuling to Tokyo" in 1928 and "On Reading *Ni Huan-chih*" in 1929.

While debating in print with leftist intellectuals back home, Mao Tun was also trying to pull himself out of despair over his own future and the future of the Party. This spiritual struggle was reflected in his fiction as well as his nonfiction. In his foreword to *The Wild Roses,* for instance, while vigorously denouncing those who peddled "promissory notes" for an illusory future of the Chinese Communist movement, Mao Tun also expressly warned himself against wandering too long in the dark valley of a present that revealed "no way out."[6]

His move to Japan gave Mao Tun the distance he needed to gain a perspective on the past, to break from the grip of his own memory and seek an open prospect to the future. His renewed research into Chinese and comparative mythology offered a structured medium for such contemplation.[7] In myth, as in poetry, reality is transformed; human experience is raised above contradictions, human consciousness is expressed in time uninterrupted by spatial differentiation, and ideas and their interrelationships need not conform to the details of the physical world. Nevertheless, as a former editor of Chinese classics, including the *Chuang-tzu* and the *Ch'u-tz'u*,[8] Mao Tun was sensitive to the danger inherent in an intellectual-activist's seeking spiritual solace in poetry and myth. Such a course, begun in the emotional and psychological realm, can easily lead in reality to intellectual and political isolation. Mao Tun knew the fate awaiting those in psychological exile: perhaps Chuang-tzu had succeeded (at least in his writings) in roaming the world of imagination and the spirit, but Ch'ü Yüan had drowned himself in despair.[9] It is not coincidental that Mao Tun's first piece written in Japan, only days after his arrival, is a short story entitled "Suicide."[10] The author must have looked hard at the classic Chinese solution to political defeat in a sordid world, which Ch'ü Yüan's fate exemplifies. Certainly he used a significantly large number of allusions to the flora and fauna of Ch'ü Yüan's mythic poetry for names of his fictional characters during this period.[11] In *The Wild Roses*, for example, there are Kuei (cassia flower) and Ch'iung-hua. He evidently thought over Ch'ü Yüan's course of action carefully and examined the psychological landscape of his journey from more than one angle. Aspects of this thinking can be found in each of the five stories collected in *The Wild Roses*—four written in Japan, one before Japan, with three set in Shanghai and the other two in unidentified Chinese towns: "Creation," "Suicide," "A Woman," "Poetry and Prose," and "Haze." In each of them Mao Tun again portrays aspects of the New Woman and her modes of emancipation, and looks to her as symbol of the revolutionary future. Using new motifs to explore realistic bases for belief in the future, he is still the conscious artist, and he is now much more experienced, and self-confident in his art. The goal of the collection, as he put it in the foreword, is to "shake free from sentimental attachment to the past and from empty boasting about the future; to focus one's gaze on reality, analyze reality, expose reality."[12]

These stories can be read as analytical studies in fictional form of the psychological impediments that afflict the revolutionary spirit in exile and unable to escape the past. Not the least formidable of these impediments, as the story "Creation" shows, is loss of confidence in a future whose value system is greatly at odds with one's own. "Suicide" depicts the iron grip of an idealized past, and "A Woman" examines the sterility of insincere flirtation and political scheming, with the resultant legacy of spite, vengefulness, and hollow nostalgia. "Poetry and Prose" ridicules the attempt to straddle the two worlds of past and future. "Haze" presents a last-minute escape from the prison of one's own mind and heart. In light of the other four stories, "Haze" seems to suggest that, whatever the future has in store, one must carry on. For to dwell on the past is futile, and to waste one's life in bitterness and revenge is tantamount to self-annihilation. When the past is closing in on the present, the only choice that carries any promise is to leap into the open future. Miss Chang in "Haze" does just that.

These stories appeared in *The Wild Roses* in their chronological order, which I believe to be no more than an editorial convention. When Mao Tun discusses the women characters in the foreword, he ignores chronology and groups them according to certain personality traits, so that the lively, bold, and emancipated Hsien-hsien of "Creation" and Madam Kuei of "Poetry and Prose" appear as one type; the weak and morbid Miss Huan of "Suicide" and the quite dissimilar Miss Chang of "Haze" another type; and the naif-turned-egoist Ch'iung-hua of "A Woman" a third type. In our discussion of the stories we will also depart from chronology and order the stories thematically, to accentuate the contrast between Mao Tun's "tragic" and "comic" approaches to his subject of the revolutionary future: "Suicide," "A Woman," "Haze," in the tragic mode; "Creation" and "Poetry and Prose" in the comic mode.

The Foreword and the Fates

In 1929, when the stories were collected in one volume, given the title *The Wild Roses,* and published in Shanghai, Mao Tun wrote a five-part foreword to explain the general outlook and purpose of the collection. To understand the five stories as a unit, we need to be aware that he selected them from a much larger body of fiction written at about the same period. Thus *The Wild Roses* is a deliberate and purposeful selection, with each of its parts playing a definite role, and the foreword is a stage-by-stage guide to an informed reading of the stories.

Mao Tun had developed his schematic overview while writing some of the later stories. His long years of struggle with the tormenting problem of the self *vis-á-vis* the revolutionary future had finally yielded a perspective on the revolutionary movement in China across historical and mythological time, and on his own position within it. To discuss these stories from the perspective of the foreword is not to dismiss all other interpretations. A different ordering of the issues is very possible, and readers are also free to relate the stories to ideas and concerns other than those the author raises. They would then mean very different things. But the purpose here is to begin with Mao Tun's own view of these works, to see how his thought processes, influenced by his intense emotional and psychological struggle over the impasse of 1927–28, led him on many seemingly divergent but sometimes converging paths to a reasoned hope for the future.

The astute critic Ch'ien Hsing-ts'un noted that the "characters in *The Wild Roses* are all suffering torture in their emotional and psychological prisons,"[13] and he took these characters to be metaphors for the decadence of the revolutionary movement. Combining this perception with an awareness of Mao Tun's psychological/political realism presents problems that scarcely exist in "Autumn in Kuling" and the *Eclipse* trilogy. There the historical references are recognizable, while the stories in *The Wild Roses* are less historically definite. Written at a time of revolution, when revolutionary tactics were still a burning issue, the stories were doubtless relevant to what had happened and was still happening in China. Connections between historical events and the episodes and characterizations in the stories must be subtly made, however, because of the psychological distancing that is part of their fictional technique. "Suicide," for example, could well be a fictional expression of Mao Tun's personal disapproval of the futility and suicidal bent of the military adventurism that began in late 1927, with the Canton Commune as its prime example, became rampant in 1928, and was identified with the putschist "Li-Li-san Line" that continued into 1930. But direct historical parallels are hard to demonstrate in any of the *Wild Roses* stories, because they are concerned not so much with the "objective representation" of reality as with the exploration of the subjective "form of consciousness" which shaped that reality. Mao Tun himself said in the foreword:

> These five stories all assume a "love story" disguise. The author wishes to reveal through the characters' actions in love their individual "form of class consciousness" *(chieh-chi i-shih)*. This is a difficult goal to achieve. But maybe a fair reader will sense that behind the descriptions of love there are a number of weighty questions.

Although Ch'ien, for polemical purposes, chose to concentrate on the political implications of Miss Huan's suicide, as if the story's main purpose were the portrayal of "decadence," it behooves later readers to follow Mao Tun's intent, implied in his foreword, to try to see the psychological permutations of his protagonists in terms of their moral significance.

The foreword, about 2,000 words, comprises five sections. Section 1 argues that catastrophe in life need not be final. Section 2 criticizes the kind of unrealistic, utopian optimism that disregards the practical problem of precisely *how* to advance into the desired future and interprets all that has happened as the result of "historical inevitability," thereby denying the creative role that people play in shaping history. Sections 3 and 4 deal with specific aspects of the personalities of the characters in the stories and what they represent in terms of the metaphor of thorns and wild roses in section 5. In a sense, these character traits are also Mao Tun's oblique answers to the central question of what one should or could do after the catastrophes of 1927–28. Section 5, which is very brief, describes the selection of the stories as the author's contribution to weaving a crown of wild roses for the revolution, his task being to identify, locate, and pull out the thorns.

The chronology of the stories and the foreword covers more than a year's time. The stories continue, as Mao Tun later pointed out, the same subject matter of revolution and the same technique of mixing allegory with realism that he used in *Eclipse*. But they are different in their conceptual objectivity and narrative distance, they have gone beyond *Eclipse* in treatment of the subject matter and in outlook. Mao Tun is no longer seeking to dramatize historical cause and effect and to define responsibility. The drama of the 1925–27 revolution is over. He is now trying to find bases for collective action in the immediate future. He is beginning to look for answers to the question of fate and revolutionary commitment in a new context.

Each of the stories focuses on a brief period of time in which the personal fate of the protagonist is decided. These stories were not written in tranquility; their narrative modes vary from tragic to comic, but the basic tone is disquietude and anguish. Mao Tun's final vision of man in a time of revolution, as presented in the foreword, lends deeper meaning to the stories. He did not construct the scheme because, as a creative writer and as an individual, he *wished* to look at man in history that way. His vision has richer implications. For one thing, history is not a series of events following blindly and automatically the dictates of uncoordinated psychological forces. The richness and diversity of human experience in a fierce revolutionary struggle may appear colorful to a spectator. But Mao Tun was more than a spectator. He was a committed revolutionary; his own fate was closely tied to the outcome of the mortal combat then raging. He therefore had to be concerned with the goals of the battle; he had to measure the distance in particularized historical time—the present—and the ultimate collective goals in infinite mythological time—the future. Time and fate are intimately related in any mythical contemplation of human destiny. Hence in the first section of the foreword Mao Tun proposed time and fate as the unifying abstract themes of the story:

If we may consider the concept of fate in the mythology of a race to be their philosophy of life, it should be very interesting to compare the concept of fate in Greek myth and the concept of fate in Nordic myth.

The goddesses of fate in Greek myth are three sisters. Clotho is the youngest, in charge of spinning the thread of life, deftly crossing the strands of light with the strands of darkness, just as there are light and darkness in human life. Lachesis is the second sister. Her task is to twist together the [strands spun by Clotho into] threads of life. Her wrist power is at times strong and at times weak; that explains why man's life force varies in degree of strength. The oldest sister, Atropos, is the cruellest one. She holds a pair of huge scissors and pitilessly snips those threads of life.

In Nordic myth also, the goddesses of fate are three sisters. But unlike their counterparts in Greek myth, they do not have three different tasks; rather, they symbolize three periods in infinite time. The eldest is Urd, who is very old and feeble and constantly reminisces; she is the personification of the "past." Skuld, the youngest, wears a veil over her face, and the direction in which she looks is exactly opposite to that of her eldest sister; she is the unfathomable "future." Verdandi is the one in the middle, in the prime of life, spirited, courageous, staring straight down the path ahead; she is the one who symbolizes the "present."

These are the different primitive philosophies of life expressed in the myths of the Greek people of the south and the Nordic people of the north. The realistic Nordic people keep a tight hold on the "present;" they neither dwell on nor lament the "past," nor do they vainly fantasize about the "future."[14]

This passage is Mao Tun's first recorded attempt to deal with the fundamental question of the ultimate destiny of the Chinese Revolution in time—namely, whether catastrophes are to be accepted as final. His attempt was cast in the form of a contrast between two concepts of fate as reflected in Greek and Nordic myths. The Greek myth, as Mao Tun presents it, judges fate to be final and irrevocable in time.[15] Man is defeated by fate, often in a setting of catastrophe, and his life is inevitably cut off by Atropos. According to the Greek view of life, man could struggle valiantly against the inexorable working of his fate. He could even achieve a degree of understanding and humility which in death would endow his prolonged suffering with dignity and ennobling humanity. This, in fact, is essentially the same concept of fate that colors the tragic life and mythical poetry of Ch'ü Yüan. However, an affirmation of the Greek philosophy of life had little relevance for a revolutionary movement in the China of 1928. Greek tragedy might honor the humanity and humanistic values of the fallen individual, but the Chinese Revolution required much more than martyrdom and dignity for its collective success. It needed life. Life had to continue; life was the moral imperative in revolution. Mao Tun could not accept the Greek concept of fate nor the notion of irretrievable time and catastrophe.

The Nordic myth, in Mao Tun's version, conceives fate not as controlling and comprehending time, but as three particularized outlooks on time, symbolized by three sister goddesses: Urd, reminiscing, the symbol of the past; Skuld, veiled, the symbol of the future; and Verdandi, staring directly ahead, the symbol of the present.[16] Mao Tun found the philosophy of life implicit in this concept of fate more congenial to the question that was foremost in his mind. For one thing, finality is not an inherent part of its scheme of time. No Atropos is there to snip the measured-out thread of life. Man's fate is defined not by catastrophe and death, but by the outlook he adopts on his own position relative to them in time. In such a perspective, fate has no control over the course of a man's life— nor over revolutionary development, for that matter. Having happened, historical events, even catastrophes, have no effect upon infinite time which is the context of human destiny, unless an individual should by choice adopt the outlook of Urd and make the remainder of his life a series of reminiscences. Otherwise, the present and the future remain free and open to his choice. Mao Tun at that point was just beginning to see that what had been tormenting him ever since the writing of *Eclipse* was not only the question of continued individual commitment to the revolutionary cause, it was also the question of commitment in a collective sense to its continuation. The latter could lie only in the sphere of life; the only way to maintain this collective commitment, in the language of the Nordic myth, was to "keep a tight hold on the 'present.'"

Having thus clarified the meaning of fate for a politically committed person as an individual and in the collective context of a living revolution, and having arrived in the process at a decisive stand on the question of time and catastrophe, Mao Tun proceeded in section 2 of the foreword to address himself to the next question, that of action and the revolutionary future. If catastrophe was not be be accepted as final, and if the collective life of the revolution was to continue, then what should be done? Should one merely rely on "historical inevitability" to shape the future? Less than a year before in "From Kuling to Tokyo," Mao Tun had bitterly attacked those who on that assumption had led the revolution into a "dead end."[17] He had berated those who blindly advocated implicit faith in a bright revolutionary future as the certain way out of defeat. And his opinion had not changed. Now as before, Mao Tun saw nothing at all inevitable about a bright future for the revolution. The human failings that had brought the revolution to catastrophic dead ends in the past could be repeated and preclude any possibility of its following a road of success. Mao Tun did not hesitate to expose once again the fallacy inherent in such blind optimism:

> Blessed are those who know enough to place their faith in the future; they deserved to be praised. However, they should be careful that they do not take "historical inevitability" as a promissory note for their own happiness, and further sell such notes without limit. In the absence of genuine

cognition, any "vitality in society" that relies on such promissory notes as morphine needles is no better than a castle built in the sand. It will all end in certain defeat. To use the brightness of the future to gloss over the darkness of reality may be considered brave by some; but to have thus concealed the darkness of reality and then attempt to use the brightness of the future as a means of agitation is nonsense! The genuinely brave are those who dare to stare unflinchingly at reality, who arrive at their realization of the inevitability of the future from [seeing] the ugliness and evil in reality, and who do not need to see the inevitability of the future as a promissory note before putting their faith in it.[18]

To reestablish a hope—not a guarantee or an assurance—for a bright revolutionary future, Mao Tun was convinced that in the present, "Truly effective work is that which will lead people to see through ugliness and evil in reality and thereby recognize the great future for mankind on their own, the faith in that future being thus engendered."[19]

The life of the revolutionary movement, as Mao Tun expressed it in the fifth section of his foreword, was like the wild rose; there were thorns and there were flowers:

> The modern Norwegian novelist Johan Bojer said something to this effect in one of his short pieces, a man praises the color and fragrance of the wild rose but detests it thorns; his friend, however, pulls out the thorns and makes a wild-rose crown. Life is like this wild rose. If one says willfully that it is without thorns, he is deceiving himself to no purpose. But to merely hate its thorns serves no purpose either. One should aim sharply at those thorns and pull them out! If my works can serve to pull such thorns, then even if I hurt my hands meanwhile, I will do it gladly.[20]

Starry-eyed naiveté, impractical idealism, and miscalculation of the ugliness and evil in society, which are the dramatic themes of the stories—and which have the charm of the blossoms in the wild-rose crown of revolution—were actually deadly thorns.[21] Hence

> Let us not lament over that which is already past, nor glorify that which has not yet come. Rather, let us stare unflinchingly at reality, analyze reality, expose reality; for there are still many who are unable to recognize reality.[22]

The task Mao Tun has set for *The Wild Roses*, then, is the identification and pulling out of the metaphorical thorns in life. Keeping this in mind, let us examine the themes, fictional devices, and see how the foreword helps to clarify key episodes.

"Suicide"

Ostensibly, the story of Miss Huan in "Suicide" (July 8, 1928) depicts her suicidal state of mind after an interrupted love affair. Miss Huan falls in love with a handsome young revolutionary and becomes pregnant by him. When he leaves for the revolution, she feels that she cannot face the world with an illegitimate pregnancy.

The story closely tracks Miss Huan's emotions of love and fear. Half is devoted to her experience of love in a tenderly and sometimes passionately remembered past; the other half deals with her fear of discovery in the present. The two halves, interacting, create the psychological drama in Miss Huan's otherwise uneventful life. In that drama Miss Huan is confronted with a real problem, her pregnancy.

Instinctively she first wants to keep "the fruit of her love." At night she dreams fondly that to bring up the child will answer the "unuttered pleading of her absent lover and of all nature," and will offer a hope of happiness and fulfillment. But when daylight comes, the social consequences of an illegitimate pregnancy appear overwhelming. The return of her beloved is uncertain; in the meantime, society will surely ostracize her and she will be denied happiness. Miss Huan feels that she would rather die than be a social outcast. As she tries to reason through the choices available to her, a drama of psychological transmutation unfolds in her consciousness:

> She was unwilling to die. Was there any way out at all? She definitely did not want to die. But death seemed the only escape. How about coming boldly forward to announce her secret, braving the sneers and scorn with an insouciant smile? Miss Huan thought it over, but she did not have that much courage. It took only a moment's courage to commit suicide, but the alternative required long-term courage. How about finding another man to cover things up? One could never be sure of succeeding in that. Besides, it wouldn't do to hurry in looking. If she got herself involved with a scoundrel, wouldn't that be worse?[23]

At the moment when Miss Huan realizes her lack of long-term courage, the issue that requires decision suddenly changes its orientation from the moral to the expedient (or in the language of the foreword, this is the pivotal moment when the thorns are distinguished from the roses). She is no longer concerned about whether or not to preserve the pregnancy, but begins to seek some expedient way to avoid the immediately feared exposure. Unfortunately, no expedient is foolproof; it also involves risk and requires a courage of its own kind. When Miss Huan sees that she is not equipped even for a marriage of convenience, she has no recourse left but suicide. In despair, she turns with intense hatred upon the ideas that originally inspired her love: "Lies, lies—liberation, freedom, light—everything is a lie! It would have been better not to have any knowledge at all . . . I shall announce to the world the crimes of those fraudulent ideas of liberation, freedom, and light. I shall announce it with my death."[24] Thus Miss Huan, an "educated" woman from a gentry family chooses the traditional solution of Chinese women since time immemorial.

As she puts the noose around her neck and feels it tighten, she becomes aware of other vague notions in her fading consciousness: "There ought to be a way out; if only one would boldly follow the tide of history and march on, if one could fall into step with this rapidly changing society. . . ."

But it was too late for Miss Huan. "Her bulging eyes stared out as if they still wanted to comprehend what was needed for one to keep pace with this tumultuous and changing life, what that IT was."[25]

C. T. Hsia held that the stories of *The Wild Roses* were similar in tone to *Eclipse,* being studies of "the vacillation and exasperation of the younger generation as it grapples with ugly reality;" Miss Huan "has to kill herself" because as "an old-fashioned girl, she has not advanced intellectually far enough to defy social ostracism."[26] More recently, John Berninghausen has interpreted "Suicide" as illustrative of Mao Tun's own "ambivalent feelings about freedom of choice in love and marriage, just as he harbored conflicting feelings about revolution."[27] Both views contrast with that of Ch'ien Hsing-ts'un, who with his usual sarcasm derided Mao Tun attempting to "induce people" to reflect on the sad state of life and the revolutionary movement by creating characters like Miss Huan:

> She was able to become conscious of the future in spite of the fact that she clung to the present. It is a pity that . . . even though Miss Huan wished to cling to the present, yet she was unable to bear the pressure of reality, nor was she able to find a way out; and so she ended up by committing suicide. . . . One can say that the protagonist in this piece of fiction is a character who is in her prime, but gloomy and dispirited, eager to display her courage by committing suicide, and staring ahead with her tongue hanging out.[28]

The gibes at Mao Tun's courageous and forward-looking Verdandi are transparent. Ch'ien Hsing-ts'un also ridiculed the futility of Mao Tun's fictional method in advancing his sociopolitical goal:

> In her suicide, there is one more thing worth noting: namely, when she inserts her neck into the silk-sash noose, an idea occurs to her, "to announce to the world the crimes of those fraudulent ideals of liberation, freedom and light," because she regards death as an "announcement." Probably this is what Mao Tun means by "exposing the darkness to induce everybody to reflect." To announce by death, to rescue mankind by committing suicide, this is the method of propelling society forward adopted by Miss Huan, who clings to the present.[29]

Deliberate distortion and polemical animus about revolutionary strategy aside, Ch'ien Hsing-ts'un remains the most attentive, though the most acrimonious, critic of the revolutionary content of Mao Tun's early fiction. His remarks here bear directly on Mao Tun's purpose as stated in the foreword: concern with the theme of time, the exposure of the surrounding darkness, and the attempt to "induce people to reflect." There is little doubt that Ch'ien understood precisely what Mao Tun was trying to accomplish with his stories. Like his criticism of *Eclipse*, his disagreement now was about the representativeness of Mao Tun's fictional characters in what Ch'ien preferred to think of as a continually heroic and successful revolution. Impatient with and contemptuous of such creative matters as the artistic distance between an author and his works, Ch'ien boldly assumed in his argument that an author's perception of reality, his fictional representation of it, and the degree to which he relates to that reality in his own life are identical.

"Suicide," in fact, can be interpreted on many levels. The most obvious, of course, is to consider it simply a realistic depiction of the social situation in the China of 1928. A would-be modern woman, inspired by progressive ideas of liberty, freedom, and light, acts accordingly and becomes pregnant without marrying; as a consequence, she is driven to suicide by the pressure of the society she lives in.[30] On this level one can readily agree with Berninghausen that her situation illustrates Mao Tun's own ambivalent feelings about Western-style liberation for women.[31] To take this position, however, is to accept on faith Miss Huan's personal perception of her situation or even to equate that perception with the author's. Miss Huan is fearful that she will be ostracized; she alternatively believes and doubts her lover; dying, she becomes vaguely conscious of a possible way out. But the story itself does not show in any tangible way that she will be ostracized; or that her aunt and cousins are capable of turning her out if they learn of her pregnancy.[32] Nor does the story show, not even in terms of a fantasy or a dream, any concrete form that the "way out" for Miss Huan could have assumed in life. All these exist only in her psychological world. It is therefore clear that what leads Miss Huan to take her own life is the subjective reality of this psychological world, not any actual ostracism or betrayal of pledged love in her objective situation.

On another level, "Suicide" can also be considered allegorically, as Mao Tun emphasizes in the foreword. Love between man and woman is a convention he uses in these stories to reveal the "form of consciousness" of the class to which each of the protagonists belongs.[33] This level too is relatively easy to get at, because we can see that class background is explicitly and objectively described in the stories, although we cannot say that it plays an equally important role in all five. One can probably understand Ch'iung-hua's tragedy in "A Woman"—the story we shall examine next—as the inevitable consequence of her failure to realize that she has lost not only her family fortune but also her class standing. In

"Suicide" class standing and class consciousness are not relevant to the working of Miss Huan's fate. We cannot say that, had Miss Huan belonged to a different class and had a different "form of consciousness," her fate would have been different. If Mao Tun had intended to show that, he would have written a different story. In fact, he did so in part in "Creation" and "Poetry and Prose" in *The Wild Roses,* and more poignantly so later in his historical tales which we shall examine in the next chapter.

Then there is the level of social realism and political allegory. Following his statement on class consciousness, Mao Tun says, "A just reader will probably feel that behind the depiction of love there are a number of weighty problems."[34] This is a very ambiguous statement. It can mean that Mao Tun is still talking about individuals and society, saying that something is wrong not only with the individual's perception of society but with society itself. (For example, in a more just society Miss Huan probably would not be driven to suicide.) But when it comes to the level of political allegory, to seeing the "weighty problems" not as social in nature but as references to current political events, the links between the stories and historical events in the larger world are not apparent. It would be hard to show, for example, that Miss Huan's pregnancy is not merely the consequence of love between a man and a woman or a dramatic setting for the exposure of evil social forces and personal weakness, but instead an allegorical representation of the political union between the KMT and the CCP during the united-front period. It would be equally hard to show that Ch'iung-hua's loss of her fortune in "A Woman" is not merely a realistic description of the loss of personal and social capital in a materialistic society, but instead an allegorical representation of the CCP's loss of its political and military capital after the searing defeats of 1927.

It is on this level of political allegory, however, that Ch'ien Hsing-ts'un's remarks have the most meaning. Whereas it is difficult to ascertain exactly which political situation Miss Huan's dilemma symbolizes (the united-front policy and military adventurism come to mind because of their similar "suicidal" outcomes), it is clear that Mao Tun was not supporting or affirming the inevitability of her choice, nor depicting her as a veritable image of contemporary political reality in the way Ch'ien's remarks imply. On the contrary, what Mao Tun has done is remind us that Miss Huan's choice could have been avoided by showing how her subjective consciousness, influenced by her psychological fear and doubt, selects and chooses from many possible factors to make that particular form of reality inevitable. Ch'ien may be correct in saying that Miss Huan is not an authentic image of the revolutionary spirit, but there is no denying that she is a realistic product of the authentic revolutionary struggle. Ch'ien's ridicule of Mao Tun draws a good part of its vehemence from a rather doctrinaire argument, popular among the radical left in the late 1920s, that it is impossible for the authentic revolutionary spirit to yield unrevolutionary results.

Mao Tun's foreword leaves no doubt that his purposes in writing the stories was not limited to realistic characterization. The portrayal of Miss Huan and her fate in "Suicide" was meant to be much more than a critical denunciation of a fallen individual in the revolutionary movement. In section 3 of the "Foreword" he said:

> The five stories collected here are all written consciously to realize these goals. Whether it is Hsien-hsien in "Creation," Miss Huan in "Suicide," Ch'iung-hua in "A Woman," Madame Kuei in "Poetry and Prose," or Miss Chang in "Haze," it does not matter how different their educational background and experiences or their personalities are, they all learn the lesson of "reality" in the school of life. Moreover, from what they assimilate from the lesson, they come to their respective ends.
>   . . . to portray a few "ordinary" people's tragedies and their dismal ends to induce people to reflect is not altogether an insignificant deed.[35]

In the collective context of a continuing revolutionary course, the question for Mao Tun was not just to recognize Miss Huan's tragic fate and what it symbolizes for the revolutionary cause, but also to see through or past the "ugliness and evil" that influence her consciousness—the possibility of other alternatives in her objective world, so that recurrence of her mistake can be avoided, life for the revolution can continue, and "faith in the future can be thus engendered." Spite, revenge, and denunciation of wrongs done (of which, by the way, not only Miss Huan's dying curse but Ch'ien's remarks are examples) are understandable reactions to critical injuries. As we shall see in the next story, they are also deadly thorns in the continuous life of the collective revolution when they become bases of action by the subjective consciousness of protagonists with little understanding of their relative position in historical time.

"A Woman"

"A Woman" is the story of a completely "politicized" life that ends in grief. Yang Ch'iung-hua is a young girl from a wealthy family who has many suitors. None, however, has been able to win her heart. In flirting with the crowd of young men around her, Ch'iung-hua has acquired consummate skill in the game of love-politics. Then one day a fire destroys her home. Ch'iung-hua's pretty face is scarred, her father dies in the accident, her mother falls ill, and her family fortunes decline. Suitors cease to visit her. At first, Ch'iung-hua is scornful of their snub; she strives to make her presence felt in her old social circle, but her reception changes from admiration to indifference. Ch'iung-hua is hurt and she is spiteful. She plans a social comeback on her next birthday and intends it to be her revenge on society. But her plan fails; few of her acquaintances appear at the party. Ch'iung-hua is mortified by the callous indifference of her former admirers. She falls ill immediately afterward and becomes delirious with fever. During her illness she yearns for someone to love her, to comfort her and sustain her through the remainder of a joyless life. Since there is no one in sight she remembers Chang Yen-ying, a former schoolmate. Chang Yen-ying was born after his father's death. Because of this social disability and because of his closeness to Ch'iung-hua in school, he had formerly been chased away by her other suitors.

Now Ch'iung-hua, in sickness and desolation, seizes upon Chang's parting words—"I shall not return until I have made something of myself"—and fantasizes that they were his pledge of love to her, that he was destined to be hers. Her obsession with Chang's return becomes a consuming passion that further damages her health. When Ch'iung-hua is near death, she hears her mother call, "Dear Ch'iung-hua, Mr. Chang has come to see you, Mr. Chang Yen-ying." Straining to see, she makes out a dimly visible face and recognizes her long-awaited lover. A smile appears on her lips, and she dies in her mother's arms.

The theme and moral of "A Woman" emerge in bolder relief when seen alongside comparable elements in "Suicide." Written one after the other within six weeks of Mao Tun's arrival in Japan, both stories employ a crisis in their protagonists' lives as the dramatic setting for the theme of fate and time. Both protagonists' crises and responses are in a context of love. Both protagonists search the past for deliverance from their present plight. In the end, both fail, and the finality of their failure is dramatized by death. In light of these parallels, one can say with reasonable confidence that the fate of the two women conveys the similar thematic message: To rely on the past for a remedy for present trouble is not only useless but fatal.

On the other hand, there are certain differences between the two characters which address different issues and say very different things about the meaning of their similar fates. There is a fundamental difference, for example, between the "form of consciousness" behind Miss Huan's outlook on love and that behind Yang Ch'iung-hua's. There is also a fundamental difference between Miss Huan's subjective perception of her world and Ch'iung-hua's practical understanding of hers.[36] Mao Tun probably hoped that his readers, particularly those who were not bystanders in the revolution, would reflect and guard against such failings in themselves and in their collective struggle.

In this perspective, Miss Huan and Ch'iung-hua emerges as two very different kinds of person. Miss Huan is revealed as not a victim of society, but rather an example of a moral failure. Miss Huan does have a real alternative; she could honor her commitment to love and bear the sufferings entailed. She declines to do so on the ground that she lacks the necessary long-term courage, yet Mao Tun shows that the real reason is that she is unwilling to sacrifice her personal happiness in life. Her failing, then, is not exclusively social, it is moral as well. She consciously betrays her emotional and moral commitments to her lover and their unborn child, and then, in a panic of self-justification, the very ideals that originally inspired those commitments.

Miss Huan's betrayal is complete. Its enormity is emphasized by the graphically gruesome details of her hanging. Mao Tun will not let his readers forget that her choice is avoidable. In reiterating in her dying consciousness the notion of following the tide of history, his condemnation peeks through the bulging eyes of Miss Huan's macabre death mask.

Ch'iung-hua, in contrast, has never placed her faith in love or abstract ideas—not because she is incapable of love or of abstract thought, but because there is no one she can entrust such notions to.[37] After her suitors chase away Chang Yen-ying, she is troubled. She detests their banality, but

> her peaceful, innocent, and virginal heart was troubled by this new lesson. However, she was willing to learn and considered learning this new lesson necessary. But she could not help feeling regretful at the same time: Is life so ugly after all? Are the people around her so demonic and horrible? Ancient saints and sages admonish us to love mankind, but Chang Yen-ying hates mankind because he gets no justice from society. Is his outlook reasonable? She could get no answers to her questions.[38]

Her friend Miss Chang tells her that man corrupts woman, which causes Ch'iung-hua to fear that one day she too will be corrupted by a man. So when her suitors slander one another to her, she loses all her trust in men.

> She did not feel like saying anything; she wanted only to run back home. She suddenly felt that people were more sinister than she had originally imagined them to be. She saw clearly that those milling around her were all demons, flattering her to her face and laughing at her behind her back.[39]

One after the other the young men of her world are shown as faithless characters; their main occupation, in Ch'iung-hua's company, is mutual slander and backbiting. But unlike Miss Huan, Ch'iung-hua has no fear of such a world. She knows her game well; she understands and knows how to manipulate the forces in her social surroundings. The "form of consciousness" (the *yi-shih-hsing-t'ai* referred to in the foreword) behind her outlook on love and society never involves any question of commitment. Mao Tun takes great care at the outset to demonstrate Ch'iung-hua's total grasp of social reality. In episode after episode we are shown how Ch'iung-hua, in her dealings with various friends, develops in her teens a consummate skill in the politics of love to replace what was once a naive belief in Rousseauian spontaneity. By emulating the ways of her world, she learns to be insincere in human relations and becomes a master at dissembling.

> She recalled that formerly when she treated others with open sincerity, she got deceit in return. Now that she dealt in craftiness and heartless intrigues, people responded with twice the respect and esteem. Was this not the normal way of life? This was exactly the kind of life that everyone praised and willingly practiced; this was the real human condition.[40]

Then the fire changes everything. Ch'iung-hua, scarred and deprived of her fortune, is suddenly shown to be no better equipped than Miss Huan to cope with change and disaster. But her subsequent failure is not a moral one. Fire is impersonal and makes no commitment of any kind in the human world. Mao Tun, by a novelistic trick, has deftly transferred the immediate cause of Ch'iung-hua's crisis from the social to the natural world, so that moral considerations no longer define the meaning of her fate. After the fire, Ch'iung-hua struggles valiantly with all her skills to maintain her social standing; but the fire has destroyed the material foundation of their effectiveness. By the time Ch'iung-hua realizes she can no longer cope, she, like Miss Huan, has retreated into the past and is vainly attempting to find succor there for the future. Mao Tun, as the contemporary critic Tsu Hsiu-hsia noted,[41] was not writing a romance in "A Woman." The final scene is not a poetic "happy ending;" it is executed with deliberate irony to expose the futility of nostalgic yearning, even when the object of yearning is a worthy life goal. Like Ch'ien Hsing-ts'un, Tsu ably captures half of the ultimate meaning of the story; his point bears cogently on the tragic fate of the protagonist as an individual in the present, but does not reach beyond to ask the question of what is to be done next.

Mao Tun admittedly was no romantic, but neither was he a cynic. In "Suicide" and "A Woman," his critical exploration never once raises questions about the intrinsic truth and value of man's hope for love, or the ideas of liberation, freedom, and light that are the timeless collective goals of the revolution. What Mao Tun does question is, given the reality of the two protagonists' worlds, how can they uphold those ideals, and what failings eventually undermine the vitality of those ideals? Miss Huan supposedly believes in love, but she betrays her faith and lets fear guide her actions instead. Ch'iung-hua believes in political strategies and in herself, but she arrogantly miscalculates the damage done by changed circumstances and is so reduced, through a series of subsequent innocent misdeeds, to futile romantic yearning. By stressing at once the differences in the two women's failings and the similarity of their ends, Mao Tun is subsuming all denunciation of guilty individuals into an effort to show how to avoid such surrenders in the future and at the same time to suggest grounds for continued hope in the future of the revolutionary cause. He is considerably less hard on the defects in Ch'iung-hua's character. She is not saved from the practical consequences of her artful arrogance and egotistical miscalculation, but she does not die a totally graceless death. The return of Chang Yen-ying and the continual presence of her loving mother stand as proof of the author's less severe judgment of Ch'iung-hua's social blunder.[42] This gesture of grace and redemption in the image of a loving mother we have already seen in the case of Miss Ching in *Disillusionment*, and in the following story, "Haze," we shall find another example of it when the heroine, prompted by the memory of her mother, makes a last-minute decision to save herself.

"Haze"

"Haze" is another story about a girl driven by circumstances to drastic action; but the action this time takes a different turn. Miss Chang, a former student activist, is under pressure from her father to marry an army commander but she is in love with an old schoolmate, Ho Jo-hua. One day she discovers that Ho Jo-hua has been seeing Lan, a girl friend of hers, and that the two have grown quite close. Betrayed, angry, and frustrated, she wants revenge—like Ch'iung-hua after the fire. She is rebellious, she wants to act. Meanwhile, paternal pressure mounts. A number of possible courses of action pass through her mind:

> Revenge! Grab Ho Jo-hua back from the hands of Lan . . .
> Revenge! Even if it means just [grabbing at] a piece of flotsam, I will avenge myself!
> But what about afterwards?
>   In her hallucinatory vision, darkness was complete. The rolling muddy waves of the Yangtze River. She recalled that someone had jumped into the river from Yellow Crane Pavilion a year ago. . . . Many fragmentary questions flashed across her consciousness, hurriedly and in disarray: leaving the family? How to make a living then? To seek a mate? To get even with Lan? With Jo-hua? . . . To go bad? Free love? Tragedy? To earn an independent living? To be an office clerk? A woman writer? A woman revolutionary party member?[43]

Miss Chang begins to see that she does not have the resources to do much. There are too many problems, and she cannot decide. But gradually her thoughts drift toward her native province and her mother. She can run away to Canton. This is a new idea. "Where there is still a haven, go to it for the time being." Canton may not be the promised land, but at least she can find temporary shelter there.

Miss Chang's escape from her oppressive surroundings is not merely a symbolic gesture. In the overall environment of *The Wild Roses*, the break is dramatic as well as psychological and spiritual. It signals the arising of new forces that can transform her personality, new strength in her beliefs, and a new future for her life. After the break, she need not fear the tragic fate of a Miss Huan or a Ch'iung-hua.

Mao Tun groups Miss Chang with Miss Huan in his foreword and describes both their characters as "weak,"—the cause of their "unfortunate" fate. Of Miss Chang, he said in particular that she "wanted to transcend her environment, but her bureaucratic family background conditioned her habits. So finally she thinks, 'Where there is still a haven, go to it for the time being.' This is an undeniable fact."

Mao Tun here might, "off the page," be using her decision to go to "Canton" to disguise a deserter's psychology. He obviously did not want the overzealous readers to take as a heroic gesture a decision that was dangerously close to what had touched off the CCP adventurism of 1927–28. He may well have feared that such incidents might recur—and this fear was strong enough to make him group Miss Chang with Miss Huan as the same character type. But readers of a later time will surely sense that the recurrence of such episodes of bloodletting as the Canton Commune is only one possibility, it is equally possible that Miss Chang, once she has cut her ties to the past, will become a free woman like Hsien-hsien or Madame Kuei in Canton. The story itself is rather less ambiguous than the author's remarks about it. It is the only time in *The Wild Roses* when I see possibilities in a story that contradict, or at least intuit far beyond the author's guideposts. Miss Chang does in fact reflect on the possibility of revenge (like Ch'iung-hua) and on the possibility of suicide (like Huan), but she acts on neither. Toward the end her thoughts are leading toward a more positive goal. And what finally triggers her decision is the thought of her mother. Since the story does not follow Miss Chang to Canton to test her revolutionary urge in a concrete situation, we can probably read Mao Tun's remarks in the foreword as primarily a warning to those who share her dilemma that they must be careful not to entrap themselves in the tragic fate of a Miss Huan.

The story itself offers good reason for us to believe that in Canton, the cradle of revolution,[44] that Miss Chang will emerge a new woman, a woman like Hsien-hsien in "Creation" and Madame Kuei in "Poetry and Prose"—who have no dark past, who bear no wounds, who have no reverence for chastity, and who revel in the liberalizing absence of the old pieties. They are the future, and they are a challenge for men like Chün-shih in "Creation," whose behavior lags far behind his ideas, and like Ping in "Poetry and Prose," who stands bewildered between the seductive allures of two opposed worlds.

"Creation"

"Creation" was written in February 1928, before Mao Tun went to Japan. Chronologically it does not belong to the same period as the other four stories in the collection. Evidently Mao Tun included it to rework a strand of thought which he had earlier cherished as innocent exaltation over a bright revolutionary future, and then discarded because of what happened in *Pursuit,* and now, after much agony and reflection, tentatively picks up again as a fictional study of a reasoned alternative to "Suicide." The motivations behind its writing and its inclusion in *The Wild Roses* are certainly different.

Hsien-hsien in "Creation" is recreated by her husband Chün-shih in accordance with his ideal of modern enlightened womanhood. Chün-shih is the courtesy-name of Ssu-ma Kuang (1018–1086), the author of *Tzu-chih t'ung-chien (Comprehensive Mirror for Aid in Government),* a monumental history of traditional China from 403 B.C. to A.D. 959. In using the name here Mao Tun intends a symbolic association between the two men's creative masterpieces and their political functions. In light of the long account of the fictional Chün-shih's own intellectual and political history in the first half of "Creation," we understand his creation—Hsien-hsien—as a symbol of the general history of modern China from the late nineteenth century to the birth of the Chinese Communist movement.[45]

So Chün-shih recreates Hsien-hsien according to his ideal. But once the ideal comes to life, the Pygmalion Chün-shih has trouble dealing with its flesh-and-blood reality. The new Hsien-hsien is too sensual, too vivacious, too pleasure-seeking, too unpredictable, and too scornful of the established ways of wifely behavior. Chün-shih, in his zeal to create an ideal woman for a new historical era, had given absolutely no thought to what she might actually *do* once given life. He certainly did not foresee that once she took life, his Galatea would no longer be his ideal but would have an independent existence of her own, and obey only the principles behind her "creation." Chün-shih is totally unprepared to lose his wife—and all that "wife" means in traditional terms.

The comedy ends with Chün-shih realizing that he has not only created a new woman, he has also created a gap the size of an entire historical era for himself as a man. If he is to live into that new era with Hsien-hsien, he must recreate himself as well.

"Poetry and Prose"

Madame Kuei in "Poetry and Prose" is another image of the new woman, born of the same ideas as Hsien-hsien, but further developed and more sophisticated. She is impudent, earthy, sensual to the extent of having no inhibitions. She is more experienced with men, and so is more aggressive in her challenge to their manhood. Like "Creation," the story is told with a comic tone.

Madame Kuei seduces the young man Ping openly and fearlessly. Ping feels that her lovemaking is "unpoetic," titillating his senses excessively and his spirit insufficiently. Nonetheless, he is irresistibly attracted to Madame Kuei; she is to him "the dance of life, the dance of the soul."[46]

Ping has another attachment, however, and tnis is to his sheltered young cousin. Madame Kuei confronts him with it and he protests that he is not the only one who has changed. "But, Kuei, you have to see that you yourself have changed recently, drastically changed. You have grown too sexy, too practical, and too vulgar by the day. You have entered this ordinary, unattractive, prosaic era too quickly."[47]

Madame Kuei couldn't care less about his criticism:

> "What change? I don't see it at all. I only know that if I want something, I just say so outright. As to you, you sing a hymn to the poetic relationship between man and woman, using such terms as divine, mystery, spiritual love. But what happens is that the minute you see a woman's flesh, you get drunk on imagination and go crazy about her body. You pant and dribble like a dog. I can remember as if it were yesterday how much you have adored my breasts, my legs, my belly. Your manner, your purity, your elegance are your hypocritical masks. You don't dare show what you really are. Giving me a lecture, how shameless."

Ping tries to defend himself with more talk, but there are no more answers. True to what she says, Kuei follows her words with whirlwind action, pushing young Ping to the floor and making love to him. Ping is completely overcome. "Darkness gradually spreads to the four corners of the room. The tall looking glass stands clear and bright, mirroring Kuei's flushed cheeks, radiant with victorious light, and also mirroring Ping, panting, slightly pale around the mouth."[48]

As Ping takes his pleasure with Madame Kuei, he cannot help feeling pangs of guilt about his cousin, who, pure and demure as the white rose she once gave him, is very dependent on him. Ping wants to go on enjoying his "dance of the soul" with Madame Kuei and at the same time keep the remembered experience of his "soul's tremor" with his cousin. But as one might expect in such a situation, before long Ping's failure to commit himself to either of the women loses him the company of both. His cousin goes to Peking with her father, and all he gets from Madame

Kuei afterward is a sarcastic remark, "When are you going to Peking, Master Ping?" She, too, is leaving him.

The Necessary Comic Vision of a Revolutionary

Ch'ien Hsing-ts'un thought that in *The Wild Roses* there was a shift in the sex of the protagonists, from Miss Huan in "Suicide" and Ch'iung-hua in "A Woman" to Chün-shih in "Creation" and the young man Ping in "Poetry and Prose."[49] Mao Tun did shift his dramatic portrayal of human failings from the female to the male characters in the stories; but the shift was not, as Ch'ien Hsien-ts'un suggests, meant to underline the universality of human failings irrespective of sex. Mao Tun made a corresponding shift in narrative mode from the tragic to the comic, and both shifts highlight a change in the subject matter as well—from man's tragic fall out of the world of values and ideals into comic attempts to seek reintegration with it.[50] The New Woman has replaced an oppressive society as the symbol of what men are up against in their struggle for self-realization and the realization of their ideals. In a deep sense, she is the alternative to Miss Huan's and Ch'iung-hua's choices, which in their stories is symbolized in the inverse image of the absent male lovers. Dramatically and thematically the New Woman represents the positive outlook on reality in the world of *The Wild Roses.* Men, with all their failings, are beginning to look away from the past and to experience, through their Skuld-like, veiled understanding of what lies ahead, a direct and yet enigmatic physical contact with seductive and emotionally frightening new modes of existence, personified by the New Woman.

Mao Tun had quite a different view of who the true protagonists are in these five stories. In the foreword he made a firm distinction between the "perceiver" and the protagonist:

> The protagonists in these five pieces are all women. The real protagonist in "Poetry and Prose" is Madame Kuei and not the young man Ping. Among the protagonists, not a single one can be considered a brave person worthy of admiration. Neither does any of them think through everything and achieve total understanding. Naturally, there are magnificently brave people in this turbulent society of ours who are genuine revolutionaries.
>
> But more plentiful are the likes of these, who are not very brave, not thoroughly enlightened. In my opinion, to create a flawless model [in fiction] for all to emulate is certainly a good idea. But to depict the tragic and obscure endings of a few ordinary persons, so as to induce people to reflect on themselves, is not altogether meaningless.[51]

The aversion to heroics which made Mao Tun say that there is no "protagonist" in *Vacillation* is here given a more positive orientation: an affirmation of the ordinary. According to the foreword, all the protagonists have taken their lessons in "reality" from "the school of the human condition."[52] With what they have absorbed into their consciousness about reality in that school, they eventually shape their own destinies. The "school" itself, as portrayed in *The Wild Roses*, is certainly not a supportive environment in which to learn about "reality" in safety and with pleasure. The educational methods of that school are fear ("Suicide"), impersonal natural calamity and personal callousness ("A Woman"), and paternal authority trying to enforce a loveless marriage ("Haze"). Counteracting those methods, on the other hand, are man's timeless desire for physical love and freedom from fear ("Poetry and Prose") and for a life that is intellectually satisfying and spiritually fulfilling ("Creation").

Time in the "school" is infinite, though man's choices are not. The presence of infinite time alongside man's outlook on fate in a particularized period of time appears in all five of the stories in *The Wild Roses*. Hsien-hsien, for example, representing the future-in-the present, has tears of memory behind her laughter of enlightment, and her heart can ache at the half-forgotten bygone days that Chün-shih tirelessly recalls with mixed feelings of pride, regret, shock, and discontent. And Madame Kuei, despite her nearly complete physical enthrallment of Ping in the present, cannot entirely free his consciousness from his remembered time with his girl cousin. Similarly, and in an inverse time perspective, both Miss Huan and Ch'iung-hua, victims of the past, retain a "romantic" yearning for a love that, despite its feeble dramatic presence, is the future envisioned in a long present-in-the-past.

The lessons in "reality" that each of the protagonists learns and the manner in which the lessons are learned vary. But from the reader's point of view, no matter how we look at them—whether dramatically as true-to-life characters in the stories, or thematically and abstractly as symbols of fate and time in the context of Mao Tun's explanation—their collective meaning is the same; that is, to continue one's struggle in the manner of Miss Huan and Ch'iung-hua is too grim a fate to endure. Short of resignation to death or perseverance to the bitter end, one simply has to look into other domains for more promising comrades to carry on the struggle. If Hsien-hsien and Madame Kuei have never existed in history before, they must be created to combat the darkness and death that would otherwise prevail. But once they have been given life, the continuation of the battle will require a successful coordination between man's reflective understanding of his past failings and a more imaginative understanding of the bold, spirited forms of action demanded by the new forces in history. Mao Tun believed that once the impact of new revolutionary forces was felt, it would be impossible for modern man to turn back to his wandering "on the road of the golden mean."[53] Madame Kuei, having broken the fetters of traditional modes of womanly behavior, would necessarily disdain "chastity." Madame Kuei, like Hsien-hsien, is a "resolute and persevering woman" who loves life passionately and who, "when the circumstances change, is capable of carrying on the revolution,"[54] for she has shattered the boundaries of the present.

The Wild Roses, written during a critical period in Mao Tun's life, bears immediate witness to the thought processes that underlay Mao Tun's reflections about the revolutionary reality of China after 1927, and to the psychological forces behind the sentiments he expressed in his lyrical prose essays of the same period. The stories are also testimony of the spiritual journey the author had to take before he was able to emerge from anguish and despair and continue on the road of "flesh-and-blood struggle" leading back home. Chronologically the five stories show alternation between dark moments of resentment and despair and moments of desperate, agonizing, yet unremitting quests for love and courage.[55] "Haze," chronologically the last of the five, shows an exceptional mode of action that sets it apart from the other four stories. In spite of Mao Tun's reservations about the real strength of Miss Chang's character, her final decision to return to the early base of the revolution, captures a parallel moment in Mao Tun's own thought and action. His lingering doubts about the "golden mean" in an age of "flesh-and-blood" revolutionary struggle were finally dispelled, and he resolved to return home.

In addition to his carefully selected *Wild Roses* stories, Mao Tun's literary record of his stay in Japan includes the short stories "Colorblindness," "Muddiness," and "The Top," all dealing with the same subject matter, and in the same style, as the stories in *The Wild Roses.*[56] The personal essays written in Japan express another aspect of the author's state of mind. It was not exactly bitterness and despondency, but rather a kind of drifting uncertainty in a sunless land, the spiritual prostration of a man who was emotionally spent. "Fog," for instance, depicts a mood that is neither sunny nor rainy but oppressively grey, as if nature too had spent its vitality.[57] The redness of "Maple Leaves" in the mountains remains brilliant and attractive, but it stirs no emotional reaction or association of any kind. The writer is a detached spectator in a foreign land, an "outcast" from his motherland.[58] The psychology behind "Knocking" is even more ambiguous, indeterminate between fearful hope and fearful disappointment, uncertain whether to advance or retreat.[59] When we compare these brief impressions of fleeting sunless moments with Mao Tun's earlier sketch, "The Afternoon of May Thirtieth," or with slightly later pieces such as "Autumn in the Public Park," "Odes to the Machine," and "In the Public Park,"[60] we are aware of the emotional coloring that can come only from a man with a well-defined communal identity. Mao Tun's Japan essays read like faint echoes of the distant signs and longings of a poet-intellectual's wanderings in classical Chinese poetry—sighs and longings that will not subside until the dislocated consciousness has reached its hoped-for destination.

Mao Tun returned to Shanghai in the spring of 1930, his elegiac mood dispelled. Although physical illness and severe nervous tension continued to plague him, he set out almost immediately to write longer, stronger, less fragmentary work than the essays and short stories. He was still Mao Tun, the man and writer of contradictions, but henceforth, he would deal with them on his home ground. With the three historical tales, published in 1930, Mao Tun began a new phase of his creative career.

VII

CONSCIOUSNESS
OF THE COLLECTIVE
REMAKING THE REBEL TRADITION

Shortly after Mao Tun returned to Shanghai in April 1930, he wrote three short pieces of historical fiction: "Lin Ch'ung the Leopard Head" (about 2,500 words), "Stone Tablet" (about 2,000 words), and "The Great Marsh District" (about 2,500 words).[1] He tried to rejoin the Communist Party but did not succeed. He was disappointed, but he had learned something about how to sidestep disappointment and cynicism and their self-destructive consequences. He patiently observed the new political struggles in the Party from the periphery and remained sharp and penetrating in his analyses. Some of his old comrades were still Party activists, and his wife continued to be active in the women's movement. His brother Shen Tse-min and his wife returned from Moscow in July 1930 as one of the Twenty-eight Bolsheviks; Tse-min would soon become active in the new Pavel Mif-Wang Ming coalition in the Party.[2]

Mao Tun's health was not good; he was suffering from attacks of acute trachoma and was nearly blinded in one eye.[3] He was also hard-pressed financially. Having been denied official reentry into the Party, he was probably not on the Party payroll and had to rely entirely on his writing to support his family. In May, the dual pressures of security and money forced him to move twice, and his mother went back to Wu Village so that the family could take a smaller apartment. Fortunately, his old friends Yeh Shao-chün and Cheng Cheng-tuo from the Literary Association group were both in Shanghai. Cheng, who as a Party sympathizer had found it prudent to spend a year in England had returned to edit the *Short Story Monthly* again; Yeh, who had replaced him as editor, was still on the staff. Between them, they saw to it that Mao Tun's work was published regularly.

After the second move, settled in a three-room apartment on Yü-yüan Road, and with his living expenses more or less covered, Mao Tun rejoined the literary world and began a new chapter in his life as a revolutionary thinker and creative writer. Mao Tun also found a new friend in

Feng Hsüeh-feng, a revolutionary writer and disciple of Lu Hsün, who would later write a very touching biographical work about Lu Hsün's years with the League of Leftist Writers. He resumed his continuing political dialogue with Ch'ü Ch'iu-po, who after more than a year in Moscow was also back in Shanghai and, though now out of power in the Party, had not lost a shred of his power with words and dialectics. Although generally in disagreement with Ch'ü's position on literature, Mao Tun nonetheless found in Ch'ü an honest antithesis to his own ideas. The presence of Lu Hsün and Ch'ü Ch'iu-po no doubt greatly speeded up Mao Tun's renewed zest in reentering the revolutionary struggle on the literary front. The League of Leftist Writers itself, founded in March 1930 to form a united front between Communist writers and their fellow-travellers, was of limited interest to Mao Tun. He joined it in May, but remained only loosely attached because of the propagandistic ploys its members used—street demonstrations, open forums, wall posters, agitation in the factories; the whole gamut Mao Tun had long since gone through in his pre-Wuhan days—and also because of the "phonograph disk" opinions of the league's dominant group—the people from the Sun Society and the Creation Society who had launched the attack on *Eclipse.* As the irony of history would have it, on one occasion Mao Tun was even assigned to a working group headed by Ch'ien Hsing-ts'un.[4]

The Chinese Communist movement had continued its confusing and uncertain journey along the "soviet" path. From 1928 to 1930, the top leadership shifted rapidly: Ch'ü Ch'iu-po, who succeeded Ch'en Tu-hsiu as the General Secretary of the CCP in August 1927, was severely criticized for putschist tendencies—ordering uprisings at a time when objective circumstances were not favorable for success—at the Sixth Congress of the CCP in July 1928. Ch'ü was then replaced by Li Li-san at the Ninth Plenum of the Executive Committee of the Comintern in February 1929[5] and remained in Moscow till August 1930. Li Li-san, closing rank with the Comintern, went to even greater extremes than Ch'ü with his "Li Li-san line," which promoted armed uprising in industrial centers and cities regardless of strength and price just to create the impression of a continuously rising revolutionary tide.

While Li's line was being carried out with the endorsement of the CCP and the Comintern, Mao Tse-tung, completely on his own initiative and unbeholden to either Shanghai or Moscow, was creating a new guerrilla strategy of revolution, a new peasant movement with the goal of surrounding the cities by an awakened and armed countryside. Mao's and Chu Te's experiments in the Chingkang Mountains on the Hunan-Kiangsi border were, in Benjamin Schwartz's words, "born under a cloud of orthodox disapproval and, at the time [1928], seemed to hold little hope of further development."[6] But by late 1929 and early 1930, Mao not only showed no sign of weakening but was growing stronger and stronger: Two new dynamic factors within the Chinese Communist movement—the Soviet areas and the Red Army—were beginning to merge. Li Li-san, however, refused to endorse or support this new development. As late as April 1930, when Mao Tun returned to Shanghai, Li was still emphatically opposing the possibility of either "encircling the city with country," as Mao Tse-tung put it, or relying on the Red Army to take the cities.[7]

Thus in 1930 the political situation of the Chinese Communist Party was complex. Its headquarters in Shanghai was directly under the Li Li-san leadership, and its soviet movement in the country was developing along a very different track. Actions were not coordinated under a centralized party line: P'eng Te-huai captured Changsha in July with the Fifth Red Army he commanded but Mao Tse-tung refused to attack Nanch'ang as a follow-up; instead he began to consolidate his own power base.

Opinions about peasant policy were divided too at the Shanghai Party headquarters. In April 1930, Chou En-lai had gone to Moscow as peace maker, and when he returned that summer, Pavel Mif and twenty-eight Chinese students who had been at Sun Yat-sen University came with him. Their assignment was to oppose Li Li-san under the flag of the Comintern, and support emerging leaders of their own. Obviously, Li had no liking for Mif or his Chinese protégés, Li's chief lieutenants, Ho Men-hsiung and Lo Chang-lung, threatened to quit over the issue of cooperation with Mif. Then Ch'ü Ch'iu-po and Teng Chung-hsia returned from Moscow in August 1930 to urge accommodation with the rich peasants, a position reflective of the current Moscow stand on the issue. This differed in fundamental ways with Mao Tse-tung's policy of open peasant revolt. With Wang Ming and the Twenty Eight Bolsheviks ready to take power, the accommodation line was in the ascendant.

This was what Mao Tun saw between the time he came home in April and the time he wrote "Lin Ch'ung the Leopard Head" in September: the internal struggle between Li Li-san and Mif and the contradiction between Mao's and Moscow's peasant policies. Apart from Mif and the Twenty Eight Bolsheviks, the other leaders on the scene were all his old comrades. The situation at the CCP Central was not altogether different from that during the period of the Great Revolution period (1925–27), with the Party split over strategy and peasant policy, and with the Comintern making the decisions. But outside the feuding leadership center in Shanghai, the vast countryside was beginning to stir.

Old Tune and New Materials.

In the autobiographical piece, "In Retrospect," Mao Tun wrote,

The great events of the several years before 1928 which shook China and the world were all familiar to me. . . . I made only partial representation of them in *Disillusionment, Vacillation,* and the unfinished *Rainbow.* . . . Yet it seems that due to the fact that I myself was dissatisfied with those old works, I subsequently steered away from the old subject matter. Besides, I had another unwarranted way of thinking: I felt that to do full justice to those "historical events" in question required novels of more than a hundred thousand words, and yet my mental state at the time did not permit me to write such long works. A last reason is that at that time I had made no confident reevaluation of the "old subject matter," so I felt that even if I did write, it would probably still be of the same "old tune," which would be worse than not writing at all. However, my determination to change the subject and the method [of fictional representation] was very strong. Meanwhile, I had returned to where the flesh-and-blood struggle was— metropolitan Shanghai. That was the spring of 1930. . . . "Lin Ch'ung the Leopard Head," "Great Marsh District," and others were written during that period, when I was recuperating from illness. They can be considered as my first attempt to write "short." My former short pieces ran at least ten thousand words. I had changed my subject; I evaded reality. Naturally there was no lack of new subject matter, but I am not accustomed to using fresh materials while they are still hot. . . ."[8]

Reviewing the historical events in the Chinese Communist movement from 1928 to 1930, we have no difficulty understanding why Mao Tun should have the weary feeling of witnessing scenes déjà vu.[9] It must have appeared to him that political struggle was going to be a permanent feature in the upper level of leadership, forever confusing and treacherous. On the other hand, the development of the peasant movement in the countryside might offer new premise for organizing the dynamic forces for the revolution.[10] Mao Tun began to see the collective as more important than the individuals making up the leadership. In particular, for the first time he saw the peasants as the premise of the future.

In 1930, Mao Tun was in no position to portray the peasants "realistically." He was not from a peasant family and the only person he had known who could associate with peasants in a positive and creative way— positive and creative by the concrete proof that he was still alive and well in the mountains with both theory and material resources well preserved from enemies without or within—was Mao Tse-tung. And he had not seen Mao in person or in action for three years. Mao Tun's intention to write "short" did not lend itself to a full, realistic portrayal. Lacking close knowledge of corollaries in current history and deficient in first-hand experiences, he was almost compelled to present his perception as "forms of consciousness (yi-shih-hsing-t'ai)."

The term "yi-shih-hsing-t'ai" plays a prominent role in Mao Tun's writing and thinking after his sojourn in Japan. He had already connected the term to the concept of "class" when he was writing his "Foreword" to *The Wild Roses.*[11] Class consciousness *(chieh-chi-i-shih)* now became one of the central themes in all three of the historical tales. In "The Great

Marsh District" for instance, "*chieh-chi* (class)" appears in a number of places as the basis of group interest versus brotherhood—*i*—of the earlier tradition. "*Ch'u-shen* (social background, social status)" serves as a synonymous variant of "class" in "Lin Ch'ung the Leopard Head" and "Stone Tablet."

Mao Tun's experiential constraints and his strong urge to write about the new dynamic forces in the Chinese Communist movement combined to produce some very unusual heroes, unusual in May Fourth fiction, normally concerned with present time, and especially unusual for Mao Tun, who had refused the notion of heroes in his trilogy and had no compunction about separating the means of perception and the central character in his stories. In the old tradition, Chinese bandit heroes are mostly men of action. Once in the mountains, few of them think about anything personal or what action they should take. But Mao Tun took these ancient models and remade them into highly reflective personages, men of conscious action. Lin Ch'ung, for example, is made to think out the question of how best to serve the rebel cause. It is not enough to kill a bad leader. Unless there is a more capable replacement, assassination merely leads to disintegration and chaos. Hsiao Jang in "Stone Tablet" recognizes that, realistically, intrigue and deception are acceptable means within the rebel camp and may even be necessary sometimes if the purpose is to achieve unity and forestall destructive rivalry among leaders. Ch'en She and the peasants in "The Great Marsh District" are awakened by the force of dire circumstance to a consciousness of their collective interest. The lesson is brought home to them that if they do not rebel together, there is no life or future, but if they do rise up, there is hope of controlling their own destiny.[12] As fictional characters, Lin Ch'ung, Hsiao Jang, and Ch'en She have each achieved a lucid understanding of their environment and themselves—an understanding never before so confidently presented in Mao Tun's fiction. This direct confrontation of revolutionary consciousness with revolutionary reality is an important link in the writer's maturing process. Mao Tun had not really changed his subject, as he had declared in "In Retrospect," nor had he evaded reality. What he had done was make a technical change in his level of narrative from the mimetic to the nonmimetic, and a corresponding adjustment in his subject from the surface actions and events in the rebel movement to the underlying forms of rebel consciousness. These new heroes have no illusions about the reality they face.

Mao Tun was always intent on creating two levels of reality in his fiction. From the beginning he experimented with combining contemporary characters and political allegory to effect a double reality: beneath the surface level, the covert political reference. But the practical difficulties were great. When he used students as protagonists in a contemporary setting, he was obliged first of all to place them in a social milieu. Then he had to provide the particular background of each of the students: they had to have parents, relatives, friends, and schoolmates, and all these on a realistic level. The more successful he was on this level of objective reality, the more fixed were his characters in their social identity, and the less free to act as allegorical representatives of political events which he was not allowed to treat openly.

To alert his readers to the allegory, Mao Tun frequently used allusions, symbols, and other devices. Sometimes they were effective but they did not always contribute to the artistic merit of his works. Realism suffered as in the case of the name symbolism and the allusive Futuristic speech of the battalion leader Ch'iang Wei-li in *Disillusionment*. There, Ch'iang Wei-li loses as a realistic character. When they do not work, as with the overnight love affair between Pao-su and Miss Ching in the same novel, allegory becomes ineffectual: the love affair is so convincing that the reader doesn't look for what it represents.

Mao Tun was aware of the technical difficulties involved in creating this double reality, especially when one of the two levels had to be disguised. He discussed these difficulties in terms of the structure of the novel *Eclipse* in "From Kuling to Tokyo"—how to make the same characters appear in different places in different parts of the novel when events have to be simultaneous—and in "On Reading *Ni Huan-chih*" he defended his failure to resolve these problems in characterization and his reason for resorting to "profile painting." From the very beginning of his career as a writer, he was conscious of the challenge facing someone who is committed to the practice of realism in art, and yet prohibited by his political purpose from being totally open with his reader about the true nature of his subject.

By 1930, Mao Tun's reflections on the future of the revolution led him to shift his emphasis from preoccupation with an authentic chronicling of the revolutionary movement to recommending a course of action that would avoid the familiar pitfalls on the road of revolution. The three historical tales can well be read as experiments with ideas about possible courses the revolution might take. In them we can find his comments and recommendations to currently active members of the Chinese Communist Party. From the artistic perspective, these tales are an experiment: a new attempt to meet the challenge of remaking the rebel tradition and consciousness in a different fictional form and with a different set of characters from students and the New Woman.

Remaking the Traditional Base

In his historical tales Mao Tun for the first time turns from contemporary reality to history and popular fiction of the oral tradition for his material and characters. "Lin Ch'ung the Leopard Head" and "Stone Tablet" are adapted from episodes in the fourteen-century popular novel about banditry, *The Water Margin*,[13] which is set in the Liang mountains surrounded by lakes and swamps. "Great Marsh District" is taken from chapter 48, "The Hereditary House of Ch'en She," in the *Records of the Grand Historian* by Ssu-ma Ch'ien (145–90 B.C.).[14] All three stories are about popular uprisings, and deal directly with political rivalry and intrigue among outlawed people.

The immediate consideration behind the shift is obviously a technical one. Using tradition and archetype in fiction gives an author the practical advantage of not having to explain everything on the very first level of communication, for tradition operates on an established level of communication. Lin Ch'ung, Wu Yung, Hsiao Jang, and probably Ch'en She and Wu Kuang, too, are familiar names to the Chinese popular reader. For centuries their exploits have been recounted by storytellers and enacted in local operas. They are archetypal political rebels, and their deeds are part of a tradition of political subversion and popular uprising. With these protagonists, Mao Tun was immediately relieved of the awkward task of having to disguise and expose at the same time the political identity of his characters. He is thus left free to exploit traditional plots and characterization for his own purposes.

In each of the stories he has changed several elements of the original. The character Lin Ch'ung, for instance, aside from the familiar Liang-shan setting and a few touches reminding one of his initial confrontation with Wang Lun, is hardly the hero familiar to us. He has acquired not only an interesting peasant ancestry but also a collective consciousness and a new pattern of behavior. Similarly, the stone tablet in the story "Stone Tablet" is no longer a heaven-sent ranking of the leaders of the Liang-shan rebels as in the original, but an artifact of human design, conceived expressly to serve a communal purpose. Looking at these changes, we must first ask why Mao Tun made them.

In modern Chinese literature, as we know, the traditional past is generally used to reflect the present. Some of Lu Hsün's "Old Tales Retold" ridicule modern-day pedantry in historical research, and Kuo Mo-jo glorified contemporary romantic rebels, male and female, in his historical plays "Ch'ü Yüan," and "Cho Wen-chün." Were Mao Tun's tales written to satirize current CCP politics or to celebrate his Party's glorious inheritance of the age-old rebel tradition?

Our answer might be: all this and more. Mao Tun is trying to clarify and combine, for himself as well as his public, two different modes of popular rebellion: (1) the individually oriented mode that characterizes the traditional rebellions as found in his sources, and which dramatizes the seizure of power by individual heroes; and (2) the new collectively oriented mode that characterized the Chinese Communist movement in the present. The new mode is based on recognition of the needs and aspirations of the masses as the moral base and unifying goal of a relentless, sometimes even sinister, struggle for power. The contrast between the two modes is revealed first by the deviations from tradition in Mao Tun's reworking of the old tales, then more pointedly in the way he perceives these deviations.

"Lin Ch'ung the Leopard Head"

"Lin Ch'ung the Leopard Head" recasts an episode from the Lin Ch'ung cycle in *The Water Margin* in terms of top-level CCP politics: how a high-ranking army commander[15] manages to keep his anger and frustration in check and thereby avert a bloody feud between himself and a civil leader whom he does not respect. The story was published in September 1930, a very troublesome time for the Chinese Communist movement, and it showed an acute awareness of the perils attendant on the actions of a political outlaw.

The original Lin Ch'ung story, occupying nearly seven chapters in *The Water Margin* (chs. 7–12 and 19) is one of the all-time favorites of Chinese audiences. Lin Ch'ung, a military instructor of the Imperial Guards in the Eastern Capital of the Northern Sung Dynasty, has married a beautiful wife and enjoys comfort and security. One day the dissolute adopted son of Grand Marshal Kao happens to see the wife in public and takes an immediate fancy to her. This is the beginning of Lin Ch'ung's troubles. Young Kao conspires with his lackeys to entrap Lin Ch'ung in a criminal offence, and Lin Ch'ung is tricked into carrying a weapon into the White Tiger Hall where arms are strictly forbidden. As a consequence he is arrested, branded, and sentenced to exile. The lackeys bribe his guards to murder him en route to his place of exile. When the attempt fails, another scheme is concocted to burn him to death in his sleep. When Lin Ch'ung finally becomes aware of the designs on his life, he kills the conspiring lackeys. Now, guilty of murder, he has no recourse but to join the bandits in the Liang-shan marshes.

The traditional Lin Ch'ung story up to the killing of the conspirators occupies five and a half chapters in *The Water Margin* and is a classic example of how a perfectly innocent man can be driven to open revolt by extreme social injustice and political persecution; hence the proverbial folk defense of lawless behavior, "driven to Liang-shan" *(pi-shang-Liang-shan).*

"Lin Ch'ung the Leopard Head," however, does not take its plot from any of these traditional incidents that drive Lin Ch'ung to Liang-shan. Mao Tun's story begins after Lin Ch'ung's arrival at Liang-shan; by that time he is no longer a citizen with a place in society but an outlaw. Clearly Mao Tun's tale is not about the workings of political corruption and injustice.

In *The Water Margin* version, Lin Ch'ung's trouble was not over after his arrival at Liang-shan. Driven out of a corrupt society, he is still well within the world of universal human iniquity. The bandit leader Wang Lun, nicknamed Scholar-in-White,[16] is jealous of Lin's martial skills and sees in him a potential rival. As a deterrent Wang makes his admission into the bandit gang conditional on offering the head of a passer-by. Yang Chih happens to pass by on the third day.[17] Wang Lun, watching the fight, is impressed by Yang Chih's prowess and decides to enlist Yang Chih into his service to counter-balance the threat from Lin Ch'ung. He stops the fight, and invites Yang Chih back to the fortress, but Yang Chih declines and continues his journey. Several chapters later, Ch'ao Kai, a wealthy landowner known for his sympathy and generosity to outlaw-heroes, takes refuge at Liang-shan and is given the same cold reception Lin Ch'ung previously received. Angry at Ch'ao Kai's treatment, Lin Ch'ung no longer hesitates to draw his sword and kills Wang Lun, the mean, imposturing bandit leader. A new leader has appeared, and to Lin Ch'ung's mind the time is ripe for a change of leadership.

Mao Tun's "Lin Ch'ung the Leopard Head" begins on the night of the third day after Lin Ch'ung arrives in Liang-shan. Lin Ch'ung's fight with Yang Chih is halted, and Yang Chih, who has just declined Wang Lun's invitation to join the outlaws, is resting in the guest quarters for the night. The parallel between Mao Tun's story and its original breaks off at this point. What follows is entirely Mao Tun's invention.

As the story opens, the crisis of Lin Ch'ung's cold reception by Wang Lun is past. Lin Ch'ung is alone at night, ruminating over his situation. A year ago he himself had been thinking the very same thoughts Yang Chih expressed earlier in the day—aspiring to a secure position under the patronage of the powers in court. But now he finds Yang Chih's ambitions contemptible. A peasant in origin, Lin Ch'ung recalls the ruin of his parents under the burden of heavy taxation and landlord exploitation. His own career as a military officer has been wrecked by corrupt court officials. Fully convinced that Yang Chih, in spite of the fact that he comes from a family of generals, will eventually suffer the same fate at the hands of those powerful at court, Lin Ch'ung can feel nothing but scorn for Yang Chih's naive resolve to curry favor with them. He feels a surge of "latent peasant rebelliousness in his blood;" someday he will certainly avenge the wrongs done to himself and to his family. His thoughts then turn to Wang Lun.

> He was not at all afraid of bloodshed, but he would not kill without a good reason. Therefore, when that Scholar-in-White, Wang Lun, refused to accept him and demanded from him some "formal application for admission," he felt from the bottom of his heart that this unscrupulous scoundrel of a scholar was no different from Kao Ch'iu, the Grand Marshal. The only difference was that he, Wang Lun, lived in the marshes.[18]

Lin Ch'ung's thoughts then swing back to Yang Chih. His anger suddenly wells up. He must kill him. Sword in hand, Lin Ch'ung begins to walk toward the guest sleeping quarters. "But which one am I going to kill?" Lin Ch'ung stops in his tracks at this unexpected self-questioning. Is he going to kill Yang Chih? The idea of killing a man while he is asleep repels him. Then is he to kill Wang Lun? Wang Lun is truly an impostor, a pretender to leadership, every inch a knave and a coward. His own family suffered a series of losses because of scholars. It seems to Lin Ch'ung that scholars are bastards, whether or not they are bandits at the same time.

With renewed indignation, Lin Ch'ung quickens his steps in the direction of the place where Wang Lun is sleeping. Then he stops a second time. Two watchmen who see him hurrying with sword in hand demand to know if he is practicing his martial arts at that late hour. He suddenly realizes that he is no longer in the world of White Tiger Hall, and that if he kills either Wang Lun or Yang Chih and creates disorder among the bandits, he will not have another Liang-shan to go to. Flushed to the ears, he realizes, to his embarrassment that in spite of his consummate martial skill, he has not been gifted with comparable intelligence:

> In this eight hundred square *li* of the Liang-shan marshes, in this sanctuary for the oppressed, there is a need for a pair of iron arms, but there is an even greater need for a great mind.[19]

Lin Ch'ung's anger subsides when he realizes his personal limitations. Wang Lun admittedly is by no means a worthy leader of the Liang-shan bandits. But who else is? He, Lin Ch'ung, has no such ambitions, much less the ability. It is better to wait, then; someday the "true emperor" is sure to appear. On this note the story ends.

Mao Tun's Lin Ch'ung bears little resemblance to the simple and forthright hero of *The Water Margin*. As a work of imaginative fiction, "Lin Ch'ung the Leopard Head" compares poorly with the original both in vividness of characterization and in force of narrative flow. To comprehend its thematic thrust and the meaning of the new Lin Ch'ung, we need to know why Mao Tun chose to write such a piece.

Mao Tun's choice of the feud between Wang Lun and Lin Ch'ung as the center of his story offers an important clue to his theme: it is about the tension and political rivalry among rebel leaders. When the story begins, Lin Ch'ung is already on the wrong side of the law, confronting his first test of survival in a rebel community. Wang Lun's rebuff and the encounter with Yang Chih brings on a state of crisis. Lin is deeply distressed by his discovery that leadership at Liang-shan falls short of his expectations: Wang Lun does not respect genuine merit, and he stands for no principle of justice or brotherhood. What is Lin Ch'ung to do under the circumstances? Mao Tun's exploration of Lin Ch'ung's situation at Liang-shan is cast in the form of interior dialogue, a probing record of Lin Ch'ung's mind. This is a device that permits the author to bring new issues to bear on the question of internal rivalry in a closed community, without significantly altering the traditional plot.

One of the new issues raised in Lin Ch'ung's stream of consciousness which deserves special attention is the matter of "class background *(ch'u-shen)*."[20] Mao Tun invented a class background for each of the main characters in the story. Lin Ch'ung is of peasant ancestry; Yang Chih comes from a family of generals; and Wang Lun is a member of the literati class. The concept of class does not exist in *The Water Margin*, with its established vantage point of classless "brotherhood." Nevertheless, Lin Ch'ung involves his class background and class history to define the cause of the antagonism between himself and Yang Chih and Wang Lun (such antagonisms will be dramatized in more explicit and explosive form in "The Great Marsh District" and "Stone Tablet"). This is the key to the difference between the new Lin Ch'ung and the traditional military commander of *The Water Margin.*

All three characters in "Lin Ch'ung the Leopard Head" have suffered reverses in their lives before they are brought together at Liang-shan. Yet the effects on these men, which are brought out in their confrontations, are quite different. Yang Chih, because of his family tradition, clings to the illusory hope of resuming his post at court. Wang Lun has been forced to abandon the career of a low-ranking literatus-administrator but retains his narrow, selfish vision in a new context by concentrating his small abilities on remaining leader of his little empire. Neither has learned from experience to reflect on the general cause of his individual suffering and displacement. Lin Ch'ung is the only one who is able to think in collective terms and to relate his personal experience to collective suffering as exemplified by the experience of his peasant ancestors.

Mao Tun has not fully developed the concept of "class" in his depiction of Lin Ch'ung's thought. It is historically and novelistically impossible for him at this point to transform Lin Ch'ung completely into a hero of the peasant class. Nonetheless, it is by means of his collective thinking that Lin Ch'ung is able to transcend the particular circumstance of his suffering (as a military commander and not as an exploited peasant) and to begin to think of himself as a member of a *class.* Once class consciousness awakens, and once he feels the "latent peasant rebelliousness in his blood," Lin Ch'ung is no longer the same person as the military commander of White Tiger Hall days and the *Water Margin* tradition. It is with his new consciousness as a peasant that he determines to someday avenge the wrongs done to himself and his family and it is also with his new peasant consciousness that he feels a historical (not merely a personal) hatred toward Wang Lun, who, aside from being an impostor and a usurper of the Liang-shan leadership, now also symbolizes the natural enemies of the peasants—literati as gentry and as lower government officials who collect rents and impose heavy taxes.

When Lin Ch'ung stops at the sudden thought of the White Tiger Hall, it is not entirely clear what Mao Tun intends to show. A provisional explanation is the very practical and immediate consideration of personal survival. But from Lin Ch'ung's subsequent thoughts, we can see that group survival is also prominent in his mind ("In this eight hundred square *li* of the Liang-shan marshes . . . there is even greater need for a great mind"). His final resolution not to act is not a sign of personal passivity and weakness, then, but a form of positive action. Lin Ch'ung has recognized the potential of timely collective action in the future and the danger of untimely individual action. If he cannot lead the heterogeneous group of Liang-shan bandits ably and successfully himself, he can at least avoid a crisis of leadership by eschewing a rash show of individual heroism and individualistic moral indignation.

Lin Ch'ung's change from a warrior hero in *The Water Margin* to a thoughtful peasant turned military leader in "Lin Ch'ung the Leopard Head" is fundamentally a change of political consciousness, an expansion from individual values to a collective goal as the basis of politically responsible action. Lin Ch'ung's final forbearance in Mao Tun's story, in contrast to his killing of Wang Lun in the traditional version, shows that he is not only capable of deeds of anger and valor, but is also able to think in terms of the larger cause and control his anger for the sake of a goal that is important not only to himself but also to his potential fellow rebels. Lin Ch'ung has become a mature revolutionary leader.

"The Great Marsh District"

"The Great Marsh District" is inspired by Ssu-ma Ch'ien's historical account of Ch'en She's rebellion in 209 B.C. against the tyrannical Ch'in Dynasty. Here again Mao Tun changes and rearranges the elements of the story to bring out his new theme of conflicting class interests. The original events took place not in an administrative center but in the countryside. Mao Tun surely had that in mind when he chose the Ch'en She story as a vehicle for his own thoughts on the development of the peasant movement in the countryside in 1930.[21]

Ssu-ma Ch'ien's chapter on Ch'en She is another story of men forced outside the law by harsh social circumstances. Ch'en She was a farm laborer with dreams of glory. He and Wu Kuang were among a group of nine hundred men conscripted for garrison duty at Yü-yang, where they had to arrive by the appointed time on pain of death. On the road, escorted by Ch'in army officers, they encountered heavy rains, which made further progress impossible; obviously they could not meet the deadline. Ch'en She and Wu Kuang decided, "Since we stand to die anyway, why not die fighting for our country?" that is, as supporters of the State of Ch'u against the State of Ch'in.

To further their plan, Chen She and Wu Kuang began to fabricate supernatural portents. Conscripts eating a fish for dinner discovered in its belly a piece of silk with the inscription "Ch'en She shall be king." Near their camp at night, the conscripts heard a fox (actually Wu Kuang imitating a fox) crying, "Ch'en She shall be king." Having thus built up Ch'en She's prestige and implanted awe among the ranks, Ch'en She and Wu Kuang killed the army officers and rallied the conscripts to their cause. Ch'en She had great military success but became arrogant and arbitrary. Within six months his original followers were disaffected; he was defeated in battle and killed by his own men. Nevertheless, the Grand Historian Ssu-ma Ch'ien commented, "Although Ch'en She himself died very early, the various rulers and commanders whom he set up and dispatched on expeditions eventually succeeded in overthrowing the Ch'in."[22] Clearly, Ssu-ma Ch'ien saw Ch'en She's life and deeds as those of an individual hero; *he* was the planner and the leader; the rebellion was *his* accomplishment. Ssu-ma Ch'ien saw history as being shaped by great men. Mao Tun moves the human dynamics from the leadership level to the masses. He has kept the bare bones of the original story. "The Great Marsh District" begins with the heavy rainfall and the resulting predicament. The counterfeit omens of fish and fox are also present, designating Ch'en She as future king. But Ch'en She and Wu Kuang are no longer at center stage. The rebellion, when it occurs, is *spontaneous*, arising from the conscripts' realization that they too have a right to live. Moreover, Mao Tun introduces two new elements that drastically reorient the political message of the story. One new element is the class background of the characters.[23] Mao Tun has made the two army officers escorting the conscripts descendants of generals and members of the wealthy landowning class. He has also, rather unsuccessfully, ascribed peasant origins to all of the nine hundred conscripts. This addition of class background serves to change the original struggle between Ch'en She and the Ch'in dynasty into a confrontation of forces represented by the conscripts and the officers respectively.

The second new element is class consciousness, which is projected as an identification of self-interest with the common interest of a group to which the individuals feel they belong. The conflict of interest between officers and conscripts that is brought on by the heavy rain constitutes the dramatic core of Mao Tun's version of the uprising. It is presented in the first two sections of the story by a juxtaposition of the thoughts and aspirations of the two groups when they contemplate the consequences of failing to meet the deadline at Yü-yang. It is clear that common predicament and common destiny are not the same thing. In "Lin Ch'ung the

Leopard Head," we have already seen one instance of how people sharing a common fate—Wang Lun, Yang Chih, and Lin Ch'ung as outlaws—do not necessarily work toward a common destiny. "The Great Marsh District" recapitulates the same motif in even more explicit terms. The rain, the fox cries, and the missing of the deadline at Yü-yang provoke very different reactions from the officers and the conscripts.

The two officers are annoyed by the heavy rain. Unable to fulfill their assigned delivery of the conscripts to Yü-yang, they begin to consider the consequences. Members of a prestigious social class, they make no identification of interest whatever with the conscripts; their military commissions are their birthright and their class privilege. Usually the men they lead are men of their own class, landowners like themselves, "youths from their own villages, bound together by class loyalties." But today they are commanding mere conscripts, "contemptible slaves who never before had the right to serve as soldiers, rabble with no feeling at all for their officers' status."[24]

As the rain falls day after day, the officers worry about two things. First, there is the deadline, and missing it is punishable by death under military law. But being officers with powerful connections in court, they know pretty well how to avoid most punishments. Then there are the nine hundred conscripts. "Another seven days of rain, and all nine hundred of them would die of hunger. But before that happened, was there anything the conscripts would not dare to do when they found themselves threatened with starvation?"[25] The rumors about Ch'en She, the portentous piece of silk, and the fox cries are much less threatening. The officers recognize in Ch'en She a handsome figure for a peasant, and possibly a good fighter too, but "the greater danger," to their minds, "lay not in Ch'en She but in the rain," and in what action the rain was likely to provoke from the doomed conscripts.

Mao Tun now turns to the class background and the thoughts and fears of the nine hundred. The conscripts are not at all happy about the heavy rain. On the one hand, they are not enthusiastic about going to Yü-yang:

> The conscripts originally had been peasants in the six kingdoms conquered by the state of Ch'in. . . . They were slaves now, conscripts who had to plunder for the rich landowners the 'free citizens' of the powerful state of Ch'in. Weren't they going to Yü-yang to protect these free citizens who held them in such contempt, to win booty for rich landowners like their officers? And weren't they going to put their poor men's bones in mortal combat against the Hsiung-nu—nomads moving south in search of pastures—in order to turn them into slaves like themselves?[26]

On the other hand, they know that if they do not get to Yü-yang in time, death will be their lot. Caught in this dilemma, the conscripts for the first time begin to think about their own position and choices.

They have heard the weird cries of the fox in the night, and they knew about the inscribed strip of silk found in the belly of the fish. Like their officers, the conscripts are not overimpressed by these supernatural omens:

> . . . these things the nine hundred conscripts considered uncanny. But that was as far as their ideas went. They had had more than their share of strife because this one or that one had wanted to be king. Their only desire was to be free again.[27]

But there is another prophecy which the conscripts are more interested in:

> Hadn't a stone fallen from the sky two years before inscribed with these words: "When the First Emperor dies, the land will be divided"? And hadn't the wizard who lives east of Hua Mountain and drives a chariot with a white horse predicted, "The Dragon Emperor will die next year"? Well, the First Emperor of Ch'in had died and been succeeded by the Second. Now was the time to realize the part of the prophecy about dividing the land.[28]

Land, unquestionably, has a fundamentally different kind of appeal to peasants than does fighting for another king. In the following description of the conscripts' thought, Mao Tun defines what he understands to be the social and moral basis of mass uprising.

> It seemed to the nine hundred conscripts that the only thing worth risking their lives for was the joy of planting their own land. They were not interested in 'Emperor Ch'en She.' If they had to go on having emperors, they wanted one who would be different from the Old Emperor, one who would give them land of their own to till.[29]

It is the simple and spontaneous desire of the peasants to own their own land and partake freely of the joy of farming that is the decisive motive in bringing them to participate in an uprising. People may sometimes be rallied to action by their fear and hatred of dark exploitative forces, and they may sometimes be rallied by their natural admiration of heroic leaders. But for the common masses, it is the positive hope for a better ordinary life of labor with the assurance of their daily needs being met that has the broadest appeal and the greatest sustaining power after the first and easily dissipated wave of hatred and admiration. Mao Tun has shown in "Lin Ch'ung the Leopard Head," and is going to show again in "Stone Tablet," that without the masses at the base, without their weight behind the momentum, and without their interest in the collective goal, all historical rebellions are no more than a game of intrigue, played for the sake of individual interests by would-be kings posing as popular heroes.

This, not Ch'en She's heroism and defeat as in Ssu-ma Ch'ien's *Records,* is the new political message of "Great Marsh District."

The outcome of "The Great Marsh District" is predictable. The officers, realizing that "they could not stand with folded hands . . . and wait for the hatred of the slaves to rise and throw them into the flood," decide to do away with the nine hundred before it is too late. The conscripts, in their simple way, also conclude that "If we stay here, we'll starve. If we get to Yü-yang late, we'll die too. But if we act together we will all live."[30] In the climactic scene of physical confrontation, the officers are killed by the representative hero of the peasants, Wu Kuang. The better known traditional hero, Ch'en She, is not in the picture as the story ends on a resounding note of hope for the millions like the nine hundred: "The Emperor is dead! The land will be divided!" The story of Ch'en She the leader has turned into a story of his peasant followers.

"Stone Tablet"

The last of the historical tales again takes as its point of departure a section of *The Water Margin.* Mao Tun adapts from chapter 39 and chapter 71 of the novel. Chapter 39 tells about a legal clerk, Sung Chiang, nicknamed Timely Rain because of his ready assistance to any outlaw in bad straits, and the subversive verse he once in drunkenness scribbles on the wall of a wine shop and as a consequence is arrested and jailed. Wu Yung, chief adviser and second in command of the Liang-shan bandits, devises a plan to rescue him. By rather devious means, Wu recruits two skilled craftsmen, the master seal carver Chin Ta-chien and the calligrapher Hsiao Jang, who, before Wu Yung lures them to Liang-shan, are both solid citizens in town. As part of the plan to get Sung Chiang out of jail, they forge a letter with an official seal. But the forgeries are detected, the plan falls through, and Sung Chiang, at the end of the chapter, is in even worse trouble because of Wu Yung's effort.

Later, however, Sung Chiang is rescued from execution and becomes the bandits' leader. In chapter 71, an epilogue to the seventy-chapter version of *The Water Margin,* the ground is opened up by a thunderbolt from Heaven and a stone tablet is found. On it are inscribed the names of the hundred and eight leading Liang-shan bandits in the hierarchical order of the stars with which they are associated in Heaven. Sung Chiang's name is at the head of the list as a sign of the Mandate of Heaven.

Mao Tun borrows the two characters Hsiao Jang and Chin Ta-chien and fragments of their deeds from chapter 39 and throws them together with the stone tablet story from chapter 71. The way he does it totally undermines "Heaven's will," which in the original is the justification for power among rebel leaders. The narrative content—a dialogue between

Chin and Hsiao on the subject of political intrigue and morality—is entirely Mao Tun's creation. What links his tale to the original is that he uses a situation of bandit leaders in conspiracy as the point of departure for his own story.

At the beginning of "Stone Tablet," Chin Ta-chien is carving a stone tablet as Hsiao Jang looks on. As the scene develops, we learn from their conversation that the tablet is the instrument of a secret scheme concocted by chief adviser Wu Yung.[31] Evidently there has been serious disagreement among different factions of the bandits over who should be their paramount leader. The controversy threatens to destroy the unity of the whole group and thus jeopardize its survival. The tablet will be "discovered" in the ground—a fabricated message from Heaven like the fox cries in the Ch'en She story—and is intended to settle peacefully the hierarchy of rank among the bandit leaders of Liang-shan.

As Chin carves, he chuckles to himself, and Hsiao Jang begins to worry about Chin's attitude toward his task. Wishing to be sure of Chin's total commitment to the project, Hsiao Jang repeatedly insists upon its importance and the need for secrecy. Chin says nothing. In fact, Hsiao is worried about whether this stratagem violates the principle of justice and equality among brothers and smacks of dishonest intrigue. To his mind, the ranking of brothers, even in the interest of group discipline, should be put to an open vote. But now that the vote is out of the question, Hsiao supports Wu Yung's scheme and wishes to be sure of Chin's feelings on the subject, and so he asks Chin's opinion on the relative merits and faults of their superiors. Chin expresses a thought that has long been in his mind: "People tend to go in groups. Those close to Squire Lu would naturally favor Lu." Hsiao quickly corrects him, saying, "No, no! Only those from the same class background as Squire Lu hold him in higher esteem."[32] Chin looked bewildered, and so Hsiao patiently analyzes for him the two main groups of bandits at Liang-shan in terms of their backgrounds and functions: those who come from the nonpropertied class and had lived by mean and disreputable professions, and those who come from a background of wealth and power and had occupied high and influential positions. Among the former group, Hsiao mentions various shiftless characters, lakeside thieves, a cutthroat innkeeper, and an itinerant Taoist; among the latter group he mentions two former government generals and Squire Lu himself, who had at first opposed the gathering of the bandits at Liang-shan and then himself "driven" to join them.

Having heard Hsiao's analysis, Chin is still noncommittal about adviser Wu's scheme. Hsiao now tries to justify it in terms of "carrying out the way of Heaven" and "demonstrating the will of Heaven." His skepticism aroused, Chin throws a question back at Hsiao: "Leaving aside all the other questions, just let me ask you this: To what group do *we* belong?"[33] Hsiao winces at Chin's abruptness. He has no ready answer.

He cannot quite bring himself to endorse brother Sung Chiang's group, even though he is caught up in the plan for a forged mandate. Seeing Hsiao's embarrassment, Chin bursts out laughing and answers his own question, saying that he himself belongs to no group. He follows orders and does what is asked of him, not concerning himself with whose will he is carrying out, be it that of Heaven, Earth, or Man. If there is anything to be said about the "Liang-shan way," then it is Chin Ta-chien's studied opinion that self-interest is supreme: "You may call it 'class background' if you like. But to me, that [self-interest] is the 'Way of Heaven' we are trying to practice here."[34]

"Stone Tablet" is probably the wittiest of Mao Tun's three historical tales. In it, Mao Tun plays with the method of class analysis with great irony. The stone tablet in the novel, as we know, functions as the ultimate sanction by Heaven of the earthly order of the hundred and eight principal Liang-shan brothers. But "Stone Tablet" deliberately subverts the traditional tale and discloses the human reality behind the myths of bandit leadership. The lucid, dispassionate, and almost sarcastic tone of the dialogue strongly suggest that Mao Tun has finally reconciled himself to the fact that intrigue is an inevitable part of high rebel politics. The moral worth of a rebel group is not to be judged by its political intrigue and intrigue should not be grounds for disparaging a rebel group with a just cause. It is not for an intellectual (like Chin Ta-chien or Hsiao Jang, or himself), whose primary value lies in his professional skill, to question which leader's will he is serving or in what intrigue he is participating. If intrigue in the leadership helps to unify contending groups, and thereby advances the rebel cause, no one should withhold his support because of personal misgivings. When called upon, one may serve the cause unquestioningly, like Chin Ta-chien; or one may go even further, like Hsiao Jang, and try to persuade others to serve, despite one's own reservations.

From Heroics to the Quotidian

The three historical tales are not among Mao Tun's major fictional works. But it was in these three short pieces that Mao Tun first dramatized the distinction between individual heroism and class interests, and between individual morality and collective goals.

He has settled his quarrel with the revolutionary movement in the final affirmation of "The Great Marsh District." He has decided that the welfare of the oppressed masses, of which the poor peasants are the majority in China, is ultimately the collective goal of all dedicated rebels, be they leaders or followers. Feuds and intrigues among leaders are common features of any political body. It is not always possible to judge the justice of the cause of a body by the morality of its leadership and the righteousness of its means. But when such a decision must be made, Mao Tun has shown in the interplay between his tales and their historical sources what the choices are and on what grounds they should be based.

After the three historical pieces Mao Tun wrote the short novels *The Road* and *In Company of Three* as his final examinations of the problem of factional struggle. Subsequently he turned his attention to the daily life of plain people, beginning with sketches and short stories of people who reside outside the isntellectual realm—hoodlums, pirates, vagabonds, and gangsterlike local bullies.[35]

In December 1932, Mao Tun wrote in "In Retrospect":

> I am confident that . . . I will never dare to forget the social significance of literature. . . . This is no longer a time when fiction is to be treated as something for amusement. Therefore, a fiction writer needs not only broad life experience; he must also have a disciplined mind that is capable of analyzing complex social phenomena. Especially in our rapidly changing society, those who have not seriously studied social science [Marxism] generally cannot correctly analyze them. What society urgently demands from our writers is precisely a correct and purposeful reflection of those social phenomena.[36]

Mao Tun in the early 1930s clearly recognized the economic nature of politics. To him revolutionary literature is no longer a realm where things are measured by moral standards determined by personal emotions or inherited from the past. Politics is not ethics. Success in political matters generally comes from a proper balancing of economic interests, not merely from people who can be martyrs for absolute moral good and evil. Martyrs who do not understand the relationship of politics to economic interests have no place in political struggles. In contemporary China, they can at most become fictional legendary figures,[37] or, worse, a radical in words who is really a romantic stereotype. In humanistic terms, they are representatives of a historical epoch, the crystallized images of certain social phenomena in a dated time. They are dramatic characters on the way to revolution, but not revolutionaries.

There were no supermen among those deeply involved in the Chinese revolution up to the beginning of the 1930s. At least Mao Tun saw no superman. They were the Devil's Clique, the Scholar's Clique, and the overbearing and corrupt school administrator Dean Thorn *(The Road)*, all of them Mao Tun's allegorical representations of the forever feuding factions within the CCP.[38]

The creative work of Mao Tun in the 1930s no longer depicts the political action and moral consciousness of heroes. As he turns from "students" and would-be revolutionaries to tradition-bound and "new" women, and from heroes old and remade to the life experiences of workers, peasants, and petty bourgeois, along with the economic factors that underlie their behavior and ethics, Mao Tun has moved from politics to society to economic, from ideals to reality to mass-as-center. There is a clear record of this change in his creative work, essays, and literary criticism of 1932 to 1942.

This second period of his creative life is soundly based on that first creative flow of hope-despair-new hope, the years 1927–1930 in the life of a young, growing writer. Indeed, the second period is so closely connected to the first that it may not be presumptuous to say that the first period, with which we have been concerned in this book, ends with a resolution of many of the contradictions that the pen name implies, and an even more important recognition that some contradictions are part of life, perhaps especially radical life. Some may even be desirable as well as permanent. The pen name assumed in confusion, elation, and despair will not be discarded during a long life that saw both oppression and triumph. The name Mao Tun still identifies the author of the last document, the *Memoirs*, written at the end of his life, when he was fully recognized as one of the enduring figures of modern Chinese literature.

APPENDIX: INTERVIEW WITH MAO TUN

In September 1977, I heard that my visa application to China to see Mao Tun had been approved. At that time, none of my friends believed that Mao Tun would consent to see me. He had not received any foreign visitors since the mid-1960s and there was no reason why he should want at that juncture to divulge his rigorously guarded secrets about his early life and political activities to a stranger. I, however, held on to my conviction that no writer of Mao Tun's stature would want to have his most important works forever misunderstood. If his early novels and stories were about the Chinese Communist movement, then he would want to have that fact known.

I arrived in Peking on September 17, 1977. At first there was no news on my request. Then one evening when I was having dinner at my brother-in-law's house, a message came that I should pack to leave for Ta-chai early the next morning, but before I left, I should leave behind in writing the questions I wanted to ask Mao Tun. I was quite tipsy when I got the message, having drunk more than half a bottle of the er-kuo-t'ou (a strong liquor distilled from sorghum) my host had procured as a particular treat for me. I had no idea that Mao Tun himself would read my questions. I assumed that his assistant or some security officials would do the screening.

When I got back to the hotel that night, it was already past eleven. I had no paper with me so I tore several pages out of my Chinese diarybook. As I was writing my questions, it completely escaped my mind that Mao Tun had served since 1949 as Minister of Culture. I only remembered him as a writer of the 1920s, the author of the Eclipse *trilogy and* The Wild Roses. *What I wanted to know from him more than anything else was if he had in his early fiction been writing about his active participation in Party affairs and if, for instance, Miss Huan in "Suicide" was a different projection of Shih Hsün in* Pursuit. *My husband thought that my drunken handwriting was a disgrace; he took over the pen and wrote over some of the less legible characters.*

After I came back from Ta-chai, I was told that Mao Tun would see me at 2 P.M. on September 29 at Conference Room 4 in the Political Consultative Conference Building. Three of us went—myself, my husband, and an escort. As we approached the designated room, I saw three people standing in the doorway. Mao Tun was at the center, a walking stick in his hand. He handed me four pages of written response to my questions. I looked at the pages and saw the neatly written lines. Later during the two-and-a-half-hour interview Mao Tun told me that he was almost blind in his left eye and that the vision in his right eye was very much impaired. He had to use a magnifying glass to do his reading and writing. I thought about my unruly scribbles and felt utterly ashamed.

That day Mao Tun did not directly admit to anything about his political activities in the 1920s. But from what he told me about the company he had kept in those critical months in 1927 (for example, he would say that he conferred with Tung Pi-wu in Wuhan and "ran into" Li Li-san in Nan-ch'ang), I knew that he was the very high-level Party propagandist I had earlier postulated him to be.

In June 1979, my article on The Wild Roses *was published. In the same month, I had a chance to forward to Mao Tun a copy each of my three studies of his "Autumn in Kuling,"* The Wild Roses, *and the three historical tales. In September of that year, Mao Tun began to publish his "Memoirs." I never learned what connection, if any, existed between the publication of his "Memoirs" and his covert activities as a Party coworker having already been exposed to an irrefutable degree in the West.*

The questions I wrote in September 1977 and Mao Tun's answers were his first exchange with an outsider on the covert content of his early fiction and may be of historical and biographical interest to scholars in the field.

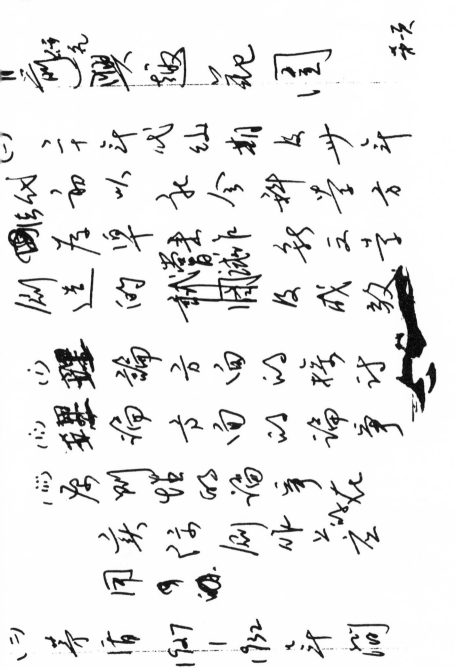

(二) 問題

(i) ...

(ii) ...

(iii) ...

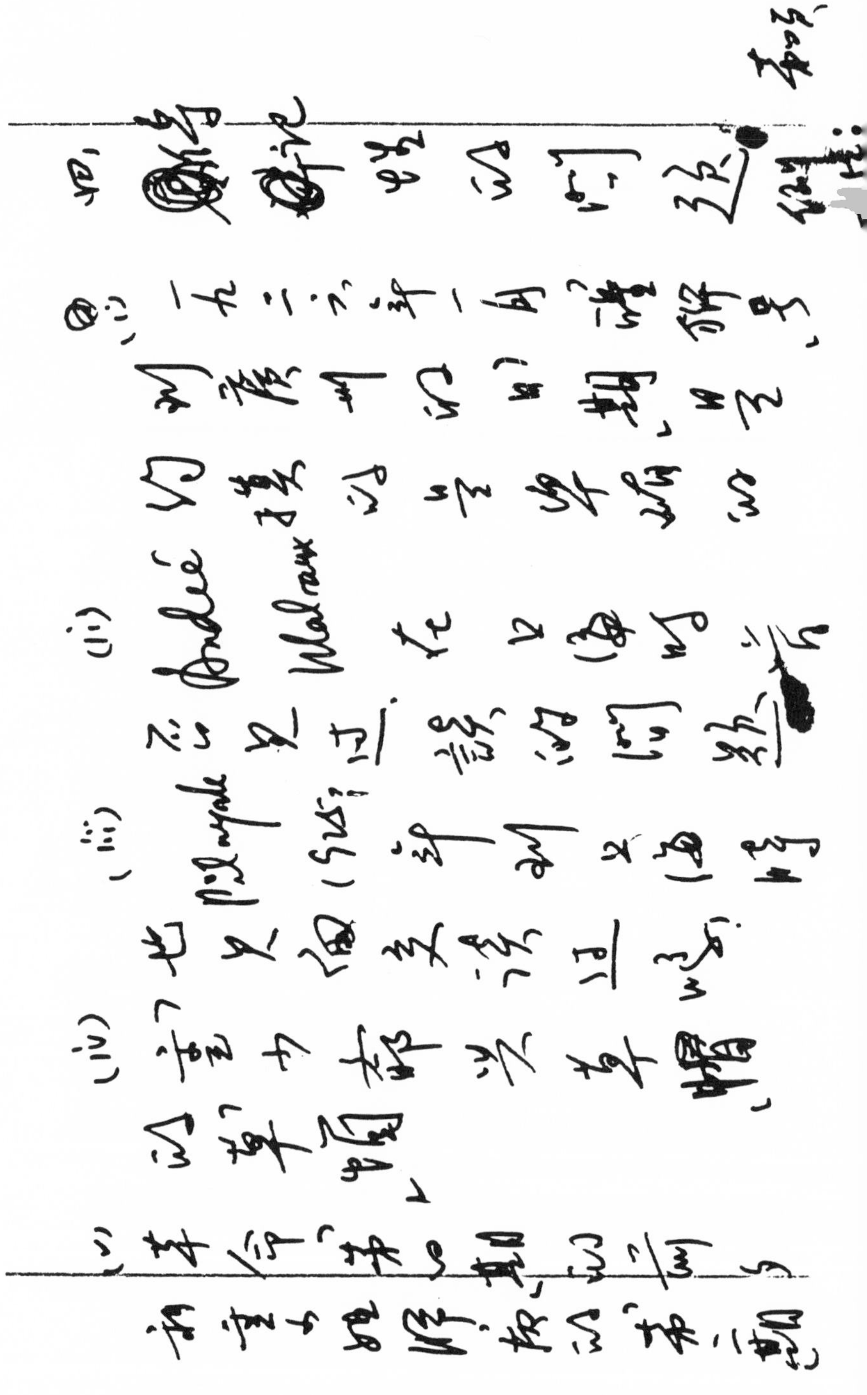

NOTES

1. From Shen Yen-ping to Mao Tun:
Literature–Politics–Literature

1. *Mingpao Monthly* 119 (Hongkong, November 1975), pp.10–11. Paul Bady, "Should Chinese People be Awarded the Nobel Prize for Literature?" Translated by Ho Ch'i. The list of names reads:

AUBERT Claude	Att. Rech.	INRA
AUBIN Francoise	Mait. Rech.	CNRS
BADY Paul	Mait. Ass.	ENS (Ulm)
BASTID-BRUGUIERE Marianne	Mait. Rech.	CNRS
BERGERE Marie-Claire	Prof.	INLCO-Paris III
BISSAT Violette	Mait. Ass.	INLCO-Paris III
BOULNOIS Lucette	Ing.	CNRS
BOURGEOIS Pénelope	Mait. Ass.	Paris VII
CARTIER Michel	Mait. Ass.	Hautes Etudes
DAVID Madeleine	Chargée mission	Musée Guimet
ETIEMBLE René	Ecrivain, prof.	Paris III
HERVOUET Yves	Prof.	Paris VIII
HOLZMAN Donald	Dir. Et.	Hautes Etudes
JIDKOFF Georges	Chef Trav.	Hautes Etudes
LARRE R. P.		Institut Ricci
LEVY André	Mait. Conf.	Bordeaux
MAGNIN Paul	Att. Rech.	CNRS
PIRAZZOLI-T'SERSTEVENS Michele	Conservateur	Musée Guimet
PUYRAIMOND Guy	Mait. Ass.	INLCO-Paris III
ROUX Alain	Mait. Ass.	Paris VIII
SCHIPPER Kristofer	Dir. Et.	Hautes Etudes
SOYMIE Michel	Dir. Et.	Hautes Etudes
TCHANG Fou-jouei	Mait. Ass.	Paris VII
THOMAS Léon	Mait. Conf.	Lyon III
TROLLIET Pierre	Mait. Ass.	Paris X
VALLETTE-HEMERY Martine	Professeur certifié	
VANDERMEERSCH Léon	Prof.	Paris VII
WILL Pierre-Etienne	Chef Trav.	Hautes Etudes
WU Chi-yu	Charge Rech.	CNRS

2. Donald W. Klein and Anne B. Clark (eds.), *Biographic Dictionary of Chinese Communism 1921–1965*, 2 vols. (Cambridge, Mass., Harvard University Press, 1971), vol. 2, pp.759–764.
According to Mao Tun's "Memoirs VI," *Source Materials on the History of the*

New Literature (January 1980), Mao Tun met Mao Tse-tung for the first time on August 5, 1923, when the latter attended the sixth meeting of the Executive Committee of the Greater Shanghai Region as a delegate from the CCP Central Committee. In 1924, when the Shanghai Executive Department of the reorganized and expanded KMT was formed, Mao Tse-tung became secretary of its Organization Department. This means that the two of them had already worked together in Shanghai in 1923–24 in propaganda and organizing work.

3. A fuller autobiography, entitled *Roads I Have Traveled,* which does start with Mao Tun's ancestry and childhood and includes a whole chapter on his marriage, was published in Hong Kong by the Joint Publishing Company in August 1981. Why the book was published in Hongkong and not by the People's Literature Press in Peking, which has been publishing all of Mao Tun's official editions, is a fascinating new puzzle for students of the politics of publication in China. To me it indicates that the authorities in China felt some urgency in getting the official version of Mao Tun's life and works during the 1920s on the public record in China, before Western research outruns what is being done at home. Mao Tun, *Wo tzou-kuo ti tao-lu (Roads I Have Traveled)* (Hongkong, Joint Publishing Co., 1981).

4. K'ung Ch'ang (pseudonym), "Biography of Hauptmann," "Hauptmann's Naturalistic Writing," and "Hauptmann's Symbolist Writing." All three articles were published in *Short Story Monthly* 13.6 (June 1922), a month before Mao Tun's famous article, "Naturalism and Modern Chinese Fiction."

5. Matsui Hiromitsu (ed.), *Collection of Mao Tun's Critical Essays* (Mao Tun p'ing-lun chi), 5 vols., and *A Bibliographical Supplement to Mao Tun's Critical Essays* (Tokyo, 1957–1966). Professor Hiromitsu's bibliographical effort continues with *A Bibliography of Mao Tun's Creative Writing, Critical Essays and Prose Works* (Tokyo, 1974–76) of which only the first two volumes have appeared.

6. Mao Tun, "Memoirs I" (Hongkong, May 1979), pp.8–9.

7. Mao Tun, "Memoirs II," *Source Materials* (Hongkong, August 1979), p.52.

8. *Ibid.,* pp.52–53.

9. Mao Tun, "Chi-chü chiu-hua" ("Remarks on the Past"), *Yin-hsiang, kan-hsiang, hui-i (Reflections and Reminiscences)* (Shanghai, 1936), pp.1–5.

10. Mao Tun, "Memoirs II." For the Saturday School of popular literature, also known as the Mandarin Duck and Butterfly School, see Perry Link's excellent *Mandarin Ducks and Butterflies: Popular Fiction in Early Twentieth-century Chinese Cities* (Berkeley: University of California Press, 1981).

11. *Ibid.*

12. Mao Tun, *Midnight* (abridged), translated by Hsu Meng-hsiung (Peking, Foreign Language Press, 1957).

In the West, C. T. Hsia's chapter on Mao Tun illustrates the standard view held of *Midnight* outside of China. See C. T. Hsia, "Mao Tun," *A History of Modern Chinese Fiction 1917–1957* (New Haven: Yale University Press, 1961) pp.155–160.

In China, the high evaluation of *Midnight* began with the short essay by Ch'ü Ch'iu-po, "*Tzu-yeh* ho kuo-huo-nien" ("*Midnight* and the Year for Chinese Native Goods"), *Collected Works of Ch'ü Ch'iu-po,* vol. 2, pp.435–438. Ch'ü's praise for *Midnight* was faithfully echoed by most leftist critics in the 1930s and reiterated in both Yeh Tzu-ming's *Mao Tun ssu-shih-nien te wen-hsüeh-tao-lu (On Mao Tun's Forty Years Literary Road)* (Shanghai, Shanghai Wen-i-ch'u-pan-she, 1959) and Shao Po-chou's *Mao Tun te wen-hsueh tao-lu (Mao Tun's Literary Road)* (Ch'ang-chiang-wen-i ch'u-pan-shu, 1959), pp.73–103.

Recently Yüeh Tai-yün of Peking University again expressed the opinion that *Midnight* is a greater work than *Eclipse* in her *"Shih* ho *Tzu-yeh* te pi-chiao fen-hsi" ("A Comparative Analysis of *Erosion* and *Midnight*") (*Wen-hsüeh p'ing-lun* [*Journal of Literary Criticism*]) 1981.1, pp.110–120.
The only critic who differed in his critical appraisal of *Midnight*, as far as I know, is Chu Tzu-ch'ing. In his short essay "On Tzu-yeh," *Literature Quarterly* (*Wen-hsüeh chi-k'an*) II (April 1934), pp.405–498, he wrote:

> In the past few years, we have seen an increase in long novels. Of those, only Mao Tun's *Eclipse* and *Midnight* are able to speak for the time. *Eclipse* deals with the Wuhan of 1927 and Shanghai of 1928; its subject is "the three stages which youth has experienced in the strong tide of revolution." Mao Tun is not the only one who is able to make use of this kind of material, but he is the only one who has done it with considerable success. Under his brush, people appear who are made of flesh and blood, are able to speak their mind and act, not at all flat characters and blurred shadows.
>
> *Midnight* deals with the Shanghai of 1930. Its subject matter is the foreshortened development and collapse of national capitalism. Like *Eclipse*, *Midnight* attempts large-scale analysis and depiction, except that it has a much smaller scope, with a limited emphasis on the "industrial and financial city of Shanghai" and covering a period of only a little more than two months. By this time, the author was more systematic in his observation and more meticulous in his analysis. The first novel [*Eclipse*] was written after the author had experienced the events in life whereas in this case [*Midnight*], the author went to experience life for the sake of writing the novel.
>
> I heard that many of his relatives played around in the stock market and he himself too had been to the stock market many times. This novel of his is the result of careful research, it is not an "impressionistic" work of creative writing. *Eclipse* consists of three novelettes but in all does not have as many pages as *Midnight*. The reason is precisely because of this.

Chu Tzu-ch'ing obviously did not place a well-researched documentary novel above the achievement of one that is deeply felt by the author.
Mao Tun's *Memoirs* also by its discussion of *Eclipse* attests though not in so many words to the fact that his experience as a revolutionary and a CCP member is more central and overwhelming than his two-month observation of the Shanghai stock market. By contrast *Midnight* is dealt with in the installment of *Memoirs* 1981.4 (November 1981) which was published posthumously (#13, in HWHSL). This chapter goes on at great length about the "circumstances" surrounding the writing of *Midnight*. The attention devoted to this work is unprecedented, totally overshadowing Mao Tun's own earlier discussion of *Eclipse*. Since the chapter was published posthumously and its rather unwieldy format differs so strikingly from the chapters published in Mao Tun's lifetime, it is not clear to me how much of the writing was by Mao Tun himself or how much he could have revised the rambling emphasis on *Midnight* before publication. The broad coverage of his revolutionary experiences in the "Memoirs" is not evidence to support the argument that *Eclipse* is a greater novel, but it points out that to Mao Tun it is a more important novel than *Midnight* in his early fiction.
13. Other stories include "Spring Silkworms" (1932), "Autumn Harvest" (1933), and "Lin's Store," which are all widely anthologized. "Lin's Store" was made into a movie in the 1950s. See Mao Tun, *Spring Silkworms and Other Stories*, translated by Sidney Shapiro (Peking, Foreign Language Press, 1956).
14. Chou Erh-fu, "When Critically Ill: In Memory of Comrade Mao Tun," *Shou-huo (Harvest Bimonthly)* 1981.3 (May 1981), pp.86–92. See especially p.90. Chou Erh-fu is himself a novelist. His own four-volume *Shanghai ti tsao-ch'en*

(Morning in Shanghai), a 1,700,000 word novel about the three-anti and five-anti campaigns, was published in its entirety only in 1983.

15. In his recent article, Yeh Tzu-ming listed five possible birth dates and two possible birthplaces for Mao Tun. Since the year of his birth is undisputed, I am not trying to be more specific than that.

Yeh Tzu-ming, "A Few Questions Concerning the Biography of Mao Tun," *Wen-hsüeh p'ing-lun ts'ung-k'an (Collected Essays on Literary Criticism)* 8, Special Issue on Modern Chinese Literature (Peking, 1981).

This part of chapter 1 generally follows the middle part of my article, "Mao Tun and the Use of Political Allegory in Fiction: A Case Study of His 'Autumn in Kuling'," in Merle Goldman (ed.), *Modern Chinese Literature in the May Fourth Era* (Cambridge, Mass., Harvard University Press, 1977). There are some minor changes, and information that has become available with the publication of Mao Tun's "Memoirs" is incorporated.

16. Mao Tun, "Memoirs I," *Source Materials* 1979.1 (Hongkong, May 1979), pp.1–2. A fuller account of his years at Peking University can be found in *Roads I Have Traveled*, pp.79–88; the section on the first years at the Shanghai Commercial Press is the same.

17. According to the "Memoirs," his contact with Marxism had already begun before the arrival of Ch'en. However, it was only after his acquaintance with Ch'en Tu-hsiu that he began to translate what had been an intellectual and patriotic interest in Marxism into concrete action. See "Memoirs IV," *Source Materials* 1980.1 (Hongkong, February 1980), pp.1–2.

18. According to Mao Tun's "Memoirs IV," *ibid.*, the Shanghai Communist Party nucleus *(Kung-ch'an-chu-i hsiao-tsu)* and the Marxist Study Group *(Ma-k'e-ssu-chu-i yen-chiu-hui)* were founded in May 1920 by Ch'en Tu-hsiu, Li Han-chün, Li Ta, Ch'en Wang-tao (translator of the Communist Manifesto), Chang Tung-sun, and Tai Chi-t'ao. Mao Tun joined the party nucleus sometime between February and March of 1921, after being recommended by Li Han-chün.

In "Memoirs VI," *Source Materials* 1980.1 (Peking, February 1980) Mao Tun suggested a different date for his joining the Party nucleus. There he said that in the winter of 1920, an underground publication of the Shanghai Communist Party nucleus called *Kung-ch'an-tang (yüeh-k'an) (Communist Party Monthly)* was published under the editorship of Li Ta. It introduced Communist theory and practice, relayed news of the Comintern and informed readers of the workers' movement in the Soviet Union and other countries. The contributors, Mao Tun said, were all exclusively "members" of the Shanghai Party nucleus. Mao Tun was one of the contributors in December 1920, hence we can infer that he was a member of the nucleus by December 1920.

19. Mao Tun, *Roads I Have Traveled*, p.123.

20. *Ibid.*, pp.150–151.

21. Mao Tun, "Wo-ti-hsiao-chuan" ("A Brief Autobiography"), *Mao Tun hsüan-chi (Selected Works of Mao Tun)* (Shanghai, 1940), p.265.

22. Mao Tun, "Memoirs VI," pp.165–168. Also, Klein and Clark, *op. cit.*, pp.760–761.

23. Mao Tun, "Memoirs IV," 1980.1 (Hongkong, February 1980), pp.1–2.

24. Chang Kuo-t'ao, *Wo-ti-hui-i (Memoirs)*, 3 vols. (Hongkong, 1971). See vol. 1, p.97.

In "Memoirs IV," Mao Tun did not mention precisely when he joined the CCP. See "Memoirs IV," p.4. Nor did he supply as much detail about the circumstances surrounding the founding of the CCP itself as Chang Kuo-t'ao did in his *Memoirs.* The founding of the CCP was implied, however, when Mao Tun wrote,

"The First Congress (I-ta) elected Ch'en Tu-hsiu as the Secretary General but Ch'en Tu-hsiu was at the time in Canton hence was not present at the First Congress" (p.5).

When we compare Mao Tun's "Memoirs" (1979–1982) to Chang Kuo-t'ao's *Memoirs* (1968–1971) for information about this period of 1921–1930, we find that they differ in two essential aspects: (1) Mao Tun provides more information about his own political activities than about the CCP's activities as a whole, whereas Chang Kuo-t'ao treats the latter at such length that they sometimes overshadow his own; (2) there is a conspicuous absence of any mention of the Comintern's role in any aspect of the CCP movement in Mao Tun's "Memoirs" (beyond the mention of Marin's name), whereas Chang Kuo-t'ao continually berated the Comintern for interfering in and imposing its will on the CCP's policies. Chang's *Memoirs* is more useful to the present study for the light it sheds on the subject and substance of Mao Tun's early fiction, which deals with the Chinese Communist movement and not his part in it. What Mao Tun tells us in his "Memoirs" that he himself was doing is less directly relevant.

25. *Roads I Have Traveled*, pp.150–154 and 195ff. "Memoirs, IV, VI, IX, XII–XV," Klein and Clark, *Dictionary* II, pp.757–759.

26. The impression of Mao Tun's being prudent derives from the comments by Ch'en Pi-lan in an interview published in 1967. See A. Fairen, "The Literary Policy of Mao Tse-tung and the Cultural Revolution" (Mao Tse-tung ti wen-i-chen-ch'e chi wen-hua-ko-ming," tr. Kuo Hsiung, *Mingpao Monthly* 21 (Hong-kong, September 1967), pp.22–27. Ch'en Pi-lan joined the Chinese Communist Party in October 1922 and was a leader of the women's movement in the 1920s. She seems to have known Mao Tun well, though he does not mention her in his "Memoirs."

Chang Kuo-t'ao shows a different facet of Mao Tun's character when he remarks that in 1922 Mao Tun supported Ch'en Wang-tao in the latter's protest against a Party resolution to increase discipline and ideological indoctrination. See Chang Kuo-t'ao, *Memoirs*, I, p.217.

27. Ch'en Pi-lan, for instance, mentioned in the interview with A. Farien (see n. 26) that she had known Mao Tun well since the early 1920s. She and Ting Ling were roomates at Shanghai University in 1923–1924 when Mao Tun was teaching Marxism, fiction, and possibly also English there. Teng Yin-ch'ao at that time was the Chairman of the Committee for the Women's Movement. Ch'en Pi-lan, Ting Ling, and K'ung Te-chih (Mao Tun's wife) were all members of the Committee. Mao Tun knew them all since he and they worked for the May Thirtieth Movement. For Mao Tun's own account of his activities and his involvement with the women's movement, see his "Memoirs VI," pp.165–183.

28. *Roads I Have Travelled*, p.201. Also "Memoirs VI," pp.165–166.

29. *Roads I Have Travelled*, pp.207–213. Also "Memoirs VI," pp.168ff.

30. A quick check of the issues of *Short Story Monthly* shows a near blank of contributions from Mao Tun in the second half of 1925. The same is true for 1926 and for the first eight issues of 1927.

31. Mao Tun, "Tu *Ni Huan-Chih*" ("On Reading *Ni Huan-chih*"), *Wen-hsüeh chou-pao (Literature Weekly)* (WHCP) 8.20 (May 1929). Collected in *Collection of Mao Tun's Critical Works*, vol. 1, pp. 64–80.

Chang Kuo-t'ao did not mention Mao Tun in his account of the May Thirtieth Movement in his *Memoirs*, but Mao Tun provides a most detailed eyewitness account in his "Memoirs VII," *Source Materials* 1980.2 (May 1980), pp.7–9. He also goes into great detail about the strike at the Commercial Press which he organized after the May Thirtieth Incident.

32. "On Reading *Ni Huan-chih*," p.10.

From Mao Tun's "Memoirs VII," we learn that after the May Thirtieth Incident, he was involved in mobilizing the teachers to join protesting students in the "Save-the-nation" movement. He gave lectures in the streets. Since most of the Shanghai newspapers shied away from publishing news about the Incident, the CCP in June 1925 sponsored two new publications—the *"Je-hsüeh jih-pao"* (*"Hot-Blooded Daily"*), with Ch'u Ch'iu-po as its editor, and *Kung-li jih-pao* (*Justice Daily*), privately funded by the Commercial Press. Mao Tun probably wrote for these papers to protest and to publicize the Incident. Funding problems caused the *Justice Daily* to close on June 24. After that, he became involved in the labor strike at the Commercial Press. See "Memoirs VII," pp.9–12, also *Roads I Have Travelled*, pp.231–241.

Kuo Mo-jo and Ch'eng Fang-wu were not involved in these activities.

33. The announced reason for the decision was that Mao Tun wanted to devote more time to social movements. But pressure from the board of directors of the Commercial Press must have contributed to it; they had been criticized for Mao Tun's political outspokenness. See Yeh Tzu-ming, *Lun Mao Tun Ssu-Shi-Nien ti Wen-Hsüeh Tao-Lu* (*On Mao Tun's Forty-Year Literary Road*) (Shanghai, 1959), p.13.

According to Mao Tun's "Memoirs IV, VI," his resignation from the editorship of *Short Story Monthly* was caused primarily by his fight with the Saturday School. See especially "Memoirs IV," pp.11–15, and "Memoirs VI," p.171.

34. Yeh Tzu-ming, *op. cit.*, p.39.

"On Proletarian Literature," *WHCP* 172, 173, 175, 196 (May 10, 17, 31, October 25, 1929). I was able to obtain a copy of this long article in the spring of 1982, through the Chinese Academy of Social Sciences at Peking. My summary of the article differs from the one that appears in Yeh Tzu-ming's book on pp.39–41.

In Part 1, Mao Tun surveys the rise of proletarian literature, he distinguishes proletarian literature from the "people's literature" of Romain Rolland on the basis of its "class" concept. He names Gorky as the only writer who was able to write about the proletariat with authenticity. He lists about half a page of other self-proclaimed proletarian writers whose works did not yet approach the standard of art.

In Part 2, Mao Tun presents a formula for conditions necessary for proletarian literature: new, lively images + the author's creative selectivity + selections imposed by the society in which the literature belongs = literature and art. (The formula greatly resembles what Filippo Tommaso Marinetti has in his "Technical Manifesto of Futurist Literature" (May 11, 1912). See Filippo Tommaso Marinetti, *Marinetti, Selected Writings*, ed. By R. W. Flint (New York, 1971) p.85: "To accentuate certain movements and indicate their directions, mathematical symbols will be used: + − × : = the musical symbols."

In Part 3, Mao Tun discusses the domain (*fan-ts'ou*) of proletarian literature. It is first of all not "peasant literature." "Peasant literature" describes only the hardships of peasant life, uninformed by the proletarian spirit. Peasants are selfish, clan-oriented, and superstitious. Because of their economic life and mode of production, they do not have class consciousness (*chieh-chi i-shih*). They are nostalgic about plundering of the romantic Robin Hood type, unorganized, primitive revolutionary action which is insufficient to uproot the capitalist class. As we shall see in chapter 7, this point bears cogently on Mao Tun's reinterpretation of the Water Margin tradition of banditry in his three historical tales. It is a pity that anthologies which include "Spring Silkworms" and "Autumn Harvest" tends to omit "Winter Ruins," an integral part of Mao Tun's "trilogy." The former two describe exactly what Mao Tun saw in "peasant literature"—the hardships of peasant life, uninformed by the proletarian spirit, and peasants who are selfish, clan-oriented, and superstitious. "Winter Ruins" depicts the first awakening of peasants' "class consciousness" in a peasant riot. Unfortunately, the true significance of the rioting scene is poorly understood, and the scene is generally regarded as an uncomplimentary picture of the peasant spirit.

Nor is proletarian literature the same as revolutionary literature. Revolutionary literature rebels against the past and is in essence destructive. The proletariat as a class seeks freedom, growth, and the realization of its historical mission. Physical force is its means to peace, not its goal. Much post-October Revolution poetry celebrates the heroic killing of its enemies by the Red Army. This cannot be considered mainstream proletarian literature. (Here we anticipate the Futuristic ode to blind destruction in Ch'iang Wei-li's speech toward the end of *Disillusionment*, an imaginative rendition of this position. See chapter 3 in this volume.)

Furthermore, proletarian literature is not identical with socialist literature. Verhaeren's play *Daylight*, for example, in celebrating the success of a workers' strike overemphasizes the importance of the leader and hence is lacking in the collective spirit that characterizes true proletarian literature.

This part ends with three necessary conditions for proletarian literature: (1) it lacks the peasant's clan-oriented thinking and religiosity; (2) it lacks the soldier's hostility toward individual capitalists; (3) it lacks the intellectual's individualistic liberalism.

Part 4 discusses the content of proletarian literature. Mao Tun succinctly points out that proletarian literature should neither limit itself to take material from toilers' lives nor content itself with the role of *agent provocateur*. Class struggle does not mean vilification of capitalists and the bourgeoisie. Class struggle aims to uproot the exploitive system and those interest groups that guard this system, not any one individual. Agitation devoid of reality does not make literature.

In Part 5, Mao Tun discusses the artistic form of proletarian literature. Mao Tun considers artistic form more than the subject matter to be tradition-bound. There can be no new art form overnight. If there is, it is not a genuine art form but a pathological phenomenon. (Italian and Soviet Futurism are named here as an example.)

> Why do we say that the Futurist School and the other schools like Expressionism and Symbolism cannot be considered models for proletarian literature? It is because they are only reflections of the abnormal psychology generated in a time of decline of the old social class. Whenever a social class has completed its mission in history and is approaching its last phase of decline, its artistic content necessarily declines also . . . and with it, its art form. . . . This phenomenon is particularly noticeable in the past forty years, a period of decline of the European middle class. What is called new art is all a product of this decline. The more a social class loses its sustaining force, the more such bizarre "New [art] schools" appear. The literary world of 1910 Russia is the best example.
>
> Therefore, if the proletarian class wants to make use of the achievements of its predecessors, it should not go looking among the so-called "new-schools". . . . The genuine literary heritage for the proletarian class, to the contrary, lies with the "old school" literature, damned by modern New Schools as behind the times. This is the literature of revolutionary romanticism and of classicism of the previous ages. Why so? This is because revolutionary romanticism is the product of the capitalist class at its peak of prosperity. It is the product of the healthy spirit of a social class. We want what is healthy as our model, not what is decaying and abnormal. (*WHCP*, 196, p.201).

"On Proletarian Literature" contains much of the ideological material that in 1927–1928 gave rise to the polemics between Mao Tun and Lu Hsün on the one side and members of the Creation Society and the Sun Society on the other. Aside from the controversial issues of what constitutes orthodox revolutionary literature and what is authentic proletarian literature, we can see here how Mao Tun's analytical mind works on the subject of literary theory and criticism to digest and assimilate it. "On Proletarian Literature" shows that Mao Tun was influenced by other than the purely Marxist literary theory that critics in China today are preoccupied with.

35. Compare the events narrated in "Remarks on the Past" with Mao Tun's "Memoirs VIII," *Source Materials* 1980.3 (Peking, August 1980) pp.1ff.

36. *"Hsing-shih" ("Awakened Lion")* was also the title of a periodical being published in 1926, which was very much to the right politically and whose main thesis was national revolution by the KMT (as against Communist-Socialist revolution).

In Mao Tun's "Memoirs VIII," we learn that Mao Tun was one of the five delegates elected by the Shanghai Communist Party Congress at the end of December 1925 to attend the Second National Congress of the KMT in Canton. The ship they boarded was the *"Awakened Lion"* (p.1). At the Second National Party Congress, the CCP and its supporters scored a victory. The extreme right-wing Hsishan group was expelled from the KMT. The Congress also reiterated its support for the three policies of the late Sun Yat-sen: (1) alliance with Soviet Russia, (2) admittance of CCP members into the KMT, and (3) promotion of the labor and peasant movements.

37. Italics added.

38. For a detailed account of the duties and activities of a Party propagandist, see Martin Wilbur and Julie Lien-ting How, *Documents on Communism, Nationalism, and Soviet Advisers in China 1918–1927* (New York, Columbia University Press, 1956), pp.97–98. And also, Jane L. Price, *Cadres Commanders and Commissars: The Training of the Chinese Communist 1920–45* (Boulder, Colorado, Westview Press, 1976).

For Mao Tun's account of his duties and activities as a Party propagandist, see his "Memoirs VIII," pp.3–4.

39. For training programs in the Party schools and activities of Party cells, see Wilbur and How, *op. cit.*, pp.97–98. See also Mao Tun, "Memoirs IV–VIII," *passim.*

40. Ch'ien Hsing-ts'un, "Mao Tun yü Hsien-shih" ("Mao Tun and Reality," renamed from "Returning from Tokyo to Kuling"), *Hsien-tai Chung-kuo Wen-hsüeh Tso-chia (Contemporary Chinese Literary Writers)*, vol. 2 (Shanghai, 1930), p.121.

In Chapter 5 of *Disillusionment*, a group of students in S University calls a meeting to discuss and pass a resolution on a triangle love relationship among three classmates. See the discussion of the political allegory in that scene in Chapter 3 of this book.

41. Ch'ien Hsing-ts'un, *op. cit.*, pp.153–154:

> As to the respected and sympathetic character Wang Shih-t'ao, her desperate recourse to prostitution certainly moves one's heart. But that is definitely not the way of life for someone who has truly grasped the meaning of life, nor a revolutionary in the revolutionary camp. I do not dare to say that there do not exist today people like Wang. ∴ . . . If her career is the author's way of portraying her attitude toward sex, then that is altogether another matter. Or if the author was using her to hint at one way of coming to terms with life, that is also acceptable. However, if she is meant to demonstrate the revolutionary spirit of women, then it becomes . . . ridiculous. . . .

42. Mao Tun, *Mao Tun hsüan-chi (Selected Works of Mao Tun)* (Peking, 1951), p.7.
Note that this is not the same *Selected Works of Mao Tun* as in note 21 above. This volume was published by K'ai-ming-shu-tien in Peking and is a title in the *Library of Selections from New Literature (Hsin-wen-hsüeh hsüeh-chi)*, while the 1940 *Selected Works of Mao Tun* was published by Wan-hsiang-shu-wo in Shanghai and is a title in the *Library of Contemporary Creative Writings (Hsien-tai Ch'uang-tso wen-k'u)*. The latter shows less political bias in its selections than the former.

43. The correlation between history and fiction finds further support in his later reminiscences about September–October 1928.

44. Mao Tun, "From Kuling to Tokyo." Mao Tun's own account of the events of 1927–1928 in his "Memoirs IX," *Source Materials* 1980.4 (Peking, November 1980), pp.1–15, and his own discussion of *Eclipse* in "Memoirs X" *Source Materials* 1981.1 (Peking, February 1981), pp.1–10, however, are curiously devoid of passion. In old age he seemed to prefer keeping his distance from events that had once reduced him to despondency.

45. Wu T'ien-wei, "Chiang Kai-shek's March Twentieth Coup d'Etat of 1926," *Journal of Asian Studies* 27.3 (May 1968) pp.585–602.
In his "Postscript to the New Edition of *Eclipse*," Mao Tun Wen-chi, vol. 1 (Peking, 1958), Mao Tun also pointed to Chiang Kai-shek as the principal cause of the failure of the Great Revolution: "The Great Revolution of 1927 was frustrated by Chiang Kai-shek's anti-Communist treason."
Mao Tun was in Canton at the time of the Chungshan Gunboat Incident. He gave a rather detailed account of the events of those days in his "Memoirs VIII," *Source Materials* 1980.3 (Peking, August 1980), pp.1–14. Mao Tse-tung was very prominent in Mao Tun's account even though he did not seem to have much to do with the movements of the Gunboat.

46. For discussion of the Comintern-CCP relationship in the 1920s, see Chang Kuo-t'ao, *Memoirs;* Benjamin Schwartz, *Chinese Communism and the Rise of Mao* (Cambridge, Mass., Harvard University Press, 1951); Robert C. North, *Chinese Communism* (New York, World University Library Paperback, 1966); Harold Isaacs, *The Tragedy of Chinese Revolution*, Second Revised Edition (New York, Atheneum Paperback, 1968).
Books in Chinese include Li Yün-han, *Ts'ung jung-kung tao ch'ing-tang (From Admission of the CCP to the Purge of the CCP)* (Taipei, 1966); Chiang Yung-chin, *Pao Lo-t'ing yü Wuhan chen-ch'üan (Borodin and the Wuhan Regime)* (Taipei, 1963).

47. Mao Tun, "Kuling chih-ch'iu" ("Autumn in Kuling") *Wen-hsüeh (Literature)* 3,5,6 (September, November, December 1933), pp.371–374; 752–761; 922–925.

2. "Autumn in Kuling": From Life to Fiction

1. The story was later added to a collection of Mao Tun's short stories bearing the title *Kuling chih-ch'iu (Autumn in Kuling)* (Shanghai, 1975), pp.1–65. I have translated this text for use in this chapter.
In his "Postscript to Volume Eight," *Mao Tun wen-chi (Collected Works of Mao Tun)* (Peking, 1959), Mao Tun wrote:

> In these ten years [1934–1944], I had written two other pieces, namely, "Autumn in Kuling," and "Yen-yün" (Misty Cloud). The former in fact was not finished. I

myself am unsatisfied with these works. Besides, they are too long, not really worth wasting paper to reprint them. Hence they are not collected here.

Thus the official edition, the *Collected Works*, still omits the story. It seems that Mao Tun's difficulties with censorship did not end in 1949.

2. Mao Tun, *Autumn in Kuling*, p.65.

3. It has been suggested that these sections were never written, since Mao Tun seemed to have a predilection for incomplete works—his novel *Rainbow* (1929) is one example. But there was another, closely related withdrawal. Ch'ien Hsing-ch'un omitted a section of his vehement attack on Mao Tun's *Eclipse* and "From Kuling to Tokyo" when it was published in January 1929. Ch'ien mentioned the omission in a postscript to his "Mao Tun and Reality" and added that as a result he had changed the article's title from "Returning from Tokyo to Wuhan":

> The content of Section 4 in this article was originally divided into two parts. But at the time of publication, I felt that this was not a suitable place or time for the latter part of the article to appear, so I withdrew that part, adding the section on *The Wild Roses* instead. I also rearranged the preface.

The "latter part" turns out to be a vociferous sixty-page attack on Mao Tun's "betrayal" of his revolutionary commitment since his days of illness in Kuling. It was later collected in Fu Chih-ying (ed.), *Mao Tun p'ing-chuan* (Critical and Biographical Essays on Mao Tun) (Shanghai, December 1931), pp.255–314. It was never reincorporated into "Mao Tun and Reality."

When we juxtapose Ch'ien's "Postscript" with Mao Tun's "footnote," the comparison strongly suggests that the missing parts of Mao Tun's story were also deliberately withdrawn. There seems to have been a secret feud going on between Mao Tun and Ch'ien's Sun Society group, and the most controversial parts of both men's works were probably kept out of print by the Party authority to avoid public scandal. In any event, there is a discrepancy between what Mao Tun said in 1933 and in 1959, and the "reasons unknown" version of 1933 seems more reliable. Probably, as Ch'ien Hsing-ts'un put it, this was "not a suitable place or time."

4. Mao Tun, "Chi-chü ch'iu-hua" (Remarks on the Past) *Mao Tun hsüan-chi* (Selected Works of Mao Tun) (Shanghai, 1935), pp.1–5.

Compare Mao Tun's "Memoirs VIII," *Hsin-wen-hsüeh shih-liao* (Source Materials on the History of the New Literature) 1980.3 (August 1980), pp.1ff.

5. Ting Ling, "The Diary of Miss Sophia," *Tsai hei-an-chung* (In the Darkness, a collection of short stories) (1982). Translated by A. L. Chin in Harold Isaacs (ed.) *Straw Sandals: Chinese Short Stories, 1918–1933* (Cambridge, Mass., M.I.T. Press, 1974), pp.129–169.

6. Mao Tun, "Memoirs IX," *Source Materials* 1980.4 (November 1980), p.13.

7. *Ibid.*, p.13.

Also "Remarks on the Past," *op.cit.*, p.4.

8. Ch'ien Hsing-ts'un, "Returning from Tokyo to Wuhan," collected in Fu Chih-ying, *op. cit.*, p.258.

9. When I was searching in China in 1982 for the text of "Master Cloud and the Straw Hat," I did not mention the flea-catching newsletter, assuming that if I could find the one I could find the other too, and that it would complicate matters too much if I asked for more than one item at a time. In any case, I was more interested in the Cloud-Straw Hat allusion.

10. Ch'ien Hsing-ts'un, *op. cit.*, pp.256–258. This is the source of the poem.

11. In "Memoirs X," 1981.1 (February 1981), p.9, Mao Tun wrote, "When I

arrived in Japan I lost contact with the Party organization. Moreover, the Party organization did not try to contact me." But it seems that the tie was broken earlier, when Mao Tun got back to Shanghai in mid-August 1927. That is the point in the "Memoirs" where he ceases to mention the "Party organization."

12. Ch'ü Ch'iu-po, "T'an-t'an *San-jen-hsing*" (Notes on *In Company of Three*), *Hsien-tai (Contemporary)* 1.1 (March 10, 1932). Collected in *Ch'ü Ch'iu-po wen-chi (Collected Works of Ch'ü Ch'iu-po)*, vol. 2, pp.334–341. See especially p.334.

13. Mao Tun, *San-jen-hsing (In Company of Three)* (Shanghai, K'ai-ming shu-tien, March 1929, "First edition"). This edition has, on the back of its title page, the note: *Nei-chen-pu chu-cho-ch'üan chu-ts'e-che-chao chin-tzu ti 1118 hao* (Ministry of Interior Affairs Authorship Registration Number Chin-1118). The "first edition" is Mao Tun, *San-jen-hsing* (Shanghai, K'ai-ming shu-tien, October 1931).

14. Several incidents are highly suggestive of Mao Tun's muted but nonetheless stubborn defiance of censorship. In chapter One, I mentioned the way he treated the manuscript of his play on the three-anti and five-anti campaigns of the 1950s. In 1980, when the official People's Literature Press wanted to reissue his *Eclipse* and offered to reinstate all the deletions it had made in the 1954 edition, he firmly rejected the proposal and mentioned both the offer and his rejection in a post-script to the new edition, putting the responsibility for what had been called "stylistic revisions" where it belonged. Then in his "Memoirs VI," *Source Materials* 1980.1 (February 1980), when he was talking about the very important Third Party Congress of 1923 and listing the names of delegates, he left out the list of the delegates from Shanghai who went to Canton to attend the Congress and inserted in its place a parenthetical remark "wang-ch'i-ming" (names forgotten). From Chang Kuo-t'ao's *Memoirs*, we know that Ch'en Tu-hsiu, Ch'ü Ch'iu-po, Chang Kuo-t'ao Ta'ai Ho-shen, and Mao Tse-tung were all present at the Congress. The figure who most infuriated Chang Kuo-t'ao, and hence has the most space in Chang's account, was Marin, the Comintern representative. It is simply impossible that Mao Tun could have forgotten the names of these close comrades and of his Comintern antagonist.

Cf. Chang Kuo-t'ao, *Wo-ti-hui-i (Memoirs)*, vol. 1 (Hongkong, Mingpao ch'u-pan-she, 1971), pp.283–302.

It is quite conceivable that the stubborn Mao Tun took the opportunity to publish in 1933 when he had the chance what had been prohibited in 1927–1928.

15. Vladimir Mayakovsky, "The Cloud in Trousers," *The Bedbug and Selected Poetry*, edited by Patricia Blake, translated by Max Hayward (Bloomington, Indiana University Press), pp.61–169. The quotation is from pp.61–63.

16. Fang Pi (pseudonym), *Hsi-yang wen-hsüeh t'ung-lun (Outline of Western Literature)* (Shanghai, 1929?), p.254.

17. *Ibid.*, pp.59–61.

18. When I interviewed Mao Tun on September 29, 1977, I asked him if *Hsiang-yang-wan* was really the name of the ship that took him to Kiukiang and whether it had any symbolic significance. Mao Tun said that it was really the name. Hsiang-yang is a city in Hunan, but the suffix "wan" meant that it was a Japanese ship. Only Japanese ships were sailing at the time, so Mao Tun had no choice but to take it.

19. *Autumn in Kuling*, pp.58–59.

20. The date August 8 is inferred from Master Cloud's remarks about Fuchow. The retreating troops arrived in Fuchow about August 8, 1927. See, for instance, "Chou Yi-ch'ün's Report," in Martin Wilbur, *Ashes of Defeat* (Institute of East

Asian Studies, Columbia University, New York, 1964). Reprinted from *The China Quarterly* 18 (April–June 1964), pp.3–54.

21. *Ibid.*, p.9. Also Chang Kuo-t'ao, *Memoirs*, vol. 2, p.706.

22. Chang Kuo-t'ao, *Memoirs*, vol. 2, p.710. See also note 20 above.

23. *Ibid.*, p.658. Cf. Harold Isaacs, *The Tragedy of the Chinese Revolution*, Second Revised Edition (Atheneum, New York, 1968), pp.252ff.

24. Mao Tun, "Tu *Ni Huan-chih*" (On Reading *Ni Huan-chih*), *Wen-hsüeh chou-pao (Literature Weekly)* 370 (Vol. 8, No. 20) (May 1929).

25. Mao Tun, "T'an Wo-ti yen-chiu" (My Understanding [of Fiction Writing] (1934), in *Yin-hsiang, kan-hsiang, hui-i (Impressions, Reflections, and Reminiscences)* (Shanghai, Wen-hua shen-huo ch'u-pan-she, 1936), pp.49–52. Mao Tun had much earlier published a rather long article, "Study in Characterization [in Fiction]," *Short Story Monthly* 16.3 (March 1925). Ideas similar to those in the 1936 publication already appear there, but the article is much more formal and more verbose.

26. *Autumn in Kuling*, p.9. Apparently the censor did not object to the expression "*not* an X-tang." Had it been in the positive, "is an X-tang," things would probably have been different.

27. Dr. Marián Gálik in a personal communication of May 21, 1974, identifies Master Yün as Sun Yün-pin, a CCP member who went to Kiukiang on board the same ship with Mao Tun and then went up to Kuling with him. Mao Tun in his "Memoirs IX" also says that the "Master Yün" of his "newsletter" was Sun Yün-pin. This contradicts Mao Tun's earlier, very strong insistence in "From Kuling to Tokyo" that characters in his stories and novels are types, composite pictures of men and women he knew at the time, rather than specific individuals. We are here confronted with a dilemma: whether to interpret Mao Tun's early fiction in the light of how he himself conceived and wrote in the 1920s, or to accept the perspective of his "Memoirs" and take it as reflections of his personal life.

The latter choice can be dangerously misleading, especially in discussing Mao Tun's fiction between 1927 and 1933. Mao Tun's "Memoirs" frequently give the names of real persons as models or partial models for his fictional characters. Besides Sun Yün-pin, he mentions, for example, Fan Chih-ch'ao, a woman co-worker in the "International Office," whom he met in Kuling and who told him about the Nanchang Uprising and other news; and a young man named Ku Chung-ch'i, first a worker in Shanghai and then a low-ranking military officer in the KMT Northern Expedition army, whom Mao Tun seemed to know fairly well and who he said provided a partial model for the Futurist battalion leader Ch'iang Wei-li in *Disillusionment* (see "Memoirs X").

The danger of these fragments of biographical information is that readers and critics may be satisfied with such neat alignments with the fictional characters and not explore their deeper dimensions. For example, Master Yün and his straw hat carries a much more subtle and important message than an identification with the historian and literary man Sun Yün-pin. And the Futuristic speech of Ch'iang Wei-li in *Disillusionment* surpasses any significance we can get from the designated life model Ku Chung-ch'i, especially in view of the fact that Ch'iang's distinguishing characteristic is his Futuristic passion for the battlefield, not an attribute of the worker-turned-soldier Ku Chung-ch'i.

In his essays of the 1920s and the 1930s, Mao Tun emphasizes that relationships among characters are thematically even more important than single characters. His later attempt to supply life models—acceptable to the national government in all cases—for his characters should not be mistakenly used as a basis for interpreting his early fiction. Doing this would be reducing the fiction to autobiography.

28. In July 1927, Lushan was a meeting ground for political negotiations, intrigues, and party reorganization. The Nanchang Uprising was partly planned there. Borodin and Ch'ü Ch-iu-po met there to discuss pending top-level leadership turnover; Wang Ching-wei, Sun Yat-sen's son Sun K'o, and Chang Fa-k'uei also went there later in July to discuss new political alliances and ways of dealing with the ominous movements of CCP troops preparing for the Nanchang Uprising.

In "Autumn in Kuling," Yün buys a travel guide to Lushan and studies it with great care. But once he gets there, all he can do is play chess in the hotel. His situation serves as an ironic comment on the general futility of the CCP activities.

Chang Kuo-t'ao, who as a CCP Central Committee representative from Shanghai was deeply involved in the attempt at remote control by the CCP Central Committee and the Comintern of the field action of the Front Committee for the Nanchang Uprising, gives a detailed account of the planning and execution of the historic event in his *Memoirs*, vol. 2, pp.695–734.

Mao Tun, on the other hand, eschews in his "Memoirs X" the larger events as a whole and concentrates only on his own itinerary and his errands, such as delivering two thousand dollars for the Party to a connection in Kiukiang. He particularly avoids any reference to interference by the Russians and any mention of the principal engineers of the uprising—Li Li-san, Chou En-lai, and Yün Tai-ying.

29. *Autumn in Kuling*, p.15.

30. *Ibid.*, p.17. Following the first remarks, Hsü goes on to say, "I am not finished yet. The Honan people stirred up only a little bit of trouble, and our Director Teng immediately compromised. . . ." That Teng is Teng Yen-ta, see Chang Kuo-t'ao, *Memoirs II*, p.547ff.

31. See the reconstruction and description of the Nanch'ang Uprising by Colonel J. Guillermaz, *The China Quarterly* 11 (July–September 1962), pp.161–169.

32. A parallel account can be found in Chang Kuo-tao's *Memoirs*, vol. 2, pp.698–705. Or see *Mingpao Monthly* 25 (January 1968), pp.90–96, where it was first published.

3. Disillusionment

1. Mao Tun, "From Kuling to Tokyo," *Short Story Monthly* 19.10 (October 1928), pp.1138–1146. Section 5, p.1141.

2. Mao Tun, *Huan-mieh (Disillusionment)* (Shanghai, K'ai-ming shu-tien, 1930), p.5.

"Miss" is used here to translate "*nü-shih*," which implies a woman of education. "Mr." is added to male characters' names for gender identification.

3. *Ibid.*, p.6.

4. *Ibid.*, p.7.

5. *Ibid.*, p.15.

6. *Ibid.*, p.18.

7. *Ibid.*, pp.23–24.

8. *Ibid.*, p.27.

9. The fly dashing itself against the glass pane was used in "From Kuling to Tokyo (Section 4)" as a symbol for those in the Great Revolution who, in their desperation to find a way out of the impasse of the CCP-KMT alliance, rushed into armed resistance and death. The "west side of the room" is also significant, because in *Pursuit* it will be the corner where, after the Wuhan purge of the CCP

in July 1927, the former S University students who had worked with the Wuhan government recongregated and planned their next step.

Mao Tun, however, in "Memoirs X," *Source Materials for the History of New Literature* 1981.1 (February 1981), remarked that Fu K'e-hsing—a member of the Sun Society and a returned student from Japan who viciously attacked *Eclipse*—"was apparently one of such flies heavily drugged by putschism." The remark, in my opinion, is a pointer to the symbolism rather than a genuine identification because Fu K'e-hsing was not involved in the Great Revolution.

10. *Disillusionment*, pp.33–35. The color red, as we would expect, is symbolic of the revolutionary forces.

11. This is the first mention of "fate" in the trilogy. Later, in chapter 8 of *Disillusionment* a crushing sense of fate overwhelms the sick Miss Ching. The crescendo of "fate" continues to build in Mao Tun's early fiction till it reaches suicidal proportions in *Pursuit* and in the short stories in *The Wild Roses.* Then the spell breaks. See chapter 6 of this book.

12. *Disillusionment*, p.42.

13. *Disillusionment*, p.42.

14. *Ibid*, pp.43–444. The signature "Kuo-liang," meaning "pillar of the nation," may carry an ironic jibe at Chiang Kai-shek or the factions he represents. At the time he was referred to as a "pillar of the national revolution." See Benjamin Schwartz, *Chinese Communism and the Rise of Mao* (Cambridge, Mass., Harvard University Press, 1951), p.56. It is not a name a revolutionary would adopt.

15. *Ibid*, pp.45–46. Miss Ching's reaction to "fate," as we see, is very different from Hui's. On one level, this is an aspect of her character that distinguishes her from Hui. She struggles against the power of "fate" whereas Hui either resigns herself to it or sports with it. On the level of political allegory, it distinguishes one line of development of the CCP from another line.

16. The reference to "the people" is to the mass movements organized by the CCP in support of the Northern Expedition. See Robert C. North, *Chinese Communism* (New York, World University Library, 1971), pp.63–94.

17. *Disillusionment*, pp.52–53.

18. I have summarized in some detail the plots of all three novels in the trilogy and quote as much as possible from them before analyzing their bearing on historical events, so the reader will understand the total context of what has gone into the analysis, hoping to avoid the objection that I have selected from Mao Tun only what serves my purposes, and not what Mao Tun wrote for his purposes, an objection that could be made of Ch'ien Hsing-ts'un, for instance. The summaries are rather detailed, but given the complexity of the issues involved, I believe they will be helpful for readers who do not have access to the Chinese originals.

It may also be well to note here that the problem that divided the Chinese Communist Party in 1926–27 was altogether different from the so-called putschist tendencies that characterized the thinking of the CCP Central Committee after August 1927 (when *Disillusionment* ends), under the leadership first of Ch'ü Ch'iu-po and then of Li Li-san. And the problems that confronted the still-divided Chinese Communist Party in 1930–31 (when Mao Tun wrote the three historical tales) were different again. When the group of returned students from Sun Yat-sen University in Moscow who called themselves the "28 Bolsheviks" arrived in the early summer of 1930 in Shanghai under the personal direction of Pavel Mif, the new Comintern delegate, to "correct" the putschism of Li Li-san, they created quite separate problems from those that grew out of Li Li-san's own leadership (see Benjamin Schwartz, *op.cit.*, pp.127–172). In Mao Tun's fictional representation of such shifting of lines, subtle but necessary distinctions are always preserved. The Li Li-san line, for example, appears in the image of banditry, *Water Margin* style in two of the three historical tales (see chapter 8). And, Mao Tse-tung's peasant movement, earlier represented by the "banditry" of Ts'ao Chih-fang in *Pursuit* has moved to the countryside and is represented by the peasant uprising of "Great Marsh District." *Water Margin*, though a historical "romance" and hence portraying life in a mode that Mao Tun considered too remote from reality, still falls into a literary genre that he did not completely disapprove. But it certainly carries a distinctly different flavor from the historical records of Ssu-ma Ch'ien that supplies the source to the story in "Great Marsh District." Mif and the 28 Bolsheviks, on the other hand, were not so kindly treated in their fictional images in *The Road*, where they were reduced to the level of high school students, with Mif (projected fictionally as Dean Thorn) recognizable as their principal. (A firsthand account of Mif's high-handed administration at Sun Yat-sen University and in 1930 Shanghai can be found in Chang Kuo-t'ao, *Memoirs II*, Hongkong, Mingpao yüeh-k'an-she, 1973, pp.777–860.)

During my 1977 interview with Mao Tun, I specifically asked him whether he had met Mif in Shanghai when he came back from Japan in the summer of 1930. To my great surprise, he answered that Mif was never in China. His denial gave me the impression that he absolutely detested Mif. His brother Shen Tse-min was at Sun Yat-sen University in Moscow when Mif was its head, and when Tse-min came back as one of the 28 Bolsheviks, he must have told Mao Tun about life in those years under Mif. According to Chang Kuo-t'ao's account, Mif was hated by all the Chinese students at the University, even by the 28 Bolsheviks. I have always suspected that Dean Thorn, the corrupt administrator in *The Road*, is modeled on Mif.

19. See especially Chang Kuo-t'ao, *Memoirs* I and II; Harold Isaacs, *The Tragedy of the Chinese Revolution* (Second Revised Edition, New York, Atheneum, 1968); Hua Kang, *Chung-kuo ta-k'o-ming-shih (A History of the Great Revolution in China)* (Shanghai, Ch'un-keng shu-tien, 1936); and Robert C. North, *Chinese Communism*.

20. Compare Chang Kuo-t'ao's account in his *Memoirs* II with Mao Tun's account in "Memoirs VI," pp.175–176.

21. See Note 20.

22. When we compare references to the presence and activities of Comintern delegates through the Great Revolution years and afterward—as here with Voitsinski and Maring and the 1923 Third Party Congress—we see a striking contrast between the exhaustive details in Chang Kuo-t'ao's *Memoirs* and the conspicuous omissions from Mao Tun's "Memoirs." Chang Kuo-t'ao, writing in Hongkong as a non-Party member, apparently enjoyed and fully exercised a degree of freedom of speech that was not available to Mao Tun on the perennially sensitive topic of Soviet ambition in China. In the West, nearly every important book on this period goes into great detail about the Comintern role in China. See, for example, any of the books listed in note 19, and Conrad Brandt, *Stalin's Failure in China 1924–1927* (Cambridge, Mass., Harvard University Press, 1958). See also Tai Chi-t'ao, *Kuo-min ko-ming yü Chung-kuo Kuo-min-tang*, preface July 23, 1925.

23. The term *"tzu-sha"* (suicide) occurs with great frequency in Chang Kuo-t'ao's account of the KMT-CCP collaboration period. Apparently it captures the peculiar color of many CCP members' feelings about the collaboration policy. Mao Tun used the expression in a variety of ways later in the trilogy—in words, in dramatic episodes such as Shih Hsün's attempted suicide in *Pursuit*—and also as

the title of the short story "Suicide" in the volume *The Wild Roses.* Chang's *Memoirs* is helpful in supplying a political frame of reference for Mao Tun's trilogy via such verbal echoes as well as factual details. *"Tung-yao"* ("vacillation") is another example, and *"t'u-fei"* ("banditry") still another.

24. Such public intervention often occurs in internal Party cell meeting, where possible political ramifications are assumed. The student assembly in chapter 5 is thus plausible when read as an allegory.

25. C. T. Hsia, *A History of Modern Chinese Fiction* (New Haven, Conn., Yale University Press, 1961), p. 143.

26. Ch'ien Hsing-ts'un, "Mao Tun yü hsien-shih" ("Mao Tun and Reality," renamed from "Ts'ung Tokyo hui-tao Wuhan") *Hsien-tai Chung-kuo Wen-hsüeh Tso-chia (Contemporary Chinese Literaty Writers),* II (Shanghai, T'ai-tung t'u-shu-chü, 1930), pp. 113–178. See pp. 120–121.

27. Chang Kuo-t'ao, *Memoirs* I, pp. 283–302; Benjamin Schwartz, *op.cit.,* p. 50; Mao Tun, "Memoirs VI," p. 175ff. Mao Tun's direct responsibility for implementing the united-front policy sheds additional light on why he shows such an intimate knowledge of its failures in *Disillusionment.* Later, in chapter 8, we have a follow-up: the CCP's position of noncollaboration with the KMT overruled by the Comintern was registered in the novel under the allegorical disguise of a report by Li K'e to Ching in the hospital, in which Li says that Shih Chün's proposal to punish Miss Wang for getting herself into such a situation was finally defeated.

28. Betrayal is the central note of Mao Tun's revelation scene here. When Pao-su's identity is discovered, and when we recall the sympathy he expressed for criminals like Raskolnikov, we see that what is being condemned here is not merely an impostor in the revolutionary camp but the kind of thinking and behavior (Hui's cynical philosophy) and the kind of illusion (Ching's trusting naïveté) within the camp itself that made Pao-su's betrayal possible.

Ch'ien Hsing-ts'un's criticism, however, was not primarily concerned with the issue of responsibility in the betrayal. Ch'ien had probably never expected anything different from the KMT to begin with, but he was rueful because Mao Tun did not bring the "correct" ideology to bear on the historical facts. The collaboration policy was decreed at the First Nationalist Congress of January 1924 and Chiang Kai-shek did not show his first signs of betrayal till March 1926 and April 1927. Hence in Ch'ien's opinion, Mao Tun's compression of the lovemaking and the discovery into an overnight affair did not adequately represent the time involved. Besides, the betrayal did not take place in CCP headquarters. It was not an insider's act. Hence Ch'ien objected to Ching's room as "the place of discovery"—that is too close to home.

Mao Tun and Ch'ien Hsing-ts'un are interested in very different aspects of the disastrous CCP-KMT collaboration policy. The discussion of *Crime and Punishment* that serves as a prelude to the triangular love affair highlights Mao Tun's moral and intellectual concern with questions of means and responsibility in a revolutionary situation. At the time he was writing the trilogy he evidently believed that the individual *is* responsible for the means he lets himself be persuaded to adopt. The motive of the individual at the time he is persuaded to act is the only test for the authenticity of his belief. The profound moral ambiguity of Raskolnikov's murder obviously intrigued Mao Tun: Is it an act of freedom or is it an act of crime? He had studied and written about Dostoevsky extensively and has been fascinated by Dostoevsky's exploration into the human irrational. As his two articles in the Special Issue on Dostoevsky in *Short Story Monthly* 13.1 (January 1922) show, he was particularly attracted to Dostoevsky's political thinking and his insight into the pathological state of mind of his characters.

Ch'ien Hsing-ts'un apparently did not share Mao Tun's literary taste. He was not interested in questions of moral ambiguity and psychological complexity in a fictional character. To him good and evil in revolutionary literature was simply a matter of whether you were with the revolution and the Party line (which is incapable of doing wrong) or not. He seems to have been the very type of revolutionary socialist writer that Mao Tun had cautioned aspiring writers of proletarian literature not to be in "On Proletarian Literature," *Literature Weekly* 172, 173, 175, 196 (May 10, 17, 31, October 25, 1925). See summary of the article in chapter 1, note 34, especially that of parts 3 and 4.

29. Huang-po and Huang-kang in Hupeh Province are not mentioned in most Chinese Communist histories of the peasant movement. Peasant organization is associated almost exclusively with the Hunan movement led by Mao Tse-tung. I have found only one instance where Huang-po and Huang-kang are mentioned, and it is in a Hongkong publication, probably not generally available on mainland China, Ho Kan-chih's *Chung-kuo hsien-tai ko-ming-shih (A History of the Contemporary Chinese Revolution)* (Hongkong, Joint Publishing Co., 1958), p. 111. The place name "Huang-po" was deleted from the 1954 Peking official edition of *Eclipse* ostensibly for stylistic streamlining. Considering the kinds of deletions made throughout the trilogy in that edition, it seems more likely that the aim is to eliminate all traces of the novel's linkage with Party history, especially those aspects of it that have been changed or omitted in the intervening years.

30. "From Kuling to Tokyo," Section 3: "Miss Hui, Sun Wu-yang, and Chang Ch'iu-liu are not revolutionary women either. However, neither are they superficial women. If the reader does not find them lovable or worthy of sympathy, then the author has failed in his characters." Most critics ignored Hui in their discussion of *Disillusionment*, concentrating only on Ching.

31. The same two questions persist through the trilogy. They are again raised and discussed in chapter 5 of this book when *Pursuit* is examined.

32. Interestingly, Chang Kuo-t'ao also used the term "purity" when he wrote about the CCP and the sullying effect of the collaboration. Apparently he and Mao Tun shared the same memories of how the issue was discussed and the language the arguments were cast in. See Chang, *Memoirs* I. Chang Kuo-t'ao incidentally identifies the red necktie Pao-su wore as that worn by cadres of the Whampoa Military Academy (see *Memoirs* II, p.414).

33. For this part of the history, see Benjamin Schwartz, *op. cit.*, pp.73ff.

34. For a firsthand account of the Fifth Party Congress, see Chang Kuo-t'ao, *Memoirs* II, p.363. Robert North in *Chinese Communism* also has a short section on the Fifth Party Congress, pp.86–90.

There is a very brief allegorical representation of the Fifth Party Congress and its political significance in chapter 6 of *Disillusionment* (p.32). Since in essence the Fifth Party Congress merely reendorsed the collaboration policy formulated at the Third Party Congress, the scene outside of Classroom Number Five is not on the same scale as the debate scene in Classroom Number Three. Nevertheless, Mao Tun's distaste for the policy is expressed again through Ching's fear of the sinister side of man-woman relationships when she sees a couple embracing in a dark corner outside of Classroom Number Five and considers it "ugly."

35. Robert North, *Chinese Communism*, pp.86–90. Benjamin Schwartz, *Chinese Communism and The Rise of Mao*, p.64.

36. "*Tung-yao*" ("vacillation") is also Chang Kuo-t'ao's expression for the CCP policies on mass movements during the Wuhan period. *Memoirs* II.

37. Chang Kuo-t'ao, *Memoirs* II. Benjamin Schwartz, *op.cit.*, pp.65–68.

38. *Disillusionment*, p.63. Here we see how the pen name for the author of the trilogy "Mao Tun" ("Contradiction") was conceived.

39. *Ibid.*

40. Changsha appears quite a few times in the second half of *Disillusionment.* In chapter 11, for example, Ching's mother wrote Ching asking her to come home to Changsha. Earlier, when Ching was in the hospital, her mother specifically asked her not to come home. Certainly Mao Tun attached special significance to Ching's relationship with her mother in Hunan, where the CCP movement had successes and failures in quick succession during 1926 and 1927.

41. Chang Kuo-t'ao records the CCP's active participation in the Honan battles of the Second Northern Expedition; see *Memoirs* II, p.656.

42. *Disillusionment,* p.42.

43. Ch'ien Hsing-ts'un, "Mao Tun and Reality," p.122.

44. *Disillusionment,*chapter 13, p.77.

45. *Ibid.,* chapter 14, p.83. This line was deleted from the 1954 edition and was not restored in the 1980 reprint. In latter-date official taste, tenderness is not something that inspires military action, and sensual pleasure between the sexes makes a totally unacceptable metaphor for battle.

46. Mao Tun's attitude toward Futurism has attracted little attention, though all through *Eclipse* we can find the emotional weight of "energy," "strength," "machine civilization," and "blind destruction" as the means of revitalization. Marián Gálik, in his thorough study of Mao Tun's literary theory, referred to Mayakovsky and Mao Tun's interest in Futurism (e.g., p.90 and p.107) but did not devote as much attention to it as he did to Naturalism and Realism.

Yeh Tzu-ming and Shao Po-chou also emphasized Mao Tun's investigation of Naturalism and Realism, and "proletarian literature," without discussing the influence of Futurism on Mao Tun's literary theory and practice. This tendency is continued in Sun Chung-t'ien's recent *Lun Mao Tun ti Sheng-huo yü Ch'uang-tso (On Mao Tun's Life and Creative Writings)* (T'ien-chin, Pai-hua-wen-i-ch'u-pan-she, 1980), and in Yüeh Tai-yün's "Mao Tun tsao-ch'i ssu-hsiang yen-chiu" ("A Study of Mao Tun's Early Thought"), *Chung-kuo hsien-tai wen-hsüeh yen-chiu ts'ung-k'an (Anthology of Essays on Modern Chinese Literature)* 1979.1 (Peking, Peking-ch'u-pan-she, 1979), pp.134–158.

Mao Tun in fact paid a great deal of attention to the development of Futurism in the West and to its possible use for China. On more than one occasion, he traced Futurism from Marinetti in Italy to the Futurist poets in Soviet Russia. Since the October Revolution in Russia offered the closest model for Chinese revolution, and since Russian fictional characters like Bazarov and Sanin came closest to the pre-revolutionary youth Mao Tun knew in the 1920s, it is only to be expected that he should have early become involved with Russian literature and with the Futurist announcement of revolutionary changes. He wrote a great deal on Futurism and Mayakovsky. *"Wei-lai-p'ai wen-hsüeh te hsien-shih"* ("The Current Development of Futurist Literature"), first published in *Short Story Monthly* 13.10 (October 1922), was collected together with his articles on Tolstoi, Hauptmann, and Maeterlinck into a small volume *Hsin-wen-i p'ing-lun (Critical Essays on New Literature),* complied by Liang Kung (Shanghai, Min-chih-shu-chü, 1923). There is also his *"Su-wei-ai O-lu-ssu ko-ming-shih-jen* Mayakovsky" ("Mayakovsky, A Revolutionary Poet of Soviet Russia"), *Literature Weekly,* no.130 (July 1924).

In his book *Hsi-yang Wen-hsüeh T'ung-lun (An Outline of Western Literature)* (Shanghai, Shih-chieh-shu-chü, 1929? 1930?), published under one of his work-for-hire pseudonyms, Fang Pi, there is a long section on Futurism (pp.237–259) in chapter 9, *"Tzu-jan-chu-i i-hou"* ("After Naturalism"). There Mao Tun wrote that Mayakovsky was the poet "who brought Futurism into the street to make contact with the broad masses," that Mayakovsky's poetry expresses the shouts of strong and heroic giants, not susceptible to ordinary evaluation of "good or bad." He uses the strong, living language of the people, Mao Tun said, recreating it for his own poetic purposes, completely free from tradition. "His poetry is written in a new colloquial language which he himself created. The assonance and alliteration in his verse, together with his specially selected consonantal sounds, orchestrate into a din like that of the drum in a military march, with a sweep like that of a storm." Hence Mayakovsky "is a poet of the crossroad, roaring out his speeches . . . In the first years of the Russian revolution, Mayakovsky's school was the most powerful one on the literary scene, totally in support of the Soviet government and calling themselves the most revolutionary poets. . . . Russian Futurism therefore joined in with the proletarian revolution, whereas Italian Futurism, with its fascist tendency, has now provided court poets for Mussolini . . ." (pp. 254–255).

Mao Tun's attitude toward Futurism and Mayakovsky changed before and after the Great Revolution, as Mayakovsky himself changed before and after the October Revolution. In *Disillusionment,* Mao Tun could still cast the Futurist in an ironic light and in general hold the Futurist faith in the power of revolution and violence in willing suspension of disbelief. Futurist mentality like Futurist slogans was part and parcel of the CCP reality in 1927. Hence Mao Tun's portrayal of the Futurist battalion leader is not without its basis in reality. After 1925, however, his enthusiasm for Russian Futurism and Russian literature dwindled as he became disillusioned with the leadership of the Comintern and the Moscow government.

47. In 1922, with his brother Shen Tse-min and his friend Wang Ch'iung-ch'üan, Mao Tun wrote a series of articles introducing Futurist literature and painting of the West. They were published in the September and October issues of *Short Story Monthly.*

48. Wang Ch'iung-ch'üan, tr. *"Hsien-tai Pu-kuei-tse shih-p'ai"* (Contemporary Avant-Garde Poetry), *Short Story Monthly* 13.9 (September, 1922).

The article says that the principal tenet of Futurist poetics is based on a *sensation dynamique.* A sense of time dominates Futurist pictorial art. For example, when a painter looks at an apple, what he sees is not merely a red object on a plate, but all associations, past or present, with the object. At the time the painter may be thinking of a girl he knew in his younger days. The girl then belongs in the painting. Futurist literature likewise emphasizes movement. The characteristic fanaticism of Futurist literature of the day celebrates machine power, insults women, and praises physical force. It rejects everything gentle and fragile, identifying only with violence and brute force that is considered masculine, proclaiming a philosophy of science and will.

The notion of time and associations across time in Futurist art is of particular interest here when we think ahead about the topsy-turvy time-scheme in *Pursuit* when past becomes part of the present in Wang Shih-t'ao's pregnancy, and especially in Chang Ch-iu-liu's hallucinatory vision of Tung-fang Ming's death.

Mao Tun's article, "The Current Development of Futurist Literature" treats a different phase of Futurist literature as it developed in the post-World War I world of Bolshevik Russia. Russian Futurism was unlike Italian Futurism in that its reaction against post-Naturalistic European subjectivism in literature and art had developed into a demand for a total destruction of the past. In particular, Mao Tun said,

The artistic world of the Russian workers and peasants was almost completely monopolized by the Futurist School. Whether the ideals of the Futurist School, basically speaking, have anything to do with the ideals of Bolshevism is hard to say in one short sentence. Some hold that their basic spirit is diametrically opposite. On the surface, both agree about the demolition of old institutions. Probably this is the reason why Futurism has become prominent in a worker-peasant government." (p.3)

49. *Ibid.*
50. *Ibid.*
51. See note 34 in chapter 1 for the correlation between musical symbol and Futurist literature mentioned in Marinetti in his "Technical Manifesto of Futurist Literature," and also Marinetti's 1909 "The Founding and Manifesto of Futurism," in which the sound of the machine as pleasing to the ear is emphasized. Filippo Tommaso Marinetti, *Marinetti, Selected Writings,* edited with an introduction by R. W. Flint, translated by R. W. Flint and Arthur A. Coppotelli (New York, Farrar, Straus and Giroux, 1971, 1972).
52. Shen Yen-ping, "The Current Development of Futurist Literature." Cf. Marián Gálik's brief discussion of Futurism and Mao Tun's literary theory (1924–1925) in chapter 8, "On Revolutionary and Proletarian Literature," of his book *Mao Tun and Modern Chinese Literary Criticism* (Wiesbaden, 1969), pp.90–94, and of Mayakovsky in chapter 9, "Contemporary Proletarian Chinese and World Avant-garde Literature," pp.106–110.
53. Marián Gálik, *ibid.,* chapter 8, p.93.
54. *Disillusionment,* chapter 12, pp.74–75.
55. *Ibid.,* p.75. Cf. Marinetti, "The Founding and Manifesto of Futurism," *op.cit.,* pp.39–44, and "Let's Murder the Moon Shine," pp.45–54.

4. Vacillation

1. Mao Tun, "On Reading *Ni Huan-chih,*" *Wen-hsüeh-chou-pao (Literature Weekly)* 8.20 (May 1929), Section 7.
2. Mao Tun, "From Kuling to Tokyo," *Short Story Monthly* 19.10 (October, 1928), pp.1138–1146. Section 5.
3. *Ibid.*
4. Vladimir I. Lenin, *"Kung-ch'an yün-tung chung ti tso-ch'ing yu-tzu-ping"* ("Infantile Leftism in Communist Movement") *Collected Works of Lenin,* Vol. 31 (Peking, Editorial Committee of the CCP Central Committee for The Works of Marx, Engels, Lenin, and Stalin, 1960), pp.1098.
5. For Mao Tun's personal experiences in the Wuhan period of the Great Revolution, see his "Memoirs IX," *Source Materials on the History of the New Literature* 1980.4 (November, 1980), pp.1–15.

After the Northern Expedition forces took Wuhan in October 1926, the Nationalist Government was moved from Canton to Wuhan. The Central Committee of the CCP also decided to send a work force there, and Mao Tun left Shanghai to join it at the end of 1926.

Mao Tun first taught at the Central Military-Political Academy in Wuhan and supervised a weekly "Literary Supplement" to the *Central Daily,* a KMT organization paper at Wuch'ang. Soon he was reassigned by the CCP Central Committee to serve as editor-in-chief of the *Hankow Republic Daily (Min-kuo jih-pao),* working with Tung Pi-wu as the Director and Mao Tse-min as the manager. Ch'ü Ch'iu-po was then the head of the Propaganda Department of the CCP. It was understood between Ch'ü Ch'iu-po and Mao Tun that one of the tasks of the *Republic Daily* was to promote the mass movements and to be a propaganda organ for the revolution. Much of the raw material that went into the depiction of the mass movements in *Vacillation* was therefore originally news that came to

Mao Tun for possible publication in the *Republic Daily.* See especially "Memoirs IX," pp.2–11.

Marián Gálik first noted Mao Tun's teaching at the military academy in his *Mao Tun and Modern Chinese Literary Criticism* (Wiesbaden, 1968). I have relied heavily on his book and on Yeh Tzu-ming's *Lun Mao Tun Ssu-shih-nien ti Wen-hsüeh Tao-lu (On Mao Tun's Forty-Years On The Literary Road)* (Shanghai: Shanghai Wen-i-ch'u-pan-she, 1959), both published before the "Memoirs," for information on Mao Tun's life and works during this period.

6. During the Manchu Ch'ing Dynasty (1644–1911), men were required to grow a queue. When the revolutionary movement began in the early twentieth century, activists and their followers cut off their queues to signify their determination to join the revolutionary ranks. Until the fall of the Manchus the absence of a queue was punishable by death.

7. Mao Tun, *Tung-yao (Vacillation)* (Shanghai, K'ai-ming shu-tien, 1930), pp.4–5.

8. *Ibid.,* p.9.

9. *Ibid.,* chapter 5, p.42.

10. The red cloth that Communist cadres and followers tied around their necks for identification during the mass movements in May and June 1927, and later during the Canton Commune of December 1927, became a fatal badge during the brutal suppressions of the commune by the KMT forces. The red line of dye left by the neckerchiefs after they were discarded exposed the wearer's identity to the KMT soldiers coming to round them up for execution. See Robert C. North, *Chinese Communism* (New York, World University Library, 1966, 1970, 1971), p.103.

In chapter 5 of *Pursuit,* we shall see that the red ring around Tung-fang Ming's neck which Chang Ch'iu-liu sees in a hallucinatory vision is produced precisely by one of these strips of red cloth.

11. *Vacillation,* p.65.

12. *Ibid.,* p.66.

13. This is one of the slogans in Sun Yat-sen's Land Reform Program, which represents the original KMT position on peasant problems.

14. *Vacillation,* pp.108–109.

15. *Ibid.,*p.110.

16. May 1 is Labor Day in China after the Soviet tradition; May 4 commemorates the May Fourth Movement of 1919; May 7 and May 9 are both memorial days for *"kuo-ch'ih"* (national humiliation), having to do with President Yüan Shih-k'ai's agreement to sign Japan's infamous Twenty-one Demands.

17. *Vacillation,* Chapter 9, p.122.

18. *Ibid.,* Chapter 11, p.134.

19. *Ibid.,* p.145. This speech reads like a parody of what Lenin is castigating in his long essay on "infantile leftism;" all its points are taken from Stalin's letter of June 1 to the CCP Central Committee.

20. *Ibid.,* chapter 11, pp.151–152.

21. See "From Kuling to Tokyo," Section 5; also Mao Tun, "Memoirs IX."

22. C. T. Hsia, *A History of Modern Chinese Fiction* (New Haven, Conn., Yale University Press, 1961), pp.144–146.

23. Ch'ien Hsing-ts'un, "Mao Tun and Reality," *Contemporary Chinese Literary Writers II* (Shanghai, T'ai-tung t'u-shu-chü, 1930), p.129.

24. "From Kuling to Tokyo," Section 5.

25. Mao Tun, *Disillusionment* (Shanghai, K'ai-ming shu-tien, 1930), Chapter 10, pp.62–63.

26. C. T. Hsia, *op.cit.*, p.145. Hsia also has a section on the triangular relationship of Fang Lo-lan, Mrs. Fang, and Sun Wu-yang, which he praises as perceptive in terms of love psychology, pp.143–146.

27. *Vacillation*, chapters 2 and 6.

28. Ssu-ma Ch'ien "Tz'u-k'e lieh-chuan" (Biographies of Assassins) *Shih-chi (Records of the Grand Historian)*, *chüan* 86.

29. Ch'ien Hsing-ts'un, "Mao Tun and Reality," p.137.

5. Pursuit

1. For the history of the Great Revolution at this period, see Benjamin Schwartz, *Chinese Communism and the Rise of Mao* (Cambridge, Mass., Harvard University Press, 1951), pp.79–108; Chang Kuo-t'ao, *Memoirs II* (Hongkong, Mingpao yüeh-k'an ch'u-pan-she, 1973), pp.611–774; Robert C. North, *Chinese Communism* (New York, World University Library, 1966), pp.72–118. The Hai-lu-feng Soviet incorporated the surviving troops from the Swatow retreat; see Robert C. North, pp.97–98.

2. Chang Kuo-t'ao has the most detailed account of the final fate of these one-time comrades of his. See his *Memoirs II*, pp.748-774. His *Memoirs*, like Hua Kang's *A History of the Chinese Great Revolution 1925–1927* (Shanghai, Ch'un-keng shu-tien, 1936), show deep feelings of pride as well as sorrow at the deaths of the Chinese Communists. Both give a moving roll call of the martyrs; Chang blames the Comintern as strongly as Mao Tun does.

3. Benjamin Schwartz, *op.cit.*, pp.86–116; Chang Kuo-t'ao, *op.cit.*, pp.735–772.

4. See in particular Schwartz, *op.cit.*, pp.86–116.

5. *Ibid.*, p.96.

6. *Ibid.*, p.94. Here we cannot but recall the "second phase" of Miss Cloud's tuberculosis in Mao Tun's "From Kuling to Tokyo," and the story of her life as she tells it.

7. Benjamin Schwartz, *op.cit.*, p.106.

8. Mao Tun, "From Kuling to Tokyo," *Short Story Monthly* 19.10 (October 1928), pp.1138–1146. See section 1. See also his "Memoirs X" *Source Materials on the History of the New Literature* 1980.1 (February 1980), p.2.

9. Mao Tun, "Memoirs X," p.8.

10. Chang Kuo-t'ao, *Memoirs II*, pp.727 ff.

11. "From Kuling to Tokyo," section 6.

12. *Ibid.*, section 4.

13. *Ibid.*, section 6.

14. Mao Tun, *Tsui-ch'iu (Pursuit)* (Shanghai, K'ai-ming shu-tien, 1930), p.5. *Tsui-ch'iu* has been variously translated as *Quest* or *Searching*. "Quest" carries a religious connotation which *Tsui-ch'iu* does not have, and "searching" does not have the sense of momentum that "pursuit" or "pursue" has.

15. *Ibid.*, pp.5–6.

16. *Ibid.*, p.3.

17. *Ibid.*, pp.9–10.

18. *Ibid.*, p.11.

19. *Ibid.*, pp.14–15.

20. *Ibid.*, p.15.

21. The group's going to the movie here reminds us of the movie scene in chapter 3 of *Disillusionment*, where Pao-su and Miss Ching and Miss Hui went to

see *Crime and Punishment.* The title of the movie Miss Chang Ch'iu-liu and the "west-side" group go to see here, Tang-ren-hun (Souls of Late Party Members) reads like an apt subtitle to the first movie: crime in the name of revolution, punishable by death, is not absolved by invocation of the goal.

22. *Pursuit,* p.19.
23. *Ibid.,* p.20.
24. *Ibid.,* pp.20–21.
25. The name of Dr. Gold is reminder of how Sun Wu-yang appeared in the eyes of Hu Kuo-kuang in *Vacillation*—glittering like a pile of silver. The reflection of "gold" (idealism) and silver in the eyes of the gazers—Chang Man-ch'ing in *Pursuit* and Hu Kuo-kuang in *Vacillation*—is certainly not meant to be complimentary. The "international" theme in both cases subtly underscores the continuing presence of the Comintern in CCP politics and the Russian aid.
26. *Pursuit,* p.104. The expression used in the novel is: "with the courage befitting a martyr walking up to the guillotine."
27. *Ibid.,* p.96.
28. *Ibid.,* p.105.
29. *Ibid.,* p.107.
30. *Ibid.,* p.104.
31. *Ibid.,* p.109.
32. *Ibid.,* p.110.
33. *Ibid.,* p.160.
34. Mao Tun began to work at the Commercial Press in 1916 and resigned in 1925. He was then involved in Party newspaper work, first in Canton and later in Shanghai, Wuch'ang, and Hankow, till July 1927.

Mao Tun's "Memoirs VIII" mentions his editorship of *Cheng-chih chou-pao (Politics Weekly)* in Canton in January 1926 at the request of Mao Tse-tung, at that time head of the Central Propaganda Department of the Nationalist Party. After the Chungshan Gunboat Incident, which he reported in great detail in the same installment of the "Memoirs," he went back to Shanghai to take charge of the Nationalist Party Communications Bureau there. One of the functions of the Communications Bureau was to reprint and distribute material from *Politics Weekly* and other propagandas from the Central Propaganda Department. While in charge of the bureau, Mao Tun asked to have a special field investigator sent to the North and to the provinces along the Yangtze Valley to do some on-site investigation. The request and its refusal are reflected in Wang Chung-chao's request and in his subsequent dance-hall visits to gather material for his special column. See "Memoirs IX."

What Mao Tun was instructed to do for the Wuhan *Republic Daily* in 1927 also bears interesting comparisons with Wang Chung-chao's assignment in *Pursuit.* The *Republic Daily* had ten pages, six pages of news and four pages of advertisements. One of the news sections was called "local city news," one was "mass movements," and one was "news of Party business." See "Memoirs IX," pp.3–4. The last item may have been the fictional "advertisement for imported goods."
35. *Pursuit,* p.94.
36 These are the very prerequisites Mao Tun laid down in his article "On Reading *Ni Huan-chih*," *Wen-hsüeh chou-pao (Literature Weekly)* 8.20 (May, 1929), for would-be writers of new literature. In Section 7, he wrote:

> One who prepares to devote himself to the new art and literature must first have a head capable of organization, judgment, observation and analysis; it is not enough to be equipped with a trumpet that will serve to transmit his voice. He must first be able

to analyze by himself the mixed noises of the masses, quietly listen to the dripping of the underground spring [covert mass movements], and then structure these into the consciousness of his fictional characters.

Wang Chung-chao's views about committed writers contrast with the "big hat" speech of Chang Man-ch'ing and the phonograph disk that he and Chang Ch'iu-liu hear in their heads, as well as the ugly grinding gritty voice of Miss Chu Chin-ju. See note 41.

The most immediate provocation for Mao Tun's attack on the "phonograph disk" in *Pursuit* and then in "On Reading *Ni Huan-chih*" was a famous article, "Liu-sheng-chi ti hui-yin" [Echoes of the Phonograph Disk], an essay on the proper attitude for young writers by the recent convert to revolutionary literature, Kuo Mo-jo, published in *Wen-hua-p'i-p'ing (Cultural Review)* no.3 (March 1928), pp.1–12, under the pseudonym Mai-k'o-ang. The opening line of the article says, "Be a phonograph—this is the best credo for young literary writers." "Phonograph," the article goes on to explain, is a metaphor for "dialectic materialism," its characteristics being "objective." All young writers need to be a phonograph to overcome their innate property-classed consciousness. So the article exhorts: "Don't blow at will on your time-worn trumpet [a metaphor for the consciousness of the propertied-class]. Be a phonograph for the time being."

Such opinions are reason enough for Mao Tun's absolute scorn of the vocal qualities of the thoughts expressed by various characters in *Pursuit*.

37. *Pursuit*, chapter 1, pp.21–22.

38. The working environment was probably modeled either on Mao Tun's working environment at the Commercial Press or his newspaper offices, or a combination of both.

39. *Pursuit*, chapter 2, pp.29–30.

40. *Ibid.*, p.32.

Mao Tun wrote in his "Memoirs IX" about the warnings from his Party superior about his *Republic Daily* reportage on the workers', peasants', and women's movements. Ch'en Tu-hsiu, still the Secretary General of the CCP, advised Mao Tun to cut down on such "radical" news. According to the "Memoirs," Mao Tun sought the opinion of Tung Pi-wu, the Communist director of the *Republic Daily*, who told him to disregard Ch'en. See "Memoirs IX," pp.6–8. People from the Nationalist Party had protested against such news because they helped to spread communism, and in May 1927 there were already protests against the overradicalization of the workers' and peasants' movements. (Mao Tun used the heading "The Struggle between Light and Darkness" for news about these movements against landlords and capitalists; the metaphor of light-and-darkness was to recur in his *Wild Roses* short stories.)

41. For the significance of the phonograph disk, see note 36 above. The adjectives "grinding, gritty," we may note, are the same ones applied to the voice of Miss Chu Chin-ju.

42. *Pursuit*, pp.32–33.

43. *Ibid.*, p.37.

In "Memoirs IX," Mao Tun wrote that he was greatly vexed by the kinds of items he had to put into the section on "Urgent News": "Announcements by the Central Executive Committee of the Nationalist Party, the Nationalist Government and their sundry orders, instructions, and speeches by Nationalist V.I.P.'s . . . ." (p.8). But I suspect that what Mao Tun was talking about in the novel in terms of "newly arrived goods" was new instructions from the Comintern and the Moscow government telling the CCP how to carry on its revolution and propaganda.

44. *Pursuit,* p.43.

45. C. T. Hsia was the first critic to notice that Wang Chung-chao attended Chang Ch'iu-liu's wild beach party and Chang Man-ch'ing's wedding on the same day. See C. T. Hsia, *A History of Modern Chinese Fiction* (New Haven, Conn., Yale University Press, 1961), p.147.

Moscow's order for the CCP to begin the "soviet phase" meant literally the death in action of many CCP members from pre-Wuhan days. Hence the wedding of the Party man Chang Man-ch'ing to his gritty-voiced partner with an interest in international history is simultaneous with Chang Ch'iu-liu's effort to create a new Shih Hsün.

46. *Pursuit,* pp.115–117.

47. This ambiguity was eliminated in the 1954 and 1957 editions of the trilogy by giving Miss Chang [Ching of *Disillusionment*] the name Chang Ch'iu-liu, so that two Miss Changs were reduced to one at the very beginning. The 1928 *Short Story Monthly* serialized version calls Chang Ch'iu-liu Chang *nü-shih* (Miss Chang), as Chang Ching is called in chapter 1 of *Disillusionment;* so in the beginning pages, there are moments of ambiguity in the reader's mind whether this Chang *nü-shih* is not related in some way to the Chang *nü-shih* of *Disillusionment.* Or in the case of more careless readers, for those initial moments, they might indeed be taken as the same one. The 1930 K'ai-ming edition follows the *Short Story Monthly.* It introduces at the beginning of *Pursuit* Chang Ch'iu-liu as Chang *nü-shih* except when she is addressed directly as Ch'iu-liu by another character. The effect of a double montage there with the Chang *nü-shih* in the first chapter of *Disillusionment* cannot be accidental. Mao Tun said in "From Kuling to Tokyo" that he had hoped to use the same characters throughout the three novels but was forced to give up the idea. Of course it is difficult to say with certainty that the two Miss Changs represent the same "type" of person under two different historical circumstances—that is, two different stages of development of the same Great Revolution—but if we take seriously the author's own references to the problem, this is the most logical reason for the discrepancy. I believe the name symbolism of Chang Ch'iu-liu (discussed later in this chapter) helps to track the development of Mao Tun's thoughts about his double character.

Mao Tun specifically mentioned in his postscript to the new 1980 edition of *Eclipse* that the editors had proposed to restore the earlier deletions and he had refused. Thus he implicitly puts responsibility for the deletions on the editors. The total effect of the deletions as they still stand today is to obscure the links between the novel and the CCP history.

48. Compare Wang Shih-t'ao's reflections about her pregnancy here with Miss Huan's thinking about her pregnancy in the story "Suicide" in *The Wild Roses* (see my discussion in chapter 6). Mao Tun apparently reasoned through many alternatives for action for the CCP and for himself following the apocalyptic Canton Commune. If Miss Huan's reasoning represents a retreat from Wang's faint but determined hope for the future, a stronger hope appears in the short novel of 1931, *In Company of Three,* where K'o's optimism reflects the author's own mental journey. K'o, a young revolutionary who is perhaps one of the heirs of such characters as Tung-fang Ming and Wang Shih-t'ao, has vanished. After his disappearance his Friend Hui finds K'o's diary and reads this passage:

> You say that we did not bring happiness to the masses; that life for the masses is still poor. Yes, I not only admit that the masses have not yet had happiness, but also that the masses are making a great sacrifice now during the struggle, an extremely great sacrifice. However, why is it that you do not see that what the masses are suffering now comes from the enemies? We have not added any burden to the masses; we have

only saved them from some of their old burdens. One more thing. You have to understand that there is a qualitative difference between the suffering of the people now and the suffering of the people before. Their former suffering was suffering from exploitation. Now, it's from heroic struggle—it is an inevitable stage in the birth of a new society . . . Do you think a new society will simply fall from the sky? That perfection will be here with a turn of your hand? Do you think the torch of revolution will draw a line between the hell of yesterday and the heaven of today in one stroke? . . . When a tiny life is born from the body of a mother, much blood is shed and much suffering has to be endured. How much the more a new society, a society that has never existed in history before.

49. This alternative as a possible form of action in the wake of revolutionary defeat is given a full treatment in the story "Haze" in *The Wild Roses* (see the discussion in chapter 6).

50. *Pursuit*, p. 117. This section was deleted in the 1957 edition and remained deleted in the 1980 edition.

51. *Ibid.*, p. 119.

52. *Ibid.*, p. 120.

53. Here we may well be reminded of the two questions Mao Tun raised with regard to Maeterlinck's play *Mona Vanna* (see *Tung-fang tsa-chih* 18.4 (1920), pp. 59–60). Can a woman remain spiritually chaste when her body is sullied? Should a woman sacrifice her body as courageously as she would sacrifice her life in order to save others and her country? The metaphor is quite clear when transposed to the context of the Chinese Great Revolution: How much bodily and spiritual violation can a committed Party member endure without self-deception in the name of the revolutionary cause? (See also the discussion of this issue in chapter 3).

54. "From Kuling to Tokyo," section 3.

55. *Ibid.*, chapter 6, p. 128.

56. Here a rather forced link is established between the Wang-Lu relationship and the Chang-Shih adventure. Later on, a similar link was established between the Chang-Shih adventure and the Chang-Chu wedding. Evidently Mao Tun was trying very hard to compress the three parallel sets of love relationship into one exposure by manipulating the time of the climactic incidents. The pursuit of Chang Ch'iu-liu is in one sense the pursuit of Chang Man-ch'ing on a different level, which in turn is the pursuit of Wang Chung-chao, all being part and parcel of the complex, multilinear development of the Great Revolution and its aftermath. Similarity here assumes the form of either simultaneity or mistaken identity.

57. That Miss Lu resembles not only Miss Chang but also Miss Chu further reinforces the above point.

Mao Tun as propagandist was supervised by people very much like Wang's editor, and he had to listen to the "social science" expertise of people like Dr. Gold and supply data to substantiate the Party line as advocated by Chang Man-ch'ing. In his private world of personal identity, his love is for the Party (the girl at Chia-hsing where the CCP was first founded); his sympathy is with his die-hard, wrong-headed comrades who rushed to their death in the 1927–28 soviet movement (the women Ch'ang Ch'iu-liu and Wang Shih-t'ao); his contempt is for the gilded authority of the ideologue (Dr. Gold) and the slogan-mongering CCP disciple (Chang Man-ch'ing); and his unremitting hatred is reserved for Miss Chu, the harsh voice of the Comintern that will wreck the Party as she will destroy her partner.

58. *Pursuit*, p. 133.

59. *Ibid.*, p.134.
60. *Ibid.*, p.135.
61. The possible significance of these simultaneous events is discussed in note 45 above. Here I want to call attention to the meaningful simultaneity of Chang Man-ch'ing's wedding, which Wang Chung-chao attended, and the beach party of Chang Ch'iu-liu and Shih Hsün, which Wang also attended. They are both "profile" painting of the disaster that was meant to inaugurate the "soviet" movement.

The Canton Commune was the result of a host of historical factors, of course, but the most prominents ones were, first, the blind orders of the Comintern (Miss Chu's willful manipulation of Chang Man-ch'ing and her own shallowness of mind and character); second, the indigenous CCP's aspirations for independence and emancipation of the masses (Miss Lu in Chia-hsing as the offstage goal of the realist Wang Chung-chao); and third, the Futuristic self-destructiveness of those who set off the Canton Commune, the same people who had founded and led the Red Army in the Nanch'ang Uprising only a few months before (young Party veterans like Chang Ch'iu-liu, Shih Hsün, and the west-side group).

62. *Pursuit*, pp.137–138. This section was deleted in the 1957 and 1980 editions.
63. *Pursuit*, p.139.
64. *Pursuit*, p.145.
65. *Ibid.*, pp.150–151.
66. The date is important because the Sixth Congress of the CCP and the Sixth Congress of the Comintern both took place in Moscow in June 1928. CCP leadership was formally transferred from Ch'ü Ch'iu-po to Li Li-san at this congress. By anchoring the events to around the Tsinan Incident, Mao Tun makes it clear that he was talking about the Party history prior to the congress. For Ch'ü's curious indifference to the Incident, see Chang Kuo-t'ao, *Memoirs II*, p.770.
67. In China, syphilis is called *mei-tu* after a fruit *yang-mei* because of the red pimples or pustules that are often symptoms of the primary stage. The final stage of this disease fatally affects the female reproductive organ and causes death. An article called "Syphilis and Pulmonary Consumption" ("Mei-tu yü fei-chieh-he,") *Tung-fang tsa-chih* 18.16 [August 1921] was published in one of the Commercial Press magazines in 1921. In it, Hsü Sung-ming discussed the symptoms and phases of development of the two diseases in Western medical terms. As a matter of fact, *Tung-fang tsa-chih* carried quite a number of articles on Western science, medicine, and technology, in the late teens and early 1920s, reflecting the general public's interest in learning from the West.

Western medicine was especially fascinating to the Chinese. The new definition of diseases (typhus, venereal diseases, and tuberculosis) and the discovery of viruses was mind-boggling in China, since Chinese medicine had a totally different way of diagnosing illness and a totally different theory of "cure." One interesting feature of the May Fourth generation of writers is that their characters have begun to get sick with Western diseases. Appendicitis, typhus, and tuberculosis are particularly popular (Ting Ling's "Miss Sophia" is best known of many examples), but there is also the typhus of Yeh Shao-chün's Ni Huan-chih, the "depression" of Yü Ta-fu's hero in the famous novella *Sinking*, and the appendicitis that quite unscientifically stripped Shih Hsün of vitality in *Pursuit*. Lu Hsün's characters, however, who generally live in the countryside, still become ill with the old Chinese names for their sicknesses—for example, the son in the story "Medicine."

68. [Shen] Yen-ping, K'ung Ch'ang, and Ch'en Ku, *Chin-tai hsi-chü-chia lun (On Modern Playwrights)* (Shanghai, Tung-fang Wen-k'u, Commercial Press, 1923), p.23.

Hauptmann's play *Der Saemann*, originally entitled *Vor Sonnenaufgang*, is translated as *Tung-fang wei-ming (The East is Not Yet Bright)*. Mao Tun in the 1930s also took "Tung-fang wei-ming" as one of his pseudonyms. The implication of the name, of course, is that the East is soon going to be bright. The chapter on Hermann Sudermann and Gerhart Hauptmann originally appeared as an article in *Tung-fang tsa-chih* 17.15–16 (August 1921).

69. Men Ch'i (*circa* 755), "Chapter 1: On Matters of Personal Feelings (Ch'ing-kan-ti-i)," *Pen-shih-shih (Stories about Poets and Their Poems)* (Shanghai, Ku-tien-wen-hsüeh ch'u-pan-she, 1957), pp.8–11.

The association between the names Chang Ch'iu-liu in *Pursuit* and the title of the poem "Chang-t'ai Liu" ("The Willow of Chang-t'ai") in the story about the T'ang poet Han Yi is indirect, as is the association of Sun Wu-yang in *Vacillation* with Ch'in Wu-yang in *Shih-chi*, and the connection cannot be proved.

70. In the short novel *The Road* (Shanghai, Kuang-hua shu-chü, 1932), the overbearing dean or supervisor of the school who ravishes a girl student is named Chin (Thorns). He is the thorn in the rose crown of revolution and also the thorns that cover the path of revolution. But evil as he is, the Dean's influence is soon limited, because he is aliented from and distrusted by both the "Devil's Clique" and the "Scholars' Clique" of the students. The Dean still persecutes them, but he is no longer able to become part of their consciousness and thus lay claim over the pattern of their behavior.

6. *The Wild Roses:* The Psychology of Revolutionary Commitment

1. Mao Tun, "Memoirs XI," *Source Materials for the History of the New Literature (HWHSL)* 1981.2 (May 1981), pp.1–2.

2. *Ibid.,* p.2.

3. *Ibid.,* pp.3–17.

4. Mao Tun arrived in Japan nearly a year after the Wuhan retreat and the Canton Commune of 1927. The situation of the CCP worsened in early 1928, when a member of the upper echelons of the Party informed on her comrades, leading in one instance to the arrest of the CCP Shanghai Branch Secretary, Lo Chüeh. One might suggest that the motif of internal betrayal among "schoolmates" in Ho Jo-hua's unexplained change of heart in the story "Haze" is based on a political reality which Mao Tun in his mental and spiritual agony preferred not to remember clearly and could not in any case refer to directly. The informer against Lo Chüeh was Ho Chih-hua (very close to Ho Jo-hua). See Chang Kuo-t'ao, *Wo ti hui-i (Memoirs)* (Hongkong, 1973) vol. II, pp.759–64.

Mao Tun in his "Memoirs X-XI" writes about the period after the Wuhan retreat and about his departure for safety in Japan but does not mention the Lo Chüeh incident, *HWHSL* 1981.1 and 1981.2.

Recently Professor Satoru Nagumo published an article on *The Wild Roses*, incorporating much biographical information from Mao Tun's "Memoirs." Satoru Nagumo, "Mao Tun and his First Collection of Short Stories, *Ye Qiang Wei*," *The Nippon-chūgoku Gakkai-hō* (Bulletin of the Sinological Society of Japan) no. 33 (1981), pp.263–277.

5. Mao Tun, *"Mai tou-fu ti shao-tzu"* (Whistle of the Bean-curd Seller) *Short Story Monthly* 18.2 (February 1929). Also see "Memoirs XI," p.8.

6. Many of the essays attacking *Eclipse* and "From Kuling to Tokyo" were collected by Fu Chih-ying in a volume called *Mao Tun P'ing Chuan (Critical and Biographical Essays on Mao Tun)* (Preface dated Shanghai, October 20, 1931; reissued Hongkong, Nan-tao ch'u-pan-she, 1968). The most detailed literary criticism of *Eclipse*, *The Wild Roses* and *Rainbow* in that volume was in an essay by Ho Yü-po, "Mao Tun ch'uang-tso ti k'ao-ch'a" ("A Critical Investigation of Mao Tun's Creative Works"), pp.7–51, and the most controversial was Ch'ien Hsing-ts'un's "Mao Tun yü hsien-shih" ("Mao Tun and Reality"), pp.195–216. K'o Hsing's "P'ing Mao Tun ti 'Ts'ung Ku-ling tao Tokyo'" ("On Mao Tun's 'From Kuling to Tokyo'"), pp.217–243, and Ch'ien Hsing-ts'un's "Ts'ung Tokyo hui-tao Wu-han" ("Returning from Tokyo to Wuhan"), pp.255–314, typified the kind of literary polemics propounded by writers and critics on the radical left.

The direct and immediate bearing of communist politics on leftist literature and criticism of the period is attested to in a statement written by Mao Tun and given to Yu-shih Chen during an interview in September 1977 when the latter asked him, also in writing and delivered ahead of the interview, about the relationship of his fiction in the later 1920s and early 1930s to the situation of the Chinese Communist movement" "Literary polemics during the period were intimately related to the different outlooks on the situation of the revolution. . . . The reason is that when literature is at the service of revolution, different lines in party policy-making cannot but be concretely reflected in the subject matter and methods of creative writing."

Mao Tun, "Hsieh tsai *Yeh ch'iang-wei* ti ch'ien-mien" ("Foreword to *The Wild Roses*"), *Yeh ch'iang-wei (The Wild Roses)* (Shanghai, 1929), pp.i–vii. See especially section 3, Mao Tun's self-admonishment appears in Yu-shih Chen, (trans.), "From Kuling to Tokyo," *Revolutionary Literature in China: An Anthology*, John Berninghausen and Ted Huters (ed.) (White Plains, N.Y., N.E. Sharpe, 1976), pp.37–43. The relevant passages are on pp.4, and 43.

7. Mao Tun worked on mythology during the 1920s. He referred to it in his "Chi-chü chiu-hua" ("Remarks on the Past") *Wen-hsüeh* (1933), saying that he had begun his serious research in Chinese mythology sometime after April 1926 (see Yu-shih Chen in Goldman, ed. *Modern Chinese Literature*, p.266). In a later autobiographical piece he referred to his mythology studies thus: "The second half of 1928 was an exception. I was not sick at the time, but I was not writing novels either. At that time I wrote a few monographs on subjects of academic interest (I feel ashamed to mention this), for example, *A Study of Chinese Mythology*" (Mao Tun, "In Retrospect," *Self-Selected Works of Mao Tun* [Reissued Hongkong: Hsin-yüeh ch'u-pan-she, 1962], p.1).

Between 1925 and 1930, Mao Tun published several articles and at least two books on mythology: The *A.B.C. of Chinese Mythology* (Shanghai: Shih-chieh shu-chü, 1929), and The *A.B.C. of Nordic Mythology* (Shanghai, Shih-chieh shu-chü, 1929). He also published *Greek Mythology* (Shanghai: Commercial Press, 1926). In 1928, he published an article, "Greek Mythology and Nordic Mythology," *Short Story Monthly* 19.8 (August 1928), pp. 942–969. The article shows that Mao Tun had been thinking about the various aspects of the two mythologies in a comparative framework—their creation myths and their mythical representation of natural phenomena such as the sun, the moon, the clouds, and the earth. Their goddesses of Fate appear on pp.950–951. The comparative perspective behind the article is more interesting than details of its content. It is clear that in the mid- to late 1920s Mao Tun was preoccupied with the meaning of mythology, and we may assume that his borrowing of mythical names for his fictional character (see note 11 below) was conscious and deliberate.

8. Shen Yen-ping (ed.), *Chuang-tzu* (Shanghai: The Commercial Press, 1926) and *Ch'u Tz'u* (Shanghai, The Commercial Press, 1926).

There is a terse exposition of Chuang-tzu's "escapist" philosophy by Chün-shih in "Creation" which certainly reflects Mao Tun's own rejection of its view of the ultimate spiritual detachment of man in his world. But Mao Tun's most telling statement on the subject is in his "Preface" to *Chuang-tzu*, where he remarks on Chuang-tzu's lack of involvement in times of disorder and concludes that he was "not revolutionary" (a most amusing way to characterize Chuang-tzu). For a discussion on Mao Tun's involvement with Chuang-tzu studies in high school and later, see Marián Gálik, "From Chuang-tzu to Lenin: Mao Tun's Intellectual Development," *Asian and African Studies* (Brastislava) Vol. 3 (1967), pp. 98–109.

9. How Ch'ü Yüan died is still debated by some scholars. Mao Tun raised no questions about the circumstances of Ch'ü Yüan's death when he included the biography of Ch'ü Yüan from the *Shih-chi* in his *Ch'u Tz'u*. My hypothesis about the significance for Mao Tun of Chuang-tzu's philosophy and Ch'ü Yüan's tragic death helps to explain a great deal about Mao Tun's early works and what he said about them during this period.

10. Mao Tun, "Suicide," *Short Story Monthly* 19.9 (September 1928).

11. These allusions later reappeared and became even more pronounced in two novelettes he wrote after his return to Shanghai, *The Road* (1930) and *In Company of Three* (1930–31). The names of the principal characters in *The Road* are Hsing, Tu-jo, and (Chiang) Yung, all flowers in *Ch'u Tz'u*. There is also an explicit reference, though it is made in joking allusion to a line in a *Ch'u Tz'u* poem about wading the river to pick the *yung* flower. See Mao Tun, *The Road* (Shanghai, Wen-hua sheng-huo ch'u-pan-she, 1935), p. 32. *Hsing* (a graph that is identical to the Hsing in *The Road*), Hsü's girl friend in *In Company of Three*, and Ch'iu-chü (autumn chrysanthemum), the maid who commits suicide, in particular, carry definite *Ch'u Tz'u* overtones. There are many other mythical and historical references in the names of Mao Tun's character such as Chün-shih in "Creation" which we have already discussed.

Mao Tun himself in his "Memoirs XI–XII" identified the symbolism in many of the proper names used in his stories and essays of this period. See *HWHSL* 1981. 2–3 (May, August, 1981).

12. "Foreword," *The Wild Roses*, Section 2, p. iv.

13. Ch'ien Hsing-ts'un, "Mao Tun and Reality," *Contemporary Chinese Literary Writers* (Shanghai, T'ai-tung-t'u-shu-chü, 1930), vol. II, p. 172; also Fu Chih-ying, *op. cit.*, p. 215.

14. "Foreword," pp. i–ii.

15. In Greek myth, Lachesis measures the thread of life spun by Clotho and determines its length. Mao Tun, however, describes her as "twisting together the thread of life. Her wrist-power is at times strong and at times weak; that explains why man's life force varies in degree of strength." As a revolutionary, Mao Tun was more concerned with the strength than the length of life when the issue at stake was power in the political as well as the military field; but it is impossible to say whether he changed the myth deliberately or inadvertently. My guess is that he did it deliberately ("Foreword," p. i).

For a short account of the Greek Fates, see Robert Graves, *The Greek Myths*, vol. I (New York: George Braziller, Inc., 1955), p. 48.

16. "Foreword," p. ii. Mao Tun's version of the Nordic fates probably also contains elements of free variation of his own. I have not been able to find a description of Urd, Verdandi, and Skuld that conforms closely to his concept of mythological time. In Brian Branston's *Gods of the North*, the sisters' being

symbols of the Present, Past, and Future is there, but not the open relationship between man and his fate in mythological time. Instead, the following is said about the Fates: "The names of the three Nornir are Urdr, Verdandi and Skuld, words which may be translated Past, Present and Future: so that when 'the three giant maids came from Giantland' they brought with them *time;* then the timeless existence of the youthful gods in the Ancient Asgard ceased, and they put off their immortality. From the 'coming of the women' the predestined events must take place one after the other until the Doom of the Gods" (Brian Branston, *Gods of the North* [New York: The Vanguard Press, 1955], p.209). The Larousse *World Mythology* (New York: G. P. Putnam's Sons, 1965) gives a slightly different version of "the mistresses of human destiny" (pp.390–391), but it also differs from Mao Tun's version.

Mao Tun may have seen an early illustrated edition of the Nordic myths which I have not seen. Since I have not been able to locate his *A.B.C. of Nordic Mythology,* which according to his "Memoirs XI," shows eight sources, I do not know his exact sources. Here again, Dr. Marián Gálik came to my last-minute rescue. In a letter dated September 26, 1984, he said that there was indeed an illustrated book of Nordic mythology which Mao Tun had seen: "It was a book by H. A. Guerber, entitled *Myths of the Norsemen* (London 1919), where are also pictures you have rightly anticipated in *China Quarterly.*" I am very grateful to Dr. Gálik for his continuing supply of rare information concerning now obscured references in Mao Tun's early works.

17. Yu-shih Chen (reanal.) "From Kuling to Tokyo," p.39.

18. "Foreword," p.iii.

19. *Ibid.,* p.iii. I have used John Berninghausen's translation of this sentence from his conference paper, "Mao Tun's Early Fiction: A Dialectic Between Politics and Love," which was revised and published as "The Central Contradiction in Mao Tun's Earliest Fiction," in Goldman, *Modern Chinese Literature,* pp.233–229. In the published version the long quotation is considerably cut (see pp.242–243). Translations of other passages from the "Foreword" are my own.

20. "Foreword," p.vii.

21. The interpretation of the dramatic personalities in the stories as metaphors for flowers is my own; the phrase and the idea of a "rose-flower crown" are in the text ("Foreword," p.vii). I made a simple inference.

22. *Ibid.,* pp.iii–iv.

23. "Suicide," *The Wild Roses,* p.75.

24. *Ibid.,* p.76.

25. *Ibid.,* p.77.

26. C. T. Hsia, *A History of Modern Chinese Fiction* (New Haven: Yale University Press, 1961), pp.140–164 (p.161).

27. John Berninghausen, "Central Contradiction," pp.233–259.

28. Ch'ien Hsing-ts'ung, vol. II, p.161; also Fu Chih-ying, p.204.

29. Ch'ien Hsing-ts'un, *ibid,* pp.161–162; also Fu Chih-ying, pp.204–205.

30. This view is represented by C. T. Hsia's statement, cited in note 26. Hsia regards Mao Tun's characterization of Miss Huan in essentially the same way that Wayne Booth looks upon Henry James's characterization of the governess in "The Turn of the Screw" (see Wayne C. Booth, *The Rhetoric of Fiction* [Chicago: University of Chicago Press, 1961], p.312). I find Booth's chapters on "The Price of Impersonal Narration, Ch. I: Confusion of Distance," (pp.311–319) and "Ch. II: Henry James and the Unreliable Narrator" (pp.339–346) helpful in understanding similar technical problems confronting Mao Tun in his characterization of Miss Huan and other women in *The Wild Roses.*

31. Cf. note 27. Berninghausen's position can be challenged by invoking Booth's discussion of the use of the "unreliable narrator" as a device in fiction to effect a double focus—the unreliable narrator (in this case, Miss Huan) as the protagonist, and the author (Mao Tun) uncontrollably "breaking out" of his narrative to speak on a different level (cf. Booth, *Rhetoric of Fiction*, p.346). Applying Booth's analysis of the James story to Mao Tun's "Suicide," we can see that ambivalence about revolution, freedom, love, or women's emancipation does not necessarily have to be a part of Miss Huan's dramatic character nor a part of Mao Tun's personal feeling as the author. It can very well reside in the fictional device of the unreliable narrator. What Mao Tun wants his dénouement in "Suicide" to address is the nature and structure of commitment and its betrayal. The ambivalence reflected in Miss Huan's situation can be resolved once we see it in that perspective.

32. The theoretical issues involved in the uses of "telling" and "showing" in realistic fiction are many and complicated. Mao Tun obviously employed some such device as the double focus discussed in n.31 to communicate on more than one level of reality. Also, he left no record of his technical planning of his fiction beyond the Chinese terms "profile painting," "allusion" *(an-shih)*, and the like. Cf. Wayne Booth, "Telling and Showing," *Rhetoric of Fiction*, pp.3–20.

33. "Foreword," p.v.

34. *Ibid.*, p.v.

35. *Ibid.*, p.iv.

36. Mao Tun puts them in two separate groups of character types in section 4 of his "Foreword." Miss Huan is called a "weak" character, and Ch'iung-hua a victim of circumstance and egocentrism who once was innocent and loving. Their different outlooks on love and their different kinds of tragic death may point toward allegories for two different Party lines in different periods of revolutionary struggle. In light of the parallels that inform the other early fiction, Miss Huan's suicidal psychology could be interpreted as the lesson Mao Tun wanted his readers to learn from the putschist tendencies in late 1927 and early 1928 that cost the lives of many of his long-time comrades and caused large casualties among the rank and file of the party. Both Miss Huan and the putschist advocates mistook the road to death for the road out of a critical situation. By the same token, Ch'iung-hua's "egocentrism" could be regarded as another lesson on the deadly consequences of the politically egocentric "Li Li-san Line" which was obsessed with the idea of making comebacks by capturing urban centers, despite the fact that CCP military forces were not equipped for such large-scale undertakings after the setbacks of 1927. It is tempting to speculate in this direction, especially when we ask the reason for Mao Tun's preoccupation with suicide and sickness-unto-death motifs in these stories. Moreover, it is difficult to understand otherwise what Mao Tun meant by "egocentrism" in Ch'iung-hua: the story itself hardly supports such a description.

37. In the story, she is frequently shown to be lonely for love. See "A Woman," *The Wild Roses*, pp.90–92, 100 and 112–14.

38. *Ibid.*, p.91.

39. *Ibid.*, p.99.

40. *Ibid.*, p.162.

41. Tsu Hsiu-hsia, "Mao Tun ti 'I-ko nü-hsing,'" ("Mao Tun's 'A Woman'"), in Fu Chih-ying, p.130.

42. In Mao Tun's early fiction the image of the mother is invariably projected as warm and comforting, and she plays a positive role in the lives of the protago-

nists. "Mother" seems to stand for a relationship between the revolution and its goal that is spontaneous, natural, loving, healing, and rejuvenating. Miss Ching in *Disillusionment* is reminded of her mother whenever she is in distress, as Ch'iung-hua is in "A Woman." The latter's partial will to survive after the fire springs largely from her concern for her aging mother. The father figure in Mao Tun's early fiction generally fares less well. Fathers are nonexistent in *Eclipse,* and Miss Chang's father in "Haze" is an ugly tyrant.

43. "Haze" *The Wild Roses,* p.184.

44. In contrast to the legendary cradle of Chinese revolutionary movement, Canton, Peking, and Nanking are the bases of the warlords and the KMT respectively. As Pao-su in *Disillusionment* is an agent from Nanking, Ping's girl cousin in "Poetry and Prose"—his tie to the conservative past—finally goes with her father to Peking. Thus it is auspicious for the revolution that Miss Chang decides to go to Canton and her mother. Mao Tun does not have her think of marrying someone in Nanking nor of leaving for Peking; she does not betray herself.

45. Hsien-hsien's leftist and Communist affiliation and activities have been commented upon by C. T. Hsia in his "On the 'Scientific' Study of Modern Chinese Literature, a Reply to Professor Průšek," *T'oung Pao* L.4–5 (1963), pp.466–467.

46. "Poetry and Prose," *The Wild Roses,* p.145.

47. *Ibid.,* pp.136–137.

48. *Ibid.,* pp.139–140.

49. Ch'ien Hsing-ts'un, "Mao Tun and Reality," p.162; also Fu Chih-ying, pp.205–206.

50. Chün-shih's obsession with his "creation" conforms closely to the concept of humors in Western comedy. Northrop Frye's definition of humors and his penetrating study of the sources of absurdity in the role of humors in a changing society as reflected in the works of Dickens shed a great deal of light on Mao Tun's conception of his comic characters in *The Wild Roses,* such as Chün-shih and young man Ping: "The humor is a character identified with a characteristic, like the miser, the hypochondriac, the braggart, the parasite, or the pedant. He is obsessed with whatever it is that makes him a humor, and the sense of our superiority to an obsessed person, someone bound to an invariable ritual habit, is, according to Bergson, one of the chief sources of laughter. But it is not because he is incidentally funny that the humor is important in New Comedy: he is important because his obsession is the feature that creates the conditions of the action, and the opposition of the two [congenial and obstructing] societies" (Northrop Frye, "Dickens and the Comedy of Humours," in *The Stubborn Structure: Essays on Criticism and Society* [Ithaca, New York: Cornell University Press, 1970], p.223).

Frye's observation about the possibility for "comic action" to overcome or evade the sinister forces in a highly structured society bears cogently on the social and political function of the combined role of Chün-shih and Hsien-hsien in "Creation," and of Ping and Madame Kuei in "Poetry and Prose." "In most of the best Victorian novels, apart from Dickens, the society described is organized by its institutions: the church, the government, the professions, the rural squirearchy, business, and the trade unions. It is a highly structured society, and the characters function from within those structures. But in Dickens we get a much more free-wheeling and anarchistic social outlook. For him the structures of society, as structures, belong almost entirely to the absurd, obsessed, sinister aspect of it, the aspect that is overcome or evaded by the comic action. The comic action itself moves toward the regrouping of society around the only social unit that Dickens really regards as genuine, the family." (pp.227–28).

51. "Foreword," pp.iv–v.

52. *Ibid.*, p.iv.

53. *Ibid.*, p.v. The Chinese concept of the Golden Mean *(chung-yung)*—the middle road, moderation instead of taking to extremes—is close to the Aristotelian principle of the Mean.

54. *Ibid.*, p.vi.

55. "Creation," February 3, 1928 (following *Disillusionment*, September–October 1927, and *Vacillation*, November–December, 1927).

"Suicide," July 8, 1928 (following *Pursuit*, April–May 1928, and departure for Japan in June 1928).

"A Woman," August 20–25, 1928 (following "From Kuling to Tokyo," July 16, 1928).

"Poetry and Prose," December 15, 1928 (following "Whistle of The Bean-curd Seller," "Maple Leaves," "Knocking," and "Fog").

"Haze," March 9, 1929 (following "Colorblindness," March 3, 1929).

"Foreword to *The Wild Roses*," May 9, 1929 (following "Muddiness," April 3, 1929, and "On Reading *Ni Huan-chih*," May 4, 1929).

We see that "Creation" was written immediately after *Disillusionment* and *Vacillation*, or possibly at the same time as *Vacillation*, before Mao Tun had learned about or thought through the events that threw him into the despair of *Pursuit*. In these three works he was quite optimistic about the future, convinced of the value and reality of love and courage. But in the period of *Pursuit*, "Suicide," and "From Kuling to Tokyo," spontaneous love and courageous struggle had become the road to sickness and death. In Japan, physical distance from the center of revolutionary struggle created the initial elegiac mood of an "exile from home" that was reflected in his lyrical essays of the first half of his stay, and also the later, more creative psychological distancing from history that is reflected in the neither-love-nor-hate philosophy of "A Woman." The direction Mao Tun was striving for is captured briefly in "Poetry and Prose," in Madame Kuei's bold, uninhibited mode of sexuality and life. Biographically, the creation of Madame Kuei in the image of Hsien-hsien implies that Mao Tun had not given up, or had reenvisioned, the future that the endings of *Disillusionment* and "Creation" point toward. Finally, as exemplified in "Haze," Mao Tun's decision to recommit himself to his originally revolutionary course was conclusive, despite all reservations about a possible reversion to "suicidal" tendencies among friends, "schoolmates," and loved ones. If nothing else, "Haze" is a declaration of the renewed courage to take risks.

After "Haze," Mao Tun's writings became more spirited. "Muddiness" looks ahead to his three historical tales, and "On Reading *Ni Huan-chih*" and the foreword to *The Wild Roses*, written only five days apart, are full of strong, nonillusionary belief in the revolution, and renewed belief in the author's ability to influence events for the better.

56. "In Retrospect," *Self-selected Works*, pp.4–5; "Afterward [i.e., after the *Eclipse* and 'Creation'], I wrote four or five short pieces, such as 'Suicide.' In subject matter and technique they all belong to the same kind of writing. It is a waste indeed of brush and ink. . . . In subject matter, 'The Top' [November 5, 1929] is not any different from 'Creation' and the other. . . ."

57. "Wu" ("Fog" December 14, 1928), *Su-mang* (Shanghai: K'ai-ming shu-tien, 1931), pp.125–27.

58. "Hung-yeh" ("Maple Leaves") *Short Story Monthly* 20.3 (March 1929). Also collected in *Su-mang,* pp.130–133. "The Sound of the Bean-curd Seller's Whistle," *Short Story Monthly* 20.2 (February 1929): "In an outcast like me, without home, without motherland, refined sentiments like homesickness are not natural to the heart any more."

59. "K'ou men" ("Knocking," January 1929), *Su-mang,* pp.121–123.

60. "Ch'iu-ti-kung-yüan" ("Autumn in the Public Park"), *Mao Tun San-wen-chi (Collected Essays of Mao Tun)* (Shanghai: T'ien-ma shu-tien, 1933); reissued as *Mao Tun Tzu-hsüan San-wen-chi (Self-selected Essays of Mao Tun)* (Hongkong: 1954), pp.77–82.

"Chi-chieh-sung" ("Odes to Machines"), *ibid.,* pp.25–29.

"Tsai kung-yüan-li" ("In the Public Park"), *ibid.,* p.88.

"Wu-yüeh san-shih-jih ti hsia-wu" ("The Afternoon of May Thirtieth"), *Mao Tun hsüan-chi (Selected Works of Mao Tun)* (Shanghai: Hsien-tai ch'uang-tso wen-k'u edition, 1933), pp.259–262.

7. Consciousness of the Collective: Remaking the Rebel Tradition

1. "Pao-tzu-t'ou Lin Ch'ung" ("Lin Ch'ung the Leopard Head") *Short Story Monthly* 21.8 (August 10, 1930); "Shih-chieh" ("Stone Tablet") *Short Story Monthly* 21.9 (September 10, 1930); "Ta-tse-hsiang" ("The Great Marsh District") *Short Story Monthly* 21.10 (October 10, 1930).

2. Mao Tun, *Lu (The Road)* (Shanghai: Wen-hua sheng-huo ch'u-pan-she, 1935). In the postscript of this edition, Mao Tun outlined the vicissitude that visited the printing of the novel and also severe eye trouble he suffered: "I began writing this novel in the winter of 1930. When it first went to print, I had the following passage in my 'Notes written after reading the galley proofs'—'The novel was only half written when my old ailment, trachoma, again broke out. I was almost blinded in one eye. It took three months of medical care before I recovered from the attack. As a result, the second half of the novel was completed in the spring of 1931.'" Mao Tun apparently had eye trouble throughout his life. When I interviewed him in September 1977, he told me that he could not see with one eye, and the other eye had only 0.2 vision.

3. Mao Tun, "Memoirs XII," *Source Materials for the History of the New Literature (HWHSL)* 1981.3 (August 1981), pp.81–104.

4. *Ibid.,* p.83.

5. Benjamin Schwartz, *Chinese Communism and the Rise of Mao* (Cambridge, Mass. Harvard University Press, 1951). See especially chapter 8, "A New Shift in Line," pp.109–126.

6. *Ibid.,* p.108.

7. *Ibid.,* p.139. I am puzzled to find that Mao Tun in "Memoirs XII" denies knowledge of the activities of Mao Tse-tung and Chu Te in Chingkang mountains but highlights the Fifth Red Army commander P'eng Te-huai and his attack on Changsha (see "Memoirs XII," pp.89–90).

8. Mao Tun, "Wo-ti-hui-i" ("In Retrospect"), *Self-Selected Works of Mao Tun* (Reissued Hongkong: Hsin-yüeh ch'u-pan-she, 1962), pp.5–7. Italics added.

9. For background to the history behind "In Retrospect," see Benjamin Schwartz, *op.cit.,* pp.109–163. Also, Chang Kuo-t'ao, *Memoirs II* (Hongkong, Mingpao yüeh-k'an ch'u-pan-she, 1973), pp.777–860.

10. Benjamin Schwartz, *op.cit.*, pp.172–188. From his writing of "The Great Marsh District" and later his trilogy of the countryside in short story form— "Spring Silkworms," "Autumn Harvest," and "Winter Ruins"—we can infer that Mao Tun's outlook on the future of the peasant movement in 1930–32 had greatly improved from his apocalyptic view of 1927–28.

11. "Foreword," *The Wild Roses* (Shanghai, 1929), p.vii: "All five stories in this collection appear in the guise of love stories. The author attempts to reveal the *chieh-chi ti i-shih-hsing-t'ai* (class consciousness of each of the characters through their actions in a love relationship."

12. "Ta-tse-hsiang" ("The Great Marsh District"), *Collected Short Stories of Mao Tun II* (Shanghai, 1939), p.107: "If we wait here, it will be death for sure. Why don't we take action together? Only then can we escape death." There is a very similar speech between Ch'en She and Wu Kuang in *Shih-chi*.

13. *Shui-hu-chuan (The Water Margin)* (Peking: Jen-min wen-hsüeh ch'u-pan-she, 1957).

14. Ssu-ma Ch'ien, *Records of the Grand Historian*, translated by Burton Watson (New York: Columbia University Press, 1961), I, pp.9–30.
For the Chinese version see "Ch'en She shih-chia," *Shih-chi hui-chu K'ao-cheng*, 48.1–25.

15. The person who comes first to mind as the model for Mao Tun's Lin Ch'ung is Mao Tse-tung. Some Japanese scholars have actually said so. However we find significant discrepancies between their positions and background.
Lin Ch'ung, both in the source and in Mao Tun's story, is always where the central court is. In *Water Margin*, he begins as the captain of the Imperial Guards right in the capital of the Northern Sung dynasty. In Mao Tun's story, he is in Liang-shan, at the headquarters of the rebel group, contending actively for leadership. Neither case adequately reflects Mao Tse-tung's situation in 1930, who at that time was out in the countryside, away from the CCP headquarters in Shanghai.
For an account of Mao Tse-tung's activities in 1930 up to the Fut-ien Incident, see Benjamin I. Schwartz, *Chinese Communism and the Rise of Mao* (Cambridge: Harvard University Press, 1951), pp.172–188, especially pp.172–178.
Li Li-san is my candidate as model for Mao Tun's Lin Ch'ung if a candidate need be found. It was he and not Mao Tse-tung who repeatedly ran afoul of "scholars" at the leadership level: first Ch'ü Ch'iu-po, then in 1930, Wang Ming. He was also the one who had held military command after the Nanchang Uprising of August 1927. The details of his role in the CCP better fit Mao Tun's portrayal of Lin Ch'ung in the fictional version of the intra-party feud.

16. There was only one set of people on the scene on the leadership level in the CCP that approximated the image of Wang Lun, namely, Wang Ming and the group of returned students from Moscow. The feud between this group and the Li Li-san group was fictionalized in *The Road*, with Mif presiding as Dean Ching.

17. Yang Chih is a good fictional projection of those like Ch'ü Ch'iu-po and Teng Chung-hsia who in 1930 still clung to the practice of deferring to the wishes of Moscow and the Comintern as the orthodox way of advancing the cause of the communist movement in China.

18. Mao Tun, *Collected Short Stories, II*, p.442.

19. *Ibid.*, p.445.

20. See note 11.

21. See note 15.

22. Burton Watson (tr.) *Records of the Grand Historian I*, pp.29–30.

23. See note 11 for the variant forms of expression for "class" in Chinese.

24. Mao Tun, *Spring Silkworms and Other Stories* (Peking: Foreign Languages Press, 1956), pp.267–268.

25. *Ibid.*, p.269.

26. *Ibid.*, p.270.

27. *Ibid.*, p.271.

28. *Ibid.*, p.271.

29. *Ibid.*, p.275.

30. *Ibid.*, p.275.

31. It is difficult to resist the temptation to speculate on the person behind Mao Tun's "chief advisor Wu Yung." There is one person throughout the Chinese Communist movement who fits consistently into this role of a master negotiator excelling in the art of *ho-hsi-ni* (making thin mud mixture), and that is Chou En-lai. Reviewing his activities in 1930, his role of a master peace-maker certainly stands out. See Chang Kuo-t'ao, *Wo ti hui-i (Memoirs)* (Hongkong, 1973) vol. 2, pp.777–857, especially pp.821–857.

32. *Collected Short Stories of Mao Tun I* (Shanghai: K'ai-ming shu-tien, 1934), p.339.

33. *Ibid.*, p.340.

34. *Ibid.*, p.341.

35. The three historical tales were first published in *Short Story Monthly.*

"Pao-tzu-t'ou Lin Ch'ung" (Lin Ch'ung the Leopard Head), first appeared in *Hsiao-shuo yüeh-pao (Short Story Monthly)* XXI.8 (August 10, 1930), and was later collected in *Mao Tun tuan-p'ien hsiao-shuo-chi II (Collected Short Stories of Mao Tun, II)*, pp.439–445.

"Shih-chieh" (Stone Tablet) first appeared in *Short Story Monthly* XXI.9 (September 10, 1930) and later on collected in *Mao Tun tuan-p'ien hsiao-shuo-chi I (Collected Short Stories of Mao Tun, I)* (Shanghai: K'ai-ming shu'tien, 1934), pp.336–341. "Stone Tablet," probably because of its cynical attitude towards political ideology and revolutionary leadership, is the least anthologized of the three historical tales. It is overlooked by leftist publishers to the extent of deliberate oblivion.

"Ta-tse hsiang" (Great Marsh District), *Collected Short Stories of Mao Tun, II*, pp.429–438. It was first published in *Short Story Monthly* XXI.10 (October 10, 1930). It was much anthologized, and was the only of the three pieces translated in *Spring Silkworms and Other Stories* (Peking: Foreign Languages Press, 1956), pp.267–276. Its popularity is easily explained by the glorification of the peasant movement and the cult of Mao Tse-tung's leadership developed since the mid-1930s.

The shift in Mao Tun's fictional characters from the upper strata of society to the lower and middle strata in mid-1930s is reflected in the following examples: "Hsiao-su" (The Little Witches) (1932.2.29); "Lin-chia p'u-tzu" (1932.6.18) and "Ta-pi-tzu ti ku-shih" (Story of the Big-nosed Boy) (1936.5.27).

"The Little Witches" is a story about the lawless behaviors of the village powers along the lower Yangtze who controlled the local militia. The title "Hsiao-wu" is somewhat puzzling because the allusion is not apparent. There is a saying in Chinese "hsiao-wu chien ta wu" meaning something like one is surpassed by another in his realm of expertise. Chang Kuo-t'ao has an interesting phrase in his *Memoirs* (Volume 2) which may elucidate the reference of Mao Tun's use of the term *Hsiao-wu.* Chang says, "I have been to the rural villages to visit collective farms, to study the actual happenings in the struggles against rich peasants and against religious practices. They reminded me of some of the excessive measures taken in the peasant movement of the Wuhan period. By comparison, the latter appears like little witches in the presence of master witches." Chang Kuo-t'ao, *Memoirs, II*, p.839.

"Lin's Store" is a story about the bankruptcy of small town storekeepers. *Collected Short Stories of Mao Tun, I*, pp.204–250. Translated in *Spring Silkworms and Other Stories*, pp.113–163.

"The Story of the Big-nosed Boy" is about a child tramp in Shanghai in the 1930s. *Collected Short Stories of Mao Tun, II*, pp.271–294. Translated in *Spring Silkworms and Other Stories*, pp.189–210.

36. Mao Tun, "In Retrospect," pp.2–3.

37. Mao Tun, *San-jen-hsing (In Company of Three)* (Shanghai: K'ai-ming shu-tien, 1930).

Hsü attempted to combat the evils around him singlehandedly. After repeated failures, he was duly martyred for his cause. The moral of Hsü's story is obvious: deeds of individualistic heroism are futile in a society dominated by organized interest groups and repressive forces.

38. Mao Tun, *Lu (The Road)* (Shanghai: Wen-hua sheng-huo ch'u-pan-she, 1935).

These are student groups and characters in *The Road*. In *The Road* Mao Tun goes back to the allegorical method of *Eclipse*, using student activities to represent Party politics. It is not a very well written novel. Its "tune" is certainly old. From the novelistic viewpoint, it breaks no new ground. Hence it is not included in this study.

BIBLIOGRAPHY

Works by Mao Tun

Novels

Huan-mieh 幻滅 (Disillusionment). Shanghai: K'ai-ming shu-tien 開明書店 ,1930.

Tung-yao 動搖 (Vacillation). Shanghai: K'ai-ming shu-tien, 1930.

Tsui-ch'iu 追求 (Pursuit). Shanghai: K'ai-ming shu-tien, 1930.

Shih 蝕 (Eclipse). Shanghai: K'ai-ming shu-tien, 1930. Reprinted Peking:
Jen-min wen-shüeh ch'u-pan-she 人民文學出版社 , 1954. Collected in
Mao Tun Wen Chi 茅盾文集 (Collected Works of Mao Tun) in ten volumes.
Peking, Jen-min wen-hsüeh ch'u-pan-she, 1957.

Hung 虹 (Rainbow). Shanghai: K'ai-ming shu-tien, 1930.

San-jen-hsing 三人行 (In Company of Three). Shanghai: K'ai-ming shu-tien,
1931.

Lu 路 (The Road). Shanghai: Kuang-hua shu-chü 光華書局 , 1932.

Tzu-yeh 子夜 (Midnight). Shanghai: K'ai-ming shu-tien, 1933.

Tuo-chiao-kuan-hsi 多角關係 (Polygonal Relations). Shanghai: Sheng-huo
shu-tien 生活書店 , 1937.

Ti-i chieh-tuan ti ku-shih 第一階段的關係 (Story of the First Stage of
the War). Shanghai: K'ai-ming shu-tien, second printing, 1939.

Fu-shih 腐蝕 (Putrefaction). Shanghai: Hua-hsia shu-tien 華夏書店 ,1941.

Shuang-yeh hung-shih erh-yüeh hua 霜葉紅似二月花 (Frosty Leaves Red
as February Flowers). Kuei-lin 桂林: Hua-hua shu-tien 華華書店, 1943.

Tuan-lien 鍛鍊 (Discipline). Peking: Wen-hua i-shu ch'u-pan-she 文化藝術
出版社 , 1980. First serialized in Wen-hui-pao 文匯報 (Hongkong,
September 9 - December 29, 1948).

Collections of Short Stories

Yeh Hsiang-wei 野薔薇 (The Wild Roses). Shanghai: Ta-chiang shu-p'u
大江書舖, 1929.

Su-mang 宿莽 . Shanghai: K'ai-ming shu-tien, 1935.

Mao Tun tuan-p'ien hsiao-shuo chi 茅盾短篇小說集 (Collections of
Short Stories by Mao Tun) in 2 volumes. Shanghai: K'ai-ming shu-tien,
1935.

Mao Tun hsüan-chi 茅盾選集 (Selected Works of Mao Tun). Shanghai:
Wan-hsiang shu-wo 萬象書屋 , 1935.

Mao Tun ch'uang-tso hsüan 茅盾劇作選 (A Selection of Creative Writing
      by Mao Tun). Shanghai: Wen-hua sheng-huo ch'u-pan-she 文化生活出版社
      1936.

P'ao-muo 泡沫 (Foams and Other Stories). Shanghai: Sheng-huo ch'u-
      pan-she 生活出版社, 1936.

Hsiao-ch'eng ch'un-ch'iu 小城春秋 (Story from a Small Town). Shanghai:
      Wen-hua sheng-huo ch'u-pan-she, 1937.

Shao-nü-ti hsin 少女的心 (Heart of the Maiden). Shanghai: Wen-hua sheng-
      huo ch'u-pan-she, 1937.

Kuling chih-ch'iu 牯嶺之秋 (Autumn in Kuling). Shanghai: Wen-hua sheng-
      huo ch'u-pan-she, 1937.

Ts'an-tung 殘冬 (Winter Days). Shanghai: Wen-hua sheng-huo ch'u-pan-
      she, 1937.

Mao Tun tai-piao-tso 茅盾代表作 (Representative Works of Mao Tun).
      Shanghai: Ch'un-ch'iu shu-tien 春秋書店, 1937. Reprinted by
      Shanghai: Ch'en-kuang ch'u-pan-kung-ssu 晨光出版公司 ', 1946.

Yen-yün-chi 煙雲集 (Misty Clouds and Other Stories). Shanghai: Ch'en-
      kuang ch'u-pan kung-ssu, 1937.

Shen-ti mieh-wang 神的滅亡 (The Death of God). n.p. Liang-yu t'u-shu-
      kung-ssu 良友圖書公司, 1944.

Wei-ch'ü 委屈 (Grievance and Other Stories). Chungking, Chien-kuo
      shu-tien 建國書店, 1944.

T'ien-shu-hua 鐵樹花 (Flower from the Barren Tree). Shanghai: Wen-hua
      sheng-huo ch'u-pan-she, 1945.

Yeh-su chih-ssu 耶穌之死 (The Death of Jesus). Shanghai: Tso-chia shu-wo
      作家書屋 , 1945.

Mao Tun Wen Chi 茅盾文集 (Collected Works of Mao Tun). Shanghai; Ch'un-
      ming shu-tien 春明書店 , 1947.

Mao Tun hsüan-chi 茅盾選集 (Selected Works of Mao Tun). Peking: K'ai-
      ming shu-tien, 1952.

Mao Tun tuan-p'ien hsiao-shuo hsüan 茅盾短篇小說選 (A Selection of
      Short Stories by Mao Tun). Peking: Jen-min wen-hsüeh ch'u-pan-she,
      1955.

Mao Tun tzu-hsüan-chi 茅盾自選集 (Works Selected by Mao Tun Himself).
      Hongkong: Hsin-yüeh ch'u-pan-she 新月出版社, 1962.

Mao Tun tuan-p'ien hsiao-shu-chi 茅盾短篇小說集 (Collections of Short
      Stories by Mao Tun) in 2 volumes. Peking: Jen-min wen-hsüeh ch'u-
      pan-she, 1980. This set includes practically all the stories in
      the 1934 K'ai-ming shu-tien edition of Collections with the
      exceptions of "Tzu-sha" 自殺 ("Suicide"), "Hsi-chü" 喜劇 ("Comedy"),
      "Kuling chih-ch'iu" 牯嶺之秋 ("Autumn in Kuling") and "Kuang-ming
      tao-lai ti shih-hou" 光明到來的時候 ("When the Light Is Here"). It
      also includes a dozen or so stories written after 1933.

Essays

Hua-hsia-tzu 話匣子 (Chatter Box). Shanghai, Liang-yu t'u-shu kung-
      ssu, 1934.

Mao Tun san-wen-chi 茅盾散文集 (Collected Essays of Mao Tun). Shanghai: T'ien-ma shu-tien 天馬書店, 1933.

Su-hsieh yü sui-pi 速寫與隨筆 (Sketches and Notes). Shanghai: K'ai-ming shu-tien, 1935.

Chung-kuo-ti i-jih 中國的一日 (One Day in China and Other Essays). Shanghai: Sheng-huo shu-tien, 1936.

Yin-hsiang, kan-hsiang, hui-i 印象感想回憶 (Impressions, Reflections, Reminiscences). Shanghai: Wen-hua sheng-huo ch'u-pan-shê, 1936.

P'ao-huo-ti hsi-li 炮火的洗禮 (Baptism by Gunfire). Chungking: Feng-huo-she 烽火社, 1939.

Chieh-hou shih-i 劫後拾遺 (Pieces Picked-up after the Calamity). Kuei-lin: Hsüeh-i ch'u-pan-she 學藝出版社, 1942.

Chien-wen tsa-chi 見聞雜記 (Miscellaneous Notes on What I see and Hear). n.p. Wen-kuang shu-tien 文光書店, 1945.

Mao Tun wen-hsüen 茅盾文選 (Selected Essays by Mao Tun). Shanghai: Ch'ing-ch'un ch'u-pan-she 青春出版社, 1946.

Pai-yang li-tsan 白楊禮讚 (Odes to the Poplar Trees). Shanghai: Hsin-hsin ch'u-pan-she 新新出版社, 1946.

Fang-sheng wei-ssu chih-chien 方生未死之間 (Between Coming to Life and Death). Nanking, Hsiao-ya shu-tien 小雅書店, 1947.

Su-lien chien-wen-lu 蘇聯見聞錄 (Travels in the Soviet Union). Shanghai: Chih-yung shu-tien 致用書店, 1949.

Mao Tun tzu-hsüan san-wen-chi 茅盾自選散文集 (Essays Selected by Mao Tun Himself). Hongkong, Hsien-tai-wen-chiao-she 現代文教社, ;954.

Yeh-tu ou-chi 夜讀偶記 (Notes While Reading at Night). T'ien-ching 天津, Pai-hua wen-i ch'u-pan-she 百花文藝出版社, 1958.

Ku-ch'uei-chi 鼓吹集 (Essays 1949-1958). Peking: 1959.

Ku-ch'uei-hsü-chi 鼓吹續集 (More Essays 1958-1961). Peking: Tso-chia-ch'u-pan-she 作家出版社, 1962.

Others

Ch'u Tz'u hsüan-chu 楚辭選註 (Annotated Selections from the Songs of Ch'u). Shanghai: Commercial Press 商務印書館, 1928.

Chung-kuo shen-hua yen-chiu A.B.C. 中國神話研究ABC (Introduction to the Study of Chinese Mythology). Shanghai: Shih-chieh shu-chü 世界書局, 1929.

Ch'i-shih wen-hsüeh ABC 騎士文學ABC (Introduction to Chivalric Literature). Shanghai: Shih-chieh shu-chü, 1929.

Shen-hua tsa-lun 神話雜論 (Miscellaneous Notes on Mythology). Shanghai: Shih-chieh shu-chü, 1929.

Hsi-yang wen-hsüeh t'ung-lun 西洋文學通論 (Outline of Western Literature). Shanghai: 1929? 1933? Pseudonym, Fang Pi 方璧.

Chung-kuo wen-hsüeh pien-ch'ien-shih 中國文學變遷史 (History of the Development of Chinese Literature). Shanghai: Hsin-wen-hua ch'u-pan-she 新文化出版社, 1934.

Ch'uang-tso-ti chun-pei 創作的準備 (Preparation for Creative Writing). Shanghai: 1937 (Second edition). Reprinted by Peking, San-lien shu-tien 三聯書店, 1951.

Kuan-yü li-shih ho li-shih-chü 關於歷史和歷史劇 (On History and Historical Plays). Peking: Tso-chia ch'u-pan-she, n.d..

Autobiographical, Bibliographical Works and Recent Collections of Mao Tun's Works

Autobiographical Works:

Hui-i-lu 回憶錄 ("Memoirs"), Hsin-wen-hsüeh-shih-liao (Quarterly)新文學史料 (Documents on the [Study of] New Literature). Peking: Jen-min wen-hsüeh ch'u-pan-she, 1978-

Wo tsou-kuo-ti tao-lu 我走過的道路 (Roads I Have Travelled On). Hongkong: San-lien shu-tien, 1981.

Bibliographical Works:

Matsui Hiromitsu 松井博光 ed. Mao Tun p'ing-lun-chi 茅盾評論集 (Collections of Mao Tun's Critical Essays), 5 vols. and A Bibliography of Mao Tun's Critical Essays. Tokyo: Toritsu Daigaku 東京都立大學 1957-1966.

_____. Mao Tun Ch'uang-tso, P'ing-lun, San-wen Mu-lu I (1892-1935) 茅盾創作評論散文目錄 I (A Bibliography of Mao Tun's Creative Writing, Critical Essays and Essays:I). Tokyo Toritsu Daigaku, Jinbun gakuhō 98 人文學報 (1974).

_____. Mao Tun Ch'uang-tso, Ping-lun, San-wen Mu-lu II (1936-1949) 茅盾創作評論散文目錄 II (A Bibliography of Mao Tun's Creative Writing, Critical Essays and Essays: II). Tokyo Toritsu Daigaku, Jinbun gakuhō 112 (1976).

Collections of Mao Tun's Works since 1958

Mao Tun wen-chi 茅盾文集 (Collected Works of Mao Tun) in ten vols. Peking: Jen-min-wen-hsüeh ch'u-pan she, 1958-1961.

Mao Tun P'ing-lun chi I & II (November 1949- fall, 1962) 茅盾評論集上下 (Collection of Mao Tun's Critical Essays in two vols.) Peking: Jen-min-wen-hsüeh ch'u-pan-she, 1978.

Mao Tun 茅盾. Shih-chieh ming-chu tsa-lun 世界名著雜論 (Essays on Great Works of World Literature). T'ien-ching, Pai-hua wen-i ch'u-pai she, 1980.

Yeh Tzu-ming ed. 葉子銘(編). Mao Tun lun ch'uang-tso 茅盾論創作 (Essays by Mao Tun on Creative Writing). Shanghai: Shanghai wen-i ch'u-pan-she 上海文藝出版社, 1980.

Yüeh Tai-yün ed. 樂黛雲 (編) Mao Tun lun Chung-kuo hsien-tai tso-chia tso-p'in 茅盾論現代中國作家作品 (Mao Tun on the Works of Contemporary Chinese Writers). Peking: Peking University Press, 1980.

Mao Tun i-wen hsüan-chi 茅盾譯文選集 (Selection of Mao Tun's Translated
Works). Shanghai: Shanghai I-wen ch'u-pan-she, 上海譯文出版社,1981.

Mao Tun wen-i p'ing-lun-chi in 2 vols 茅盾文藝評論集 (Essays on
Literature and Arts by Mao Tun in 2 vols). Peking: Wen-hua i-shu
ch'u-pan-she 文化藝術出版社, 1981.

References

Aristophanes. Five Comedies of Aristophanes. Translated by Benjamin
Bickley Rogers with introduction and notes. Anchor Books, 1956.

Ayers, Williams. "The Society for Literary Studies," Papers on China
7:34-79 (February, 1953). Cambridge, Mass.: East Asian Research
Center, Harvard University.

Beardsley, Monroe. Aesthetics. New York: Harcourt, Brace & World, Inc.,1958.

Berdyaev, Nicolas. The Russian Idea. New York: The Macmillan Co., 1948.

Berninghausen, John & Huters, Ted, ed. Revolutionary Literature in China:
An Anthology. White Plains, New York: M.E. Sharpe, 1976.

Booth,Wayne. The Rhetoric of Fiction. Chicago: University of Chicago
Press, 1961.

Brandt, Conrad, Schwartz, Benjamin, and Fairbank, John K. A Documentary
History of Chinese Communism. Cambridge, Mass.: Harvard University
Press, 1952.

_____. Stalin's Failure in China 1924-1927. Cambridge, Mass.:
Harvard University Press, 1958.

Branston, Brian. Gods of the North. New York: The Vanguard Press, 1955.

Brostrom, Kenneth N. "Boris Pil'njak's A Chinese Tale: Exile as Allegory,"
Mosaic (University of Manitoba Press) IX.3 (1976), pp.11-25.

Brown, Edward J. Mayakovsky, A Poet in the Revolution. Princeton, New
Jersey: Princeton University Press, 1973.

Carr, E.H. Socialism in One Country, 1924-1926, in three vols. Penguin
Books, 1970.

Chang Jo-ying 張若英. Chung-kuo hsin-wen-hsüeh yün-tung-shih tzu-liao
中國新文學運動史資料 (Source Materials on the History of the New
Literature Movement in China). Shanghai: 1934.

Chang Kuo-t'ao 張國燾. Wo-ti hui-i 我的回憶(Memoirs) in three vols.
Hongkong, Mingpao yüeh-k'an-she 明報月刊社, 1971-1974.

Ch'en Kung-po & Chou Fuo-hai 陳公博,周佛海. Hui-i-lu ho-pien 回憶綜合編
(Memoirs in One Volume). Hongkong, Ch'un-ch'iu ch'u-pan-she 春秋出版社
1967.

Ch'en Tu-hsiu. "Chin-jih-chih chiao-yü fang-chen"近日之教育方針 ("The
Tendency of Contemporary Educational Policies") HCN 新青年 1.2
(October, 1915), pp.1-6.

_____. "Wen-hsüeh ko-ming lun" 文學革命論("On Literary Revolution")
HCN 2.6 (February, 1917), pp.1-4.

Ch'eng Fang-wu 成仿吾 . "Hsin-wen-hsüeh-chih shih-ming" 新文學之使命
("The Mission of New Literature")CTCP 創造周報 2.1-7 (May, 1923).

_____. "Ts'ung wen-hsüeh-ko-ming tao ko-ming-wen-hsüeh"
從文學革命到革命文學("From Literary Revolution to Revolutionary
Literature) CTYK 創造月刊 9.1-7.

Chiang Yung-ching 蔣永敬 . Pao Lo-t'ing yü Wuhan cheng-ch'üan 鮑羅廷
與武漢政權(Borodin and the Wuhan Regime). Taiwan: Commercial Press, 1963.

Ch'ien Hsing-ts'un 錢杏邨 . Hsien-tai Chung-kuo wen-hsüeh tso-chia, 現代
中國文學作家 上下 (Contemporary Chinese Literary Writers) in 2 vols..
Shanghai: T'ai-tung t'u-shu-chü 泰東圖書局 , 1929, 1930.

_____. "Chung-kuo hsin-hsing wen-hsüeh-chung-ti
chi-ko chü-t'i wen-t'i" 中國新興文學中的幾個具體問題
("A Few Concrete Questions in The Newly Developed Chinese Literature")
To-huang-che 拓荒者 1 (January, 1930), pp.341-382.

_____. "Ts'ung Tung-ching hui-tao Wuhan" 從東京回到武漢
("Returning from Tokyo to Wuhan) in Fu Chih-ying 伏志英 ed., Mao Tun
P'ing-chuan 茅盾評傳 , pp.250-314.

Chiang Kuang-tz'u 蔣光慈 . Shao-nien p'iao-po-che 少年飄泊者 (The Youthful
Tramp). Shanghai: Pei-hsin shu-tien 北新書店 , 1933.

_____. Ch'ung-ch'u yün-wei-ti yüeh-liang 衝出雲圍的月亮
(The Moon Emerging From the Clouds). Shanghai: Pei-hsin-shu-tien, 1939.

_____. Chiang Kuang-tz'u hsüan-chi 蔣光慈選集 (Selected
Works of Chiang Kuang-tz'u). Peking: K'ai-ming shu-tien, 1955.

Chou Erh-fou 周而復 . "Tsai ping-wei-ti shih-hou" 在病危的時候("When
Critically Ill"), Shou-huo Bimonthly 收穫 (Harvest) 1981.3 (May, 1981),
pp.86-92.

Chou Tse-tsung. The May Fourth Movement. Cambridge, Mass.: Harvard
University Press, 1960.

_____. Research Guide to the May Fourth Movement. Cambridge,
Mass.: Harvard University Press, 1963.

Chu P'ei-hsien (Tzu-ch'ing) 朱佩弦(自清) . "Tzu-yeh"子夜 Wen-hsüeh-
chi-k'an 文學季刊 2 (April, 1934), pp.405-408.

Chung-kuo Hsin-wen-hsüeh ta-hsi 中國新文學大系 (A Compendium of Modern
Chinese Literature) in ten vols: Wen-hsüeh lun-cheng-chi(vol.2)
文學論爭集, (Literary Controversies). Shanghai: 1935-1936.

Chung-kuo hsien-tai wen-hsüeh ts'an-k'ao tzu-liao 中國現代文學史參攷資料
(Source Materials on the History of Modern Chinese Literature). Edited
by Peking Normal University, Department of Chinese Literature,
Committee on the Revision of the Teaching of Modern Literature 北京.
師範大學中文系,現代文學教學改革小組 2 vols., Peking: 1959.

Chung-kuo hsien-tai-wen-hsüeh ch'i-k'an mu-lu 中國現代文學期刊目錄
(A Catalogue of Modern Chinese Literary Periodicals), edited by
Joint Research Committe on Modern Literary Periodicals 現代文學
期刊聯合調查小組 , 2 vols.. Shanghai: 1961.

Chung-kuo hsien-tai-wen-i tzu-liao ts'ung-k'an 中國現代文藝資料叢刊
(An Anthology of Modern Chinese Literature Source Materials). Shanghai
wen-i-ch'u-pan-she, 1962.

"Mao Tun yen-chiu tzu-liao hui-pien" 茅盾研究資料彙編 "A Compendium of Research Materials on Mao Tun", Chung-kuo hsien-tai-tso-chia yen-chiu tzu-liao ts'ung-shu 中國現代作家研究資料叢書 (Library of Research Materials on Modern Chinese Writers). Shantung: Shantung Normal College, Department of Chinese 山東師範大學中文系 , 1960.

Ch'ü Ch'iu-po wen-chi 瞿秋白文集 (Collected Works of Ch'ü Ch'iu-po) 4 vols. Peking: Jen-min-wen-hsüeh ch'u-pan-she, 1957.

Davis, A.R.. "Revolution and Literature in Twentieth Century China," JOSA 3.2 (December, 1963), pp.55-65.

Deutscher, Isaac. The Prophet Unarmed, Trotsky: 1921-1929 (Vol.2 of a three-volume biography of Trotsky). Oxford University Press, 1959.

_____. Stalin. Oxford University Press, 1949.

Doležalová, Anna. "Subject-matters of Short Stories in the Initial Period of the Creation Society's Activities," Asian and African Studies (AAS) (Brastislava) 6 (1970), pp.131-144.

Dostoyevsky, Fyodor. Crime and Punishment. Translated with an introduction by Ernest J. Simmons. New York: The Modern Library, 1950.

Erlich, Victor. Russian Formalism, History-Doctrine. New Haven: Yale University Press, 1981, third edition.

Ehrmann, Jacques. Literature and Revolution. New Haven: Yale French Studies, 1967.

Fan Chün 樊駿 . "Mao Tun ti Shih ho Hung" 茅盾的蝕和虹 ("Mao Tun's Eclipse and Rainbow), Wen-hsüeh yen-chiu (Quarterly) 文學研究 (Research and Studies in Literature) 4 (1956.11).

_____. "Liang-pen kuan-yü Mao Tun wen-hsüeh-tao-lu ti shu" 兩本關於茅盾文學道路的書 "Two Books on the Literary Road of Mao Tun") Wen-hsüeh-p'ing-lun 文學評論 (Literary Review) (1960.2), pp.112-116.

Fang Pi 方璧 (pseudonym of Mao Tun). Hsi-yang wen-hsüeh t'ung-lun 西洋文學通論 (Outline of Western Literature). Shanghai: 1929? 1933.

Frye, Northrop. The Stubborn Structure, Essays on Criticism and Society. Ithaca: Cornell University Press, 1970.

Fu Chih-ying 伏志英 (ed.) Mao Tung P'ing Chuan 茅盾評傳 (Critical and Biographical Essays on Mao Tun). Shanghai: Hsien-tai-shu-chü 現代書局, 1931.

Gálik, Marián. Mao Tun and Modern Chinese Literary Criticism. Wiesbaden: 1969.

_____. The Genesis of Modern Chinese Literary Criticism. London: Curzon Press; Bratislava: Veda, Publishing House of the Slovak Academy of Sciences, 1980.

_____. "The Names and Pseudonyms Used by Mao Tun," Archiv Orientalni (AO) 31 (1963), pp.81-108.

_____. "A Comment on Two Collections of Mao Tun's Works," AO 33 (1965), pp.614-638.

_____. "On the Influence of Foreign Ideas on Chinese Literary Criticism, 1894-1904," Asian and African Studies (AAS) (Bratislava) 2 (1966), pp.38-48.

_____. "A Comment on Two Studies on the Works of Mao Tun," AAS 1
(1965), pp. 81-101.

_____. "Naturalism: A Changing Concept," East and West, New Series
16. 3-4 (September -December, 1966), pp.310-328.

_____. "The Expressionistic Criticism of Kuo Mo-jo,"
Shinagakuhō (Bulletin of the Tokyo Sinological Society) (Tokyo)
13 (1967), pp.231-243.

_____. "From Chuang-tzu to Lenin, Mao Tun's Intellectual
Development," AAS 3 (1967), pp.98-109.

_____. "Studies in Modern Chinese Literary Criticism: III.
Ch'ien Hsing-ts'un and the Theory of Proletarian Realism," AAS 5 (1969).

_____. "Studies in Modern Chinese Literary Criticism: V.
The Socio-Aesthetic Criticism of Ch'eng Fang-wu," AAS 7 (1971),
pp.41-78.

_____. "Studies in Modern Chinese Literary Criticism: VII.
Liang Shih-ch'iu and New Humanism, " AAS 9 (1973), pp.29-51.

_____. "A Comment on Recent Books on Chinese Literary Criticism,"
AAS 9 (1973), pp.151-169.

_____. "Studies in Modern Chinese Literary Criticism VI:
Chiang Kuang-ch'ih's Concept of Revolutionary Literature," AAS 8
(1972), pp.43-69.

Goldman, Merle. Literary Dissent in Communist China. Cambridge, Mass.:
Harvard University Press, 1967.

_____. "Left-wing Criticism on the Pai-hua Movement," in Benjamin
Schwartz (ed.) Reflections on the May Fourth Movement, Cambridge:
1973, pp.85-94.

_____ (ed.) Modern Chinese Literature in the May 4th Era. Cambridge,
Mass.: Harvard University Press, 1977.

Graves, Robert. The Greek Myths. New York: George Braziller, Inc., 1955.

Colonel Jr. Guillermaz. "The Nanchang Uprising," The China Quarterly 11
(July-September 1962), pp.161-169.

Hua Kang 華崗. Chung-kuo Ta-ko-ming-shih 中國大革命史 (A History of the
Great Revolution in China). Shanghai: Ch'un-keng shu-tien 春耕書店 ,
1936.

_____. Wu-ssu-yün-tung-shih 五四運動史 (A History of the
May Fourth Movement) 4th edition. Shanghai: 1952.

Hu Shih 胡適 . "Chien-she-ti wen-hsüeh-ko-ming-lun" 建設的文學革命論
("A Constructive Theory of Literary Revolution") Chung-kuo Hsin-wen-
hsüeh-ta-hsi, Vol.1, pp.127-140.

_____. "She-mo she wen-hsüeh" 什麼是文學 ("What is Literature")
Chung-kuo Hsin-wen-hsüeh-ta-hsi, Vol.1, pp.214-216.

_____. "Wen-hsüeh-kai-liang ch'u-i" 文學改良芻議 ("A Draft
Proposal for Literary Reform") Chung-kuo Hsin-wen-hsüeh-ta-hsi,
Vol. 1, pp.34-43. Originally published in HCN 2.5 (January, 1917)
pp. 1-11.

Hu Yü-shih 胡剣之. "Chin-tai wen-hsüeh-shang-ti hsieh-shih chu-i" 近代文學上 的寫實主義 ("Realism in Modern Literature") <u>Tung-fang tsa-chih</u> 東方雜誌 (<u>TFTC</u>) 17.1 (1920), pp.64-75.

Harrison, James P. "The Li Li-san Line and the CCP in 1930 Part I," <u>The China Quarterly</u> 14 (April-June, 1963), pp.178-194.

_____. "The Li Li-san Line and the CCP in 1930 Part II," <u>The China Quarterly</u> 15 (July-September, 1963), pp.140-159.

Hsü, Immanuel, C.Y.. <u>The Rise of Modern China</u>. Oxford, England: Oxford University Press, 2nd. edition, 1975.

Issacs, Harold. <u>The Tragedy of the Chinese Revolution</u>. New York: Atheneum, 2nd. revised edition, 1968.

<u>Kindai Chūgoku shisō to bungaku</u> (<u>Modern Chinese Thought and Literature</u>). Ed., Tokyo Daigaku bungakupo Chūgoku bungaku kendyū shitsu (Research Division of Humanities, Tokyo University), Tokyo, 1961.

Klein, Donald Walker & Clark, Anne B. (ed.). <u>Biographic Dictionary of Chinese Communism 1921-1965</u>, 2 vols. Cambridge, Mass.: Harvard University Press, 1971.

Konishi Noboru 小西昇. "Shoki no Bōjun (1) (2)" 初期の矛盾(ーに)("The Early Phase of Mao Tun), <u>Chūgoku bunka zadanda nōto</u> Vol. 6, pp.10-34.

Knapp, Bettina. <u>Maurice Maeterlinck</u>. Boston: Twayne Publishers, 1975.

Krimerman, Leonard I. & Perry, Lewis (ed.). <u>Patterns of Anarchy</u>. New York: Anchor Books, 1966.

<u>Kuang-chou-shih-pien yü Shanghai Hui-i</u> 廣州事變與上海會議(<u>The Canton Coup and the Shanghai Conference</u>). n.p., 1928.

<u>Kuang-chou-ch'i-i</u> 廣州起義 (<u>The Canton Uprising</u>). Kuangtung: Jen-min ch'u-pan-she, 1957.

K'ung Ling-ching 孔另境. "Huai Mao Tun" 懷矛盾 ("Thinking of Mao Tun"), <u>Yung-yüan-chi</u> 廣園集 (<u>Common Park and Other Essays</u>), Shanghai: 1946, pp.64-71.

_____. "I-wei tso-chia-ti mu-ch'in" 一位作家的母親 ("The Mother of a Writer"), <u>Common Park and Other Essays</u>, pp.29-39.

Kuo Mo-jo 郭沫若. <u>Ch'uang-tsao shih-nien</u> 創造十年 (<u>Ten Years of The Creation Society</u>). Chungking: 1943.

_____. "Liu-sheng-chi-ch'i-ti hui-yin" 留聲機器的迴音 ("Reverberations of the Gramophone"), <u>Collected Works of Kuo Mo-jo</u> 郭沫若文集, Vol. 10, pp.344-356. Originally published in <u>Wen-hua p'i-pan</u> 文化批判3 under the pseudonym Mai-k'e-ang

_____. "I-shu-ti p'ing-chia" 藝術的評價"The Evaluation of Art"), <u>Ch'uang-tsao chou-pao</u> (<u>CTCP</u>) 創造周報(<u>Creation Weekly</u>) 3 (May, 1923), pp.13-15.

_____. "Ko-ming yü wen-hsüeh" 革命與文學("Revolution and Literature") <u>Chung-kuo hsien-tai-wen-hsüeh-shih ts'an-k'ao tzu-liao</u> 中國現代文學史參攷資料 (<u>Source Materials for the History of Modern Chinese Literature</u>). Peking: 1959, Vol. 1, pp.210-219.

_____. "Ying-hsiung-shu" 英雄樹 ("The Hero Tree"), <u>Collected Works</u>, Vol. 10, pp.324-330.

Liang Kung 侭工 (Compile). Hsin-wen-i-p'ing-lun 新文藝評論 (Studies of New Literature). Shanghai: Min-chih-shu-chü 民智書局, 1923.

Lao She 老舍. Lao-niu p'o-ch'e 老牛破車 (Old Ox and the Broken Cart). Shanghai: Jen-chien-shu-wo 人間書屋, 1939.

Lee, Leo Ou-fan. The Romantic Generation of Modern Chinese Writers. Cambridge, Mass.: Harvard University Press, 1973.

_____. "Lin Shu and his Translations: Western Fiction in Chinese Perspective," Papers on China 19 (1965), pp.159-193. East Asian Research Center, Harvard University.

_____. "Literature on the Eve of Revolution: Reflections on Lu Xun's Leftist Years, 1927-1936," Modern China Vol.2 No.3 (July, 1976), pp.277-326.

Leong, Sow-theng. Sino-Soviet Diplomatic Relations 1917-1926. The University of Hawaii Press, 1976.

Evans, Leon & Block, Russell (ed.). Leon Trotsky on China, with an introduction by Pen Shu-tse. New York: Monad Press, 1976.

Li Ch'u-li 李初梨. "Tsen-yang-ti chien-she ko-ming wen-hsüeh" 怎樣的建設革命文學 ("How to Build a Revolutionary Literature"), Wen-hua-p'i-p'an 2 (February, 1928), pp.3-20.

Li Ho-lin 李何林 (ed.). Chung-kuo wen-i lun-chan 中國文藝論戰 (Literary Polemics in China). Shanghai: 1929.

_____. Chin-erh-shih-nien chung-kuo wen-i-ssu-ch'ao lun 近二十年中國文藝思潮論 (On Intellectual Trends in Chinese Literature in the Recent Twenty Years). Shanghai: Sheng-huo-shu-tien, 1939.

Li Tien-yi. Chinese Fiction, A Bibliography of Books and Articles in Chinese and English. New Haven, Conn.: Yale University Press, 1968.

Li Yün-han 李雲漢. Ts'ung Yung-kung tao ch'ing-tang 從容共到清黨 (From Admitting the Chinese Communist Party to the Purge). Taipei, Taiwan: The Commercial Press, 1966.

Lin Po-hsiu 林伯修 (tr.). "Tao Hsin-hsieh-shih-chu-i chih-lu" 到新寫實 主義之路 ("The Road to New Realism [i.e. Proletarian realism]"), T'ai-yang-yüeh-k'an 太陽月刊 7.1 (1928), pp.1-19.

Link, Perry. Mandarin Ducks and Butterflies: Popular Fiction in Early Twentieth-Century Chinese Cities. Berkeley: University of California Press, 1981.

Liu Chün-jo. Controversies in Modern Chinese Intellectual History. Cambridge, Mass.: East Asian Research Center, Harvard University, 1964.

Liu Shou-sung 劉綬松. Chung-kuo hsin-wen-hsüeh-shih-ch'u-kao 中國新文 學史初稿 (History of Modern Chinese Literature, A Preliminary Draft) 2 vols.. Peking: 1956.

Liu Wu-chi. An Introduction to Chinese Literature. Bloomington: Indiana University Press, 1966. See Chapter 18: "Contemporary Experiments and Achievements."

Lu Hsün-魯迅 . Lu Hsün ch'üan-chi 魯迅全集 (Complete Works of Lu Hsün), 10 vols.. Peking: 1957-58.

_____ . "Min-tsu-chu-i-wen-hsüeh-ti jen-wu ho yün-ming" 民族主義的 文學的任務和運命("The Task and Destiny of Nationalist Literature") Complete Works, Vol.4, pp.244-253.

_____ . "Wen-i ta-chung-hua" 文藝大眾化 ("On Literature's Being for the Masses"), Lu Hsün on Literature 魯迅論文學 Peking: 1959, pp.62-63.

_____ . "Wen-i yü ko-ming" 文學與革命 ("Literature and Revolution"), Complete Works, Vol.4, pp.291-294.

Lukacs, George. Studies in European Realism. New York: The University Library, 1964.

_____ . Writers and Critics and Other Essays, edited and translated by Arthur D. Kahn. New York: The University Library, 1970.

McDougall, Bonnie. The Introduction of Western Literary Theories into Modern China. Tokyo: East Asian Cultural Studies Series, Nos. 14-15, 1971.

_____ . "The Search for Synthesis: T'ien Han and Mao Tun in 1920," in A.R. Davis (ed.) Search for Identity: Modern Literature and the Creative Arts in Asia (Papers presented to the 28th International Congress of Orientalist). Sydney: Angus and R bertson, 1974, pp.225-254.

Malraux, André. Man's Fate. New York: Smith & Hass, 1934.

Maeterlinck, Maurice. "Monna Vanna," translated by Alfred Sutro. London: G. Allen, 1904.

Marx & Engels. Marx & Engels Basic Writings on Politics and Philosophy, ed. by Lewis S. Feuer. Anchor Books, 1959.

Marinetti, Filippo Tommaso. Marinetti, Selected Writings , edited with an introduction by R.W. Flint, translated by R.W. Flint and Arthur A. Coppotelli. New York: Farrar, Straus and Giroux, 1971, 1972.

Mayakovsky, Vladimir. The Bedbug and Selected Poetry, edited with an introduction by Patricia Blake, translated by Max Hayward. Bloomington: Indiana University Press.

_____ . Mayakovsky, A Poet in the Revolution by Edward J. Brown. Princeton, New Jersey: Princeton University Press, 1973.

Meng Ch'i 孟棨. Pen-shih-shih 本事詩 (Stories about How Poems Are Written). Shanghai: Ku-chi-ch'u-pan-she 古籍出版社 n.d.

Minihan, Michael A. & Mochulsky, Konstatin (tr.). Dostoevsky, His Life and Works. Princeton: Princeton University Press, 1967.

Nagumo, Satoru. "Mao Tun and his First Collection of Short Stories Ye Qiang Wei," Nippon-chūgoku-gakkai-hō (Bulletin of the Sinological Society of Japan) 33 (1981), pp.263-277.

Nasu, Kiyoshi 那須清 . "Hakin to Bōjun no bunshō" 巴金と茅盾の文章 ("The Writings of Pa Chin and Mao Tun"), Bungaku ronshū 文章論輯 Vol. 8, pp.33-40.

North, Robert C. Chinese Communism. New York: World University
    Library. 1966.

Ono Shinobu 小野忍,. "Bōjun-hito to sakuhin" 茅盾一人と作品 ("The
    Writings of Mao Tun"), Tōyō bunka 東洋文化 Vol.17, pp.25-42.

Pei-fa-hou chih ko-p'ai-ssu-ch'ao 北伐後之各派思潮 Schools of
    Intellectual Thought after the Northern Expedition). Peiping:
    Ying-shan-she 鳥山社, 1930.

Pikowicz, Paul G. "Qu Qiubai, Critique of the May Fourth Generation:
    Early Chinese Marxist Literary Criticism," in Merle Goldman
    Modern Chinese Literature in the May Fourth Era, pp.351-384.

Pilnyak, Boris. The Tale of the Unextinguished Moon and Other Stories.
    Translated by Beatrice Scott with an introduction by Robert Payne.
    New York: Washington Square Press, Inc., 1967.

_____. "Boris Pil'njak's A Chinese Tale: Exile as Allegory,"
    by Kenneth N. Brostrom. Mosaic (University of Manitoba Press)
    IX.3 (1976), pp.11-25.

Price, Don C.. Russia and the Roots of the Chinese Revolution.
    Cambridge, Mass.: Harvard University Press, 1974.

Prince, Jane L. Cadres, Commanders, and Commissars: The Training of
    the Chinese Communist Leadership 1920-1945. Boulder, Colorado:
    Westview Special Studies on China and East Asia, 1976.

Průšek, Jaroslav. "Subjectivism and Individualism in Modern Chinese
    Literature," Archiv Orientalni 25.2 (1957), pp.261-286.

_____. "On the Question of Realism in the Literature and
    Art of China Today," New Orient 3.4 (1962), pp.107-108.

_____. "A Confrontation of Traditional Oriental Literature
    with Modern European Literature in the Context of the Chinese
    Literary Revolution," AO 32.3 (1964), pp.265-375.

_____ (ed.). Studies in Modern Chinese Literature. Berlin:
    Academie-Verlag, 1964.

_____. Three Sketches of Chinese Literature. Prague: Oriental
    Institute, 1969. Mao Tun, pp.10-43.

Pollard, D.E.. "Chou Tso-jen and Cultivating One's Garden," Asia Major,
    New Series, 11.2 (1965), pp.180-198.

Reed, John. Ten Days That Shook The World. New York: International
    Publishers, 1974 printing.

Roy, David T.. Kuo Mo-jo: The Early Years. Cambridge, Mass.: Harvard
    University Press, 1971.

Sanpō, Masami 三角政美 . "Bōjun no Nihon taizai jidai," 茅盾の日本滞在時代
    ("Mao Tun's Japan Period"), Shūkan Tōyōgaku 集刊東洋學, Vol.13,
    pp.69-84.

_____. "Bōjun to Kokkyō to no aida ni torikawasareta
    kakemei bungaku ronso ni arawareta ikutsu ka no mondai megutte"
    茅盾と克興との問にとりかわされた革命文學のいつかの問題をめぐって
    ("Questions Raised in the Controversies over Revolutionary
    Literature between Mao Tun and [Fu] Ko-hsing"), Shūkan tōyōgaku,
    Vol. 17, pp.45-58.

Scholes, Robert & Kellogg, Robert. The Nature of Narrative. Oxford
University Press, 1966.

Scholes, Robert. Structuralism in Literature. New Haven: Yale
University Press, 1974.

Schultz, William R.. "Kuo Mo-jo and the Romantic Aesthetic: 1918-
1925," Journal of Oriental Literature 6.2 (April, 1955), pp.49-81.

Schwartz, Benjamin. Chinese Communism and the Rise of Mao. Cambridge,
Mass.: Harvard University Press, 1951.

_____. Reflections on the May Fourth Movement. Cambridge, 1973.

Schwartz, Harry. Tsars, Mandarins and Commissars (History of Chinese-
Russian Relations), revised edition. Anchor Books, 1973.

Schyns, Joseph et.al.ed.. 1500 Modern Chinese Novels and Plays.
Peiping: Catholic University Press, 1948. Reprinted in Hongkong:
Lun-men Bookstore 龍門話店 , 1966.

Shao Po-chou 邵伯周 . Mao Tun-ti wen-hsüeh-tao-lu 茅盾的文學道路(Mao
Tun's Literary Road). Wuhan: Ch'ang-chiang-wen-i-ch'u-pan-she
長江文藝出版社 , 1959. Reprented 1979. The work
includes an appendix of Mao Tun's works and translations.

Shen Tse-min 沈澤民. "Wen-hsüeh yü ko-ming-wen-hsüeh" 文學與革命文學
("Literature and Revolutionary Literature"), Chüeh-wu 覺悟 (Awakening,
a supplement to the newspaper Min-kuo-jih-pao 民國日報 (November 6,
1924).

Shih Vincent Y.C.. "Enthusiast and Escapist: Writers of the Older
Generation," China Quarterly 13 (1963), pp.92-112. Discusses
Mao Tun.

_____. "Mao Tun: The Critic," The China Quarterly 19 (July-
September, 1964), pp.84-98.

Shimamura Hogetsu 島村抱月 . "Wen-i-shang-ti tzu-jan-chu-i" 文藝上的自
然主義 ("Naturalism in Literature"), tr. by Hsieh Liu-i 謝六逸,
HSYP 12.12 (December, 1921), pp.1-16.

Slonim, Marc. Soviet Russian Literature, Writers and Problems 1917-1967.
Oxford University Press, 1964.

Sorokin, V.F.. Tvorcheskiy put' Mao Dun'a. (The Literary Road of Mao Tun).
Moscow: Izdatel'-stvo vostochnoy literatary, 1962.

Spence, Jonathan. "On Chinese Revolutionary Literature," Literature
and Revolution, Yale French Studies 39 (1967), pp.215-255.

Ssu-ma Ch'ien 司馬遷 . Shih-chi 史記 (Records of the Grand Historian).
Erh-shih-wu-shih edition 二十五史本. Taipei: I-wen yin-shu-
kuan 藝文印書館 , 1956.

Stone, Donald David. Novelists in a Changing World. Cambridge, Mass.:
Harvard University Press, 1972.

Su Wen 蘇汶 ed.. Wen-i-tzu-yu lun-pien-chi 文藝自由論辯集(Debates
on the Freedom of Literature and Arts), 2nd. edition. Shanghai: 1933.

Sun Chung-t'ien 孫中田 . Lun Mao Tun ti sheng-huo yü ch'uang-tso
論茅盾的生活與創作(On the Life and Creative Writing of Mao Tun).
T'ien-ching: Pai-hua-wen-i-ch'u-pan-she, 1980.

Sun Yün-pin 孫雲彬. "Shen Yen-ping" 沈雁冰 Jen-wen-tsa-chih 人文雜誌8 (September, 1946), pp.16-23.

_____. Chung-kuo chin-pai-nien-shih 中國近百年史 (A History of China in the Last One Hundred Years). Shanghai: Hsin-chih-shu-tien 新知書店, 1948.

Tan Yen-i. "Lu Hsün ho Mao Tun chan-tou-yu-i-tuan-pien" (Glimpses of the Friendship between Lu Hsün and Mao Tun in a Common Battle"), Jen-wen-tsa-chih (Hsi-an 西安 edition) 4 (1957), pp.77-81.

Tertz, Abram. On Socialist Realism, tr. by G. Dennis. New York: Pantheon, 1960.

Thomas, S. Bernard. Proletarian Hegemony in the Chinese Revolution and the Canton Commune of 1927. Michigan Papers in Chinese Studies, No.23, 1975.

Ti-i-tz'u kuo-nei ko-ming-chan-cheng-shih-ch'i-ti nung-min-yün-tung 第一次國內革命戰爭時期的農民運動 (Peasant Movement during the First National Revolutionary War). Peking: Jen-min-ch'u-pan-she,1953.

"Ti-san-kuo-chi yü Chung-kuo" 第三國際與中國 ("The Third Communist International and China"),Kuo-wen-chou-pao 國聞週報 Vol.1 (1928).

Trotsky, Leon. Problems of the Chinese Revolution. Ann Arbor Paperback, 1967.

_____. Literature and Revolution. Ann Arbor Paperback, 1960.

_____. The Permanent Revolution and Results and Prospects. New York: Pathfinder Press, 1969.

Tseng Hua-p'eng 曾華鵬. "Chiang Kuang-ch'ih lun" 蔣光慈論 ("On Chiang Kuang-ch'ih"), Wen-hsüeh-p'ing-lun 5 (October, 1962), pp.42-58.

Turnell, Martin. The Art of French Fiction. New York: A New Directions Book, 1959.

Ulam, Adam B. The Unfinished Revolution. Vintage Books, 1960.

Vishnyakova-Akimova, Vera Vladimirovna. Two Years in Revolutionary China 1925-1927, tr. by Stephen I. Levine. Harvard East Asian Monographs, 1971.

Wang Hsi-yen 王西彥. "Lun Tzu-yeh" 論子夜 (On Midnight), Hsin-kang 新港 12 (December 1957).

_____. "Lun Mao Tun ti tuan-p'ien-hsiao-shuo" 端著論 的短篇小說 ("On Mao Tun's Short Stories), Wen-hsüeh-p'ing-lun 1981.4 (July, 1981), pp.55-72.

Wang Yao 王瑤. Chung-kuo hsin-wen-hsüeh-shih-kao 中國新文學史稿 (A History of Modern Chinese Literature: Draft), 2 vols. Shanghai: 1951.

Wang Che-fu 王哲甫. Chung-kuo hsin-wen-hsüeh-yün-tung-shih 中國新文學 運動史 (A History of the New Literature Movement in China). Hongkong: 1965.

Wang Chih-chung 王臻中. "Lun Mao Tun tuan-p'ien-hsiao-shuo-ti i-shu t'e-tien" 論茅盾短篇小說的藝術特點 ("On the Special Characteristics of the Art of Mao Tun's Short Stories"), Wen-hsüeh-ping-lun-ts'ung-k'an Vol.6, 文學評論叢刊 1980, pp.105-130.

Wei Shao-ch'ang 韋紹昌. Yüan-yang-hu-tieh-p'ai yen-chiu-tzu-liao 舊鴛鴦蝴蝶派研究資料 (Source Materials on the Study of the Mandarin Duck and Butterfly School), Shanghai: 1962.

Watson, Burton (tr.). Shih-chi by Ssu-ma Ch'ien, 2 vols.. New York: Columbia University Press, 1961.

Wang Shih 王實. Chung-kuo Kung-ch'an-tang-shih-chien-pien 中國共產黨史簡編 (A Brief Outline of the History of the Chinese Communist Party). Shanghai: Jen-min-ch'u-pan-she, 1958.

Whiting, Allen S. Soviet Policies in China. New York: Columbia University Press, 1953. Reissued by Stanford University Press, 1968.

Wilbur, Martin C. and How, Julie Lien-ying (ed.). Documents on Communism, Nationalism, and Soviet Advisers in China 1918-1928 (papers seized in the 1927 Peking raid). New York: Columbia University Press, 1956.

Wilbur, Martin. Ashes of Defeat. New York: Columbia University Press, 1964. Reprinted from The China Quarterly (April-June, 1966).

Williams, Gwyn A. Artisans and Sans-culottes, Foundations of Modern History (Popular movements in France and Britain during the French Revolution). New York: W.W. Norton & Company, Inc., 1969.

Wilson, Edmund. To the Finland Station (A Study in the Writing and Acting of History). New York: Anchor Books, 1953.

Wu T'ien-wen. "Chiang Kai-shek's March Twentieth Cout D'Etat of 1926," Journal of Asian Studies 27.3 (May, 1969), pp.585-602.

Yang Ts'un-jen 楊邨人 . "T'ai-yang-she yü Chiang Kuang-tz'u" 太陽社與蔣光慈 ("The Sun Society and Chiang Kuang-tz'u") Hsien-tai 現代 (Contemporary) 3.4 (August, 1932), pp.470-476.

Yeh Sheng-t'ao 葉聖陶. Ni Huan-chih, translated by A.C. Barnes. Peking, Foreign Languages Press, 1958.

_____. Ni Huan-chih 倪煥之 . Shanghai: 1927. Reissued Peking: Jen-min-wen-hsüeh-ch'u-pan-she, 1953.

_____. "Lüeh-t'an Yen-ping-hsiung-ti wen-hsüeh kung-tso" 略談雁冰兄的文學工作 ("A Few Words about the Literary Endeavors of Mr. [Shen] Yen-ping") Wen-shao 1.3 (October, 1945).

_____. Hsien-hsia 線下 (On the Frontline). Shanghai: The Commercial Press, 1925.

Yeh Tzu-ming 葉子銘 . Lun Mao Tun ssu-shih-nien-ti wen-hsüeh-tao-lu 論茅盾四十年的文學道路 (On Mao Tun's Forty-year of Literary Road). Shanghai: Shanghai wen-i-ch'u-pan-she 上海文藝出版社, 1959. Revised and enlarged edition, 1978.

_____. "Kuan-yü Mao Tun sheng-p'ing-ti jo-kan-wen-t'i" 關於茅盾生平的若干問題 ("A Few Questions Concerning the Biography of Mao Tun") Wen-hsüeh-p'ing-lun-ts'ung-k'an 文學評論叢刊 Vol.8, Peking, 1981, pp.342-377.

Yüeh Tai-yün 樂黛雲 . "Mao Tun tsao-ch'i ssu-hsiang yen-chiu" 茅盾早期思想研究 ("A Study of the Early Thought of Mao Tun") Chung-kuo hsien-tai-wen-hsüeh-yen-chiu-ts'ung-k'an 中國現代文學研究叢刊 Peking: Peking-ch'u-pan-she, 1970, pp.134-158.

———————. "Ni-ts'ai yü Chung-kuo-hsien-tai-wen-hsüeh"
尼采與中國現代文學 ("Nitzsche and Modern Chinese Literature")
Peking ta-hsüeh-hsüeh-pao, che-hsüeh, she-hui·k'o-hsüeh-pan 北京大學
學報哲學社會科學版 (Bulletin of the Peking University:
Philosophy and the Social Sciences Issue) 1980.3 (June, 1980).

———————. "Shih ho Tzu-yeh ti pi-chiao-fen-hsi" 蝕和
子夜的比較分析 ("A Comparative Analysis of Erosion [i.e. Eclipse]
and Midnight") Wen-hsüeh-p'ing-lun 文學評論 1981.1 (1981),
pp.110–120.

JOURNALS AND PERIODICALS

Ch'uang-tsao chi-kan	創造季刊	Creation Quarterly	CTCK	May, 1922
Ch'uang-tsao chou-pao	創造週報	Creation Weekly	CTCP	May 13, 1923
Ch'uang-tsao jih	創造日	Creation Day	CTJ	
Ch'uang-tsao yüeh-k'an	創造月刊	Creation Monthly	CTYK	March, 1926
Fu-nü tsa chih	婦女雜誌	The Women's Journal	FNTC	Jan., 1915
Hsiang-tao chou-k'an	响導週報	Vanguard Weekly	HT	Sept., 1922
Hsiao-shuo yüeh-pao	小說月報	Short Story Monthly	HSYP	
Hsin-wen-hsüeh shih-liao	新文學史料	Source Materials on the History of the New Literature	HWHSL	Nov., 1978
Hsin-hua yüeh-pao: wen-che-pan	新華月報文摘版	New China Monthly: Literary Selections	HHWC	Sept., 1979
Hsin-ch'in-nien	新青年	New Youth	HCN	Sept., 1915
Hsüeh-sheng tsa-chih	學生雜誌	The Students Magazine	HSTC	Jan., 1911
Hsüeh-teng: Wen-shüeh (A supplement to the newspaper Shih-shih hsin-pao in Shanghai)	學燈·文學 時事新報	Lantern of Learning: Literature [Weekly]	HT-WH	July, 1923
Ming-pao yüeh-k'an	明報月刊	Mingpao Monthly	MPYK	Jan., 1966
T'ai-yang yüeh-k'an	太陽月刊	Sun Monthly	TYYK	1928
Tung-fang tsa-chih	東方雜誌	The East Magazine	TFTC	Jan., 1904
Wen-hsüeh chi-k'an	文學季刊	Literature Quarterly	WHCK	1933
Wen-hsüeh chou-pao	文學週報	Literature Weekly	WHCP	1922
Wen-hsüeh p'ing-lun	文學評論	Literary Review	WHPL	March, 1957
Wen-i yen-chiu	文藝研究	Studies in Literature and Arts	WIYC	May, 1979 '

Archiv Orientalni	AO (Bratislava)
Asia Major	AM
Asian and African Studies	AAS (Bratislava)
The China Quarterly	CQ
The Journal of Asian Studies	JAS

GLOSSARY

"A Woman"	一個女性
Chang Ch'iu-liu	章秋柳
Chang Fa-fuei	張發奎
Chang Jo-ying	張若英
Chang Kuo-t'ao	張國燾
Chang Man-ch'ing	張曼倩
Chang T'ai-lei	張太雷
Chang-t'ai liu	章臺柳
Changsha	長沙
Ch'ang-ting	長汀
Chang Tso-ling	張作霖
Chao Ch'ih-chu	趙赤珠
Ch'ao Kai	晁蓋
Chao Po-t'ung	趙伯通
Ch'en Chung	陳中
Chekiang	浙江
Ch'en Kung-po	陳公博
Ch'en Pi-lan	陳碧蘭
Ch'en She	陳涉

Ch'en Tu-hsiu 陳獨秀

Chengchou 鄭州

Ch'eng Fang-wu 成仿吾

"Chi-chieh-sung" 機械頌

"Chi-chü-chiu-hua" 幾句舊話

Chia-hsing 嘉興

Chiang Kuang-tz'u 蔣光赤

Chiang Yung-ching 蔣永敬

Ch'iang Meng (Wei-li) 強猛,惟力

chieh-chi i-shih 階級意識

Ch'ien Hsing-ts'un 錢杏邨

Ch'ien Su-chen 錢素貞

Chin K'o 荊軻

Chin Ta-chien 金大堅

Ch'in Wu-yang 秦舞陽

Ching 靜

Ching-kang-shan 井崗山

Ch'iu-chü 秋菊

"Ch'iu-ti-kung-yüan" 秋的公園

Ching-yün-li 景雲里

Ch'iung-hua 瓊華

Cho Wen-chün 卓文君

Chou En-lai 周恩來

Chou Er-fu 周爾復

Chou I-ch'ün 周逸群

Chou Shih-ta 周時達

Chou Ting-hui 周定慧

Chou Tso-jen 周作人

Chow Tse-tsung 周策縱

Chu Chin-ju 朱近如

Chu Min-sheng 朱民生

Ch'u Wang-t'ai 楚望臺

"Clear-wind Pavilion" 清風閣

"Command-obeying literature" 遵命文學

"Creation" 創造

Ch'ü Ch'iu-po 瞿秋白

Fan Chih-ch'ao 范志超

Fan Chün 樊駿

Fang Lo-lan 方羅蘭

Fang Mei-li 方梅麗

Fang Pi 方璧 (pseudonym of Mao Tun)

Feng Yü-hsiang 馮玉祥

fin-de-siecle 世紀末

Fu Chih-ying 伏志英

Fuchow 撫州

Fu K'e-hsing 傅克興

Fu-shih 腐蝕

Hai-Lu-Feng	海陸豐
Hankow	漢口
Han Yi	韓瑃
"Haze"	靉
Ho Chih-hua	賀芝華
Ho Jo-hua	何若華
Ho Yü-po	賀玉波
Ho Kan-chih	何幹之
Honan	河南
Ho Yü-po	賀玉波
Hsia Tou-yin	夏斗寅
Hsiang-t'an	湘潭
Hsiang-yang-wan	襄陽丸
Hsiao Jang	蕭讓
Hsien-hsien	嫻嫻
Hsin-wen-hsüeh hsüan-chi	新文學選集
Hsin-wen-hsüeh shih-liao	新文學史料
Hsü Pai-hao	許白昊
Hsü Tzu-ts'ai	徐子材
Hu Kuo-kuang	胡國光
Hua Han (Yang Han-sheng)	華漢 (陽翰笙)
Huang Ch'i-hsiang	黃琪翔
Huan (Miss)	環小姐

Huang-kang　　　　　　　　　黃岡

Huang-p'o　　　　　　　　　　黃陂

Hui-ch'ang(Kiangsi Province)　會昌(江西省)

"Hung-yeh"　　　　　　　　　紅葉

Hupei　　　　　　　　　　　　湖北

I-wen　　　　　　　　　　　　譯文

Je-hsüeh jih-pao　　　　　　熱血日報

Jen-min wen-hsüeh　　　　　　人民文學

Jui Chen　　　　　　　　　　瑞澂

Jung　　　　　　　　　　　　蓉

Kao Ch'iu　　　　　　　　　　高俅

Kiangsi　　　　　　　　　　　江西

Kiukiang　　　　　　　　　　九江

Kuang-chou (Canton)　　　　廣州

Ku Chung-ch'i　　　　　　　顧仲起

Kuei (Madam)　　　　　　　桂

Kuling　　　　　　　　　　　牯嶺

Kuling chih-ch'iu　　　　　牯嶺之秋

Kuo-liang　　　　　　　　　國樑

kung-ch'an　　　　　　　　　共產

K'ung Ling-ching　　　　　孔另境

K'ung Te-chih	孔德沚
kuo-ch'ih	國恥
Kuo Mo-jo	郭沫若
Lao She	老舍
Lao-niu p'o-ch'e	老牛破車
Li Ch'u-li	李初梨
Li Han-ch'ün	李漢俊
Li Ho-lin	李何林
Li K'e	李克
Li Li-san	李立三
Li Ta	李達
Li Ta-chao	李大釗
Li Yün-han	李雲漢
Liang-kung	俍工
Liang-shan	梁山
lieh-sheng	劣紳
Lin Ch'ung	林沖
Lin Pu-p'ing	林不平
Lin Po-hsiu	林伯俏
Lin Tzu-ch'ung	林子沖
Lin-ying (in Honan)	臨潁(河南)
Liu Po-ch'eng	劉伯承
"Liu-pye Yün-mei"	留別雲妹

Liu Shao-ch'i	劉少奇
Liu Shou-sung	劉綬松
local ruffian	土豪
Lo Chüeh	羅覺
Lu Chün-ch'ing	陸俊卿
Lu Chün-yi	盧俊義
Lu Hsün	魯迅
Lu Mu-yu	陸慕游
Lushan	盧山
Lu Ting-yi	陸定一
Lung Fei	龍飛
Mahweiling	馬迴顏
Mai K'e-ang	麥克昂
Mao Tse-min	毛澤民
Mao Tse-tung	毛澤東
Mao Tun	茅盾
Meng Ch'i	孟棨
Min-kuo jih-pao	民國日報
Nanch'ang	南昌
Ni Huan-chih	倪煥之
Nieh Jung-chih	聶榮臻
nü-shih	女士

Pao-su	抱素
P'eng Kang	彭剛
P'eng Pai	彭湃
Ping	丙
pi-shang-liang-shan	逼上梁山
"Poetry and Prose"	詩與散文
"Promissaory Notes"	預約券
Shen Te-hung	沈德鴻
Shen Tse-min	沈澤民
Shen Yen-ping	沈雁冰
Shih Chün	史俊
Shih Hsün	史循
Shih-shih hsin-pao	時事新報
Ssu-ma Ch'ien	司馬遷
"Suicide"	自殺
su-mang	宿莽
Sun K'o	孫科
Sun Wu-yang	孫舞陽
Sun Yün-ping	孫雲彬
Sung Chiang	宋江
ta-jen lao-yeh	大人老爺
Tai Chi-t'ao	戴季陶

"T'an wo-ti yen-chiu' 誤我的研究

T'ao Ch'ien 陶潛

"Tang-jen-hun" 黨人魂

T'ang Sheng-chih 唐生智

Ti ch'üan 地泉

Ti-san-kuo-chi 第三國際

Tien-shih-chai hua-pao 點石齋畫報

Ting Ling 丁玲

Tsai-hei-an-chung 在黑暗中

"Tsai-kung-yüan-li" 在公園裏

Ts'ai Ho-shen 蔡和森

Ts'ao Chih-fang 曹志芳

Tsinan 濟南

Tsu Hsiu-hsia 祝秀俠

Tzu-chih t'ung-chien 資治通鑑

tu-jo 杜若

Tung-fang Ming 東方明

Tung-fang Shuo 東方朔

Tung Pi-wu 董必武

tung-yao 動搖

tzu-sha 自殺

Wang Ching-wei 汪精衛

Wang Ch'iung-ch'üan 汪馥泉

Wang Chung-chao 王仲昭

Wang Hsi-yen 王西彦

Wang Jung-ch'ang 王縈昌

Wang Lun 王倫

Wang Shih-t'ao 王詩陶

Wei-lai-p'ai 未來派

wei-yüan 委員

Wen-hsüeh 文學

Wen-yi chen-ti 文藝陣地

"wu" 霧

Wuhan 武漢

Wu Kuang 吳廣

Wu P'ei-fu 吳佩孚

Wu-sung Harbor 吳淞港

"Wu-yüeh san-shih-jih ti hsia-wu" 五月三十日的下午

Wu Yung 吳用

Yang Chih 楊志

Yeh Sheng-t'ao (Shao-chün) 葉聖陶 (紹鈞)

Yeh T'ing 葉挺

Yeh Tzu-ming 葉子銘

Yü-yang 漁陽

Yü Yu-jen 于右任

Yüan Shih-k'au 袁世凱

Yün   雲

"Yün-shao-yeh yü-ts'ao-mao"   雲少爺與草帽

Yün Tai-ying   惲代英

"yün-yu"   雲游

INDEX